Complete
German

Paul Coggle
and Heiner Schenke

For UK order enquiries: please contact Bookpoint Ltd, 130 Milton Park, Abingdon, Oxon OX14 4SB. *Telephone:* +44 (0) 1235 827720. Fax: +44 (0) 1235 400454. Lines are open 09.00–17.00, Monday to Saturday, with a 24-hour message answering service. Details about our titles and how to order are available at www.teachyourself.com

For USA order enquiries: please contact McGraw-Hill Customer Services, PO Box 545, Blacklick, OH 43004-0545, USA. *Telephone:* 1-800-722-4726. Fax: 1-614-755-5645.

For Canada order enquiries: please contact McGraw-Hill Ryerson Ltd, 300 Water St, Whitby, Ontario L1N 9B6, Canada. *Telephone:* 905 430 5000. Fax: 905 430 5020.

Long renowned as the authoritative source for self-guided learning – with more than 50 million copies sold worldwide – the *Teach Yourself* series includes over 500 titles in the fields of languages, crafts, hobbies, business, computing and education.

British Library Cataloguing in Publication Data: a catalogue record for this title is available from the British Library.

Library of Congress Catalog Card Number: on file.

First published in UK 1998 as Teach Yourself German by Hodder Education, part of Hachette UK, 338 Euston Road, London NW1 3BH.

First published in US 1998 by The McGraw-Hill Companies, Inc.

This edition published 2012.

The *Teach Yourself* name is a registered trade mark of Hodder Headline.

Copyright © 1998, 2003, 2007, 2010, 2012 Paul Coggle and Heiner Schenke.

Advisory Editor: Paul Coggle, University of Kent at Canterbury.

Typeset by Integra Software Services Pvt. Ltd., Pondicherry, India.

Printed in Dubai for Hodder Education, an Hachette UK Company, 338 Euston Road, London NW1 3BH.

The publisher has used its best endeavours to ensure that the URLs for external websites referred to in this book are correct and active at the time of going to press. However, the publisher and the author have no responsibility for the websites and can make no guarantee that a site will remain live or that the content will remain relevant, decent or appropriate.

Hachette UK's policy is to use papers that are natural, renewable and recyclable products and made from wood grown in sustainable forests. The logging and manufacturing processes are expected to conform to the environmental regulations of the country of origin.

Impression number	10 9 8 7 6 5 4 3 2 1
Year	2014 2013 2012

Contents

BEGINNER

Meet the authors

So you are thinking of learning German? As the authors of **Complete German**, we are very keen to help you achieve your objectives. We are both enthusiastic and experienced teachers of German and we like to think we have produced an excellent course that has been tried, tested and recently updated.

Of course, different people learn in different ways and we have tried to take this fact into account by offering a variety of language activities. You will find a lot of listening, speaking, reading and writing practice, information on how the language works plus some facts about present-day German culture and society.

Those who like to know the ins and outs of the grammar will find what they want here, but those who just want to know enough to be able to meet their basic needs are also catered for. As long as you are up for a bit of work, complete the exercise materials, and put in some practice, you will make progress.

Whether you are an adult learner with no previous knowledge of German or someone who is a 'false beginner', we hope that you will feel we are taking you carefully through the essentials to the point where you can cope on your own.

The going will sometimes be tough, but with a bit of encouragement from us and perseverance from you, you will get there!

Good luck with learning German!

Paul Coggle and Heiner Schenke

Introduction

Welcome to *Complete German!*

Is this the right course for you?
If you are an adult learner with no previous knowledge of German and studying on your own, then this is the course for you. Perhaps you are taking up German again after a break from it, or you are intending to learn with the support of a class? Again, you will find this course very well suited to your purposes.

DEVELOPING YOUR SKILLS

The language introduced in this course is centred around realistic everyday situations. The emphasis is first and foremost on using German, but we also aim to give you an idea of how the language works so that you can create sentences of your own.

The course covers all four of the basic skills – listening and speaking, reading and writing. If you are working on your own, the recordings will be all the more important, as they will provide you with the essential opportunity to listen to German and to speak it within a controlled framework. You should therefore try to obtain a copy of the recordings if you haven't already got one.

The structure of this course

The course book contains 23 course units plus a reference section at the back of the book. There are also two CDs which you really do need to have if you are going to get maximum benefit from the course.

THE COURSE UNITS

The course units can be divided roughly into the following categories, although of course there is a certain amount of overlap from one category to another.

Statement of aims

At the beginning of each unit you will be told what you can expect to learn, in terms of a) what you will be able to do in German by the end of the unit and b) the language points that are being introduced.

Presentation of new language

This is usually in the form of text material, often supported by illustrations, or of a dialogue. Most of the dialogues are recorded on the audio (indicated with) and also printed in the book. Some assistance with vocabulary is also given. The language is presented in manageable chunks, building carefully on what you have learned in earlier units.

Practice of the new language

Practice is graded so that activities which require mainly **recognition** come first. As you grow in confidence in manipulating the language forms, you will be encouraged to produce both in writing and in speech.

Description of language forms and grammar

Information on the forms of the language is presented in two ways: i) in the *Language discovery* sections which encourage you to discover language patterns yourself and ii) in the *Learn more* sections which explain the grammar concepts in detail.

Learning the **forms** of the language actively will enable you to construct your own sentences correctly. For those who are daunted by grammar, assistance is given in various ways. See pages xiv for more details about our unique Discovery Method.

Pronunciation and intonation

The best way to acquire good pronunciation and intonation is to listen to native speakers and to try to imitate them. But most people do not actually notice that certain sounds in German are pronounced differently from their English counterparts until this is pointed out to them. For this reason we include specific advice within the course units.

Vocabulary

To help you monitor your own learning of vocabulary, much of the new vocabulary is presented as it occurs. At the end of the book there is also a short English-German reference vocabulary.

Monitoring your progress

You will of course want to monitor your own progress. We provide a 'Test Yourself' section and a checklist at the end of every unit to help you be sure that you have mastered the main points.

The reference section

This contains:

▶ a list of German irregular verbs
▶ a key to the activities
▶ transcripts of the recordings
▶ an English–German vocabulary

How to use this course

Make sure at the beginning of each course unit that you are clear about what you can expect to learn.

Read any background information that is provided. Then either read the text material or listen to the dialogues on the recording. With the recording try to get the gist of what is being said before you look at the printed text in the book. Then refer to the printed text and the *New Expressions* in order to study the dialogues in more detail.

Don't fall into the trap of thinking you have 'done that' when you have listened to the recording a couple of times and worked through the dialogues in the book. You may **recognize** what you hear and read, but you almost certainly still have some way to go before you can **produce** the language of the dialogues correctly and fluently. This is why we recommend that you keep listening to the recording at every opportunity – sitting on the train or bus, waiting at the dentist's or stuck in a traffic jam in the car, using what would otherwise be 'dead' time. Of course, you must also be internalizing what you hear and making sense of it – just playing it in the background without really paying attention is not enough!

Some of the recordings are listen-only exercises. The temptation may be to go straight to the transcriptions in the back of the book, but try not to do this. The whole point of listening exercises is to improve your listening skills. You will not do this by reading first. The transcriptions are there to help you if you get stuck.

As you work your way through the exercises, check your answers carefully in the back of the book. It is easy to overlook your own mistakes. If you have a 'study buddy', it's a good idea to check each other's answers. Most of the exercises have fixed answers, but some are a bit more open-ended, especially when we are asking you to talk about yourself. We then, in most cases, give you a model answer which you can adapt for your own purposes.

We have tried to make the grammar explanations as user-friendly as possible, since we recognize that many people find grammar daunting. But in the end, it is up to you just how much time you spend on studying and sorting out the grammar points. Some people find that they can do better by getting an ear for what sounds right, others need to know in detail how the language is put together.

Before you move on to a new unit, always make sure that you know all the new words and phrases in the current unit. Trying to recall the context in which words and phrases were used may help you learn them better.

Language learning is a bit like running – you need to do it regularly for it to do any good!

Commonly used instructions in *Complete German*:

Hören Sie (zu)	*Listen*
Lesen Sie...	*Read...*
Schreiben Sie...	*Write...*
Spielen Sie die Rolle von...	*Play the role of...*

German in the modern world

German is spoken as a first language by approximately 110 million people who live mainly in Germany, Austria and Switzerland. But German is also spoken elsewhere – for instance in Luxembourg, Liechtenstein, the South Tyrol region of Italy and in border regions of Belgium. German-speaking communities are also to be found in Eastern Europe, particularly in Romania, in North America (e.g. the Pennsylvania Dutch) and in southern Africa (Namibia).

After English, German is the most widely spoken language within the European Union and is an important language in business and commerce, particularly in Eastern Europe.

Learn to learn

THE DISCOVERY METHOD

There are lots of approaches to language learning, some practical and some quite unconventional. Perhaps you know of a few, or even have some techniques of your own. In this book we have incorporated the **Discovery Method** of learning, a sort of DIY approach to language learning. What this means is that you will be encouraged throughout the course to engage your mind and figure out the language for yourself, through identifying patterns, understanding grammar concepts, noticing words that are similar to English, and more. This method promotes *language awareness*, a critical skill in acquiring a new language. As a result of your own efforts, you will be able to better retain what you have learned, use it with confidence, and, even better, apply those same skills to *continuing* to learn the language (or, indeed, another one) on your own after you've finished this book.

Everyone can succeed in learning a language – the key is to *know how to learn* it. Learning is more than just reading or memorizing grammar and vocabulary. It's about being an *active* learner, learning in real contexts, and, most importantly, *using* what you've learned in different situations. Simply put, if you figure something out for yourself, you're more likely to understand it. And when you use what you've learned, you're more likely to remember it. However, once you have discovered the main rules and patterns yourself, you will also be given sound and detailed explanations that will consolidate and extend your knowledge.

And because many of the essential details, such as grammar rules, are taught through the Discovery Method, you'll have more fun while learning. Soon, the language will start to make sense and you'll be relying on your own intuition to construct original sentences *independently*, not just listening and repeating.

Enjoy yourself!

BECOME A SUCCESSFUL LANGUAGE LEARNER

1 Make a habit out of learning

Study a little every day, between 20 and 30 minutes if possible, rather than two to three hours in one session. **Give yourself short-term goals**, e.g. work out how long you'll spend on a particular unit and work within the time limit. This will help you to **create a study habit**, much in the same way you would with a sport or music. You will need to concentrate, so try to **create an environment conducive to learning** which is calm and quiet and free from distractions. As you study, do not worry about your mistakes or the things you can't remember or understand. Languages settle differently in our brains, but gradually the language will become clearer as your brain starts to make new connections. Just **give yourself enough time** and you will succeed.

2 Expand your language contact

As part of your study habit try to take other opportunities to **expose yourself to the language.** As well as using this book you could try listening to German radio and television or reading articles and blogs. Perhaps you could find information in German about a personal passion or hobby or even a news story that interests you. In time you'll find that your vocabulary and language recognition deepen and you'll become used to a range of writing and speaking styles.

3 Vocabulary

To organise your study of vocabulary, group new words under:

a *generic categories, e.g. food, furniture.*

b *situations in which they occur, e.g. under restaurant you can write waiter, table, menu, bill.*

c *functions, e.g. greetings, parting, thanks, apologizing.*

Say the words out loud as you read them.

Write the words over and over again. Remember that if you want to keep lists on your smartphone or tablet you can usually switch the keyboard language to make sure you are able to include all special characters.

Listen to the audio several times.

Cover up the English side of the vocabulary list and see if you remember the meaning of the word.

Associate the words with similar sounding words in English, e.g. *schwimmen* is **swimming**, *neun* is **nine** or *Schuh* is **shoe**.

Create flash cards, drawings and mind maps.

Write words for objects around your house and stick them to the objects.

Pay attention to patterns in words, e.g. nouns ending in -e are usually feminine, such as *die Adresse* or nouns ending in -or are usually masculine, such as *der Motor*.

Experiment with words. Use the words that you learn in new contexts and find out if they are correct. For example, you learn in Unit 7 how to say *Ich möchte ...* (**I'd like ...**) in the context of ordering drinks in a café. Experiment with *Ich möchte ...* in new contexts, e.g. **when buying groceries from a shop** (*Ich möchte ein Brot, bitte.*) or **ordering a meal in a restaurant** (*Ich möchte ein Omelett und einen Salat, bitte.*) Check the new phrases either in this book (in this case in Unit 8), a dictionary or with German speakers.

4 Grammar

To organise the study of grammar, write your own grammar glossary and add new information and examples as you go along.

Experiment with grammar rules. Sit back and reflect on the rules you learn. See how they compare with your own language or other languages you may already speak. Try to find out some rules on your own and be ready to spot the exceptions. By doing this you'll remember the rules better and get a feel for the language. Try to find examples of grammar in conversations or other articles.

Keep a 'pattern bank' that organises examples that can be listed under the structures you've learned.

Use old vocabulary to practise new grammar structures.

When you learn a new verb form, write the conjugation of several different verbs you know that follow the same form.

5 Pronunciation

When organising the study of pronunciation, keep a section of your notebook for pronunciation rules and practise those that trouble you.

Repeat all of the conversations, line by line. Listen to yourself and try to mimic what you hear.

Record yourself and compare yourself to a native speaker.

Make a list of words that give you trouble and practise them.

Study individual sounds, then full words.

Don't forget, it's not just about pronouncing letters and words correctly, but using the right intonation. So, when practising words and sentences, mimic the rising and falling intonation of native speakers.

6 Listening and reading

The conversations in this book include questions to help guide you in your understanding. But you can go further by following some of these tips:

Imagine the situation. When listening to or reading the conversations, try to imagine where the scene is taking place and who the main characters are. Let your experience of the world help you guess the meaning of the conversation, e.g. if a conversation takes place in a snack bar, you can predict the kind of vocabulary that is being used.

Concentrate on the main part. When watching a foreign film, you usually get the meaning of the whole story from a few individual shots. Understanding a foreign conversation or article is similar. Concentrate on the main parts to get the message and don't worry about individual words.

Guess the key words; if you cannot, ask or look them up.

When there are key words you don't understand, try to guess what they mean from the context. If you're listening to a German speaker and cannot get the gist of a whole passage because of one word or phrase, try to repeat that word with a questioning tone; the speaker will probably paraphrase it, giving you the chance to understand it. If for example you wanted to find out the meaning of the word *Mineralwasser* (mineral water), you would ask *Entschuldigung, was ist Mineralwasser?* or *Entschuldigung, was bedeutet Mineralwasser?* (**Excuse me, what does mineral water mean?**)

7 Speaking

Rehearse in the foreign language. As all language teachers will assure you, the successful learners are those students who overcome their inhibitions and get into situations where they must speak, write and listen to the foreign language. Here are some useful tips to help you practise speaking German:

Hold a conversation with yourself, using the conversations of the units as models and the structures you have learnt previously.

After you have conducted a transaction with a salesperson, clerk or waiter in your own language, pretend that you have to do it in German, e.g. *buying groceries, ordering food, drinks* and so on.

Look at objects around you and try to name them in German.

Look at people around you and try to describe them in detail.

Try to answer all of the questions in the book out loud.

Say the dialogues out loud, then try to replace sentences with ones that are true for you.

Try to role play different situations in the book.

8 Learn from your errors

Don't let errors interfere with getting your message across. Making errors is part of any normal learning process, but some people get so worried that they won't say anything unless they are sure it is correct. This leads to a vicious circle as the less they say, the less practice they get and the more mistakes they make.

Note the seriousness of errors. Many errors are not serious as they do not affect the meaning; for example if you use the wrong article (*der* for *die* or *der*), wrong pronouns (*ich kaufe ihn* for *ich kaufe es*) or wrong adjective ending (*ein guter Buch* for *ein gutes Buch*). So concentrate on getting your message across and learn from your mistakes.

9 Learn to cope with uncertainty

Don't over-use your dictionary.

When reading a text in the foreign language, don't be tempted to look up every word you don't know. Underline the words you do not understand and read the passage several times, concentrating on trying to get the gist of the passage. If after the third time there are still words which prevent you from getting the general meaning of the passage, look them up in the dictionary.

Don't panic if you don't understand.

If at some point you feel you don't understand what you are told, don't panic or give up listening. Either try and guess what is being said and keep following the conversation or, if you cannot, isolate the expression or words you haven't understood and have them explained to you. The speaker might paraphrase them and the conversation will carry on.

Keep talking.

The best way to improve your fluency in the foreign language is to talk every time you have the opportunity to do so: keep the conversations flowing and don't worry about the mistakes. If you get stuck for a particular word, don't let the conversation stop; paraphrase or replace the unknown word with one you do know, even if you have to simplify what you want to say. As a last resort use the word from your own language and pronounce it in the foreign accent.

1 Mein Name ist ...
My name is ...

In this unit you will learn how to:
- ▶ *say what your name is.*
- ▶ *greet people and say goodbye.*
- ▶ *ask people where they come from and where they live.*
- ▶ *use the words I and you.*
- ▶ *understand basic German word order.*

CEFR: *Can introduce oneself (A1); Can ask and answer questions about personal details (A1); Can produce simple phrases to describe personal details (A1)*

Greetings

Germans often shake hands when they meet and when they say **Auf Wiedersehen** (*goodbye*). They also often give only their **Nachname** (*surname*) when they introduce themselves. The courtesy titles **Herr** and **Frau** are used rather like *Mr* and *Mrs* in English. **Fräulein** (*Miss*) is hardly used any more. Women irrespective of whether they are married or not are addressed with **Frau**.

The standard greetings in German are **Guten Morgen** (*good morning*), **Guten Tag** (*good day*), **Guten Abend** (*good evening*) and **Gute Nacht** (*good night*). As you can probably see they are quite similar to English.

In addition there are many regional and less formal ways to greet or to say farewell. In Austria and southern Germany people often say **Grüß Gott**, which means *May God greet you.* In Austria **Servus** is commonly used and can mean *good day* or *goodbye*. Swiss people frequently use **Grüezi**. In less formal situations you will also hear **Hi** (*hi*), **Hallo** (*hello*) or **Ciao**.

What words in the text mean *Mr* and *Mrs*? And where would you use Grüß Gott, Servus and Grüezi?

Vocabulary builder

GREETINGS AND FAREWELLS

  1 01.01 **Listen and read how these people introduce themselves and repeat.**

Guten Tag. Ich heiße Helga Kirsch.

Hallo. Mein Name ist Steffi Schmidt.

Guten Tag. Mein Name ist Gerd Baumann.

Hallo. Ich heiße Markus.

 2 01.02 **Now complete the greetings. Listen to check your answers. Then listen and repeat.**

Hallo.	*Hello.*
Guten Morgen.	*Good morning.*
Guten Tag.	*Good day.*
Guten Abend.	*_____ evening.*
Gute Nacht.	*Good night.*
Ich heiße ...	*I am called ...*
Mein Name ist ...	*My _____ is ...*
Auf Wiedersehen.	*Goodbye.*

The greeting **Guten Tag** is used from about 10 am until 6 pm. Note there is no German equivalent for *Good afternoon*.

3 **Did you notice the different ways the people gave their names? Now have a go at giving your own name in German.**

    a Hallo. Mein Name _____ .

    b Hallo. Ich _____ .

4 **Which greetings or farewells go with which? Match the numbers and the pictures.**

a

b

c

d

1 A Gute Nacht, Frau Naumann!
    B Auf Wiedersehen!

2 A Auf Wiedersehen, Frau Hermann!
    B Auf Wiedersehen, Herr Schneider!

3 A Guten Abend, Frau Naumann!
    B Guten Abend!

4 A Guten Morgen, Herr Schneider!
   B Guten Morgen, Frau Hermann!

5 **When would you use the following greetings? Choose the appropriate boxes.**

	Guten Morgen	Guten Tag	Guten Abend	Gute Nacht
14:00				
8:00				
23.00				
10.00				
18.00				

INTRODUCTIONS

1 **01.03 Listen to the audio. What are the two ways of asking someone's name in German?**

a _____   b _____

Woman 1	Guten Tag. Wie heißen Sie?
Woman 2	Ich heiße Elisabeth Schuhmacher.
Man 1	Wie ist Ihr Name, bitte?
Man 2	Mein Name ist Paul Matthiesen.
Woman 3	Und Sie? Wie heißen Sie?
Woman 4	Ich heiße Bianca Schulz.
Man 3	Guten Tag. Wie ist Ihr Name, bitte?
Man 4	Mein Name ist Deichmann, Oliver Deichmann.

2 **01.04 Now complete the translations. Listen to check your answers. Then listen and repeat.**

bitte	*please*
Und Sie?	*And you?*
Wie ist Ihr Name?	*What is your _____?*
Wie heißen Sie?	*What are _____ called?*

3 **01.05** Listen to the policeman taking down names at the scene of an accident. Then choose the correct answers to complete the sentences.

    a What is the name of the first person?
       It's (Gertrud Gruber / Gerda Gruber / Gertrud Huber).

    b The name of the second person is (Martin Baumann / Markus Braun / Martin Braun).

    c The third person's name is (Boris Schulz / Boris Schwarz / Moritz Schulz).

All nouns begin with a capital letter in German. Nouns are naming words which refer to persons, concepts or objects:

Guten Tag. Guten Morgen. Guten Abend. Gute Nacht.
Mein Name ist Claudia.

Note that the polite forms **Sie** (*you*) and **Ihr** (*your*) also start with a capital letter:

Wie heißen Sie? Wie ist Ihr Name?

4 **01.06** **Hören Sie zu!** Listen to these people introducing themselves and read along. Then answer the questions with *True* or *False*.

    a Danielle comes from Dijon and lives in Hamburg. _____

    b Tony Linneker comes from Berlin but now lives in London. _____

    c Bettina comes from Austria and lives in Germany. _____

    d Peter lives in Germany but comes from the USA. _____

> Ich heiße Danielle Bouvier. Ich komme aus Frankreich, aus Dijon. Ich wohne in Hamburg.

> Mein Name ist Tony Linneker. Ich komme aus Großbritannien, aber ich wohne jetzt in Berlin.

Ich heiße Bettina Merkel. Ich komme aus Wien in Österreich. Ich wohne jetzt in Hannover.

Ich heiße Peter Kramer. Ich komme aus den USA, aus Chicago. Ich wohne jetzt in Hamburg.

5 01.07 Now complete the translations. Listen to check your answers. Then listen and repeat.

Ich komme aus ...	*I come from ...*
Frankreich	*France*
Ich wohne in ...	*_____ live in ...*
Großbritannien	*Great Britain*
... aus den USA ...	*... _____ the USA*
aber	*but*
Wien	*Vienna*
Österreich	*Austria*
jetzt	*now*

6 01.08 How would you say what your name is, where you come from and where you live? Try answering the questions in the audio. Then write your answers down.

Ich heiße ...

NEW EXPRESSIONS

Look at the expressions that are used in the next interviews. Note their meanings.

Entschuldigen Sie	*excuse (me)*
ein paar Fragen	*a few questions*
Darf ich Ihnen ein paar Fragen stellen?	*May I ask you a few questions?*
Ja.	*Yes.*
Wo?	*Where?*
Wo wohnen Sie?	*Where do you live?*
Woher?	*Where ... from?*
Woher kommen Sie?	*Where do you come from?*
Danke schön.	*Thank you.*

Interviews

 1 **01.09** Listen to a reporter from a German radio station as he interviews two visitors to Hanover. Then answer the question. Apart from asking the names, what other two questions does the reporter ask each person?

a _____   b _____

INTERVIEW 1

Reporter	Entschuldigen Sie, bitte. Guten Tag, Radio N–4. Darf ich Ihnen ein paar Fragen stellen?
Passant	Ja, bitte.
Reporter	Wie heißen Sie?
Passant	Ich heiße Jochen Kern.
Reporter	Und woher kommen Sie?
Passant	Ich komme aus Aachen.
Reporter	Wo wohnen Sie, bitte?
Passant	Ich wohne jetzt in Bonn.
Reporter	Danke schön.

Reporter	Wie ist Ihr Name, bitte?
Passantin	Ich heiße Dana Frye.
Reporter	Ah. Und woher kommen Sie?
Passantin	Ich komme aus Stuttgart.
Reporter	Und wo wohnen Sie?
Passantin	Ich wohne jetzt hier in Hannover.

2 **01.09** Now listen to the audio again and supply the information missing from the grid below. Try not to look at the text. Note that the German for *place of birth* is **Geburtsort** and for *place of residence* is **Wohnort**.

Name	Geburtsort	Wohnort
(Ich heiße ...)	*(Ich komme aus ...)*	*(Ich wohne jetzt in ...)*
1		
2		

 Language discovery

1 **Look at the sentences from the conversation. Notice the underlined words. Which word means *you*? Which word means *I*?**

  a Wie heißen <u>Sie</u>?
  b <u>Ich</u> heiße Jochen Kern.
  c Und woher kommen <u>Sie</u>?
  d <u>Ich</u> komme aus Aachen.

2 **Look at the interviews to find the words to complete the sentences. Which verb ending goes with *Sie*? Which verb ending goes with *ich*?**

  a Und woher komm_____ Sie?
  b Ich komm_____ aus Stuttgart.
  c Und wo wohn_____ Sie?
  d Ich wohn_____ jetzt hier in Hannover.

Learn more

1 PERSONAL PRONOUNS

The personal pronouns (words for *I, you,* etc.) in German are:

Singular (one person)		Plural (more than one person)	
ich	*I*	wir	*we*
du	*you* (informal)	ihr	*you* (informal)
Sie	*you* (formal)	Sie	*you* (formal)
er, sie, es	*he, she, it*	sie	*they*

So far you have met **ich** and **Sie** (the formal *you*). Note that **Sie** is written with a capital letter. You will learn about the others in the next few units.

2 VERB ENDINGS

A verb normally expresses an action or state. In German you need to learn which endings to put on the verb for each pronoun. In this unit you have met the verbs **heißen**, **kommen** and **wohnen**. The form of the verb that you find in a dictionary or glossary is called the infinitive: e.g. **wohnen** (*to live*).

The infinitive can be divided into two parts: **wohn-** the *stem*, **-en** the *ending*. The endings change according to the *subject* used (i.e. **ich**, **Sie**, etc.). For most verbs the endings you add with **ich** and **Sie** are:

Pronoun	Verb ending	Examples		
ich	-e	wohne	komme	heiße
Sie	-en	wohnen	kommen	heißen

3 BASIC WORD ORDER

In a German sentence the verb is usually in the second position. *Wh*-questions are questions which in English start with *What?, Who?, Where?,* etc. Hence the name *Wh*- questions, even though the question *How?* also comes into this category. In German these question words tend to start with *W*-. As you can see, the verb is the second element in both of these structures.

Statements			Wh- questions		
subject	verb		Wh – word	verb	
Ich	heiße	Schmidt.	Wie	heißen	Sie?
Ich	komme	aus Bonn.	Woher	kommen	Sie?
Ich	wohne	in Köln.	Wo	wohnen	Sie?

Practice

1 **You are going to ask a new German colleague a few questions about herself. Can you get your endings right?**

   a Guten Tag. Wie heiß_____ Sie, bitte?

   b Woher komm_____ Sie?

   c Und wo wohn_____ Sie jetzt, bitte?

2 **Timo Schmidt is introducing himself. Fill in the missing endings.**

   Hallo, ich heiß _____ Timo Schmidt. Ich komm _____ aus Hamburg, aber ich wohn _____ jetzt in Liverpool.

Pronuncation

01.10 **Hören Sie zu und wiederholen Sie.** Listen and repeat. Listen to the German words several times and try to get as close to the sounds as possible.

Hallo!

Guten Morgen!

Guten Tag!

Guten Abend!

Gute Nacht!

Auf Wiedersehen!

Listening and writing

 01. 11 Hören Sie zu. How many different greetings do you hear? What are they? Make a list.

Guten ...

Test yourself

1 Welche Antwort passt? *Which answer fits?*

  a *Guten Morgen, Herr Liebmann.*
    1 Hallo, wie ist dein Name?
    2 Guten Morgen, Frau Münch.

  b *Hallo, mein Name ist Mats. Wie heißt du?*
    1 Ich heiße Bernd.
    2 Ich heiße Herr Ahrens.

  c *Auf Wiedersehen und gute Nacht, Frau Renke.*
    1 Guten Morgen, Herr Müller.
    2 Gute Nacht, Herr Müller.

2 Wo? Woher? or Wie? Write in the missing words.

  a _____ heißen Sie?
  b _____ wohnen Sie?
  c _____ kommen Sie?
  d _____ ist Ihr Name?

3 -e, -en? Fill in the missing endings.

  a Ich heiß_____ Simone Becker. Wie heiß_____ Sie?
  b Ich wohn_____ in Berlin. Wo wohn_____ Sie?
  c Ich komm_____ aus Großbritannien. Woher komm_____ Sie?

4 Welche Worte fehlen? *Which words are missing?*

Reporter	Wie heißen ___?
Passant	___ heiße Jochen Kern.
Reporter	Und woher kommen ___?
Passant	___ komme aus Aachen.

SELF CHECK

I CAN...

○ . . . say what my name is.

○ . . . greet someone and say goodbye.

○ . . . ask people where they come from.

○ . . . ask people where they live.

○ . . . use the words for *I* and *you.*

○ . . . understand basic German word order.

2 Mir geht's gut.
I'm fine.

In this unit you will learn how to:
▶ *ask people how they are*
▶ *say how you are*
▶ *say which cities and countries people come from*
▶ *use the correct verb endings for he, she and it*

CEFR: *Can ask how people are and react (A1); Can ask and answer questions about personal details (A1); Can use basic introduction and leave-taking expressions (A1); Can produce simple phrases to describe personal details (A1)*

German-speaking countries

The three main German-speaking countries are **Deutschland** (*Germany*), **Österreich** (*Austria*) and **die Schweiz** (*Switzerland*). However, German is also spoken in **Luxemburg** (*Luxembourg*) and parts of **Belgien** (*Belgium*) and **Italien** (*Italy*). With approximately 92 million native speakers, **Deutsch** (*German*) represents the largest language group within the European Union.

Out of the three main German-speaking countries Germany is also by far the largest with more than 82 million **Einwohner** (*inhabitants*). The biggest city is Berlin with approximately 3.4 million people, followed by Hamburg and **München** (*Munich*). The largest city in Austria is **Wien** (*Vienna*) with 2.1 million people. Other well-known places are Innsbruck and Mozart's birthplace, Salzburg. Apart from German there are three more official languages in Switzerland. In the German-speaking part the two main cities are **Bern** (*Berne*), the **Hauptstadt** (*capital*), and **Zürich** (*Zurich*).

What words in the text mean Germany, Munich, Austria, Vienna and Switzerland? And what is the word for German?

Vocabulary builder

SAYING HOW YOU ARE

 1 **02.01** Here are some words people use to say how they are feeling. Listen and read what the people are saying.

a

+++
sehr gut
ausgezeichnet
prima (informal)

b

+
gut

c

+ −
es geht

d

−
nicht (so) gut

e

− − −
schlecht
furchtbar

 2 **02.02** Now listen and match the English meanings to the words about feelings. Then listen and repeat.

a sehr gut _____	**1** terrible
b ausgezeichnet _____	**2** good
c prima _____	**3** very good
d gut _____	**4** (it's) ok
e es geht _____	**5** excellent
f nicht (so) gut _____	**6** great
g schlecht _____	**7** bad
h furchtbar _____	**8** not (so) good

NEW EXPRESSIONS

Look at the expressions that are used in the next conversations. Note their meanings.

Conversations 1, 2, and 3

Wie geht es Ihnen?	*How are you?*
Und Ihnen?	*And (how are) you?*
Wie geht's?	*How are you?* (less formal version)
Das freut mich.	*I am pleased.*
nicht	*not*
heute	*today*
na ja	*oh well*

Conversation 4

nicht mehr	*no longer*
am Main	*on the (river) Main*
noch	*still*
liegen	*to lie, be*
nicht ..., sondern	*... not ..., but ...*
in der Schweiz	*in (the) Switzerland*
aber	*but, however*
dort	*there*
arbeiten	*to work*
nein	*no*
ist	*is*
schön	*beautiful, nice*

Conversations

 1 **02.03 Listen to the greetings. Then answer the question.**
In which conversation does the speaker use a less formal version of *How are you?*

CONVERSATION 1

Frau Müller	Guten Tag, Frau Renger. Wie geht es Ihnen?
Frau Renger	Gut, danke, Frau Müller. Und Ihnen?
Frau Müller	Sehr gut, danke.
Frau Renger	Das freut mich.

CONVERSATION 2

Frau Koch	Guten Morgen, Herr Schulz. Wie geht es Ihnen heute?
Herr Schulz	Nicht so gut, Frau Koch. Und Ihnen?
Frau Koch	Danke. Es geht.

CONVERSATION 3

Herr Akdag	Guten Abend, Herr Krämer. Wie geht's?
Herr Krämer	Ausgezeichnet. Vielen Dank, Herr Akdag. Und Ihnen?
Herr Akdag	Na ja, es geht.

2 **02.03 How is each person? Listen to the conversations again and supply the information missing from the grid below. Try to do this without looking at the printed text. You'll probably need to listen to each dialogue several times.**

	ausgezeichnet	sehr gut	gut	es geht	nicht so gut	schlecht
a Frau Renger			✔			
b Frau Müller						
c Herr Schulz						
d Frau Koch						
e Herr Krämer						
f Herr Akdag						

3 02.04 **Where do these people come from? Listen to the audio and find out.**

a Rainer Görner _____

b Martina Schümer
_____

c Susanna Vermeulen _____

d Michael Naumann
_____

CONVERSATION 4

Woman 1	**Rainer Görner** kommt aus Berlin. Aber er wohnt nicht mehr in Berlin. Er wohnt jetzt in Frankfurt am Main. Frankfurt ist in Deutschland.
Man 1	**Martina Schümer** kommt aus Basel. Sie wohnt noch in Basel. Basel liegt nicht in Deutschland, sondern in der Schweiz.
Woman 2	**Susanne Vermeulen** kommt aus Brüssel in Belgien. Sie wohnt aber nicht mehr dort. Sie arbeitet jetzt im Hotel Lindenhof in Düsseldorf.
Man 2	**Michael Naumann** kommt aus Leipzig. Er wohnt jetzt in Salzburg. Liegt Salzburg in der Schweiz? Nein! Es ist in Österreich und es ist sehr schön.

4 **Read the text and decide whether these statements are richtig (*true*) or falsch (*false*). Correct the false statements.**

Statement *Rainer Görner kommt aus Wien.*

Answer *Falsch. Rainer Görner kommt aus Berlin.*

a Rainer Görner wohnt jetzt in Frankfurt am Main. _____

b Zürich liegt nicht in Deutschland, sondern in Österreich.
_____

c Martina Schümer kommt aus Basel und wohnt noch in Basel.
_____

d Susanne Vermeulen kommt aus Delft in den Niederlanden.
_____

e Sie wohnt jetzt in Düsseldorf und arbeitet im Hotel Lindenhof.
_____

f Michael Naumann kommt aus Dresden und wohnt jetzt in Linz, in Österreich. _____

💡 Language discovery

1 **Look at these sentences from the last conversation. Notice the underlined words. Which words mean *he* and *she*? Which word means *it*?**

  a Martina Schümer kommt aus Basel. <u>Sie</u> wohnt noch in Basel.

  b <u>Es</u> ist in Österreich und <u>es</u> ist sehr schön.

  c Michael Naumann kommt aus Leipzig. <u>Er</u> wohnt jetzt in Salzburg.

2 **Look at the conversation again and fill in the missing endings. Which verb ending goes with er, sie and es?**

  a Martina Schümer komm＿＿ aus Basel.

  b Er wohn＿＿ jetzt in Salzburg.

  c Rainer Görner komm＿＿ aus Berlin.

  d Lieg＿＿ Salzburg in der Schweiz?

Learn more

1 VERB ENDINGS

For the third person singular (*he* = **er**, *she* = **sie**, *it* = **es**) you add a **-t** to the stem of the verb:

komm-**en**	er komm-**t**
wohn-**en**	sie wohn-**t**
lieg-**en**	es lieg-**t**

Note that **er**, **sie**, **es** are usually written with a small letter, unless they start a sentence.

The verb **arbeiten** (*to work*) is slightly different. You add **-et** rather than just **-t** to the stem so that it's easier to pronounce:

Er arbeit-et.

Here is a summary of the verb endings you have met so far:

ich	komm**e**	heiß**e**	wohn**e**	arbeit**e**
Sie	komm**en**	heiß**en**	wohn**en**	arbeit**en**
er/sie/es	komm**t**	heiß**t**	wohn**t**	arbeit**et**

2 NEGATION

Note that the negative **nicht** (*not*) is usually placed after the verb in German:

Ich wohne in London. *I live in London.*

Anke wohnt nicht in London. *Anke doesn't live in London.*

The equivalent of *not ..., but ...* is **nicht ..., sondern** in German:

Wien liegt <u>nicht</u> in Deutschland, *Vienna is <u>not</u> in Germany, <u>but</u>*
<u>sondern</u> **in Österreich.** *in Austria.*

Practice

 1 Answer the question **Wie geht es Ihnen heute?** for each of these people. Give the reply suggested by the picture. Use the expressions given.

a

Danke, mir geht's ...

b

c

_____

d

_____

Ach, es geht.	Mir geht es gut.
Mir geht's heute nicht so gut.	Mir geht's heute schlecht.
Danke, mir geht's wirklich sehr gut.	Danke, gut.

2 This is what Oliver Schmidt has written about himself. Introduce him by supplying the missing endings.

> Ich heiße Oliver Schmidt. Ich komme aus Berlin. Ich wohne jetzt aber in Hannover. Ich arbeite in Hannover.

  a Er heiß___ Oliver Schmidt.
  b Oliver komm___ aus Berlin.
  c Er wohn___ jetzt aber in Hannover.
  d Oliver arbeit___ in Hannover.

3 Put the following sentences in the negative using **nicht**. Start each sentence with **Nein, ...**
  a Er wohnt in London. Nein, er wohnt nicht in London.
  b Wien liegt in Deutschland.
  c Sie heißt Claudia.
  d Frankfurt liegt in Österreich.
  e Ich komme aus Berlin.
  f Sie arbeitet im Hotel Lindenhof.

4 How many words can you find? They have all occurred in this unit. You should be able to find at least 15.

M	E	I	N	S	I	E	A	N	H	D	Z	G
G	E	H	T	E	S	P	R	I	M	A	S	U
A	U	S	G	E	Z	E	I	C	H	N	E	T
H	W	I	R	K	L	I	C	H	L	K	H	O
T	N	O	C	H	H	E	U	T	E	E	R	P

Pronunciation

 02.05

ei in German is pronounced like the English letter *i*:

Beispiel, heißen, Einstein, Wein

ie is pronounced like the English letter *e*:

Dietrich, Sie, Wien (Vienna)

How would you pronounce this sentence (which means *I drink wine in Vienna*)? Have a go and then listen to check your answer.

Ich trinke Wein in Wien.

Listening

02.06 Listen to these three colleagues greeting each other as they arrive at the office. Which three of the six responses below did you hear in the audio and in what order?

   a Danke, gut. _____
   b Ach, es geht. _____
   c Mir geht's wirklich sehr gut. _____
   d Mir geht's heute wirklich schlecht. _____
   e Mir geht es heute nicht so gut. _____
   f Nicht schlecht. Und Ihnen? _____

Mir geht es gut.	*I am fine.*
Mir geht's gut.	*I'm fine.*
wirklich	*really*
Das tut mir leid.	*I'm sorry about that.*

Go further

1   02.07 Listen and mark the names of the countries you hear. Then listen again. Where do German speakers mostly put the stress in each name? Underline the correct stressed part in the names of the countries you hear.

Beispiel *(example)*   <u>Deutsch</u>land

Belgien		Irland		Schweden	
Dänemark		Italien		die Schweiz	
Deutschland		die Niederlande		Spanien	
England		Österreich		die Tschechische Republik	
Frankreich		Polen		die Türkei	
Griechenland		Portugal		Ungarn	
Großbritannien		Schottland		Wales	

Some place names are spelt the same in both English and German, but are pronounced differently: e.g. **Berlin**, **Frankfurt** and **England**. Others are different in German from their English versions: e.g. **Köln** (*Cologne*); **München** (*Munich*); **Hannover** (*Hanover*); **Wien** (*Vienna*); **Braunschweig** (*Brunswick*); **Nürnberg** (*Nuremberg*).

Note that for most countries you would just say:

▶ **Ich komme aus Irland, Großbritannien, Deutschland**, *etc.*
▶ **Ich wohne in Irland, Großbritannien, Deutschland**, *etc.*

There are a few exceptions, including Switzerland, Turkey, the Czech Republic and the Slovak Republic, the Netherlands and the USA.

▶ **Ich komme aus der Schweiz/aus der Türkei/aus der Tschechischen Republik/aus der Slowakischen Republik.**
▶ **Ich wohne in der Schweiz/in der Türkei/in der Tschechischen Republik/in der Slowakischen Republik.**
▶ **Ich komme aus den Niederlanden/aus den USA.**
▶ **Ich wohne in den Niederlanden/in den USA.**

2 **Which statements are richtig (*true*) or falsch (*false*)? Correct the wrong statements.**

   a Zürich liegt in Deutschland. *Zürich liegt nicht in Deutschland, sondern in der Schweiz.*
   b Innsbruck liegt in Österreich. *Richtig.*
   c Brüssel liegt in Belgien. _____
   d Heidelberg liegt in Österreich. _____
   e Köln liegt in den Niederlanden. _____
   f Salzburg liegt in Österreich. _____
   g Amsterdam liegt in Belgien. _____

Writing

 Woher kommen diese Leute und wo wohnen diese Leute jetzt?
Where do these people come from and where do these people live now?
Write sentences.

Beispiel: Boris Becker. D / USA, D

Boris Becker kommt aus Deutschland. Er wohnt jetzt in den USA und in Deutschland.

a Naomi Campbell (GB / USA) _____

b Johnny Depp (USA / F) _____

c Karl Lagerfeld (D / F) _____

d Michael Schuhmacher (D / Ö) _____

e Arnold Schwarzenegger (Ö / USA) _____

f Heidi Klum (D / USA) _____

Speaking

 02.08 You meet Ulrike Peters in a hotel lobby and get into conversation with her. **Was antworten Sie?** *What do you answer?* Fill in the answers and play the part of Sheena MacDonald in the audio. Sheena comes from **Edinburg**, **Schottland** (*Edinburgh, Scotland*).

Ulrike	Guten Tag! Mein Name ist Ulrike Peters.
Sheena	*Return the greetings and say your name.*
Ulrike	Und woher kommen Sie?
Sheena	*Say that you come from Edinburgh in Scotland. Then ask her where she lives.*
Ulrike	Ich wohne hier in München.
Sheena	*Say Munich is beautiful.*
Ulrike	Ja, München ist sehr schön. Aber Edinburg ist auch sehr schön!

Test yourself

1 **Here are some extracts from the conversation earlier in the unit. Fill in the missing words.**

a *Rainer Görner kommt* **1** _____ *Berlin,* **2** _____ *er wohnt nicht mehr in Berlin. Er wohnt* **3** _____ *in Frankfurt am Main.*

b *Susanne Vermeulen kommt* **1** _____ *Brüssel in* **2** _____ *.Sie wohnt* **3** _____ *nicht mehr dort. Sie* **4** _____ *jetzt im Hotel Lindenhof in Düsseldorf.*

2 **Schreiben Sie die Fragen!** *Write out the questions.* **Find the questions that these sentences would answer.**

Frage (question)	**Wie geht es Ihnen? / Wie geht's?**
Antwort (answer)	**Mir geht's gut, danke.**

a _____ ?

Ich heiße Susi Reinhardt.

b _____ ?

Ich komme aus Köln.

c _____ ?

Ich wohne jetzt in Bonn.

d _____ ?

Mir geht es heute nicht so gut.

3 **Verbendungen.** **Add the appropriate verb ending.**

a Peter komm___ aus München, aber er wohn___ jetzt in Stuttgart.

b Er arbeit___ in Köln, aber ich arbeit___ in Bonn.

c Edinburg lieg___ in Schottland.

d Ich komm___ aus England, aber Julia komm___ aus Österreich.

3 Wie schreibt man das?

How do you write that?

In this unit you will learn how to:
▶ *count from 0 to 100*
▶ *spell names and words*
▶ *use* yes/no questions
▶ *give your phone number and email address*
▶ *use plural verb forms for* we *and* they

CEFR: *Can read isolated phrases (A1); Can identify main points of news items (A2); Can handle numbers, quantities, cost and time (A1)*

German pronunciation and spelling

In German spelling and pronunciation is much more consistent than in English. Most **Wörter** (*words*) are pronounced as they are spelled and the **Aussprache** (*pronunciation*) doesn't vary from one word to the next. The German **Alphabet** (*alphabet*) uses the same 26 **Buchstaben** (*letters*) as the English alphabet, but there are four additional letters. Three of these are formed by adding an **Umlaut**, two dots, above the vowels *a, o* and *u,* which become **ä, ö** and **ü**. These are used in words such as **Bäckerei** (*bakery*), **Österreich** or **Zürich** (*Zurich*).

The fourth extra letter is **ß**, which is called **scharfes s** (*sharp s*) or **sz,** and sounds like the *s* in *bus.* This is used after a long vowel in words such as **Straße** (*street*) and **Fußball** (*football*).

What are the four additional letters in the German alphabet?

Vocabulary builder

NUMBERS 1–10

1 03.01 Numbers are important in any language. Here are the numbers 1–10 in German. Hören Sie zu und wiederholen Sie! *Listen and repeat.*

1 eins	2 zwei	3 drei	4 vier	5 fünf
6 sechs	7 sieben	8 acht	9 neun	10 zehn

Note that the word for *nil* or *zero* is **null** in German.

2 03.02 Listen to the audio. Which six of these numbers do you hear?

1 9 7 3 10 1 8 5 4 7 6 1 5 2

In spoken German, on the phone or the radio for example, **zwo** is sometimes used instead of **zwei** to distinguish it from **drei**.

3 03.03 Hören Sie zu! *Listen.* **Supply the results of the football matches.**

BUNDESLIGA			
Bayern München	2	Stuttgart	2
Köln	3	Leverkusen	4
Hamburg		Dortmund	
Bochum		Hannover	
Duisburg		Mönchengladbach	
Bielefeld		Wolfsburg	
Schalke		Freiburg	
Nürnberg		Hertha Berlin	
Bremen		Frankfurt	

THE ALPHABET

1 03.04 Hören Sie zu und wiederholen Sie!

A-B-C D-E-F G-H-I J-K-L M-N-O P-Q-R S-T-U V-W-X Y-Z

Other letters used in German:

▶ **Ä Ö Ü:** the two dots or **Umlaut** over these letters change the pronunciation, as you may have already noticed in words like **schön** and **Übung.**

▶ ß (**sz** or **scharfes s** *sharp s*) is used instead of a double *s* after a long vowel or a diphthong.

▷ **Long vowels**	Straße, Fußball
▷ **Diphthong**	heißen
▷ **Short vowel**	Wasser

Note how you pronounce the letters *A*, *E* and *I* in German: *A* as in ***Africa***; *E* as in ***Elephant***; *I* as in ***Israel***.

2 **03.05 Listen to these people checking in at a conference. Number the names as you hear them.**

…

Baumgart, Waltraud	☐
Henning, Sebastian	☐
Hesse, Patrick	☐
Hoffmann, Silke	☐
Ludwig, Paul	☐
Schanze, Martin	☐
Schidelowskaja, Tanja	☐
Schulte, Christel	☐

…

NEW EXPRESSIONS

Look at the expressions that are used in the next conversation. Note their meanings.

wir	*we*
sind	*are*
sprechen	*to speak*
Französisch	*French (language)*
nur ein wenig	*only a little*
ziemlich	*fairly*
Englisch	*English (language)*
kein Englisch	*no English*
ein bisschen	*a bit (of)*

Conversation

1 **03.06** **These German tourists are visiting Paris. Two couples are getting to know each other while they wait in the hotel foyer for the tour bus. Listen to the conversation. Then answer the questions.**

a Where do the two couples come from?

_____

b Do they speak French? _____

Jochen	Guten Morgen! Ich heiße Jochen Klempner und das ist meine Frau, Katja.
Marga	Guten Morgen! Wir heißen Marga und Peter Krumbacher. Wir kommen aus Jena. Wir arbeiten bei Carl Zeiss. Woher kommen Sie?
Katja	Wir sind aus Stuttgart. Sprechen Sie Französisch?
Peter	Nur ein wenig. Wir sprechen aber ziemlich gut Englisch. Und Sie?
Jochen	Wir sprechen kein Französisch und nur ein bisschen Englisch.

2 **Richtig oder falsch? Korrigieren Sie die falschen Aussagen.** _True or false? Correct the wrong statements._ **Then answer the last question.**

a Jochen und Katja kommen aus Stuttgart. _____

b Sie sprechen ziemlich gut Französisch. _____

c Marga und Peter sind aus Weimar. _____

d Sie sprechen nur ein wenig Französisch. _____

e Sie sprechen kein Englisch. _____

f Arbeiten Marga und Peter bei Jenapharm oder bei Carl Zeiss?

_____

 Language discovery

1 **Look at the last conversation and the following questions again. Which verb ending goes with wir (we)? And what ending do you use when you refer to two people or more by name or as sie (they)?**

a Wir heiß_____ Marga und Peter Krumbacher.

b Wir komm_____ aus Jena.

c Wir arbeit_____ bei Carl Zeiss.

d Wir sprech_____ kein Französisch.

e Marga und Peter komm_____ aus Weimar.

f Marga und Peter sprech_____ kein Englisch.

g Arbeit_____ Marga und Peter bei Jenapharm oder bei Carl Zeiss?

Learn more

1 *YES/NO* QUESTIONS

Yes/No questions, as their name suggests, are those questions which require a *yes* or a *no* answer.

Statement	**Peter und Marga sprechen Englisch.**
Question	**Sprechen Peter und Marga Englisch?**
Statement	**Katja spricht kein Französisch.**
Question	**Spricht Katja Französisch?**

As you can see, *Yes/No* questions in German start with a verb followed by the subject. They don't use a structure like 'Do you....?' as in English. Note that **ja** and **nein** are separated from the main part of the sentence by a comma.

Yes/No Questions			
Verb	**Subject**		
Sprechen	**Sie**	Deutsch?	
Wohnen	**Sie**	in Hamburg?	
Kommen	**sie**	aus Berlin?	
Statements			
	Subject	**Verb**	
Ja,	**ich**	**spreche**	Deutsch.
Nein,	**ich**	**wohne**	nicht in Hamburg.
Nein,	**sie**	**kommen**	aus München.

2 SAYING WE AND THEY

So far you have learned to talk about yourself (**ich**) and about a third person (**er**, **sie**) and to talk directly to someone (**Sie**). What if you wanted to talk about yourself together with somebody else? In German you use the word **wir** (*we*). In the **wir** form the verb takes an **-en** ending.

Wir wohnen in Bonn.   *We live in Bonn.*

Wir arbeiten in Köln.   *We work in Cologne.*

To talk about two or more other people, you use **sie** (*they*). Again, the verb takes an **-en** ending.

Sie heißen Gerd und Sabine.   *They are called Gerd and Sabine.*

Sie kommen aus München.   *They come from Munich.*

3 VARIOUS MEANINGS OF SIE

You might think it a little confusing that the word **Sie/sie** has so many different meanings. In practice, there are several ways of distinguishing between them. Firstly, the formal **Sie** (*you*) always takes a capital initial letter; secondly, the ending of the verb for **sie** (*she*) is **-t** as opposed to **-en** for **sie** (*they*). Thirdly, and probably most importantly, the context nearly always makes the meaning clear.

4 VERB ENDING REVIEW

You have now met the verb endings for most personal pronouns. Here is an overview.

Singular				Plural			
ich	komm**e**	sprech**e**	arbeit**e**	wir	komm**en**	sprech**en**	arbeit**en**
Sie	komm**en**	sprech**en**	arbeit**en**	Sie	komm**en**	sprech**en**	arbeit**en**
er/sie/es	komm**t**	sprich**t**	arbeit**et**	sie	komm**en**	sprech**en**	arbeit**en**

Remember **arbeiten** needs an extra **e** in the **er/sie/es** form. Also note that **sprechen** has a vowel change to **spricht** in the **er/sie/es** form.

The verb **sein** (*to be*) is irregular.

Singular		Plural	
ich	**bin**	wir	**sind**
Sie	**sind**	Sie	**sind**
er/sie/es	**ist**	sie	**sind**

PRACTICE

1 **Imagine you are somewhat surprised by the information given in these statements, so you query each one. Use wirklich (*really*) to emphasise your point.**

Statement *Tim und Julia sprechen sehr gut Englisch.*

Question *Sprechen Tim und Julia wirklich sehr gut Englisch?*

  a Tim und Julia wohnen in München.
  b Tim und Julia arbeiten im Apple Store.
  c Julia kommt aus Italien.
  d Tim spricht ein bisschen Spanisch.

2 **Look at the underlined words. Decide if Sie/sie means *you*, *she* or *they* in each of the sentences.**

  a <u>Sie</u> heißt Nadine.
  b Guten Tag. Heißen <u>Sie</u> Carsten Neumann?
  c Jetzt wohnen <u>sie</u> in Edinburg, in Schottland.

3 **Lilo and Carmen, two sisters, are introducing themselves. Supply the missing endings.**

Hallo, wir heiß_____ Lilo und Carmen Weiland. Wir komm_____ aus Linz, in Österreich. Wir sprech_____ sehr gut Englisch and Französisch. Wir wohn_____ jetzt in Berlin und arbeit_____ hier.

Speaking

 03.07 Answer the two questions in the audio, first giving your name and then spelling your surname. Here is what you would say if your name were Karen Franks.

Other person	Wie ist Ihr Name?
You	Franks, Karen Franks.
Other person	Und wie schreibt man das?
You	F-R-A-N-K-S.

 03.08 Try answering the questions in the audio. Then listen again and note down the numbers given by Jochen:

 Telefon _____ Handy _____

Fax _____ E-Mail _____

Note that the @ sign in German is pronounced as in English.

Listening

 1 **03.09 Hören Sie zu!** Listen to the radio excerpt from a stock market report. Which of the companies, whose logos appear below, are mentioned?

AEG	☐	DER	☐
DB	☐	MAN	☐
BMW	☐	DZ BANK	☐
VW	☐	E-ON	☐

AEG   Die Bahn DB

[reproduced with permission of Volkswagen AG]

 2 03.10 **Welche Namen und Telefonnummern hören Sie? What names and phone numbers do you hear in the audio?**

a Name _____ Telefonnummer _____
b Name _____ Telefonnummer _____

V **Wie ist Ihre Telefonnummer?**

Wie ist Ihre Handynummer?

Wie ist Ihre Faxnummer?

Wie ist Ihre E-Mail-Adresse?

Meine Telefonnummer,
number, **Handynummer,**
Faxnummer, E-Mail-Adresse ist...

What is your telephone number?

What is your mobile number?

What is your fax number?

What is your e-mail address?

My telephone mobile number, fax number, e-mail address is ...

Go further

1 03.11 **Hören Sie bitte zu und wiederholen Sie.**

11 elf	14 vierzehn	17 siebzehn
12 zwölf	15 fünfzehn	18 achtzehn
13 dreizehn	16 sechzehn	19 neunzehn
20 zwanzig	50 fünfzig	80 achtzig
30 dreißig	60 sechzig	90 neunzig
40 vierzig	70 siebzig	100 (ein)hundert

In German, numbers such as 24 and 48 start with the last number and work backwards (a bit like the four-and-twenty blackbirds of nursery rhyme fame).

21 einundzwanzig	43 dreiundvierzig
32 zweiunddreißig	54 vierundfünfzig

Numbers in German are written as one word. German speakers don't seem to mind long words, as you will discover! Please note the following spelling variations: the *s* at the end of **eins** is dropped in **einundzwanzig**, **einunddreißig** etc.; **dreißig** is written with *ß* and not with the letter z.

In German you can say your phone number in single digits:

7 – 6 – 2 – 8 – 3 – 4
sieben – sechs – zwei/zwo – acht – drei – vier,

or in pairs:

76 – 28 – 34 sechsundsiebzig – achtundzwanzig – vierunddreißig.

This also applies to dialling codes. The number 0521 could be:
null – fünf – zwei/zwo – eins

or

null – fünf – einundzwanzig.

2 03.12 **How do you think you say these numbers in German? Make a guess and then listen to the answers in the audio.**

99 _____	87 _____	52 _____
48 _____	26 _____	

3 03.13 **You will hear a recording from a German Lotto draw. Choose six numbers first and then listen and see if you have won.**

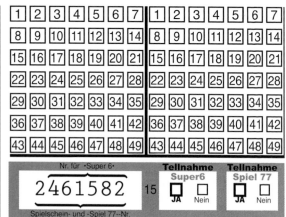

Test yourself

1 Choose the correct verb to complete these *yes/no* questions.

Arbeiten – Sprechen – Wohnen – Kommen – Heißen

- **a** _____ Sie aus Großbritannien?
- **b** _____ Sie Englisch?
- **c** _____ Sie Frank Linneker?
- **d** _____ Sie bei BMW?
- **e** _____ Sie in Deutschland?

2 What are these numbers?

- **a** fünfzehn = _15_
- **b** dreiundzwanzig = _____
- **c** siebenundzwanzig = _____
- **d** achtunddreißig = _____
- **e** zweiundneunzig = _____
- **f** neunundfünfzig = _____
- **g** sechsundvierzig = _____

3 Can you remember the verb endings you have used so far?

- **a** Ich komm_____ aus London.
- **b** Ich heiß_____ Henrietta.
- **c** Komm_____ Sie aus Schottland?
- **d** Er heiß_____ Robert.
- **e** Christine sprich_____ sehr gut Französisch.
- **f** Wir wohn_____ in Frankfurt.
- **g** Carmen und Lilo komm_____ aus Linz, in Österreich.

4 Here are the **Visitenkarten** (*business cards*) of two people. Pretend that you are each person in turn and write as much as you can about yourself at this stage.

δ **Delta Software GmbH**

Matthias Peters
Marketing

Burchardstraße 34 20095 Hamburg
Telefon 040-300526 Fax: 040-376284
E–Mail m.peters@delta.com

ANTIQUITÄTEN CENTER
Marienstraße 21 44000 Münster

Dorothea Johannsen
ART DECO, ART NOUVEAU

Telefon 02 51/51 43 86
E-Mail johannsen@artdeco.de

SELF CHECK

I CAN...
. . . count from 0 to 100.
. . . spell names and words.
. . . use yes/no questions.
. . . give my phone number and email address.
. . . use plural verb forms for we and they.

Sprechen Sie Deutsch?
Do you speak German?

In this unit you will learn how to:
▶ *say what languages you speak and ask others what they speak*
▶ *say whether you are working or studying*
▶ *say what nationality you are*
▶ *use the formal and informal forms of* you

CEFR: *Can ask and answer questions about personal details (A1); Can write short notes about personal details (A1); Can understand short simple texts (A1); Can understand frequently used expressions about geography (A1)*

Saying *you*

While in English people use *you* when addressing someone formally or informally, there are different words in German. When addressing someone *formally,* Germans say **Sie** (singular and plural) and when addressing someone informally, they use **du** for one person and **ihr** for two persons or more.

Here are a few tips for when to use the formal and informal modes of address:

▶ Use **Sie** with people you are not particularly close to. **Sie** is spelt with a capital **S** wherever it comes in the sentence. Use **Sie** to address one or more persons.
▶ Use **du** to a person you feel close to, and to a child or a pet; **du** is also used among young people and students; **du** can only be used to address one person.
▶ Use **ihr** to two or more people who you would address individually as **du**.
▶ When you are not sure, use **Sie**.

What would you use with the people below? Write du, ihr or Sie.
one of your parents _____ a group of people at a meeting _____
a person you don't know _____ two of your good friends _____

In everyday situations where English speakers might immediately adopt first name terms, many German speakers tend to prefer a certain degree of formality. For instance, work colleagues often call each other **Herr X** or **Frau Y** and use the **Sie** form to each other even after years of working together.

Vocabulary builder

NATIONALITIES AND LANGUAGES

1 04.01 **Here are some nationalities and languages that you already know together with some new ones. Listen and repeat.**

Men	Women	**Sprache** (language)
Ich bin **Deutscher**.	Ich bin **Deutsche**.	**Deutsch**
Bernd ist **Österreicher**.	Susi ist **Österreicherin**.	**Deutsch**
Er ist **Engländer**.	Sie ist **Engländerin**.	**Englisch**
Sind Sie **Amerikaner**?	Sind Sie **Amerikanerin**?	**Englisch**
David ist **Waliser**.	Sîan ist **Waliserin**.	**Englisch/Walisisch**
Iain ist **Schotte**.	Una ist **Schottin**.	**Englisch**
Padraig ist **Ire**.	Maire ist **Irin**.	**Englisch**
Gür ist **Türke**.	Yildiz ist **Türkin**.	**Türkisch**
Jean-Claude ist **Franzose**.	Nadine ist **Französin**.	**Französisch**
Miguel ist **Spanier**.	Manuela ist **Spanierin**.	**Spanisch**
Masahide ist **Japaner**.	Kumi ist **Japanerin**.	**Japanisch**

2 **Now answer the questions. What can you figure out about the expressions?**

   a What are the two endings on the nationalities used for men? _____

   b What is the main ending for female nationalities? _____

   c What do almost all the languages end in? _____

NEW EXPRESSIONS

Look at the expressions that are used in the next conversation. Note their meanings.

Part 1

ich bin ...	*I am ...*
Deutscher	*(a) German (male)*
in der Nähe von ...	*near ...*
ich kann ...	*I can (speak) ...*
auch	*also*
Russisch	*Russian (the language)*
verheiratet	*married*
seit zwei Jahren	*for (lit. since) two years*

Part 2

Deutsche	*(a) German (female)*
ledig	*single, unmarried*
natürlich	*of course*
Französisch	*French (the language)*
verstehen	*to understand*
Spanisch	*Spanish (the language)*
studieren	*to study*

Conversation

 1 **04.02 Listen to the audio, then answer the question. What are the people doing?**

    a introducing themselves   **b** introducing each other

PART 1

Man	Guten Abend! Mein Name ist Norbert Schicker und ich bin Deutscher. Ich komme aus Potsdam in der Nähe von Berlin, aber ich wohne jetzt hier in Leipzig. Ich spreche Deutsch und ich kann auch sehr gut Russisch. Ich bin verheiratet und ich bin seit zwei Jahren pensioniert.

| Woman | Hallo! Ich heiße Heike Berger und bin Deutsche. Ich bin ledig und komme aus Merseburg, in der Nähe von Leipzig. Ich spreche natürlich Deutsch und ein wenig Französisch. Ich verstehe auch ein bisschen Spanisch. Ich studiere hier in Leipzig. |

2 **Check if you understood what Heike and Norbert said about themselves. Write an N if the description fits Norbert or an H if it fits Heike.**

1 ___ versteht ein bisschen Spanisch.

2 ___ ist Deutscher und kommt aus Potsdam.

3 ___ ist verheiratet.

4 ___ kann sehr gut Russisch.

5 ___ studiert in Leipzig.

6 ___ ist seit zwei Jahren pensioniert.

Language discovery

1 **In German there is a formal and informal way of saying you. Can you figure out what ending goes with du? And what ending goes with ihr?**

1 Woher <u>kommst</u> du?

2 Wo <u>wohnst</u> du?

3 <u>Sprichst</u> du Englisch?

4 <u>Studierst</u> du Medizin?

5 Woher <u>kommt</u> ihr?

6 Wo <u>wohnt</u> ihr?

7 <u>Versteht</u> ihr Spanisch?

   a ending with du: _____

   b ending with ihr: _____

Learn more

1 NATIONALITIES AND LANGUAGES

The endings for nouns indicating nationality are:

For males		For females	
-er	*-e*	*-erin*	*-in*
Amerikan**er**	Franzose	Amerikan**erin**	Französ**in**
Engländ**er**	Türke	Engländ**erin**	Türk**in**
Spani**er**	Griech**e**	Spani**erin**	Griech**in**

The main exception to this is the female version of a German: **eine Deutsche**. Most languages end in **-isch**: **Englisch, Französisch, Japanisch**, etc. The exception is *German*: **Deutsch**.

Note that **Franzose** does not have an umlaut (¨), but **Französin** and **Französisch** do.

2 INFORMAL WAYS OF SAYING YOU (DU, IHR)

As you've discovered in German, there are formal and informal ways of saying you: **Sie** (*formal*) and **du** (*informal*) are used when addressing one person; **Sie** (*formal*) and **ihr** (*informal*) are needed when talking to more than one person. As you might expect the verb endings for **Sie**, **du** and **ihr** are different. Here are some examples of all three forms, starting with the **Sie** form that you have practised already.

Sie **–en**	du **-st**	ihr **-t**
Woher komm**en** Sie?	Woher komm**st** du?	Woher komm**t** ihr?
Wo wohn**en** Sie?	Wo wohn**st** du?	Wo wohn**t** ihr?
Wie heiß**en** Sie?	Wie heiß**t** du?	Wie heiß**t** ihr?
Sprech**en** Sie Deutsch?	Sprich**st** du Deutsch?	Sprech**t** ihr Deutsch?

If the stem of a verb ends in **ß**, **ss** or **z**, only **-t** is added to the stem in the **du** form: **du heißt, du tanzt.**

With **sprechen** the vowel changes to an **i** in the **du** form, just as it does in the **er/sie/es** form: **du sprichst, er/sie/es spricht.**

3 SUMMARY OF VERB ENDINGS

Here is a summary of verb endings in German. Most verbs follow the regular pattern like **wohnen**, but some verbs, like **sprechen**, have a vowel change in the **du** and the **er/sie/es** forms.

Also note that verbs whose stem ends in **t**, such as **arbeiten**, add an extra **-e** in the **du, ihr** and **er/sie/es** forms. We have included the irregular verbs **sein** (*to be*) and **haben** (*to have*) because they occur so frequently.

		wohnen	sprechen	arbeiten	sein	haben
Singular						
ich	-e	wohne	spreche	arbeite	bin	habe
du	-st	wohnst	sprichst	arbeitest	bist	hast
Sie	-en	wohnen	sprechen	arbeiten	sind	haben
er/sie/es	-t	wohnt	spricht	arbeitet	ist	hat
Plural						
wir	-en	wohnen	sprechen	arbeiten	sind	haben
ihr	-t	wohnt	sprecht	arbeitet	seid	habt
Sie/sie	-en	wohnen	sprechen	arbeiten	sind	haben

3 DIFFERENT WORDS FOR YOUR

Words for *your* and *my* are called *possessive adjectives*. There are three words for the possessive adjective *your* in German. When they are used with certain nouns you have to add an **e** to them. The reason for this is that these nouns are feminine. You will learn about the gender of nouns in the next unit.

Sie – Ihr(e)*	du – dein(e)	ihr – euer/eure
formal, 1 or more people	informal, 1 person	informal, 2 or more people
Wie ist **Ihr** Name?	Wie ist **dein** Name?	Wie ist **euer** Name?
Wie ist **Ihre**	Wie ist **deine**	Wie ist **eure**
Handynummer?	Handynummer?	Handynummer?
Wie ist **Ihre** E-Mail-Adresse?	Wie ist **deine** E-Mail-Adresse?	Wie ist **eure** E-Mail-Adresse?

* For a more detailed list of possessives in German see Unit 15, Learn More.

Note that an e is dropped from **euer** when there is an e at the end.

4 ASKING HOW SOMEONE IS

There are three ways of asking *How are you?* in German, depending on the context (formal, informal) and the number of people being addressed.

Sie → Ihnen	du → dir	ihr → euch
Wie geht es Ihnen?	Wie geht es dir?	Wie geht es euch?

Practice

1 **Jan is introducing his colleagues. Fill in the missing nationalities.**

    a Martin kommt aus Deutschland. Er ist *Deutscher*.

    b Fiona kommt aus England. Sie ist _____ .

    c Yuko kommt aus Japan. Sie ist _____ .

    d Iain kommt aus Schottland. Er ist _____ .

    e Jennifer kommt aus den USA. Sie ist _____ .

    f Karl kommt aus Österreich. Er ist _____ .

2 **While travelling you meet a young German and ask her a few questions. Fill in the correct endings and the other missing words.**

    a Wie geht es <u>dir</u>?

    b Wie heiß_____ du?

    c Woher komm_____ du?

    d Wohn_____ du in Deutschland?

    e Sprich_____ du Englisch?

    f Studier_____ du oder arbeit_____ du?

    g Wie ist_____ Handynummer?

    h Wie ist_____ E-Mail-Adresse?

3 **How would you ask these people how they are?**

    a an elderly person you don't know: Wie geht es _____?

    b a good friend: Wie _____?

    c two friends from school: Wie _____?

    d two strangers in a hotel bar: Wie _____?

Pronunciation

04.03 A **W** in German is pronounced more like an English *v*. And a **V** in German is pronounced like an *F* in English. Listen and repeat these words.

wie?	wo?	wer?
verheiratet	verwitwet	vierzig

St and **sp** in German are pronounced as *sht* and *shp* at the beginning of a word or syllable. Listen and repeat these words.

Straße	**studieren**	**verstehen**
Sport	**Spanisch**	**versprechen** (*to promise*)

How are these words pronounced? Have a go and then listen to check your answers.

viel, wirklich, Sprachen, Beispiel, Studium

Speaking

1 04.04 **Play the role of Jürgen Krause and answer the questions in the audio.**

Name	Jürgen Krause
Staatsangehörigkeit	Österreicher
Geburtsort	Wien
Wohnort	Salzburg
Sprachen	Deutsch und Englisch
Familienstand	seit drei Jahren verwitwet
Arbeit?	Ja, in Salzburg

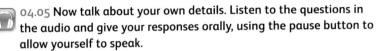

04.05 **Now talk about your own details. Listen to the questions in the audio and give your responses orally, using the pause button to allow yourself to speak.**

Familienstand	*marital status*
verwitwet	*widowed*
geschieden	*divorced*
pensioniert	*retired*
arbeitslos	*unemployed*
Staatsangehörigkeit	*nationality*

Listening

04.06 Listen to the two evening students introducing themselves. Supply the information missing from the grid below.

	Dialog 1	Dialog 2
Name	Gür Yalezan	Susi Merkl
Staatsangehörigkeit (**nationality**)	Türke	_____
Geburtsort	_____	_____
Wohnort	Taucha	Rötha
Sprachen (**languages**)	_____	_____
Familienstand (**marital status**)	_____	_____
Arbeit? (**work**)	_____	_____
Studium? (**study**)	_____	_____

In English you do not in general say 'I'm a German' or 'He's a Turk'. You prefer to say 'I'm German' or 'He's Turkish' – using the adjective rather than the noun. In German, it is normal to use the noun, but the word for 'a' is not needed:

Ich bin Deutscher / Deutsche.

Gür ist Türke.

Susi ist Österreicherin.

 # Reading and writing

1 Read the following text. Which languages does Michael speak?

> **Michaels Blog – Ich über mich**
>
> Ich heiße Michael Schulmeyer und bin 23 Jahre alt.
>
> Ich bin Österreicher und komme aus Wien.
>
> Ich studiere auch in Wien (Fremdsprachen).
>
> Meine Muttersprache ist Deutsch.
>
> Ich spreche auch Englisch und Französisch.
>
> Ich verstehe ein wenig Spanisch.
>
> Ich lerne im Moment Japanisch.
>
> Mehr über mich? Hier <u>klicken</u>.

ich über mich	*about me*
alt	*old*
auch	*also*
Fremdsprachen	*foreign languages*
meine Muttersprache	*my mother tongue*
lernen	*to learn*
im Moment	*at the moment*

2 Beantworten Sie die Fragen. Answer the questions in full sentences.

Frage	Ist Michael 23 Jahre alt?
Antwort	Ja, er ist 23 Jahre alt.
Frage	Kommt Michael aus Salzburg?
Antwort	Nein, er kommt aus Wien.

a Ist Michael Deutscher? _____

b Ist er arbeitslos? _____

c Studiert er in Innsbruck? _____

d Spricht er Deutsch? _____

e Spricht er auch Russisch? _____

f Versteht er ein wenig Spanisch? _____

g Lernt er im Moment Türkisch? _____

 3 Rachel Jenkins has written down details about herself. Write down your own details following the same pattern.

> _Mein Name ist Rachel Jenkins. Ich bin Engländerin._
> _Ich komme aus Preston. Ich wohne jetzt in Manchester._
> _Ich spreche Englisch und ein bisschen Deutsch._
> _Ich bin ledig und ich arbeite hier in Manchester._

Go further

1 Read a dialogue between two students, Markus and Christian, meeting in a London hotel foyer. They are using the **du** form. Look at the sentences from their conversation below and number them so they're in the correct order.

Markus	Aus München. Kommst du auch aus München?
Markus	Hallo! Ich heiße Markus. Und wie heißt du?
Markus	Ja, ziemlich gut. Und du?
Christian	Na ja, es geht.
Christian	Nein, aus Nürnberg. Sprichst du Englisch?
Christian	Ich bin Christian. Woher kommst du?

2 04.07 **Now, rewrite the dialogue for two businessmen, Klaus Thomas and Gerhard Braun, meeting in the same hotel foyer. Use the Sie form. Then check your new version with the audio.**

Klaus Thomas _____

Gerhard Braun _____

Klaus Thomas _____

Gerhard Braun _____

Klaus Thomas _____

Gerhard Braun _____

Test yourself

1 **Sagen Sie es anders. Say it another way. Match the sentences on the left with those of similar meaning on the right.**

a Wie ist dein Name? _____

b Welche Telefonnummer habt ihr? _____

c Woher kommt ihr? _____

d Wie ist deine Handynummer? _____

e Wie heißen Sie? _____

f Woher bist du? _____

1 Woher seid ihr?

2 Welche Handynummer hast du?

3 Wie heißt du?

4 Woher kommst du?

5 Wie ist eure Telefonnummer?

6 Wie ist Ihr Name?

2 **Sie, du und ihr. Look at the questions which you might ask a new colleague. Then reformulate the questions as if you were a student who has just met another student in a hall of residence.**

a Wie heißen Sie? Wie heißt du? _____

b Woher kommen Sie? _____

c Und wo wohnen Sie jetzt? _____

d Wie geht es Ihnen? _____

e Sprechen Sie Englisch? _____

f Sind Sie aus Hamburg? _____

g Wie ist Ihre Handynummer? _____

3 Now reformulate the questions yet again as if you were a young person who has just met a young couple in a hotel.

a Wie heißt ihr?

5 *In der Stadt*
In town

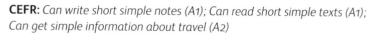

In this unit you will learn how to:

▸ *talk about places in towns and cities.*
▸ *count from 101 upwards.*
▸ *understand the gender of nouns.*
▸ *use articles.*

CEFR: *Can write short simple notes (A1); Can read short simple texts (A1); Can get simple information about travel (A2)*

München

Germany has many attractive towns and cities. One of the most popular is **München** (*Munich*). Munich is the capital of **Bayern** (*Bavaria*) and the third largest city in Germany with about 1.2 million **Einwohnern** (*inhabitants*).

Any tour should start at **Marienplatz** (*Marien Square*) in the **Altstadt** (*old town*). From here you can explore many old **Gebäude** (*buildings*), **Kirchen** (*churches*) and other **Sehenswürdigkeiten** (*sights*). The **Frauenkirche** (*Cathedral of Our Lady*) can hold up to 20000 people and from its towers you have a breathtaking view of Munich's cityscape and the **Bayerischen Alpen** (*Bavarian Alps*).

The **Viktualienmarkt** (*Victuals Market*) is only a few steps away from the Marienplatz. It's a daily outdoor market and you can buy everything from **Blumen** (*flowers*) and **Gewürzen** (*spices*) to **Käse** (*cheese*) and **Fleisch** (*meat*). While in Munich don't miss the **Englischen Garten** (*English garden*) which is one of the largest city parks in Europe and visit one of the many **Biergärten** (*beer gardens*). In most beer gardens you are traditionally allowed to bring your own **Essen** (*food*).

 What words in the text mean *churches, buildings, garden, old town* and *food*?

52

Vocabulary builder

 1 05.01 **Look at the pictures and read the texts. Then listen to the sentences and letter them as you hear them.**

____ Das ist ein Hotel. Das Hotel Schmidt in Celle.

____ Das ist ein Bahnhof. Der Bahnhof in Hannover.

____ Das ist ein Flohmarkt. Der Flohmarkt in Hannover.

____ Das ist eine Bäckerei. Die Stadtbäckerei.

____ Das ist eine Kneipe. Die Kneipe heißt 'Das Weinloch'.

____ Das ist ein Kino. Das Abaton-Kino.

2 Did you realise that there are different words for *a* and *the*? Which means *a*? And which ones mean *the*?

 3 05.02 Now listen and match the German words with the English meanings. Then listen and repeat.

a der Bahnhof _____   **1** *the cinema*

b der Flohmarkt _____   **2** *the railway station*

c die Bäckerei _____   **3** *the pub*

d die Kneipe _____   **4** *the hotel*

e das Kino _____   **5** *the flea market*

f das Hotel _____   **6** *the bakery*

 NEW EXPRESSIONS

Look at the expressions that are used in the next reading. Note their meanings.

Woche	*week*
besonders	*especially*
Stadtzentrum	*city centre*
Garten	*garden*
gehen	*to go (on foot)*
Sprachschule	*language school*
ziemlich viel	*quite a lot*
Bier	*beer*
Weizenbier	*wheat beer*
bis bald	*see you soon*
nur	*only*

Reading

 1 05.03 **Lesen Sie die E-Mail und beantworten Sie dann die Frage.** *Read the e-mail and answer the question.* Then listen and read along.

Wo ist Tracy? _____

München, 3. September

Hallo Jörg,

wie geht's? Mir geht es wirklich sehr gut. Ich bin jetzt zwei Wochen in München. Die Stadt ist sehr schön, besonders das Stadtzentrum und der ‚Englische Garten'. Ich gehe auch in eine Sprachschule. Die Sprachschule heißt ‚Superlang'. Ich spreche ziemlich viel Deutsch. Das Bier in München ist sehr gut. Es heißt Weizenbier.

Bis bald

deine Tracy

2 Beantworten Sie die Fragen. *Answer the questions.*

a Wie ist die Stadt? _____

b Was ist besonders schön? _____

c Wie heißt die Sprachschule? _____

d Spricht Tracy nur Englisch? _____

e Was ist auch sehr gut in München? _____

Language discovery

Read the email again. Write the words **der**, **die**, and **das** that appear before the nouns. Notice which words appear with which nouns.

___die___ **Stadt**

_____ **Stadtzentrum**

_____ **Englische Garten**

_____ **Sprachschule**

_____ **Bier**

Learn more

1 GENDER OF NOUNS AND ARTICLES

All German nouns have a gender: they are masculine, feminine or neuter. The words for *the* and *a* (the so-called *definite* and *indefinite articles*) have to match the gender of the nouns:

the ...	a ...	
masculine	**der Bahnhof** *(the station)*	**ein Bahnhof** *(a station)*
feminine	**die Kirche** *(the church)*	**eine Kirche** *(a church)*
neuter	**das Café** *(the café)*	**ein Café** *(a café)*

In the plural the word for *the* is **die**: **die Bahnhöfe, die Kirchen, die Cafés**.

Here are a few guidelines to help you know the gender of nouns in German:

- ▶ **masculine nouns:**
    - ▷ *males and male animals:* **der Mann, der Tiger**
    - ▷ *many nouns ending in* **-en**: **der Garten**
    - ▷ *many nouns ending in* **–mus**: **der Optimismus**
- ▶ **feminine nouns:**
    - ▷ *females and female animals:* **die Frau, die Katze** *(cat)*
    - ▷ *most nouns ending in* **-e**: **die Kirche, Kneipe**
    - ▷ *most nouns ending in* **-ei**: **die Bäckerei**
    - ▷ *all nouns ending in* **-ung**: **die Zeitung** *(newspaper)*
    - ▷ *all nouns ending in* **-tät**: **die Nationalität**
- ▶ **neuter nouns:**
    - ▷ *most nouns ending in* **-o**: **das Kino**
    - ▷ *most nouns ending in* **-um**: **das Zentrum**

If a noun is made up of two or more nouns, it is always the last noun which determines the gender:

- ▶ **das Bier + der Garten: der Biergarten** *(beer garden)*
- ▶ **das Telefon + die Nummer: die Telefonnummer** *(telephone number)*

In general, you need to learn a new noun with its definite article: **der**, **die** or **das** when you first meet it. If you look up the gender in a dictionary, masculine nouns are usually indicated with (m), feminine nouns with (f) and neuter nouns with (nt). Note that from this unit onwards, new nouns are usually given with their gender.

2 ENDINGS FOR POSSESSIVE ADJECTIVES

Words like **mein** (*my*), **dein** (*your*, informal) and **Ihr** (*your*, formal) also have masculine, feminine and neuter forms. In German these endings don't depend on the person who speaks but on the gender of the noun that comes after **mein**, **dein** etc.:

masculine   **mein Name**

feminine   **meine Adresse**

neuter   **mein Haus**

Masculine (der Name) Mein Name ist Ulrike Weber. Wie ist Ihr Name?
Feminine (die Telefonnummer) Meine Telefonnummer ist 774876. Wie ist deine Telefonnummer?
Neuter (das Haus) Das ist mein Haus. Wo ist dein Haus?

For a list of possessive adjectives please see Unit 15.

Don't forget that the formal word for *your* takes a capital letter.

▶ **Wie ist Ihr Name?**
   Wie ist Ihre Telefonnummer?
   Wo ist Ihr Haus?

Practice

1 In the grid below, write down the German word for each of the pictures horizontally and another word will appear vertically. Then, think of the correct gender article for each noun.

a Bakery   **b** Station   **c** Hotel

d Church   **e** Beer

a						
b						
c						
		d				
		P				
	e					

2 Which endings are needed in these sentences? In some cases no ending is needed.

a Das ist ein____ Kino.

b D____ Hotel heißt Vier Jahreszeiten.

c Dort ist ein____ Bäckerei.

d Wie ist Ihr____ Name?

e Wo ist d____ Bahnhofshotel?

f Wo ist hier ein____ Café?

g Wie ist dein____ Telefonnummer?

h D____ Kneipe heißt *Blauer Engel*.

Speaking

 05.04 Six of the places on the map are represented by a number. A visitor wants you to tell him what these places are. Write down your answers and practise saying them. Then check your answers with the models in the audio.

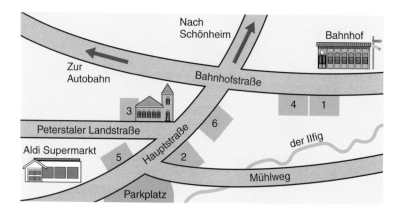

1 Kneipe – Bierstübl

2 Biergarten – Mönchbräu

3 Kirche – Jakobskirche

4 Hotel – Bahnhofshotel

5 Café – Café Krause

6 Markt – Buttermarkt

> Beispiele:
> Eins ist eine Kneipe. Die Kneipe heißt Bierstübl.
> Zwei ist ein Biergarten. Der Biergarten heißt ...

Go further

 1 05.05 Hören Sie bitte zu und wiederholen Sie! *Listen and repeat.*

101	(ein)hunderteins
102	(ein)hundertzwei
110	(ein)hundertzehn
111	(ein)hundertelf
120	(ein)hundertzwanzig
121	(ein)hunderteinundzwanzig
201	zweihunderteins
312	dreihundertzwölf
999	neunhundertneunundneunzig
1 000	(ein)tausend
2 843	zweitausendachthundertdreiundvierzig
10 962	zehntausendneunhundertzweiundsechzig
1 000 000	eine Million
4 000 000	vier Millionen
1 000 000 000	eine Milliarde

Note how even long numbers are written as one word in German.

2 05.06 Say the numbers for police, fire and emergency doctor out loud. Then check your answers in the audio.

Notrufe	
Polizei ...	110
Feuer ...	112
Notarzt ...	115

 3 05.07 Listen to the six numbers in the audio and mark the ones you hear.

1 a 237   b 273   c 327

2 a 459   b 954   c 495

3 a 642   b 624   c 426

4 a 1 321   b 1 231   c 1 132

5 a 4 762   b 4 267   c 6 462

6 a 11 329   b 11 932   c 11 293

Writing

How many inhabitants do these cities have? Write out in full the number of inhabitants for each city.

Beispiel Köln	986 000	*neunhundertsechsundachtzigtausend*
Heidelberg	143 000	_____
Dresden	502 000	_____
Frankfurt am Main	660 000	_____
München	1 326 000	_____
Hamburg	1 750 000	_____
Berlin	3 402 000	_____

Test yourself

1 Fill in the gaps with the correct versions of Ihr(e) or mein(e).

a Wie ist *Ihr* Name? – *Mein* Name ist Astrid.

b Wie ist _____ E-Mail-Adresse? – _____ E-Mail-Adresse ist h17@google.de .

c Wie ist _____ Telefonnummer? – _____ Telefonnummer ist 753412.

d Wie ist _____ Adresse? – _____ Adresse ist Hauptstraße 45.

e Wie heißt _____ Mann? – _____ Mann heißt Gerhard.

f Wie heißt _____ Frau? – _____ Frau heißt Maria.

2 **Schreiben Sie Ihre erste Postkarte.** *Write your first postcard in German.* **Supply the missing words. Choose the person you would like to write to.**

der – schön – Die – fantastisch – bald – eine – das – heißt – spreche – geht's – eine – Die

---

[✉] [← REPLY] [← REPLY ALL] [📎]

Wien, 7. Februar

Hallo _____ ,

wie _____? Mir geht es _____ . Ich bin jetzt _____ Woche in Wien. _____ Stadt ist sehr _____, besonders _____ Zentrum und _____ Stadtpark. Ich gehe jetzt auch in _____ Sprachschule. _____ Sprachschule _____ ,Eurolingua'. Ich _____ jetzt viel Deutsch.

Was machst du?

Bis _____

♀ deine _____

♂ dein _____

SELF CHECK

I CAN...

○	...name five buildings in a town with the correct articles.
○	...count from 100 onwards.
○	...give the correct articles for a few masculine, feminine and neuter nouns.
○	...name one typical ending each for masculine, feminine and neuter nouns.

6 Arbeit und Studium
Work and study

In this unit you will learn how to:
▶ *ask people about their occupation and state yours.*
▶ *ask people what they study and where.*
▶ *use the verb sein (to be).*
▶ *use plural forms of nouns.*
▶ *use the expression for since and for.*

CEFR: *Can exchange information on familiar topics and activities (A1); Can read short, simple texts (A1); Can write short, simple notes (A2); Can give simple descriptions (A2)*

Studying in Germany

Germany has a very diverse university landscape with more than 400 institutions. This includes the classically-oriented **Universitäten** (*universities*) with a broad range of degree courses, as well as **Fachhochschulen** (*Universities of Applied Science*), **Musikhochschulen** (*music colleges*) and **Kunsthochschulen** (*art colleges*). The oldest university in Germany is the **Ruprecht-Karls-Universität** in Heidelberg, founded in 1386.

In recent years, there has been widespread criticism of the length of time taken by German students to complete their studies. Nowadays, in addition to traditional German degrees which last 4 to 6 years, most universities run bachelor and master courses based on the British and American models in order to provide a faster and more flexible system. Popular subjects are **Betriebswirtschaftslehre (BWL)** (*management studies*), **Maschinenbau** (*mechanical engineering*), **Informatik** (*computer science*), **Jura** (*law*) and **Germanistik** (*German language and literature*).

What words in the text mean *law, universities, mechanical engineering* and *computer science*? And what is the oldest university in Germany?

Vocabulary builder

 1 06.01 **Was sind diese Leute von Beruf? Welches Wort passt zu welchem Bild?** *What do these people do for a living?* **Give the name of the job for each person. Then listen to check your answers.**

Automechanikerin

Kellner   Ärztin   Taxifahrer

Tischler   Musikerin

Paul Meier _____   Helga Neumann _____

Heike Müller _____   Manfred Lustig _____

Ulrike Wagner ____   **Kurt Leutner** ____

Das ist Paul Meier. Er ist Taxifahrer. Das ist Helga Neumann. Sie ist Automechanikerin. Das ist … Sie ist …

 2 Write short descriptions of the people in the pictures.

MORE PROFESSIONS

 1 Here is a list of common professions. Note the different forms for males and females.

der (masculine)	die (feminine)	English
Automechaniker	Automechaniker**in**	*car mechanic*
Friseur	Friseur**in**	*hairdresser*
Informatiker	Informatiker**in**	*IT-specialist*
Ingenieur	Ingenieur**in**	*engineer*
Journalist	Journalist**in**	*journalist*
Kellner	Kellner**in**	*waiter/waitress*
Kundenberater	Kundenberater**in**	*customer advisor*
Lehrer	Lehrer**in**	*teacher*
Manager	Manager**in**	*manager/manageress*
Maurer	Maurer**in**	*bricklayer*
Musiker	Musiker**in**	*musician*
Sekretär	Sekretär**in**	*secretary*
Student	Student**in**	*student*
Taxifahrer	Taxifahrer**in**	*taxi driver*
Tischler	Tischler**in**	*carpenter*
Verkäufer	Verkäufer**in**	*shop assistant*

The following professions are **Ausnahmen** *(exceptions)* to the usual gender rule.

Arzt	Ärztin	*doctor*
Bankkaufmann	Bankkauffrau	*qualified bank clerk*
Koch	Köchin	*chef*
Angestellter	Angestellte	*employee*
Krankenpfleger	Krankenschwester	*nurse*

2 Was sind diese Leute von Beruf? Unscramble the letters to spell out these jobs.

a NREIRLEH _____

c ANSTUJORIL _____

e HKCO _____

b ERURAM _____

d ERNISÄTERK _____

NEW EXPRESSIONS

Look at the expressions that are used in the next conversation. Note their meanings.

Part 1

willkommen	*welcome*
denn	*(here) then*
mein Mann	*my husband*
Sind Sie berufstätig?	*Do you have a job?*

Part 2

Wo arbeiten Sie?	*Where do you work?*
der Supermarkt	*supermarket*
seit wann?	*since when?*
seit drei Jahren	*for (lit. since) three years*
Was sind Sie von Beruf?	*What job do you do?*
Er arbeitet bei …	*He works for …*
Was macht Ihr Mann?	*What does your husband do?*
war	*was*

Conversation

 1 06.02 **Jutta Sammer aus Borken lernt Ingrid Baker aus Whitstable kennen.** *Jutta Sammer from Borken gets to know Ingrid Baker from Whitstable.* **Listen to the first part of the conversation to find answers to these two questions.**

a How is it that Ingrid Baker speaks German so well?

_____

b Why does she mention a period of 18 years?

_____

PART 1

Jutta Sammer	Willkommen in Borken! Mein Name ist Jutta Sammer. Hoffentlich sprechen Sie Deutsch!
Ingrid Baker	Guten Abend! Ja, ich spreche Deutsch. Ich heiße Ingrid Baker.
Jutta Sammer	Prima! Sie sprechen ja sehr gut Deutsch. Sind Sie denn Deutsche, Frau Baker?
Ingrid Baker	Ja, aber mein Mann ist Engländer und ich wohne seit 18 Jahren in England.
Jutta Sammer	Ach so. Sind Sie berufstätig?
Ingrid Baker	Ja, ich bin Verkäuferin.

2 **And now listen to the second part of the conversation and try to work out the answers to these two questions.**

   a Which of the women works – Jutta, Ingrid or both of them?

   _____

   b Whose husband is retired – Jutta's or Ingrid's?

   _____

PART 2

Jutta Sammer	Und wo arbeiten Sie, Frau Baker?
Ingrid Baker	Ich arbeite bei Sainsbury's, das ist ein Supermarkt in Großbritannien.
Jutta Sammer	Seit wann arbeiten Sie dort?
Ingrid Baker	Seit drei Jahren. Und Sie? Was sind Sie von Beruf?
Jutta Sammer	Ich bin Krankenschwester. Mein Mann ist von Beruf Mechaniker und er arbeitet bei Opel. Und was macht Ihr Mann?
Ingrid Baker	Er ist jetzt pensioniert, aber er war Journalist.

3 **Richtig oder falsch? Korrigieren Sie die falschen Aussagen.** _True or false? Correct the false statements._

   a Ingrid Baker ist Österreicherin. _____

   b Ingrid wohnt seit 18 Jahren in England. _____

   c Sie ist Verkäuferin von Beruf. _____

   d Jutta Sammer ist Bankkauffrau von Beruf. _____

   e Herr Sammer ist seit neun Monaten pensioniert.

   _____

   f Herr Baker war Journalist von Beruf. _____

 # Language discovery

The verb **sein** _to be_ is very frequently used in German and like in English quite irregular. Look at these sentences you have all met so far. Can you fill in the missing forms in the verb table below?

   a Mein Name <u>ist</u> Jutta Sammer.

   b <u>Sind</u> Sie denn Deutsche, Frau Baker?

   c Woher <u>seid</u> ihr?

   d Wir <u>sind</u> aus Stuttgart.

   e Ja, ich <u>bin</u> Verkäuferin.

Singular	Plural
ich _____	wir _____
du bist	ihr _____
Sie _____	Sie sind
er/sie/es _____	sie sind

Learn more

1 THE VERB SEIN *(TO BE)*

Remember that this is an irregular verb so it changes according to the subject it is used with.

Singular			Plural		
Ich	bin	Student.	Wir	sind	Engländer.
Du	bist	Sekretärin.	Ihr	seid	Amerikaner.
Sie	sind	verheiratet.	Sie	sind	Japaner.
Er/Sie/Es ist		alt.	Sie	sind	arbeitslos.

2 SAYING *FOR* OR *SINCE*

There are two examples of the preposition **seit** *(for, since)* in the conversation.

Ich wohne seit 18 Jahren in England.

Seit drei Jahren.

In these examples **seit** corresponds to the English *for* (e.g. *for 18 years, for 3 years*). Note that **seit** is used with the present tense in German. The plural of **Jahr** ist **Jahre**, but when it is used with **seit** an extra **-n** is added for example **drei Jahre – seit drei Jahren**.

3 PLURAL OF NOUNS

German nouns do not simply add *-s* to form their plurals (*a book, two books*). You need to learn the plural of a noun when you first meet it, along with the gender. For instance, later in this unit you'll meet:

Singular	**Ich bin Student.**
Plural	**Seid ihr Studenten?**

A few other types of plural are:

▶ **nouns –** often ending in **-er** or **-en -** which do not change: **ein Engländer, zwei Engländer; ein Manager, zwei Manager; ein Kuchen, zwei Kuchen**

- ▶ **nouns** – ending in **–e**, usually feminine, which add **–n: eine Kirche, zwei Kirchen; eine Schule, zwei Schulen**
- ▶ **nouns** – usually referring to female professions – which add **-nen:** **eine Managerin, zwei Managerinnen; eine Studentin, zwei Studentinnen**
- ▶ **nouns** which add an umlaut (¨) and an **-e: ein Bahnhof, zwei Bahnhöfe.** Note that this pattern often applies to masculine nouns: **ein Koch, zwei Köche.**

Practice

1 Fill in the missing plural forms
- a ein Name – vier Name**n**
- b eine Schule – fünf Schule_____
- c eine Adresse – zwei Adresse_____
- d eine Kneipe – zwei Kneipe_____
- e eine Sekretärin – drei Sekretärin_____
- f eine Ärztin – zwei Ärztin_____
- g ein Ball – zwei B**ä**ll_____
- h ein Fuß – zwei F**ü**ß_____

2 Boris Sammer, Julia's husband, is introducing himself. Fill in the correct forms of sein:

Mein Name _____ Boris Sammer. Ich _____ berufstätig. Ich _____ Mechaniker bei Opel. Meine Frau _____ Verkäuferin. Wir _____ beide aus Borken. Borken _____ in Westdeutschland und es _____ sehr schön.

 Pronunciation

06.03 In German the use of the umlaut (¨) always changes the way a vowel (such as **a**, **o** or **u**) or a diphthong (such as **au**) is pronounced. Listen to the way **a** plus an umlaut is pronounced in these words:

Engländer   Universität   berufstätig   Sekretärin   Kindergärtnerin

Listen to the way **au** plus an umlaut is pronounced:

Verkäufer Fräulein

How would you pronounce these words? Have a go and then check your answers on the audio.

Ärztin, Bäckerei, Dänemark, Häuser.

Speaking

 06.04 Answer the questions on the recording as if you were Frau Murphy-Heinrichs. Here are her details:

Deutsche
Mann ist Ire
wohnt seit 17 Jahren in Münster
ist Sekretärin bei Mannesmann
Mann ist Taxifahrer

Listening

 06.05 Jochen Krenzler aus Dresden lernt Rainer Tietmeyer aus Coventry kennen. *Jochen Krenzler of Dresden meets Rainer Tietmeyer of Coventry.* Listen to the recording and find the correct answer.

  a Herr Tietmeyer ist (Deutscher / Schweizer).
  b Frau Tietmeyer ist (Deutsche / Engländerin) .
  c Herr Tietmeyer wohnt seit (14 / 20 / 24) Jahren in England.
  d Herr Tietmeyer ist (Kellner / Tischler / Bankkaufmann) von Beruf.

Writing

 Write down as much information about yourself as your German will allow. Use Vicki Farrow's model below to help you.

> **Ich über mich**
>
> Ich heiße Vicki Farrow. Ich komme aus Newcastle, aber ich wohne jetzt in Peckham. Das ist in London. Meine Eltern wohnen noch in Newcastle.
>
> Ich bin Krankenschwester und ich arbeite in Southwark. Ich spreche Englisch, Französisch und ein bisschen Deutsch. Mein Partner heißt Darren und er ist Arzt. Er arbeitet in Battersea. Er spricht sehr gut Deutsch.

Go further

 1 06.06 These are some of the most commonly studied subjects at university. Listen and repeat.

Anglistik	*English language and literature*
Betriebswirtschaftslehre (BWL)	*management studies*

Biologie	biology
Chemie	chemistry
Germanistik	German language and literature
Geschichte	history
Informatik	computer science
Jura	law
Mathematik	maths
Medizin	medicine
Romanistik	Romance studies
Volkswirtschaftslehre (VWL)	economics

Studieren means to study at a university; **lernen** is more appropriate for study at lower levels, such as in schools, further education and adult education.

2 06.07 **Nicolai lernt Karin und Anke kennen.** *Nicolai gets to know Karin and Anke.* **Listen to the recording and answer the question.**

Who lives in Gießen? _____

Nicolai	Grüß euch! Ich heiße Nicolai. Wie heißt ihr?
Karin	Hallo! Mein Name ist Karin.
Anke	Und ich bin die Anke.
Nicolai	Und woher kommt ihr?
Anke	Wir kommen aus Gießen. Und du? Woher kommst du?
Nicolai	Aus Frankfurt. Ich studiere dort Romanistik. Studiert ihr auch?
Karin	Ja, wir studieren BWL in Marburg.
Nicolai	Und ist das interessant?
Anke	Na ja, es geht, ein bisschen langweilig.

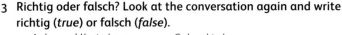

Grüß euch!	*Hello all, hi (informal more than one person)*
interessant	*interesting*
langweilig	*boring*

3 **Richtig oder falsch? Look at the conversation again and write richtig (*true*) or falsch (*false*).**

a Anke und Karin kommen aus Gelsenkirchen. _____

b Nicolai kommt aus Frankfurt. _____

c Nicolai studiert Germanistik. _____

d Anke und Karin studieren BWL. _____

e Sie studieren in Marburg. _____

f Sie finden es sehr interessant. _____

4 06.08 **Now listen to another recording and supply the information that these students give about themselves.**

Name	Paul	Daniel	Heike	Martina
Geburtsort	Hamburg	_____	_____	_____
Studienort	Bremen	_____	_____	_____
Studienfach	Informatik	_____	_____	_____

die Bildung	*education*
die Ausbildung	*training*

Test yourself

1 **Anke and Thomas meet up and ask each other a few questions. Write the numbers 1–6 to put what they say in the correct order to make a continuous dialogue. There may be more than one solution.**

_____ Anke	**a**	**Bist du Student?**
_____ Thomas	**b**	**Hallo! Mein Name ist Thomas.**
_____ Anke	**c**	**Und woher kommst du?**
_____ Thomas	**d**	**Ja, ich studiere Chemie in Leipzig. Und du?**
__1__ Anke	**e**	**Hallo! Ich heiße Anke. Wie heißt du?**
_____ Thomas	**f**	**Ich komme aus Leipzig.**
_____ Anke	**g**	**Ich bin auch Studentin. Ich studiere Anglistik in München.**

2 **Setzen Sie ein. Fit these words into the gaps.**

Kellnerin, Engländer, Studentin, Ire, Verkäuferin, Journalist, Schottin, Sekretärinnen, Studenten

A Sind Herr und Frau Brookes **a** _____?

B Nein, Herr Brookes kommt aus Dublin und ist **b** _____ und Frau Brookes ist **c** _____ .

A Sind Doris und Walther **d** _____?

B Doris ist **e** _____, aber Walther ist **f** _____ bei der Süddeutschen Zeitung.

A Sind Elke und Birgit **g** _____?

B Nein, Elke ist **h** _____ bei H&M und Birgit ist **i** _____ .

3 **Wie heißt es richtig? Supply the correct forms of the verb sein.**

  a Ich b_____ Deutscher.

  b S_____ Sie auch Deutscher?

  c Claudia i_____ ledig und Petra i_____ verheiratet.

  d Ich b_____ nicht verheiratet.

  e Peter i_____ Amerikaner.

  f B_____ du auch Engländer?

  g S_____ ihr aus Japan?

4 **Schreiben Sie die Fragen! Here is an interview with Bernd Schneider. Can you complete the questions he was asked?**

  a Herr Schneider. Was sind Sie _____ _____?
     Ich bin Ingenieur.

  b Und wo _____ Sie?
     Ich arbeite bei Volkswagen.

  c Seit _____ arbeiten Sie dort?
     Seit vier Jahren.

  d Und _____ Sie _____?
     Ja, ich bin seit zwei Jahren verheiratet.

  e Und _____ macht Ihre Frau?
     Meine Frau ist Studentin.

  f Und was _____ sie?
     Sie studiert Jura.

SELF CHECK

	I CAN. . .
○	. . . ask people their occupation and say my own.
○	. . . give both the male and female forms of five occupations.
○	. . . name at least four subjects one can study at university.
○	. . . say I have been doing something for several years.
○	. . . use the various forms of the verb sein.

7 Gehen wir ins Café
Let's go to a café

In this unit you will learn how to:
▶ *understand a menu.*
▶ *order food and drink.*
▶ *use the accusative case.*
▶ *talk about containers and their contents.*

CEFR: *Can locate specific information in texts (A2); Can handle numbers, quantities and costs (A1); Can understand directions (A2)*

Kaffee and Kuchen

The concept of **Kaffee und Kuchen** (*coffee and cake*) plays an important role in Germany, Austria and Switzerland. It is quite common to meet up with friends, relatives or work colleagues in a **Café** (*café*) or a **Kaffeehaus** (*coffee house*) and to talk about any matter over **eine Tasse Kaffee** (*a cup of coffee*) or a **Cappuccino** (*cappuccino*).

Most cafés offer a wide range of **Getränke** (*drinks*) and **Speisen** (*food*). You will of course find cakes such as **Erdbeerkuchen** (*strawberry cake*), **Käsekuchen** (cheese cake) or the well-known **Apfelstrudel** (*apple strudel*) and **Schwarzwälder Kirschtorte** (*Blackforest gateau*).

If you fancy a snack you can order **ein Brötchen mit Käse** (*a roll with cheese*) or perhaps **ein Baguette mit Tunfisch** (*a baguette with tuna*).

Cafés usually offer **alkoholische Getränke** (*alcoholic drinks*), such as **eine Flasche Bier** (*a bottle of beer*) or **ein Glas Sekt** (*a glass of sparkling German wine*). For any questions ask the **Kellnerin** (*waitress*) or **Kellner** (*waiter*).

What words in the text mean *cake, drinks, roll* and *apple strudel*? And what are the expressions for a *cup*, a *bottle* and a *glass*?

Vocabulary builder

 1 **07.01 Read the menu as you listen and repeat the food and drink expressions. Try to work out what the items mean in English. You can check your answers in the key.**

WARME GETRÄNKE	€
Tasse Kaffee	2,50
Cappuccino	2,75
Heiße Schokolade	2,80
Schwarzer Tee (Glas)	2,50

EIS-SPEZIALITÄTEN	€
Gemischtes Eis	3,00/4,00/5,00
Pfirsich Melba	4,50
Krokant-Becher	4,75

KUCHEN	€
Butterkuchen	2,25
Schwarzwälder Kirschtorte	3,50
Diverse Obstkuchen	3,00
Portion Sahne	0,90

ALKOHOLFREIE GETRÄNKE	€
Coca Cola	2,50
Limonade	2,50
Orangensaft	2,50
Mineralwasser	2,80

BIERE	€
König-Pilsener (0,33l)	2,75
Weizenbier (0,5l)	3,25

2 **What are the English meanings for these foods and drinks? Match the correct words.**

a die heiße Schokolade _____

b der Butterkuchen _____

c Gemischtes Eis _____

d die Portion Sahne _____

e der Orangensaft _____

f das Mineralwasser _____

1 *mineral water*

2 *mixed ice cream*

3 *hot chocolate*

4 *butter cake*

5 *a serving of whipped cream*

6 *orange juice*

3 07.02 **Now look at the prices for cake on the menu. Listen and repeat the prices.**

 4 07.03 **Listen to the prices and note the amounts.**

a _____   d _____

b _____   e _____

c _____   f _____

NEW EXPRESSIONS

Look at the expressions that are used in the next conversations. Note their meanings.

Conversation 1 (Part 1)

der Vater	*father*
die Mutter	*mother*
der Junge	*boy*
Ich bin durstig.	*I am thirsty.*
brauchen	*to need*
zu dick	*too fat*
gesund	*healthy*
möchte(n)	*would like*
bestellen	*to order*
nehmen	*to take; here: to have*
schön kühl	*nicely cold/chilled*
Kein Problem.	*No problem.*
bekommen	*to get*
schmecken	*to taste*
lecker	*delicious*
mit, ohne	*with, without*
finden	*here: to find/think*

Part 2

Mein Kollege hat Feierabend.	*My colleague has finished work.*
sicher	*sure(ly)*
wer was bekommt	*who gets what*
der Sohn	*son*
zu warm, zu kalt	*too warm, too cold*

1 07.04 **Herr and Frau Häfner and their children are out together. Listen to the audio and answer the question.**

    a Where is the Häfner family? _____

CONVERSATION 1 (PART 1)

Vater	Oh, bin ich jetzt durstig. Ich brauche jetzt ein Bier.
Mutter	Nicht schon wieder ein Bier, Vater. Du bist zu dick.
Vater	Ach, Bier ist gesund. Hallo. Wir möchten bestellen.
Kellner	Guten Tag. Was möchten Sie, bitte?
Mutter	Ich möchte ein Mineralwasser und einen Kaffee, bitte.
Kellner	Ein Mineralwasser und einen Kaffee. Und was nehmen Sie, bitte?
Vater	Also, ich nehme ein Weizenbier. Schön kühl, bitte.
Kellner	Kein Problem. Und was bekommst du?
Junge	Ich trinke einen Orangensaft. Mit Eis.
Kellner	Und du? Was bekommst du?
Mädchen	Ich bekomme eine Limonade. Aber ohne Eis. Limonade schmeckt lecker.

2 **Richtig oder falsch? Korrigieren Sie die falschen Aussagen.**
Correct the wrong statements.

    a Der Vater ist durstig. _____

    b Er möchte eine Limonade. _____

    c Der Vater findet, Bier ist gesund. _____

    d Die Mutter bestellt ein Eis und einen Kaffee. _____

    e Der Junge bekommt eine Cola. _____

    f Das Mädchen findet, Limonade schmeckt lecker. _____

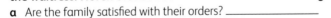

3 07.05 **The Häfner family is waiting for their order. Here comes the waitress. Hören Sie zu! Beantworten Sie dann die Frage.**

    a Are the family satisfied with their orders? _____

Kellnerin	Guten Tag! Mein Kollege hat jetzt Feierabend. Ich bin nicht ganz sicher, wer was bekommt. *(zu der Mutter)* Bekommen Sie den Orangensaft und das Eis?
Mutter	Nein, ich bekomme das Mineralwasser und den Kaffee. Mein Sohn bekommt den Orangensaft und das Eis.
Kellnerin	Gut. Bitte schön. *(zum Mädchen)* Und du? Du bekommst sicher die Limonade.
Mädchen	Ja, richtig! Die Limonade bekomme ich.
Vater	Und ich bekomme das Weizenbier.
Kellnerin	So, bitte schön.
Vater	Ach, das Bier ist zu warm!
Mutter	Und der Kaffee ist zu kalt!
Kellnerin	Oh! Entschuldigung.

4 Richtig oder falsch?

    a Der Vater bekommt den Orangensaft. _____

    b Die Mutter bekommt den Kaffee. _____

    c Das Mädchen bekommt die Limonade. _____

    d Das Bier ist zu kalt. _____

Language discovery

1 Look at conversation 1, part 1 and complete the sentences with *einen*, *eine* or *ein*. Notice which genders (masculine, feminine, neuter) the nouns that follow them are.

    a Ich trinke _____ Orangensaft. (m)

    b Ich bekomme _____ Limonade. (f)

    c Ich nehme _____ Weizenbier. (nt)

    d Ich möchte _____ Mineralwasser und _____ Kaffee. (nt, m)

2 Now look at conversation 1, part 2 and find the various words for *the* to complete the sentences. How many words are there and which word goes with masculine nouns?

    a Bekommen Sie _____ Orangensaft? (m)

    b Du bekommst sicher _____ Limonade. (f)

    c Und ich bekomme _____ Weizenbier. (nt)

Learn more

1 NOMINATIVE AND ACCUSATIVE CASES

In the sentence *I drink a coffee*, *I* is said to be the subject of the sentence and *a coffee* is said to be the direct object.

In German, the subject (often the doer of an action) has to be in the nominative case and the direct object has to be in what is called the accusative case.

Cases in German are often indicated by the words in front of the relevant noun, usually articles. So far you have learned the articles used with the subject **der**, **die**, **das** and **ein**, **eine** and **ein** (nominative case). When used for the direct object, the articles for masculine nouns **der** and **ein** change to **den** and **einen** (accusative case). This happens after most verbs in German, including **möchten**, **trinken**, **nehmen**.

		a	the
m	Ich möchte ... Meine Freundin trinkt ...	einen Kaffee einen Tee	den Kaffee den Tee
f	Ich nehme ... Mein Freund bekommt ...	eine Limo eine Cola	die Limo die Cola
nt	Ich bekomme ... Meine Frau bekommt ...	ein Mineralwasser ein Eis	das Wasser das Eis

Note that these changes also apply to the negative form which is **kein** → **keinen** (*no, not a*) and the possessive adjectives like **mein** → **meinen** (*my*) or **Ihr** → **Ihren** (*your*).

Feminine, neuter and the plural forms are the same when used as the subject (nominative) or the direct object (accusative). See the following examples.

	Nominative	Accusative
masc. sing.	**Der** Kaffee schmeckt gut.	**Den** Kaffee nehme ich.
	Ist das **ein** Wein aus Chile?	Ich bekomme **einen** Wein.
	Mein Tee ist ganz kalt!	Du trinkst **meinen** Tee!
f. sing.	**Die** Milch ist nur für Babys.	Wir kaufen **die** Milch.
	Hier liegt **eine** Flasche.	Er findet **eine** Flasche.
	Meine Cola ist lecker.	Sie bezahlt **meine** Cola.
neut. sing.	**Das** Eis kostet viel.	Ich bezahle **das** Eis.
	Da steht **ein** Bier.	Alle trinken **ein** Bier.
	Wo ist **mein** Glas?	Ihr habt **mein** Glas.
pl.	**Die** Brötchen sind hier.	Wir essen **die** Brötchen.
	Meine Kinder sind klein.	Mögen Sie **meine** Kinder?

Note that the nominative case is also used after the verb **sein** (*to be*).

Ist der Wein aus Chile?

Das ist ein Kaffee.

Das ist mein Vater.

🔓 Practice

1 **Ergänzen Sie die Endungen.** Decide which accusative endings are correct. Sometimes none is needed. The genders of the nouns are given in brackets.

   a Ich möchte *eine* Cola, bitte. (f)

   b Ich nehme ein___ Limonade. (f)

   c Ich möchte ein___ Orangensaft. (m)

   d Marco bekommt ein___ Kaffee und ein___ Mineralwasser. (m, nt)

   e Wir möchten ein___ Cappuccino und ein___ Tee. (m, m)

   f Ich nehme ein___ Eis. (nt)

2 **Wer bekommt was? Add den, die or das.**

   a Susanne bekommt *den* Orangensaft.

   b Timo nimmt d___ Kaffee.

   c Axel trinkt d___ Limonade.

   d Carsten bekommt d___ Bier.

   e Julian trinkt d___ Mineralwasser.

   f Wer bekommt d___ Tee?

3 **Nominative or Accusative? Look at the underlined masculine words and decide if they are the subject (nominative case) or direct object (accusative case) in the sentences. Choose *N* for nominative or *A* for accusative. Note the different article forms.**

   a <u>Der Kaffee</u> schmeckt gut. ( )

   b Ich bekommen <u>den Kaffee</u>. ( )

   c Er hat <u>einen Sohn</u>. ( )

   d Das ist <u>mein Sohn</u>. ( )

   e Du trinkst <u>meinen Saft</u>. ( )

   f Das ist <u>ein Saft</u> aus Südafrika. ( )

4 Read Conversation 1 again and find out the missing gender for these drinks. Use *m* for masculine, *f* for feminine or *nt* for neuter nouns.

a Tee ___
b Cola _f_
c Mineralwasser ___
d Bier ___
e Orangensaft ___
f Wein _m_
g Kaffee ___
h Schnaps _m_
i Sekt _m_
j Milch _f_

V Don't feel overwhelmed by the three different genders for nouns in German. Remember certain endings of nouns can help you identify gender (see Unit 5 for more guidelines). Sometimes, nouns belonging to a certain group of items can have the same gender. For instance, most alcoholic drinks – with the exception of **das Bier** – are masculine: **der Wein, der Sekt, der Schnaps**, etc. These non-alcoholic beverages are also masculine: **der Kaffee, der Cappuccino, der Espresso, der Tee, der Orangensaft, der Apfelsaft, der Zitronensaft**.

Go further

DIFFERENT WAYS OF ORDERING DRINKS

Did you notice that there are various expressions people can use when ordering drinks? Complete the following sentences with the correct form of the verbs **trinken** (*to drink*), **bekommen** (*to get*) and **nehmen** (*to take/have*). All three can be used as an alternative to **möchten** (*would like to*) when ordering drinks.

1 Was sagt der Kellner?
  a Was möchten Sie, bitte?
  b Was tr_____ Sie, bitte?
  c Was bek_____ Sie, bitte?
  d Was ne_____ Sie, bitte?

2 Was sagen Sie?
  a Ich möchte einen Kaffee.
  b Ich tr_____ einen Kaffee.
  c Ich bek_____ einen Kaffee.
  d Ich ne_____ einen Kaffee.

CONTAINERS AND THEIR CONTENTS

1   When talking about containers and their contents, such as a cup
   of tea, a glass of wine, a dish of ice-cream, etc., you do not use
   the equivalent of the word *of* in German:

eine Flasche Wein	*a bottle of wine*
ein Glas Mineralwasser	*a glass of mineral water*
ein Kännchen Kaffee	*a pot of coffee*
eine Tasse Tee	*a cup of tea*

2 07.06 **Listen and match the names for containers with their plural forms. Then listen and repeat.**

a eine Tasse Kaffee_____

b ein Glas Wasser_____

c eine Flasche Wein_____

d eine Dose Cola_____

e ein Becher Eis_____

1 drei Dosen Cola

2 zwei Becher Eis

3 drei Flaschen Wein

4 zwei Tassen Kaffee

5 drei Gläser/Glas Wasser

Watch out!

Sie bekommt *ein* **Eis. Aber: Sie bekommt** *einen* **Becher Eis (der Becher).**

Ich nehme *einen* **Kaffee. Aber: Ich nehme** *eine* **Tasse Kaffee (die Tasse).**

Er trinkt *einen* **Weißwein. Aber: Er trinkt** *ein* **Glas Weißwein (das Glas).**

Speaking

07.07 **Bitte bestellen Sie. How would you order the following drinks in German? Practise and then check your answers on the audio. For answers** *c* **and** *d* **use the correct form of nehmen.**

a I'd like a coffee, please.

b I'd like a mineral water and an orange juice.

c I'll have a cup of tea, please.

d I'll have a coke and a glass of beer.

❓ Test yourself

1 **The four nouns in each line all have the same gender. Decide whether they are _m_ for masculine, _f_ for feminine or _nt_ for neuter.**

  a Kaffee, Cappuccino, Espresso, Tee ( )

  b Eis, Bier, Wasser, Glas ( )

  c Wein, Sekt, Schnaps, Wodka ( )

  d Orangensaft, Apfelsaft, Zitronensaft, Becher ( )

  e Tasse, Flasche, Dose, Limonade ( )

2 **Wie heißt es richtig? Decide which endings are correct. Sometimes no ending is needed.**

  a Elmar ist müde. Er braucht ein＿＿ Kaffee.

  b Katrin bestellt ein＿＿ Glas Bier.

  c Die Kinder sind sehr durstig. Sie bestellen ein＿＿ Orangensaft und ein＿＿ Cola.

  d Bekommen Sie d＿＿ Kaffee oder d＿＿ Tee?

  e D＿＿ Kaffee ist lecker.

  f D＿＿ Tee ist auch lecker.

  g Ich bekomme d＿＿ Weizenbier und mein Mann bekommt d＿＿ Orangensaft.

3 **Singular, Plural. Decide which plural form is appropriate.**

  a ein Becher Eis – zwei ＿＿＿＿＿ Eis

  b eine Dose Cola – drei ＿＿＿＿＿ Cola

  c eine Flasche Wasser – vier ＿＿＿＿＿ Wasser

  d eine Tasse Tee – zwei ＿＿＿＿＿ Tee

4 **Was gehört zusammen? Match up the two sides to complete the sentences.**

  a **Er möchte einen Orangensaft** ＿＿＿＿＿   **1** _sehr viele Kalorien._

  b **Frau Müller nimmt ein Kännchen** ＿＿＿＿＿   **2** _Eis._

  c **Limonade ist** ＿＿＿＿＿   **3** _sehr durstig._

  d **Ich möchte einen Becher** ＿＿＿＿＿   **4** _Tee._

  e **Ein Eis hat** ＿＿＿＿＿   **5** _lecker._

  f **Ich bin jetzt** ＿＿＿＿＿   **6** _mit Wodka._

SELF CHECK

I CAN...

- ○ ... understand a simple menu.
- ○ ... order food and drink.
- ○ ... use the accusative and nominative cases.
- ○ ... talk about containers and their contents.

8 Einkaufen und Bestellen

Shopping and ordering

In this unit you will learn how to:
▶ *talk about food shopping.*
▶ *ask for and give prices.*
▶ *order food and drink in a restaurant.*
▶ *say what you like eating and drinking.*
▶ *use more plural forms of nouns.*
▶ *use correct word order.*

CEFR: *Can understand high frequency phrases (A2); Can locate specific information in texts (A2); Can handle numbers, quantities, cost and time (A2)*

Grocery shopping and dining in Germany

Tante-Emma-Läden were the traditional corner shops where people could buy lots of different things. As in other countries, these have steadily been replaced by other forms of shops, such as **Supermärkte** (*supermarkets*) or **Einkaufszentren** (*shopping centres*).

In recent years, however, neighbourhood shops have seen something of a revival in certain cities. These offer a wide variety of products, ranging from **Lebensmitteln** (*food*), including **Obst**, **Gemüse und Brot** (*fruit, vegetables and bread*), to non-food items such as **Zeitungen** (*newspapers*).

German-speaking cities offer a wide range of international **Küchen** (*cuisines*) and **Restaurants** (*restaurants*), including many options for **Vegetarier** (*vegetarians*).

 What words in the text mean *bread, fruit and vegetables*? And what is the German word for *vegetarians*?

Vocabulary builder

GROCERIES

1 08.01 **Look at the pictures and read the labels. Then listen and number the images. Then listen and repeat.**

a _____
b _____
c _____
d _____
e _____
f _____
g _____
h _____
i _____
j _____
k _____
l _____
m _____

das Brot
das Müsli
die Äpfel
der Wein
der Reis
das Öl
der Zucker
der Käse
die Tomaten
die Kartoffeln
die Karotten
der Blumenkohl
das Salz

2 Put the above items into the following categories: Lebensmittel (*food*), Obst (*fruit*), Gemüse (*vegetables*) or Getränke (*drinks*). Then add other words you know. Check genders in a dictionary if needed. Include both singular and plural forms where you can.

Lebensmittel	Obst	Gemüse	Getränke
der Reis	der Apfel /	die Kartoffel /	der Tee
das Öl	Äpfel (pl)	Kartoffeln (pl)	das Mineralwasser
_____	_____	_____	_____

3 **Was bekommt man hier? Finden Sie mindestens zwei Artikel, die man hier kaufen kann.** *What can you get here? Find at least two items you can buy from these shops.*

a Das ist eine Bäckerei. Hier kann man Brot, Brötchen und Kuchen kaufen.

b Das ist ein Markt. Hier kann man _____ kaufen.

c Das ist eine Fleischerei. Hier kann man _____ kaufen.

d Das ist ein Getränkemarkt. Hier kann man _____ kaufen.

e Das ist ein Supermarkt. Hier kann man zum Beispiel Käse, Brot, _____, und _____ kaufen.

Note that when you use **kann** (*can*), the second verb (in the examples above **kaufen**) goes to the end of the sentence.

MORE CONTAINERS AND QUANTITIES

1 08.02 **Read the sentences and look at the pictures. Listen and match the sentences to the pictures. Then listen again and repeat.**

1 Das ist eine Flasche Öl.
2 Das ist ein Stück Käse.
3 Das ist eine Dose Mais.
4 Das ist eine Tüte Gummibärchen.
5 Das ist eine Packung Cornflakes.

a _____
b _____
c _____
d _____
e _____

2 Was stimmt? Finden Sie, was zusammengehört. *Find the pairs*.

a eine Dose_____	**1** Wein
b eine Flasche_____	**2** Tomaten
c eine Packung_____	**3** Salami
d eine Tüte_____	**4** Bonbons
e ein Stück_____	**5** Cornflakes

Starting in this unit, we give the plural forms of nouns: e.g. **die Tomate** (-n) means that it is **eine Tomate** singular, **zwei Tomaten** plural. The vocabularies at the end of the book also provide the plural forms of nouns.

 NEW EXPRESSIONS

Look at the expressions that are used in the next conversation. Note their meanings.

Conversation 1

das Brötchen (-)	*roll*
Sonst noch etwas?	*Anything else?*
ganz frisch	*quite fresh*
Ist das alles?	*Is that all?*
Was kostet ...? (sing.)	*What does ... cost?*
Was kosten ...? (plural)	*What do ... cost?*
Wie teuer ist ...? (sing.)	*How much is ...?*

Wie teuer sind …? (plural)	*How much are …?*
Das macht (zusammen) …	*That is … /That comes to …*
noch einen schönen Tag	*(Have) a nice day*
Was für …	*What kind of …*

Conversation 2

bestellen	*to order*
Als Vorspeise …	*As a starter*
Als Hauptgericht …	*For my main course …*
Als Nachtisch …	*As dessert …*
die Gemüsesuppe (-n)	*vegetable soup*
das Pfeffersteak (-s)	*peppered steak*
die Grilltomate (-n)	*grilled tomato*
Pommes frites (pl)	*French fries*
der gemischte(r) Salat (-e)	*mixed salad*
stattdessen	*instead of that*
selbstverständlich	*of course*
Hat es geschmeckt?	*Did it taste good?*
die Sahne	*cream*

Conversations

 1 08.03 **Das ist der Laden von Herrn Denktash. Hier kann man viel kaufen: Brot und Brötchen, Butter, Käse, Obst, Gemüse, Getränke und vieles mehr. Hören Sie zu und beantworten Sie dann die Frage.**

a Which foods are mentioned? Identify the words you hear. Try not to look at the text.

Butter   Brötchen   Karotten   Tomaten   Salz

CONVERSATION 1

Herr Denktash	Guten Tag, Frau Berger. Was bekommen Sie, bitte?
Frau Berger	Ich möchte zehn Brötchen, bitte.
Herr Denktash	Sonst noch etwas?
Frau Berger	Was kosten die Tomaten?
Herr Denktash	Ein Kilo €1,80. Sie sind ganz frisch. Sonst noch etwas?
Frau Berger	Wie teuer ist denn der Riesling?
Herr Denktash	Der kostet €4,95.
Frau Berger	Dann nehme ich zwei Flaschen, bitte.

Herr Denktash	Ist das alles?
Frau Berger	Ja, das ist alles.
Herr Denktash	So, das macht zusammen €12,35 ... €15. €2,65 zurück.
Frau Berger	Auf Wiedersehen, Herr Denktash.
Herr Denktash	Auf Wiedersehen, Frau Berger, und noch einen schönen Tag.

2 Now look at the conversation again and answer the questions.

a Wie viele Brötchen kauft Frau Berger? _____

b Was kosten die Tomaten? _____

c Was für Wein kauft sie? _____

d Was kostet alles zusammen? _____

3 08.04 Sonja Auer is at a restaurant. Listen to the audio and then answer the question.

a How many items, including drinks, does Sonja order? _____

CONVERSATION 2

Sonja Auer	Herr Ober! Ich möchte bestellen.
Kellner	Bitte schön. Was möchten Sie?
Sonja Auer	Als Vorspeise nehme ich eine Gemüsesuppe.
Kellner	Eine Gemüsesuppe – und als Hauptgericht?
Sonja Auer	Als Hauptgericht nehme ich das Pfeffersteak mit Grilltomaten, bitte. Ich möchte aber keine Pommes frites. Kann ich stattdessen einen gemischten Salat haben?
Kellner	Aber selbstverständlich. Und zum Trinken?
Sonja Auer	Ich nehme ein Perrier.
(20 Minuten später)	
Kellner	So? Hat es geschmeckt?
Sonja Auer	Danke. Sehr gut.
Kellner	Gut. Möchten Sie vielleicht auch etwas als Nachtisch?
Sonja Auer	Ja. Als Nachtisch bekomme ich einen gemischten Eisbecher – ohne Sahne. Und ich trinke auch eine Tasse Kaffee.
(später)	
Sonja Auer	Ich möchte bezahlen, bitte.
Kellner	Einen Moment, bitte. Das macht zusammen €23,30.

4 Richtig oder falsch?

  a Als Vorspeise bekommt sie eine Suppe. _____

  b Sie isst das Pfeffersteak mit Pommes frites. _____

  c Sie trinkt ein Glas Rotwein. _____

  d Als Nachtisch isst sie einen Eisbecher mit Sahne. _____

  e Zusammen macht es €29,50. _____

Language discovery

1 Look at conversation 1 again. Can you find the plural forms of the words below?

  a Tomate - _____

  b Flasche - _____

  c Brötchen - _____

2 Look at these sentences from Conversation 2. Identify the subject (S) and the verb (V) in each sentence. The first one has been done for you.

  a Ich (S) möchte (V) bestellen.

  b Ich ( ) nehme ( ) ein Perrier.

  c Ich ( ) möchte ( ) aber keine Pommes frites.

  d Als Vorspeise nehme ( ) ich ( ) eine Gemüsesuppe.

  e Als Hauptgericht nehme ( ) ich ( ) das Pfeffersteak mit Grilltomaten.

  f Als Nachtisch bekomme ( ) ich ( ) einen gemischten Eisbecher.

Learn more

1 PLURAL FORMS OF NOUNS

In Unit 6 you were introduced to a few patterns when forming the plural in German. Here are some tips which might make it easier for you to deal with the plural. But you have to be careful as these are only broad guidelines, and there are many exceptions in German. Always make sure that you learn the plural forms of new nouns as you meet them.

Tip	Example
1 Many feminine nouns add -n or -en.	**die Flasche → die Flaschen** **die Packung → die Packungen**
2 a Many masculine nouns add an -e and very often an umlaut:	**der Saft → die Säfte** **der Markt → die Märkte**

b Sometimes no umlaut is added.	**der Salat → die Salate** **der Tag → die Tage**
3 **a** Neuter nouns often add -e, but no umlaut.	**das Geschenk → die Geschenke** **das Problem → die Probleme**
b Another common ending is -er and an umlaut where possible.	**das Glas → die Gläser** **das Haus → die Häuser**
4 **a** Nouns ending with -chen don't change in the plural.	**ein Brötchen → vier Brötchen** **ein Kännchen → zwei Kännchen**
b Nouns ending in -er or –en often stay the same or can add an umlaut on a, o, u.	**ein Eisbecher → zwei Eisbecher** **eine Mutter → zwei Mütter**
5 Nouns imported from English or French tend to add an -s in the plural.	**ein Café → zwei Cafés** **ein Taxi → zwei Taxis**

Note that the singular form is preferred to the plural in certain expressions of quantity:

Drei Pfund **Äpfel, bitte.**	*Three pounds of apples, please.*
250 Gramm **Käse.**	*250 grams of cheese.*
Zwei Stück **Kuchen.**	*Two pieces of cake.*
Drei Glas **Wein.**	*Three glasses of wine.*

2 WORD ORDER

The verb in a German sentence usually has to be the second idea or component. So if the sentence starts with anything other than the subject, the verb and subject have to be swapped around.

[1]	[2]	[3] +
Subject Ich	*Verb* nehme	eine Gemüsesuppe.
Als Vorspeise	*Verb* nehme	*Subject* ich eine Gemüsesuppe.

This swap is often referred to as subject-verb inversion. Here are some more examples.

[1]	[2]	[3] +
Subject	**Verb**	
Wir	möchten	eine Flasche Wein
	Verb	**Subject**
Zum Trinken	möchten	wir eine Flasche Wein.
Subject	**Verb**	
Wir	bekommen	ein Kännchen Kaffee.
	Verb	**Subject**
Nachher	bekommen	wir ein Kännchen Kaffee.

Remember also that the verb **können** sends the second verb to the end of the sentence:

Man **kann** jetzt hier in Hamburg sehr gute Tomaten **kaufen**.

Wo **können** wir hier Äpfel **bekommen**?

This also applies to **möchten**:

Ich **möchte** bitte ein Stück Kuchen **bestellen**.

Wir **möchten** jetzt bitte **bezahlen**.

Practice

 1 08.05 Match the customer's sentences (1–6) with those of the shopkeeper (a–f) to make a dialogue. The shopkeeper's sentences are in the right order. You can check your answers on the audio.

a Guten Tag. _____

b Ja, natürlich haben wir Eier. Wie viele nehmen Sie? _____

c 12 Stück. Sonst noch etwas, bitte? _____

d Der Sekt kostet €4,75. _____

e Zwei Flaschen. Gern. Ist das alles? _____

f Gut, das macht zusammen €10,75. _____

1 12 Stück, bitte.

2 Dann nehme ich zwei Flaschen.

3 Guten Tag. Haben Sie Eier?

4 Ja, das ist alles.

5 €10,75. Bitte schön.

6 Was kostet der Sekt?

2   **Identify the missing singular and plural forms of these containers.**

  a   eine Flasche – *zwei Flaschen*
  b   eine Dose – zwei _____
  c   eine Tüte – drei _____
  d   eine _____ – zwei Packungen
  e   ein Glas – vier _____
  f   ein _____ – drei Becher
  g   ein Kännchen – zwei _____

3   **Put the following words in the correct order. Start with the words or phrases in bold.**

  a   möchte – **ich** – bestellen
  b   mit Tomatensoße – **ich** – nehme – Spaghetti
  c   ich – nehme – **zum Trinken** – ein Glas Rotwein
  d   die Gemüsesuppe – **als Vorspeise** – ich – bekomme
  e   einen Apfelstrudel – esse – **als Nachtisch** – mit Sahne – ich
  f   bezahlen – möchten - **wir**

Pronunciation

08.06 The **s** at the beginning of a word or syllable is pronounced like an English *z*:

Saft, Sie, sehr, Sohn
gesund, lesen, Musiker, reisen

At the end of a word or syllable the **s** is pronounced like an English *s*:

es, was, das, Haus
Eisbecher, Reisplatte, Auskunft, arbeitslos

How would you pronounce these words? Have a go and then listen to check your answers.

Sekt, Supermarkt, zusammen, besonders, alles, Mais?

Go further

GELD/WÄHRUNG MONEY/CURRENCY

Man schreibt: € 7,20. Man sagt: 7 Euro 20 *oder* 7 Euro und 20 Cent.
Man schreibt: € 6,40. Man sagt: 6 Euro 40 *oder* 6 Euro und 40 Cent.

GEWICHTE WEIGHTS

Ein Pfund* = 500 Gramm, ein halbes Kilo.

*Remember! The metric pound weighs slightly more than the UK or US pound.

 08.07 *Beantworten Sie die Fragen auf der Audioaufnahme.* On the audio you will hear questions about the prices of items. Press the pause button, formulate your answers and say them out loud. Then press play and check your answers.

Beispiel Audio: Was kostet eine Flasche Wein?

You: €4,90 (*You say it as* **vier Euro neunzig**)

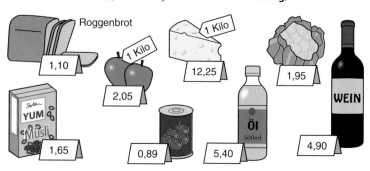

Roggenbrot
1 Kilo
1,10
1 Kilo
2,05
1 Kilo
12,25
1,95
YUM Müsli
1,65
0,89
Öl 500ml
5,40
WEIN
4,90

📖 Reading

1 Read the menu. Can you figure out what the items mean in English? Have a go and then check your answers in the list.

Gaststätte Schnitzel-Ranch	
Speisekarte	
Vorspeisen	**€**
Französische Zwiebelsuppe	3,20
Gemüsesuppe	3,00
Omelett	4,80
Salate	
Grüner Salat	2,50

Tomatensalat	3,50
Gemischter Salat	3,80

Hauptgerichte

Pfeffersteak mit Grilltomaten und Pommes frites	13,00
Paniertes Schnitzel mit Pommes frites	10,50
Nudeln mit Tomatensoße	4,50

Nachtisch

Gemischter Eisbecher	3,80
Obstsalat	4,50
Apfelstrudel	5,00

Alkoholfreie Getränke		**Alkoholische Getränke**	
Mineralwasser	1,50	Glas Rotwein	3,80
Tasse Kaffee	2,00	Glas Weißwein	3,40
Tasse Tee	1,80	Bitburger Pilsener	2,90
Coca Cola	1,70		

V NEW WORDS

die Zwiebelsuppe (-n)	*onion soup*
die Gemüsesuppe (-n)	*vegetable soup*
das Omelett (-e or -s)	*omelette*
der Salat (-e)	*salad*
grün	*green*
gemischt	*mixed*
der Pfeffer	*pepper*
die Grilltomate (-n)	*grilled tomato*
das Schnitzel (-)	*cutlet, schnitzel*
paniert	*breaded*
Pommes frites (pl.)	*French fries*
Nudeln (pl.)	*pasta*
der Eisbecher (-)	*a tub or dish of ice-cream*

2 08.08 **Martin Merlin likes eating. Take his role and order for him. Decide on the answers first, then listen to the audio, using the pause button so that you can say your responses out loud. Then listen to the audio to check your answers.**

Martin Merlin	Say that you would like to order.
Kellner	**Ja, was möchten Sie?**
Martin Merlin	Say that for a starter you'd like a French onion soup.
Kellner	**Eine französische Zwiebelsuppe. Und als Hauptgericht?**
Martin Merlin	Say that for your main course you'll have the schnitzel and French fries. And you'd also like a mixed salad.
Kellner	**Jawohl. Und was trinken Sie dazu?**
Martin Merlin	Say you'd like a glass of white wine. And for dessert you'll have the apple strudel.
Kellner	**Mit oder ohne Sahne?**
Martin Merlin	Say with cream, and afterwards you'd like a coffee.

USEFUL EXPRESSIONS

Ich möchte bestellen.	*I'd like to order.*
Als Vorspeise nehme ich …	*As a starter I'll have …*
Als Hauptgericht bekomme ich …	*For my main course I'll have …*
Als Nachtisch/Dessert möchte ich …	*For dessert I'd like …*
nachher	*afterwards*

Writing

Here is a puzzle involving words for groceries. Fill in the German words for the clues across and a further word will be revealed diagonally. What is i on the diagonal?

Waagerecht *Horizontal*

a cheese **d** fruit **g** eggs

b salad **e** tea **h** cake

c bread **f** tomatoes **i** ?

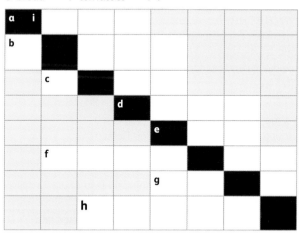

 Test yourself

1 **Identify the correct singular and plural forms.**

	Singular	Plural
a	der Apfelsaft	die _____
b	der Salat	die _____
c	die Tomate	die _____
d	die Flasche	die _____
e	die Tasse	die _____
f	die _____	die Kartoffeln
g	das Brötchen	die _____
h	das Glas	die _____
i	der _____	die Väter
j	das Restaurant	die _____
k	die Party	die _____

2 **08.09** Put these sentences in order to create a dialogue between Frau Trübner and the waiter, starting with Frau Trübner. Listen to the audio and check your answers.

Frau Trübner

  a Ja, einen Kaffee, bitte. _____

  b Ich möchte bitte bestellen. _____

  c Einen gemischten Eisbecher, bitte. _____

  d Ja, sehr gut. Ich möchte jetzt bezahlen. _____

  e Ich nehme die Nudeln mit Tomatensoße, bitte. _____

  f Ohne, bitte. _____

Kellner

  1 Mit oder ohne Sahne?

  2 Gut, als Hauptgericht die Nudeln. Und als Dessert?

  3 Einen Moment. Das macht zusammen €10,30.

  4 (*20 Minuten später*) Hat es geschmeckt?

  5 Bitte schön. Was bekommen Sie?

  6 Und möchten Sie etwas zum Trinken?

3 Move the item in bold to the beginning of the sentence and make the necessary changes to the sentence structure.

  a Ich möchte **als Vorspeise** eine Gemüsesuppe.

  b Ich nehme **als Hauptgericht** das Schnitzel.

  c Wir möchten **zum Trinken** eine Flasche Mineralwasser bestellen.

  d Wir bekommen **als Dessert** den Obstsalat mit Sahne.

  e Wir trinken **nachher** eine Tasse Kaffee und eine Tasse Tee.

  f Wir möchten **jetzt** bitte bezahlen.

SELF CHECK

I CAN...

●	. . . talk about food shopping
●	. . . name at least eight items of food with the correct gender
●	. . . ask for and give prices
●	. . . order food and drink in a restaurant
●	. . . say how some nouns often form their plural
●	. . . use correct word order for verbs in various sentences.

Freizeit
Leisure

In this unit you will learn how to:
▶ *say what people are doing.*
▶ *talk about leisure pursuits.*
▶ *state likes and dislikes.*
▶ *use irregular verb forms.*
▶ *use the expression* **gern.**
▶ *use* **in** *for focusing on movement.*

CEFR: *Can explain likes and dislikes (A2); Can write about everyday activities (A2); Can recognize significant points in articles (B1)*

Leisure activities

In their **Freizeit** (*leisure*) many Germans like relaxing activities such as **Fernsehen** (*watching TV*), **mit Freunden telefonieren** (*phoning friends*), **Lesen** (*reading*) or **Musik hören** (*listening to music*).

However, statistics show that many Germans work out at least once a week. Popular sports activities include **Joggen** (*jogging*), **Nordic Walking** (*Nordic walking*), **Skaten** (*skating*), **Wandern** (*hiking*) or **Rad fahren** (*cycling*).

There are almost 600,000 different **Vereine** (*clubs*) in Germany and about 25 million Germans are **Mitglieder** (*members*) of one club or another. Clubs cover a multitude of interests, from **Gartenarbeit** (*gardening*) to coin collection or singing. **Gesangsvereine** (*singing clubs*) alone have over 2 million members and **Sportvereine** (*sports clubs*) manage to attract many more.

As in most other countries nowadays, many young people tend to be interested in pop culture and clubbing. Facebook, Twitter and other **soziale Netzwerke** (*social networks*) play an increasingly important role in many people's lives.

What are the German words for leisure time, watching TV, cycling and hiking? And what are a *Gesangsverein* and a *Sportverein*?

Vocabulary builder

 09.01 **1 Look at the pictures and read what the people are doing. Then listen to the audio and number the pictures in the order you hear about them.**

a Frau Thielemann kocht.

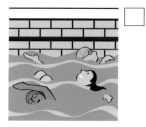

b Die Leute schwimmen im Schwimmbad.

c Frau Ihßen hört Musik. Sie hört klassische Musik.

d Sie spielen Fußball.

e Frau Copa liest eine Zeitung.

f Herr und Frau Gerber fahren nach Berlin.

g Die Leute machen ein Picknick.

h Die Leute spielen Schach. Sie spielen im Park.

MORE NEW WORDS

das Schwimmbad (¨er)	*swimming pool*
die Zeitung (-en)	*newspaper*
das Schach (no pl.)	*chess*

2 **Wie heißen die Verben?** *What are the verbs?* **Choose an appropriate verb in the infinitive form to fit in each of the spaces.**

Beispiel: ein Buch → **lesen**

a nach London → _____

b im Schwimmbad → _____

c Schach → _____

d Fußball → _____

e Rockmusik → _____

f Nudeln → _____ oder → _____

NEW EXPRESSIONS

Look at the expressions that are used in the next conversation and reading. Note their meanings.

Conversation

eigentlich	*actually*
tja,...	*well,...*
trainieren	*to train, work out*
der Roman (-e)	*novel*
fotografieren	*to take photos*
sicher	*sure, certain(ly)*
nachher	*afterwards, later*

Reading

Wie oft?	*How often?*
einmal, zweimal, dreimal usw.	*once, twice, three times, etc.*

einmal pro/die Woche	*once per/a week*
zweimal im Monat	*twice a month*
mindestens	*at least*
die Statistik (-en)	*statistics*
zeigen	*to show, to indicate*
die Lieblingsbeschäftigung (-en)	*favourite activity*
Sport treiben	*to do sports*
das Fitnesscenter (-)	*gym*
lieber	*prefer*
der Rentner (-)	*pensioner*
das Fußballstadion (-stadien)	*football stadium*
billig	*cheap*
das Abonnement (-s)	*season ticket, subscription*
die Kunst (-e)	*art*

Conversation

V NEW LANGUAGE

If you want to express in German what you do or do not like doing, you use **gern** or **nicht gern**:

Ich trainiere gern.	*I like training/working out.*
Ich lese gern.	*I like reading.*
Ich esse gern italienisch.	*I like eating Italian food.*
Ich schwimme nicht gern.	*I don't like swimming.*

09.02 **1 Frauke and Sandro are getting to know each other in a bar. Listen to the conversation and answer the question.**

a Who asks someone out to dinner and a movie? _____

Frauke	Hast du eigentlich ein Hobby?
Sandro	Tja, ich trainiere gern und ich schwimme auch gern. Und du?
Frauke	Ich lese gern Romane und ich fotografiere gern.
Sandro	Ach so! Und gehst du auch gern ins Kino?
Frauke	Oh ja! Ins Kino gehe ich sehr gern.
Sandro	Und isst du gern italienisch?
Frauke	Ja sicher, ich esse sehr gern Pizza.
Sandro	Gut, dann gehen wir ins Kino und nachher essen wir Pizza!

2 Richtig oder falsch?.

a Sandro trainiert gern. _____

b Er schwimmt auch gern. _____

c Frauke liest gern Zeitung. _____

d Ins Kino geht sie sehr gern. _____

e Sie isst gern italienisch. _____

Reading

09.03 1 Lesen Sie den Artikel aus einer deutschen Zeitung und beantworten Sie dann die Frage. *Read the article and answer the question.* **Then listen and read to check pronunciation.**

a *What is the focus of the article? Choose one answer.*

sports and fitness   *people from Berlin*   *leisure activities*

Frage der Woche: Wie oft gehen Sie im Monat aus? Und wohin gehen Sie?

Statistiken zeigen es: Die Lieblingsbeschäftigung der Deutschen in ihrer Freizeit ist das Fernsehen. Doch immer mehr Deutsche gehen in den letzten Jahren auch wieder ins Kino, treiben Sport und gehen ins Restaurant. Wir haben vier Berliner gefragt, wie oft sie ausgehen und was sie dann machen.

Herr Protschnik (37, Bankangestellter)

Ich gehe viermal pro Woche ins Fitnesscenter und habe wenig Zeit, etwas anderes zu machen. Am Wochenende gehe ich manchmal ins Kino, wenn es einen interessanten Film gibt. Ich gehe aber lieber ins Restaurant, meistens einmal die Woche. Ich esse sehr gern italienisch, aber ich koche auch viel zu Hause.

* * *

Herr Schmidt (65, Rentner)

Ins Museum oder ins Theater gehe ich nie mehr. Als ich jung war, da war ich ein großer Kino-Fan. Aber jetzt sind wir Rentner und bleiben abends meistens zu Hause und sehen lieber fern. Einmal oder zweimal pro Woche gehe ich in die Kneipe. Und wir gehen jeden Tag in den Park. Dort ist es sehr schön. Und manchmal gehe ich auch noch ins Fußballstadion.

* * *

Frau de Grille (36, Architektin)

Ich gehe auch gern ins Museum, normalerweise zweimal im Monat. Hier in Berlin gibt es sehr gute Museen. Einmal im Monat gehen mein Mann und ich auch in die Oper. Wir haben ein Abonnement. Und mit den Kindern gehen wir oft ins Kindertheater. Die finden das super.

* * *

Petra Kant (24, Studentin)

Ich bin ein großer Kino-Fan und gehe mindestens einmal die Woche ins Kino. Jeden Montag ist Kino-Tag, da ist es besonders billig. Ich liebe die Filme mit Brad Pitt. Er ist sehr attraktiv. Ins Museum gehe ich sehr selten, moderne Kunst finde ich langweilig. Ich gehe lieber mit Freunden in die Disco, meistens zweimal die Woche.

2   Wie heißen die Antworten?

    a Warum hat Herr Protschnik wenig Zeit? _____

    b Wohin geht er lieber: ins Restaurant oder ins Kino? _____

    c Was macht Herr Schmidt normalerweise abends? _____

    d Wie oft geht Frau de Grille ins Museum? _____

    e Wohin geht sie oft mit ihren Kindern? _____

    f Wohin geht Petra Kant: in die Disco oder ins Museum? _____

    g Wie findet sie Brad Pitt? _____

Language discovery

1   Read the leisure activities and the conversation again from earlier in this chapter and identify the missing verb forms of *lesen* and *essen*. Can you spot any changes, apart from the different endings?

    a Ich _____ gern Romane.

    b Frau Copa _____ eine Zeitung.

    c Ja sicher, ich _____ sehr gern Pizza.

    d Und _____ du gern Pizza?

2   Look at the following sentences from the conversation. Does *gern* appear before or after the verb in a sentence or clause?

    a Tja, ich trainiere gern und ich schwimme auch gern.

    b Ich lese gern Romane und ich fotografiere gern.

    c Ja sicher, ich esse sehr gern Pizza.

3 **Read the article again and complete the sentences with** *in die,* *ins* **or** *in den.* **Notice the gender of the nouns. What form goes with which gender?**

a Ich gehe viermal pro Woche _____ Fitnesscenter. (nt)

b Wir gehen jeden Tag _____ Park. (m)

c Einmal im Monat gehen mein Mann und ich auch _____ Oper. (f)

d Ich gehe mindestens einmal die Woche _____ Kino. (nt)

e Ich gehe lieber mit Freunden _____ Disco. (f)

Learn more

1 IRREGULAR VERBS

Some verbs in German have a change in the vowel in the **du** and **er**, **sie**, **es** forms. Here are some of the ones you have met so far:

	lesen	essen	sprechen	nehmen	fahren
ich	**lese**	**esse**	**spreche**	**nehme**	**fahre**
du	**liest**	**isst**	**sprichst**	**nimmst**	**fährst**
er, sie, es	**liest**	**isst**	**spricht**	**nimmt**	**fährt**

Now read the examples.

> Ich **lese** Krimis. **Liest** du auch Krimis?
>
> Ich **fahre** nach Hamburg. Paula **fährt** heute nach Frankfurt.
>
> Ich **spreche** Französisch. **Sprichst** du auch Französisch?

As you can see, this change does not happen at all in the plural forms:

	lesen	essen	sprechen	nehmen	fahren
wir	**lesen**	**essen**	**sprechen**	**nehmen**	**fahren**
ihr	**lest**	**esst**	**sprecht**	**nehmt**	**fahrt**
Sie/sie	**lesen**	**essen**	**sprechen**	**nehmen**	**fahren**

2 GERN AND NICHT GERN

If you want to express in German what you do or do not like doing you use **gern** or **nicht gern**. The word **gern** is used together with a verb to say that you like doing something:

Ich gehe gern **ins Kino.**   *I like going to the cinema.*

Ich lese gern.   *I like reading.*

Ich esse gern **italienisch.**   *I like eating Italian food.*

Ich koche gern.	*I like cooking.*
Ich spreche gern **Deutsch.**	*I like speaking German.*
Ich arbeite gern **im Garten.**	*I like working in the garden.*
Ich twittere gern.	*I like going on Twitter*

To say that you do not like doing something, you simply add **nicht**:

Ich lese nicht gern.	*I don't like reading.*
Ich schwimme nicht gern.	*I don't like swimming.*
Ich schwimme nicht gern.	*I don't like swimming.*
Ich jogge auch nicht gern.	*I don't like jogging either.*
Ich twittere nicht gern.	*I don't like going on Twitter*

In a positive sentence **gern** follows the verb. In a negative sentence **nicht** goes between the verb and **gern** or is directly placed before **gern**.

There is also another way in German to express likes or dislikes using **mögen**. **Mögen** is irregular.

Ich mag Musik.	**Wir mögen Musik.**
Magst du Musik?	**Mögt ihr Musik?**
Mögen Sie Musik?	**Mögen Sie Musik?**
Er / Sie / Es mag Musik.	**Sie mögen Musik.**

Gern is used with verbs. **Mögen** is normally used with nouns. Look at the following examples:

Gern	Mögen
Ich spiele gern **Fußball.**	Ich mag **Fußball.**
Ich lerne gern **Deutsch.**	Ich mag **Deutsch.**
Ich höre gern **Barockmusik.**	Ich mag **Barockmusik.**

3 VERBS AS NOUNS

Most German verbs can be used as nouns:

schwimmen	*to swim*	→	**das Schwimmen**	*swimming*
joggen	*to jog*	→	**das Joggen**	*jogging*
reisen	*to travel*	→	**das Reisen**	*travelling*

As you can see, these nouns are neuter and, of course, start with a capital letter.

4 *IN* WITH VERBS OF MOVEMENT (ACCUSATIVE ENDINGS)

In German, accusative case endings are needed after **in** when movement is indicated as if answering the question **wohin?** (*where to?*).

> Frau Norbert geht jeden Tag **in den** Stadtpark.
>
> Herr Gerber geht zu oft **in die** Kneipe.
>
> Heike geht sehr oft **ins** Kino. (in das → ins)

der	Ich gehe	**in den**	Park. Biergarten.
die	Ich gehe	**in die**	Oper. Kneipe.
das	Ich gehe	**ins**	Kino. Restaurant.

The same form is used when asking and answering questions about where someone goes.

Fragen

> Wie oft gehen Sie/gehst du **in den** Park?
>
> Gehen Sie/Gehst du oft **ins** Theater?
>
> Gehen Sie/Gehst du gern **in die** Kneipe? /**in die** Oper?

Antworten

> Ich gehe einmal die Woche/zweimal im Monat **in den** Park.
>
> Ich gehe oft/manchmal/selten/nie **ins** Theater.
>
> Ich gehe (sehr) gern **in die** Kneipe./**in die** Oper.

🔓 Practice

1 Complete the sentences with the correct form of the verb in brackets.

a Er _____ sehr gut Deutsch. (sprechen)

b _____ du Englisch? (sprechen)

c Ich _____ nach Berlin. (fahren)

d Angela _____ zweimal im Monat nach München. (fahren)

e Was _____ du als Vorspeise? (nehmen)

f Ich _____ eine Gemüsesuppe und ein Omelett. (nehmen)

g Frau Peters _____ viel Agatha Christie. (lesen)

h Was _____ Sie? (lesen)

i Er _____ viel Nudeln. (essen)

j Was _____ Susanne und Katja? (essen)

2 The sentences with *gern* and *nicht gern* are all scrambled up. Put them in the right order and start with the word or phrase in bold. Remember that the verb is the second idea or component.

a gehe – **ich** – ins Theater – gern

b gern – trinkt – **er** – französischen Rotwein

c Baguette – **wir** – sehr – gern – essen – mit Käse

d **Angela** – nicht – in die Oper – gern – geht

e nicht – **ich** – gern – koche

f gern – ins Fitnesscenter – **Thomas und Uta** – nicht – gehen

3 Wie heißt es richtig? Identify the correct form of *mögen*.

a _____ du Peter?

b Nein, ich _____ Peter nicht.

c _____ Sie Sport?

d Ja, ich _____ Sport.

e _____ ihr deutsches Essen?

f Ja, wir _____ deutsches Essen.

4 Wohin gehen die Leute wirklich? What is wrong with these sentences? Say where the people really go, by correcting the information given in bold, as shown in the example.

Beispiel Frau Jörgensen findet moderne Kunst interessant und geht oft **in die Kneipe.**

Nein, sie geht nicht in die Kneipe, sie geht ins Museum.

a Peter und Heike essen gern chinesisch und gehen einmal die Woche **ins Kino**.

b Frau Schweigert hört gern klassische Musik und geht oft **ins Café**.

c Frau Müller liebt Schwarzwälder Kirschtorte. Sie geht jeden Tag **in die Oper**.

d Herr Knobl findet Fußball gut. Er geht oft **ins Restaurant**.

e Herr Radek trinkt gern Bier und geht häufig **ins Museum**.

f Gerd liebt alte Hollywoodfilme. Er geht oft **ins Fitnesscenter**.

Listening

 09.04 **Hören Sie zu!** Listen to the interviews and identify the hobbies mentioned.

Lesen	☐	Golf	☐	Fitness	☐
Reisen	☐	Surfen	☐	Fotografieren	☐
Fußball	☐	Schwimmen	☐	Popmusik	☐
Facebook	☐	Kino	☐	Garten	☐
Klassische Musik	☐	Tennis	☐	Segeln	☐
Twittern	☐	Wandern	☐	Joggen	☐

 NEW WORDS

die Umfrage (-n)	*survey*
der Krimi (-s)	*crime story, detective story*
die Biographie (-n)	*biography*
die Fotografie	*photography*
die klassische Musik	*classical music*
das Reisen	*travelling*
das Wandern	*hiking*
das Segeln	*sailing*

 # Writing

Complete the survey with your own information. Complete your answers as done in the example.

Beispiel　**Frage**　Sprechen Sie gern Deutsch?

　　　　　Antwort　Ja, ich spreche gern / sehr gern Deutsch. *oder*

　　　　　　　　　Nein, ich spreche nicht gern Deutsch.

Fragen

1 Lesen Sie gern Zeitung?

2 Hören Sie gern Elvis Presley?

3 Essen Sie gern Pizza?

4 Reisen Sie gern?

5 Arbeiten Sie gern im Garten?

6 Trinken Sie gern Bier?

7 Twittern Sie gern?

8 Kochen Sie gern?

Go further

 09.05 **1 Listen and repeat the words for describing how often you do things.**

immer	*always*
meistens	*mostly*
oft / häufig	*often/frequently*
normalerweise	*normally, usually*
manchmal	*sometimes*
selten	*seldom*
nie	*never*

 2 Now make sentences about these activities . Say how often you do them.

Beispiel   Meistens koche ich nur am Wochenende.

Ich schwimme normalerweise einmal pro Woche.

kochen
schwimmen
Musik hören
Fußball spielen
Zeitung lesen
ein Picknick machen
Schach spielen

? Test yourself

1 Wie heißt es richtig? Identify the correct forms of the verbs in brackets.

a _____ du gern Pizza? (essen)

b Sabrina _____ oft nach Berlin. (fahren)

c _____ du Deutsch? (sprechen)

d Er _____ Karten. (spielen)

e _____ ihr Deutsch? (sprechen)

f Ich _____ gern. (fotografieren)

g Er _____ Zeitung. (lesen)

h Ihre Hobbys _____ Sport und Reisen. (sein)

2 Wie sagt man es anders? Can you write these sentences in a different way, using gern together with a suitable verb instead of *mag/mögen*?

a Ich mag Obst.   *Ich esse gern Obst.*

b Ich mag Rotwein. _____

c Ich mag Pommes frites. _____

d Wir mögen klassische Musik. _____

e Wir mögen Schach. _____

f Ich mag die Süddeutsche Zeitung. _____

g Magst du Kaffee? _____

3 Wie heißen die Hobbys? Ergänzen Sie.

a S _ h w _ m _ e n

b M u s _ _

c W _ _ d e r n

d _ o c h _ n

e T a _ _ _ e n

f F _ _ b _ l l

g T w _ t _ _ _ n

h _ e s _ n

4 Ergänzen Sie die Sätze mit in die, ins oder in den.

a Mein Hobby ist Musik. Ich gehe oft _____ Oper.

b Herr und Frau Sander gehen gern _____ Park.

c Er isst gern Kuchen und geht oft _____ Café.

d Leonore mag Shakespeare und geht oft _____ Theater.

e Tim und seine Freunde gehen gern _____ Kneipe.

f Ich mache viel Yoga. Ich gehe häufig _____ Fitnesscenter.

SELF CHECK

I CAN. . .
. . . talk about leisure pursuits and hobbies.
. . . say what I like and don't like doing.
. . . say how often I go out and where I go.
. . . name three verbs in which vowel changes in the second and third person singular forms occur.
. . . use **in** for focusing on movement.
. . . use the expression **gern.**

10 Die Uhrzeit
The time

In this unit you will learn how to:
▶ *tell the time.*
▶ *talk about daily routines.*
▶ *use separable verbs.*
▶ *understand word order after* und *and* aber.

CEFR: *Can understand the main point of radio programmes (B1); Can understand short text with high frequency and shared international vocabulary (A2); Can describe daily routines (A2)*

The working day

The **Arbeitstag** (*working day*) in Germany tends to start earlier than in most other countries. **Büros** (*offices*) and **Schulen** (*schools*), for instance, often start **um 8.00 Uhr** (*at 8.00 a.m*).

Most people will have their **Mittagspause** (*lunch break*) **um 12.00 Uhr mittags** (*at 12 noon*). Despite the changes in working practices this old habit seems to prevail in modern Germany.

The **Arbeitszeit** (*working time*) for most people varies between 38 and 40 **Stunden** (*hours*) per **Woche** (*week*). However, many **Angestellte** (*employees*) in skilled jobs and those who are self-employed will work longer hours.

The earlier start means that many people finish work earlier too. **Der Feierabend** (*the time when work is finished*) is commonly regarded as a time to be enjoyed and not to be spent doing chores. The common way of asking someone in German what time they finish work is: **Wann hast du Feierabend?** The answer will be along the lines of: **Ich habe um fünf Uhr Feierabend.**

 What are the German words for working day, lunch break and hours? And how would you say at 8 o'clock and at 12 noon?

Vocabulary builder

10.01 1 Listen for the two ways in which you can ask for the time in German. Then listen and repeat.

Entschuldigen Sie, bitte. Wie spät ist es?

Zwei Uhr.

Entschuldigung. Wie viel Uhr ist es, bitte?

Es ist zehn vor vier.

2 Complete the English expressions.

a **Wie spät ist es?**   *What's the time? (lit. How late is it?)*

b **Zwei Uhr.**   *Two _____.*

c **Wie viel Uhr ist es, bitte?**   *What is the time, _____.? (lit. How many hours is it?)*

d **Es ist zehn vor vier.**   *_____.ten to four.*

Note that **die Uhr,** apart from indicating the time, can also mean *the clock* or *watch*, whereas hour in terms of duration is **die Stunde** in German.

Das ist meine Uhr.   This is my watch.

Er braucht eine Stunde.   He needs one hour.

10.02 1 Look at the times based on the 12-hour clock and listen to them on the audio. Then listen and repeat.

Es ist zwei Uhr.

Es ist zehn nach zwei. / Es ist zehn Minuten nach zwei.

Es ist zehn Minuten vor vier.

Es ist zwei Minuten nach neun. / Es ist kurz nach neun.

Es ist Viertel nach fünf.

Es ist Viertel vor sieben.

Es ist halb zwei.

Es ist halb fünf.

2 Look at the time expressions in exercise 1. Match the German words to the English expressions.

a halb _____   1 *past*
b Viertel _____   2 *shortly past/after*
c nach _____   3 *quarter*
d vor _____   4 *half*
e kurz nach _____   5 *before*

 3 10.03 Hören Sie zu. *Number the times in the order you hear them.*

a 4:30 _____   c 8:45 _____
b 8:50 _____   d 6:28 _____

4 10.03 Schreiben Sie die Uhrzeiten. Listen to the conversations again and write out the time expressions you hear.

1 <u>sechs Uhr achtundzwanzig</u>

2 _____

3 _____

4 _____

MORGENS ODER ABENDS?

10.04 1 Listen to the German expressions for a.m. and p.m. on the next page and number them in the order you hear them. Then listen and repeat the expressions.

In German when using **Uhr** (*o'clock*) after the digit one you need to drop the **s** from **eins**.

Es ist eins.   Es ist ein Uhr.

a Es ist neun Uhr **morgens**. _____

b Es ist ein Uhr **mittags**. _____

c Es ist vier Uhr **nachmittags**. _____

d Es ist sieben Uhr **abends**. _____

e Es ist ein Uhr **nachts**. _____

 2 **Sagen Sie die Uhrzeit. Say the time**.

1 p.m.   4 p.m.   8 p.m.   11 p.m.   9 a.m.   6 a.m.

The 24-hour clock is usually used for official purposes in Germany. Look at the following examples.

21:00 – **Es ist einundzwanzig Uhr.**

17:56 – **Es ist siebzehn Uhr sechsundfünfzig./Es ist siebzehn Uhr und sechsundfünfzig Minuten.**

3 10.05 **Now practice the 24-hour clock. Check your answers on the audio.**

13:00   15:20   07:45   18:12   23:35   04:17

 NEW EXPRESSIONS

Look at the expressions that are used in the next reading. Note their meanings.

aufstehen	*to get up*
dann	*then*
duschen	*to shower*
frühstücken	*to have breakfast (lit. to breakfast)*
danach	*afterwards*
anfangen	*to start*
anrufen	*to phone*
die Kundin (-nen)	*female customer*
Um Viertel nach fünf hat sie Feierabend.	*She finishes work at a quarter past five.*
der Feierabend	*end of work*
einkaufen	*to shop*
isst sie zu Abend	*she has her evening meal/dinner*
anschließend	*immediately afterwards*
abholen	*to fetch, pick up*
fernsehen	*to watch TV*
die Nachrichten (pl.)	*news (on radio, TV)*

 # Reading

10.06 **1 Was macht Frau Haase? Read the text below and find out what Frau Haase does on ein typischer Tag (*a typical day*). Answer the question. Then listen and read to check pronunciation.**

a How long is Frau Haase's typical day?

about 12 hours   about 16 hours   about 20 hours

Es ist 7 Uhr 10. Frau Haase steht auf. Dann duscht sie und frühstückt. Normalerweise isst sie ein Brötchen und sie trinkt zwei Tassen Kaffee.

Um Viertel vor acht geht sie normalerweise aus dem Haus. Sie geht ins Büro. Ihre Arbeit fängt um halb neun an.

Frau Haase arbeitet in einer Bank. Um 10 Uhr ruft sie eine Kundin an. Danach schreibt sie E-Mails. Um zwölf Uhr macht sie Mittagspause.

Um Viertel nach fünf hat sie Feierabend. Dann geht sie in den Supermarkt und kauft ein. Um sechs Uhr ist sie wieder zu Hause. Um Viertel nach sechs isst sie zu Abend.

Um sieben Uhr holt Frau Haase eine Freundin von der Arbeit ab. Anschließend gehen sie zusammen ins Kino und dann gehen sie in die Kneipe.

Um halb elf ist sie wieder zu Hause. Sie sieht noch ein bisschen fern. Sie sieht die Nachrichten. Sie sieht aber nur selten fern. Um halb zwölf geht sie dann ins Bett.

2 **Was macht Frau Haase wann? Read the text again and decide in what order she does these activities.**
   a   Sie geht aus dem Haus. ( )
   b   Frau Haase geht in den Supermarkt. ( )
   c   Sie schreibt E-Mails. ( )
   d   Sie isst normalerweise ein Brötchen. ( )

e Frau Haase duscht. (1)

f Sie sieht die Nachrichten. ( )

g Frau Haase geht ins Kino. ( )

💡 Language discovery

1 **Look at the text and identify the missing words. Can you figure out what happens to verbs like aufstehen, anfangen, anrufen, einkaufen, abholen and fernsehen when they are used in a sentence?**

a aufstehen – Es ist 7 Uhr 10. Frau Haase _____ _____.

b anfangen – Ihre Arbeit _____ um halb neun _____.

c anrufen – Um 10 Uhr _____ sie eine Kundin _____.

d einkaufen – Dann geht sie in den Supermarkt und _____ _____.

e abholen – Um sieben Uhr _____ sie eine Freundin von der Arbeit _____.

f fernsehen – Sie _____ noch ein bisschen _____.

2 **Read these sentences from the text. Indicate the position of the subject (S) and the verb (V). Can you see what happens to the word order after und? In which position is the verb?**

a Um Viertel vor acht geht (V) sie (S) aus dem Haus.

b Frau Haase ( ) arbeitet ( ) in einer Bank.

c Danach schreibt ( ) sie ( ) E-Mails.

d Um sechs Uhr ist ( ) sie ( ) wieder zu Hause.

e Normalerweise isst ( ) sie ( ) ein Brötchen und sie ( ) trinkt ( ) zwei Tassen Kaffee.

f Anschließend gehen ( ) sie ( ) zusammen ins Kino und dann gehen ( ) sie ( ) in die Kneipe.

Learn more

1 SEPARABLE VERBS

In English you have verbs such as to get up, to pick up and to come along where the verb is made up of two parts. There are also a number of verbs in German which are called **trennbare Verben** (*separable verbs*). The first part (the verb's prefix) separates from the main part (the stem) and usually goes to the end of the sentence. However, in the infinitive (the form that appears in the dictionary) the two parts are joined together.

Look at the examples you have met in this unit:

Infinitive	German expression	English expression
abholen	**Ich hole dich um acht Uhr ab.**	*I'll pick you up at 8 o'clock.*
aufstehen	**Wann stehst du auf?**	*When do you get up?*
anfangen	**Die Arbeit fängt um 9 Uhr an.**	*Work starts at 9 o'clock.*
anrufen	**Sie ruft eine Kundin an.**	*She phones a client.*
einkaufen	**Sie kauft im Supermarkt ein.**	*She shops at the supermarket.*
fernsehen	**Sie sieht manchmal fern.**	*She sometimes watches TV.*

Other frequently used separable verbs include:

abfahren	*to depart*	**ausgehen**	*to go out*
abwaschen	*to wash up*	**einladen**	*to invite*
ankommen	*to arrive*	**vorbereiten**	*to prepare*
aufhören	*to stop*	**stattfinden**	*to take place*

From now on separable verbs will be shown as follows in the vocabulary lists:

anlfangen   *to start*

In good dictionaries separable verbs are usually indicated with (sep).

2 WORD ORDER

As you learned earlier in Unit 8, the verb in German is usually the second element in the sentence. The first element in a sentence can be the subject, a time expression or another element; it can even be an object. The verb, however, needs to be in second place and this often means putting the subject in third place.

1	2 = verb	3	4
subject Ich	trinke	*object* eine Tasse Kaffee	zum Frühstück.
prep. phrase Zum Frühstück	trinke	*subject* ich	eine Tasse Kaffee.
object Eine Tasse Kaffee	trinke	*subject* ich	zum Frühstück.
frequency expression Normalerweise	trinke	*subject* ich	eine Tasse Kaffee.

Note that **und** and **aber**, which usually connect two clauses or sentences, do not count as an element and do not affect the word order, i.e. the verb should still be the second element. **Aber** is normally preceded by a comma:

Sentence Part 1	Connecting word	1	2 = verb	3	4
Ich gehe ins Café	**und**	*time expression* danach	**gehe**	*subject* ich	ins Kino.
Zuerst dusche ich	**und**	*time expression* dann	**frühstücke**	*subject* ich.	
Ich stehe früh auf	**und**	*subject* ich	**lese**	*object* die Zeitung.	
Ich esse kein Fleisch,	**aber**	*object* Gemüse	**esse**	*subject* ich	gern.
Ich treibe keinen Sport,	**aber**	*subject* ich	**gehe**	*frequency expression* oft	ins Café.

If the subject in the first and second clause are the same it is often dropped:

Dann duscht sie und frühstückt. (Instead of: **Dann duscht sie und sie frühstückt.**)

Dann geht sie in den Supermarkt und kauft ein. (Instead of: **Dann geht sie in den Supermarkt und sie kauft ein.**)

Practice

1 Was machen die Leute? Using the appropriate separable verb, identify what the people in the pictures are doing.

a Das Mädchen _____ um sieben Uhr _____ .

b Der Mann _____ _____ .

c Die Schule _____ um acht Uhr _____ .

d Der Mann _____ im Supermarkt _____ .

2 10.07 Ein Tag im Leben von Herrn Fabione. Listen to Mr Fabione describing a typical day and answer the questions with *richtig* or *falsch*.

a Herr Fabione ist Lehrer. _____

b Seine Arbeit fängt um acht Uhr an. _____

c Mit den Kindern geht er manchmal schwimmen. _____

d Er bleibt oft zu Hause. _____

NEW WORDS

Autowerkstatt (¨en)	*garage, car repair shop*
Schwiegermutter (¨)	*mother-in-law*
passt auf die Kinder auf	*looks after the children*
später	*later*

3 10.08 **Hören Sie noch einmal zu und beantworten Sie die Fragen.**
Listen again and answer the questions.

a Wann steht Herr Fabione normalerweise auf? _____

b Wann hat er Feierabend? _____

c Sieht er viel fern? _____

d Wann geht er normalerweise ins Bett? _____

4 Sabrina talks about her routine as a student. Connect the two
sentences by using either *und* or *aber*.

Beispiel   Um acht Uhr stehe ich auf. Dann dusche ich. (und)
   Um acht Uhr stehe ich auf und dann dusche ich.

a Zum Frühstück esse ich Müsli. Ich trinke grünen Tee. *(und)*

b Ich checke meine E-Mails. Dann gehe ich aus dem Haus. *(und)*

c Ich bin in zwanzig Minuten an der Universität. Meine Seminare
fangen um zehn Uhr an. *(und)*

d Um ein Uhr habe ich Mittagspause. Meistens esse ich Sushi. *(und)*

e Normalerweise bin ich um 18.00 Uhr wieder zu Hause. Manchmal
muss ich länger studieren. *(aber)*

Pronunciation

10.09 **Here are some nouns with their plural forms. Notice what an
important difference the addition of an umlaut (¨) can make to the
pronunciation and to the meaning.**

Tochter (*daughter*)	**Töchter** (*daughters*)
Koch (*cook*)	**Köche** (*cooks*)
Mutter (*mother*)	**Mütter** (*mothers*)
Kuss (*kiss*)	**Küsse** (*kisses*)

What are the plural forms of these words?

Bruder (*brother*)   **Sohn** (*son*)   **Buch** (*book*).

Listening

 10.10 **Listen to the excerpts from various radio and TV programmes and identify the missing times.**

a   Es ist _____ Uhr. Hier ist das Erste Deutsche Fernsehen mit der Tagesschau.

b   Radio Bremen. Sie hörten die Nachrichten. Es ist _____. Und jetzt der Wetterbericht.

c   Beim Gongschlag war es _____. Hier ist die Deutsche Welle mit den Nachrichten.

d   _____. Und jetzt die Verkehrslage auf Deutschlands Straßen.

e   Das war das Aachener Nachrichtenmagazin. Es ist jetzt _____.

f   RTL. Radio-Shop. Es ist _____.

Writing

Und was machen Sie am Sonntag? Write an account of what you do on Sundays. Use words such as **dann**, **danach**, **anschließend**, **normalerweise** and **meistens** to make it more fluent, and try to connect sentences with **und** and **aber**, where appropriate. Remember that the verb has to be the second element.

> Am Sonntag stehe ich normalerweise um 10.00 Uhr auf. Dann frühstücke ich und lese die Zeitung. Meistens esse ich Toast mit Butter und Marmelade und ich trinke Orangensaft. Danach ...

Test yourself

1   **Wie gut kennen Sie trennbare Verben?** *How well do you know your separable verbs?* **Complete the verbs with an appropriate prefix. Sometimes there might be more than one possibility.**

a	_____rufen	e	_____kaufen
b	_____sehen	f	_____fangen
c	_____stehen	g	_____kommen
d	_____fahren	h	_____holen

2   **Ein Tag im Leben von Herrn Reinhard. Was macht er? Write an account of Herr Reinhard's day. Use the 12-hour clock in this exercise.**

6:30 aufstehen – 7:00 zur Arbeit fahren – 9:00 eine Kundin anrufen – 12:30 zur Bank gehen – 17:00 einkaufen – 19:00 mit Helga in die Kneipe gehen – 22:00 fernsehen

Beispiel   Um halb sieben steht Herr Reinhard auf. Um sieben Uhr fährt er …

3   **Complete the sentences by putting the words in italics in the correct order. Start with the word or phrase in bold.**

a   Ich komme aus Deutschland, aber *aus Schottland* - **mein Mann** - *ist*

b   Ich dusche und *ich* - **danach** - *frühstücke*

c   Ich bin pensioniert und *morgens* - *ich* - *lange schlafen* - **kann**

d   Ich gehe gern ins Theater, aber - *nicht* - **ich** - *gehe* - *gern* - *in die Oper*

e   Mein Mann und ich reisen viel und *fahren* - **wir** - *nach Großbritannien* - *oft*

f   Wir sind oft in London und in *die Tate Gallery oder* - **dann** - *wir* - *gehen* - *ins Britische Museum*

SELF CHECK

I CAN...

○	. . . ask for and tell the time
○	. . . talk about my daily routine
○	. . . use separable verbs
○	. . . understand word order after **und** and **aber**

11 Was machen wir heute?

What are we doing today?

In this unit you will learn how to:
▶ *describe/say what there is to do in a given town.*
▶ *make appointments.*
▶ *say what you would like to do and what you have to do.*
▶ *say why you can't do things on a date suggested.*
▶ *use the modal verbs* **können** *and* müssen.
▶ *use* in *for focusing on position.*

CEFR: *Can find and understand information in official documents (B1); Can understand the main point of speech about familiar matters (B1); Can make and respond to invitations (A2); Can indicate time phrases (A1); Can describe habits or routines (A1)*

Sightseeing and culture

Even small towns in Germany, Austria or Switzerland usually have their own **Theater** (*theatre*) and **Museum** (*museum*). You will find a rich and diverse **Kulturangebot** (*cultural activities*) almost everywhere.

In larger towns and cities there are opportunities to see interesting **Ausstellungen** (*exhibitions*), **Theaterstücke** (*plays*), **Konzerte** (*concerts*) or **Filme** (*films*).

A good way to find out what is on offer is to contact die **Touristeninformation** (*tourist information*).

Larger cities also have their own **Stadtmagazine** (*city magazines*) containing detailed information about events and attractions.

 What words in the text mean plays, exhibitions and concerts? And what is the word for tourist information?

Vocabulary builder

DIE WOCHENTAGE

11.01 1 Listen and read. Number the days of the week to put them in the right order. Then listen and repeat.

_____ Mittwoch

Samstag/Sonnabend

_____ Freitag

Sonntag

Donnerstag

1 Montag

Dienstag

_____

2 Write the days of the week in the correct order.

1 _Montag_

2 _____

3 _____

4 _____

5 _____

6 _____

7 _____

NEW EXPRESSIONS

Look at the expressions that are used in the next reading and conversation. Note their meanings.

Reading

der Höhepunkt (-e)	_highlight_
die Altstadt (¨e)	_old town_
die Stadtführung (-en)	_guided tour_ (of the town)
der Treffpunkt (-e)	_meeting point_
Ein Sommernachtstraum	_A Midsummer Night's Dream_
vergessen	_to forget_
der Regenschirm (-e)	_umbrella_
das Abenteuer (-)	_adventure_

der Samstag (-e)	*Saturday*
der Sonntag (-e)	*Sunday*
Erwachsene (pl.)	*adults*
retten	*to save*
das Theaterstück (-e)	*play*
man	*one/you*

Conversation

Kommst du mit?	*Are you coming along?*
der Geburtstag (-e)	*birthday*
vielleicht	*maybe, perhaps*
die Schwester (-n)	*sister*
zurücklkommen	*to return, to come back*
der Bruder (¨)	*brother*
Geht es am Donnerstag?	*Is Thursday all right?*
Wann treffen wir uns?	*When shall we meet?*
das ist eine gute Idee	*that's a good idea*
bis Donnerstag	*until/till Thursday*
Mach's gut.	*All the best.*

Reading

 11.02 1 Lesen Sie, was man am Wochenende in Hannover machen kann und beantworten Sie die Frage. Read the text and answer the question. Then listen and read to check the pronunciation of new words.

    a What activity is NOT offered in Hanover this weekend?

    a concert   a football match   a lecture   a city tour

HEUTE IN HANNOVER

Die Höhepunkte fürs Wochenende

Samstag

13:00	Stadtführung durch Hannovers historische Altstadt, Treffpunkt: Touristeninformation.
15:30	Fußball: Hannover 96 – Bayern München. Bayern ist der Favorit. Keine Chance für Hannover 96?
20:00	Theater: Ein Sommernachtstraum, Klassiker von William Shakespeare, Gartentheater Herrenhausen – Vergessen Sie die Regenschirme nicht!
20:30	Konzert: Tina und die Caprifischer spielen Soul, Funk und HipHop, anschließend Disco, Tanzclub Hippodrom.

Sonntag

10:00	Fahrrad-Tour, Treffpunkt: Hauptbahnhof.
15:00	Theater: Die Abenteuer von Aladdin – Für Kinder und Erwachsene; anschließend Spiele, Eis und Bratwurst, Faust-Theater.
20:30	Konzert: Melody Makers aus Frankfurt spielen Oldies und Goldies, Bar Domingo.
21:00	Kino: Mission Possible, James Bond wieder in Action – der neue Film mit dem britischen Superagenten. Kann er die Welt retten? Colosseum.

2 Richtig oder falsch? Was kann man am Samstag machen?

  a Man kann um 13.00 Uhr eine Stadtführung machen. _____

  b Man kann ein Fußballspiel sehen. Hannover 96 ist der Favorit. _____

  c Man kann ins Theater gehen. Es gibt ein Theaterstück von Goethe. _____

  d Um 20.30 Uhr kann man ins Konzert gehen und danach kann man tanzen. _____

Remember that when you use **können/kann** (*can*), the second verb (in the infinitive form) goes to the end of the sentence.

3 Was kann man am Sonntag in Hannover machen? Lesen Sie noch einmal, was man am Sonntag machen kann und beantworten Sie die Fragen.

a Was kann man um 10 Uhr machen? *Um 10 Uhr kann man eine Fahrrad-Tour machen.*

b Welches Theaterstück kann man sehen? _____

c Was kann man anschließend machen? _____

d Welche Musik kann man um halb neun hören? _____

e Was können James-Bond-Fans machen? _____

Conversation

11.03 1 Hören Sie, was Petra und Simone sagen. Beantworten Sie dann die Frage.

a Where do the two women want to go? _____

Petra	Hallo Simone. Na, wie geht's?
Simone	Ganz gut. Und dir?
Petra	Auch ganz gut. Simone, ich möchte nächste Woche ins Kino gehen. Es gibt einen neuen Film mit Cate Blanchett. Kommst du mit?
Simone	Ja, gern. Und wann?
Petra	Kannst du am Montag? Da ist Kino-Tag.
Simone	Tut mir leid. Am Montagabend muss ich zum Geburtstag von Birgit. Vielleicht am Mittwoch?
Petra	Am Mittwochabend muss ich meine Schwester abholen. Sie kommt aus Griechenland zurück. Geht es am Donnerstag?
Simone	Donnerstag ist gut. Wann fängt der Film an?
Petra	Um halb neun. Wann treffen wir uns?
Simone	Um acht vielleicht?
Petra	Ja, acht ist gut. Und wo treffen wir uns? Im Kino oder in der Kneipe?
Simone	Im Kino, das ist eine gute Idee. Also, dann bis Donnerstag.
Petra	Mach's gut. Bis dann.

2 Richtig oder falsch? Korrigieren Sie die falschen Sätze.

a Petra möchte einen Film mit Brad Pitt sehen. _____

b Am Montag muss Simone zum Geburtstag von Birgit. _____

c Am Mittwoch muss Petra ihren Bruder abholen. _____

d Sie gehen am Donnerstag ins Kino. _____

e Der Film fängt um halb neun an. _____

f Sie treffen sich um Viertel nach acht im Kino. _____

💡 Language discovery

1 **Look at the conversation and the questions that follow and identify the correct verb forms of müssen (to have to). Note the endings for the first and third person singular (I, he/she/it):**

a Am Montagabend _____ ich zum Geburtstag von Birgit.

b Am Mittwochabend _____ ich meine Schwester abholen.

c Am Montag _____ Simone zum Geburtstag von Birgit.

d Am Mittwoch _____ Petra ihre Schwester abholen.

2 **Read the conversation again and identify the missing words. Can you figure out which sentence focuses more on position/location and which one indicates movement?**

a Simone, ich möchte nächste Woche _____ Kino gehen.

b Und wo treffen wir uns? _____ Kino.

Learn more

1 MODAL VERBS *KÖNNEN AND MÜSSEN*

There is a special group of verbs called modal verbs. Modal verbs behave differently from ordinary verbs. For instance, they do not take the usual endings in the **ich** and **er/sie/es** forms:

können (to be able to)		müssen (*to have to*)	
ich kann	wir können	ich muss	wir müssen
du kannst	ihr könnt	du musst	ihr müsst
Sie können	Sie können	Sie müssen	Sie müssen
er/sie/es kann	sie können	er/sie/es muss	sie müssen

Modal verbs are normally used together with another verb. This second verb goes to the end of the sentence and is in the infinitive.

| **Er kann sehr viel Bier trinken.** | *He can drink a lot of beer.* |
| **Ich muss heute Nachmittag einkaufen.** | *I have to do some shopping this afternoon.* |

When you use **können** or **müssen** with a separable verb (**an|fangen**, **an|rufen**, etc.), the prefix of the separable verb joins up with its stem at the end of the sentence:

Ich muss morgen früh aufstehen. *I have to get up early tomorrow.*

Möchten is formed from the verb **mögen** (*to like*). It too sends the second verb to the end of the sentence:

Ich möchte heute Abend ins Kino gehen.	*I would like to go to the cinema this evening.*
Kannst du mich vom Flughafen abholen?	*Can you collect me from the airport?*

Here are the full forms of **möchten**:

ich möchte	**wir möchten**
du möchtest	**ihr möchtet**
Sie möchten	**Sie möchten**
er/sie/es möchte	**sie möchten**

2 LOCATION AND POSITION

In Unit 9 you learned how to express motion from one point to another: **Ich gehe in den Park/in die Oper/ins Kino**. However, in German it often makes a difference if a sentence is expressing movement from one point to another (e.g. **Wir gehen ins Kino**) or if the focus is on position or location (e.g. **Wir treffen uns im Kino**). This distinction is made after prepositions like **in**. Look at the following examples:

	Movement	Position/Location
masc.	Er geht **in den** Biergarten.	Er ist **im** Biergarten.
	Wir gehen **in den** Park.	Wir sitzen **im** Park.
fem.	Frauke geht **in die** Kneipe.	Sie trinkt **in der** Kneipe.
	Ich gehe **in die** Bäckerei.	Ich kaufe Brot *in der* Bäckerei.
neut.	Heike und Peter gehen **ins** Restaurant.*	Sie essen **im** Restaurant.*
	Ich gehe heute früh **ins** Bett.	Ich lese gern *im* Bett.

*Note: **ins** and **im** are abbreviations for **in das** and **in dem**.

The plural forms are **in die** if motion is indicated and **in den** for position.

Er geht oft **in die** Parks. Er sitzt oft **in den** Parks.

The examples under **Movement** are in the accusative case and those under **Position/Location** are in what is referred to as the dative case. For more information on the dative case, see Unit 12.

There are some more prepositions which behave in this way. One example is **auf.** You use **auf** for example when you say that you go to a market, party or to the countryside:

	Movement	Position/location
masc.	Wir gehen auf den Markt.	Wir treffen uns auf dem Markt.
fem.	Gehst du heute auf die Party?	Wir sehen uns dann auf der Party?
neut.	Wir fahren morgen aufs Land.** (*to the countryside*)	Wir haben ein Haus auf dem Land. (*in the countryside*)
**Aufs is an abbreviation for auf das.		

There are some other prepositions that behave in the same way as **in** and **auf**. You can find a list in Unit 16.

Practice

1 **Was passt zusammen? Match the questions with the most appropriate answers.**

a Wo kann man ein Guinness trinken? _____

b Wo kann man einen Film sehen? _____

c Wo kann man Englisch lernen? _____

d Wo kann man typisch deutsch essen? _____

e Wo kann man einen Kaffee trinken? _____

f Wo kann man einkaufen? _____

g Wo kann man tanzen? _____

h Wo kann man schlafen? _____

1 Im Restaurant *Deutscher Michel*.

2 Im Bett.

3 In der *Disco Heaven*.

4 Im Supermarkt.

5 Im *Lumiere-Kino*.

6 In der irischen Kneipe.

7 Im *Café Kaffeeklatsch*.

8 In der Sprachschule.

2 **Matthias has a busy week. His friend Jörg wants to go to the cinema with him. Look at his diary and identify what he has to do and why he can't make it this week.**

Mo:	20.00 Dr. Schmidt treffen
Di:	abends zum Geburtstag von Bernd gehen
Mi:	bis 22:00 Uhr arbeiten
Do:	mit den Kollegen essen gehen
Fr:	mit Tante Gisela in die Oper gehen
Sa/So:	nach München fahren

a Am Montag muss er um 20.00 Uhr Dr. Schmidt treffen.

b Am Dienstag muss _____ .

c Am Mittwoch _____ .

d _____ .

e _____ .

f Am Wochenende _____ .

3 **Indicate whether in refers to movement or position in these sentences. The first two have been done for you.**

a

1 Gehen wir heute **ins** Kino? (*movement*)

2 Es gibt einen neuen französischen Film **im** Kino. (*position*)

b

1 Sie arbeitet jeden Tag **im** Büro. (_____)

2 Wann gehst du **ins** Büro? (_____)

c

1 Annett kauft meistens **im** Supermarkt ein. (_____)

2 Ich gehe noch schnell **in den** Supermarkt und hole Milch. (_____)

d

1 Kommst du mit **in den** Park? (_____)

2 Ja, **im** Park kann ich gut joggen. (_____)

e

1 Treffen wir uns **im** Restaurant? (_____)

2 Morgen gehe ich **ins** Restaurant. (_____)

4 **Ergänzen Sie, bitte. Use these phrases to fill in the gaps.**

| in die Sprachschule | ins Café | ins Kino | im Café |

| im Restaurant | in der Sprachschule | im Kino | ins Restaurant |

a Ich möchte einen Film sehen. Kommst du mit _____ ?

b _____ *Müller* kann man sehr gut Kuchen essen.

c Ich möchte einen Kaffee trinken. Wir gehen _____ .

d Karsten ist Kellner _____ *Deutscher Michel*.

e Er muss Englisch lernen und geht _____ *Lingua plus*.

f Er möchte chinesisch essen und geht _____ *Shanghai.*

g _____ gibt es einen neuen Film mit Jude Law.

h _____ *Lingua plus* kann man Deutsch und andere Sprachen lernen.

 Speaking

11.04 Write down your responses for this dialogue. Then play the audio, using the pause button to enable you to say your part out loud. You can check your answers on the audio after each response.

Jutta	Hallo, hier ist Jutta. Wie geht's?
Sie	*Return the greetings, say you are fine and ask how she is.*
Jutta	Danke, gut. Klaus und ich möchten nächste Woche essen gehen. Wir möchten in die neue Pizzeria La Mamma gehen. Kommst du mit?
Sie	*Say that this is a good idea and ask when.*
Jutta	Kannst du am Dienstagabend?
Sie	*Say you are sorry but you can't make Tuesday evening. You have to work.*
Jutta	Und am Freitag?
Sie	*Say you are sorry but on Friday you have to go to Cologne. Ask if Saturday evening is all right.*
Jutta	Ja, am Samstag geht es.
Sie	*Ask what time you should meet.*
Jutta	Acht Uhr vielleicht? Und wo treffen wir uns?
Sie	*Say 8 o'clock is fine. Say you could meet in the restaurant.*
Jutta	Das ist eine gute Idee. Dann bis Samstag. Und iss nicht zu viel vorher.
Sie	*Say bye bye; until Saturday evening.*

 Writing

Was kann man noch am Wochenende machen? *What else can one do at the weekend?* Try to write at least ten sentences. You will find some ideas below.

Freunde besuchen

lange schlafen

auf eine Party gehen

zusammen

auf den Flohmarkt gehen

Man kann Freunde besuchen. Am
Wochenende kann man auf den Flohmarkt
gehen. Außerdem kann man

 Note that if you want to say that you are going to a party or a street
market, the preposition **auf** is frequently used.

Ich gehe **auf** eine Party.   Ich gehe **auf** den Flohmarkt.

Go further

 11.05 1 Kommst du mit? *Are you coming along?* Listen to the invitation and responses. Then listen and repeat.

 Invitation

Ich möchte am Samstag ins Kino gehen. Kommst du mit?

Possible responses

Ja ...	Nein ...
Ja, gerne.	Tut mir leid, aber ich habe leider keine Zeit.
Ja, ich komme gern mit.	Ich möchte mitkommen, aber ich muss lernen.
Ja, das ist eine gute Idee.	Da muss ich arbeiten, einkaufen etc.

2 Now read these invitations. Give appropriate responses using the expressions above.

    a Ich möchte am Samstag ins Kino gehen. Kommst du mit?

    b Ich möchte am Mittwoch in die Kneipe gehen. Kommst du mit?

    c Wir gehen am Dienstag ins Fitnesscenter. Kommst du mit?

    d Freitag gibt es eine Party bei Susanna. Kommst du mit?

Test yourself

1 Wie heißt es richtig? Put the sentences in the right order. Start with the word or phrase in italics.

    a ein Stück von Shakespeare / *im Theater* / man / kann / sehen

    _____

    b möchte / heute / gehen / Abend / in die Kneipe / *er*

    _____

    c sehr gut / Tango tanzen / *er* / kann

    _____

    d kann / man / *was* / machen? / in London

    _____

    e essen gehen / *ich* / möchte / am Dienstag

    _____

    f sprechen / *Frau Johnson* / Deutsch / kann / sehr gut

    _____

2 Eine harte Woche. Brigitte Mira's diary for the next few days is full of appointments that she doesn't like but which she has to keep. She has written down the things she would like to do instead. Decide what she has to do and what she would like to do.

Mo:	ins Kino gehen 🙂
	abends für das Mathe-Examen lernen ☹
Di:	Klaus treffen 🙂
	Mathe-Examen machen ☹
Mi:	lange schlafen 🙂
	morgens um 7.30 Uhr ins Fitnesscenter ☹
Do:	in die Kneipe gehen 🙂
	für Hannelore Babysitting machen ☹

> Am Montag möchte sie ins Kino gehen,
> aber sie muss abends für das
> Mathe-Examen lernen.

SELF CHECK

I CAN...

○ ... say what people can do at the weekend or any other day.

○ ... make appointments.

○ ... say what I have to do and what I would like to do.

○ ... say why I can't do things on the date suggested.

○ ... use the modal verbs **können** and **müssen**.

○ ... use **in** for focusing on movement and position.

12 Eine Fahrkarte nach Heidelberg, bitte.

A ticket to Heidelberg, please.

In this unit you will learn how to:
▶ *buy a ticket and read timetables.*
▶ *say how you travel to work or university.*
▶ *ask how you can get somewhere.*
▶ *use the dative case after prepositions.*

CEFR: *Can deal with most situations that arise when travelling (B1); Can cope with follow up questions (A2); Can understand everyday signs and notices (A2)*

German railways

If you are planning to do some travelling in Germany, it might be worth studying the **Spezialangebote** (*special fare offers*) available from the main German rail operator **Deutsche Bahn**: there are **Sparpreise** (*economy prices*) for **ICE** (*Inter-City Express*) trains or other kinds of trains, such as the **IC** (*Inter-City*), **EC** (*Euro-City*) or **IR** (*Inter-Regio*); with a **Länder-Ticket** you can travel cheaper within a German **Bundesland** (*state/land*) and a **Schönes-Wochenende-Ticket** offers special travel at weekends. The **Bahncard** offers frequent rail travellers various discounts.

There are also **Europa-Spezial** offers with **Ermäßigungen** (*discounts*) on journeys from and to Germany within **Europa** (*Europe*).

In recent years, Germany's high speed railway network has been extended and upgraded and **eine Fahrt** (*a journey*) from Frankfurt to Munich nowadays will typically only last about **drei Stunden** (three hours).

If you buy **eine Fahrkarte** (*a ticket*) online, **einfache Fahrt** normally refers to a *single ticket* and **Hin-und Rückfahrt** means *return ticket*.

 What words in the text mean *economy prices, journey, discounts* and *ticket*? And what is special about the Länder-Ticket and the Schönes-Wochenende-Ticket?

Die Bahn

Preiswert reisen am Wochenende

Mit dem Schönes-Wochenende-Ticket können bis zu fünf Personen einen ganzen Tag im Nahverkehr durch Deutschland fahren.

Das Ticket gilt samstags oder sonntags von 0.00 Uhr bis 3.00 Uhr des Folgetages für beliebig viele Fahrten.

Vocabulary builder

GETTING AROUND TOWN

1 **12.01 Wie fahren die Leute?** How do these people get where they want to go? Read the sentences and look at the pictures. Then listen and number the pictures as you hear the descriptions. Listen again and repeat.

a   Bettina fährt mit dem **Fahrrad**. _____

b   Herr Abramcik fährt mit dem **Auto** in die Stadt. _____

c   Paul fährt mit dem **Zug** von Hamburg nach Berlin. _____

d Sie fahren mit dem **Bus** für ein Wochenende nach Paris. _____

e Frau Schulz fährt mit der **U-Bahn** ins Stadtzentrum. _____

f Sabine fährt mit der **Straßenbahn**. _____

g Markus und Hans **gehen zu Fuß**. _____

Note that **Zug** and **Bus** are masculine, **U-Bahn** and **Straßenbahn** are feminine, and **Fahrrad** and **Auto** are neuter in German. If you would like to say that someone travels **by** car, bus etc., you use the preposition **mit** in German.

Notice what happens with the articles (**der**, **die** and **das**) when they appear after **mit**.

 NEW EXPRESSIONS

Look at the expressions that are used in the next conversation. Note their meanings.

die Fahrkarte (-n)	_ticket_
Ich möchte eine Fahrkarte.	_I would like a ticket._
einfach	_single (for bus or train fare)_
hin und zurück	_return_
Was kostet die Fahrkarte?	_What does the ticket cost?_
der Zuschlag (¨e)	_supplement_

Muss ich umsteigen?	*Do I have to change? (trains, coaches, etc.)*
Wann fährt der nächste Zug?	*When does the next train go?*
Von welchem Gleis fährt der Zug?	*What platform/track does the train leave from?*
Von Gleis 14.	*From platform 14.*

Conversation

1 **12.02 Auf dem Bahnhof. Bernadette Klose kauft eine Fahrkarte auf dem Bahnhof.** Bernadette Klose buys a ticket at the train station. Listen to the dialogue and answer the question.

    a What kind of ticket does Bernadette want? _____

Bernadette Klose	Ich möchte eine Fahrkarte nach Berlin, bitte.
Herr Schulze	Einfach oder hin und zurück?
Bernadette Klose	Hin und zurück, bitte. Was kostet die Fahrkarte?
Herr Schulze	Das macht €53, inklusive ICE-Zuschlag.
Bernadette Klose	Ja, gut. (*Gibt €60*) Muss ich umsteigen?
Herr Schulze	Nein, der Zug ist direkt. Hier ist Ihre Fahrkarte und €7 zurück.
Bernadette Klose	Und wann fährt der nächste Zug?
Herr Schulze	Der nächste Zug fährt in 10 Minuten.
Bernadette Klose	Und von welchem Gleis fährt er?
Herr Schulze	Von Gleis 14.
Bernadette Klose	Vielen Dank.

2 **Beantworten Sie die Fragen**
    a Wohin fährt Bernadette Klose? _____
    b Was kostet die Fahrkarte? _____
    c Muss sie umsteigen? _____
    d Wann fährt der nächste Zug? _____
    e Von welchem Gleis fährt der nächste Zug? _____

Language discovery

Look at the vocabulary exercise again. Identify the missing words for *the*. Can you figure out how the articles change after mit?
    a Sie fahren mit _____ Bus. **(m)**
    b Paul fährt mit _____ Zug von Hamburg nach Berlin. **(m)**

c Frau Schulz fährt mit _____ U-Bahn ins Stadtzentrum. **(f)**

d Sabine fährt mit _____ Straßenbahn. **(f)**

e Bettina fährt mit _____ Fahrrad. **(nt)**

f Herr Abramcik fährt mit _____ Auto in die Stadt. **(nt)**

Learn more

1 PREPOSITIONS + DATIVE

In Unit 11 you saw how some prepositions, such as **in** and **auf**, are followed by the accusative case endings when motion is involved and the dative case endings when position or location is involved. Other prepositions, such as **mit**, are followed only by the dative case endings, irrespective of whether movement or location is being talked about.

The dative form of the word for *the* is **dem** for masculine and neuter nouns, **der** for feminine nouns, and **den** in the plural.

masc.	**der** Bus	Frau Krause fährt **mit dem** Bus.
fem.	**die** U-Bahn	Rainer Krause fährt **mit der** U-Bahn.
neut.	**das** Auto	Herr Krause fährt **mit dem** Auto.
plural	**die** Kinder	Sie reist mit **den** Kindern.

As you can see, an extra **-n** is usually added to the noun in the dative plural. Other frequently used prepositions with travelling followed by dative endings are **von** and **zu**. The preposition **zu** means *to* and is often used when asking how to get to a place or location or when saying where you are going. The preposition **von** corresponds to the English *from*:

Look at these examples.

masc.	**der** Bahnhof	Ich fahre **zum** (= zu dem) Bahnhof.
fem.	**die** Universität	Sie fährt **zur (= zu der)** Universität.
neut.	**das** Stadion	Wie komme ich zum **(= zu dem)** Stadion?
masc.	**der** Park	Wie komme ich **vom (= von dem)** Park zum Supermarkt?
fem.	**die** Kirche	Wie komme ich **von der** Kirche zur Post?
neut.	**das** Hotel	Ich möchte bitte **vom (= von dem)** Hotel zum Bahnhof fahren.

As you can see the following contracted forms are commonly found:

zu dem → zum   zu der → zur

von dem → vom

Four other prepositions which are followed by the dative are: **aus** (*out [of]/from*), **bei** (*with/at/in*), **nach** (*after*), **seit** (*since*).

masc.	**der** Film	Was machst du nach **dem** Film?
fem.	**die** Firma	Er arbeitet bei **der** Firma Bräuer.
neut.	**das** Haus	Er kommt aus **dem** Haus.

The indefinite article **ein**, **eine** (*a* or *an*) becomes **einem** for masculine and neuter nouns and **einer** for feminine nouns in the dative form.

masc.	**der** Freund	Er wohnt jetzt bei **einem** Freund.
fem.	**die** Freundin	Wir essen heute Abend bei **einer** Freundin.
neut.	**das** Jahr	Er arbeitet seit **einem** Jahr in London.

To talk about means of transport in German, you use the preposition **mit**. To say *to go on foot* in German, you use **zu Fuß gehen**.

Frau Krause fährt **mit dem** Zug.

Saskia Krause geht **zu** Fuß.

abfahren *and* **ankommen**

Two useful verbs for when a train departs or arrives somewhere are: **ab|fahren** (*to depart/to leave*) and **an|kommen** (*to arrive*). They are both separable verbs:

Wann **fährt** der nächste Zug **ab**?   Er **fährt** um 15.07 Uhr **ab**.

Wann **kommt** er in Heidelberg **an**?   Er **kommt** um 18 Minuten vier nach **an**.

On a timetable the prefixes **ab** and **an** on their own are commonly used to indicate the departure and arrival of trains.

Practice

1 **Ergänzen Sie. Complete these sentences with der or dem**.

   a In Amsterdam fahren viele Leute mit _____ Fahrrad.

   b Mit _____ U-Bahn ist man in sieben Minuten in der Stadt.

   c In München kann man mit _____ Straßenbahn fahren.

   d Er fährt mit _____ Auto nach Österreich.

   e Mit _____ Zug kostet es €60 bis nach Freiburg.

2 **Was fragen die Leute? Ergänzen Sie.** Complete the questions.
Note that **Bahnhof** is masculine, **Touristeninformation** feminine
and **Hotel** and **Fußballstadion** are neuter.

a

a Entschuldigen Sie bitte, wie komme ich ___ Bahnhof?

b

b Entschuldigen Sie, wie komme ich ___ Touristeninformation?

c

c Entschuldigung bitte, wie komme ich v___ Bahnhof z___ Hotel Germania?

d

d Entschuldigen Sie bitte, wie komme ich ___ Fußballstadion?

3 **Choose the appropriate answer for the question in each instance.**

a Kann ich eine Fahrkarte nach Freiburg bekommen?

    1 Der nächste Zug fährt um 16.00 Uhr.

    2 Das macht €37.

    3 Einfach oder hin und zurück?

b Wann fährt der nächste Zug nach Innsbruck?

    1 Von Gleis 7.

    2 In 10 Minuten.

    3 Einfach oder hin und zurück?

c Von welchem Gleis fährt der Zug?

    1 Sie müssen nicht umsteigen.

    2 Gleis 10.

    3 Es ist ein Direktzug.

d Was kostet die Fahrkarte?

    1 Das macht €43.

    2 Sie brauchen einen Zuschlag.

    3 Sie können mit Ihrer Visa-Karte bezahlen.

Speaking

 12.03 Write down the answers first, then listen to the audio, using the pause button so that you can say your responses out loud. Then check your answers.

Sie	*Ask how much a ticket to Frankfurt costs.*
Verkäufer	Einfach oder hin und zurück?
Sie	*Say a single ticket.*
Verkaüfer	Das macht €42,50, inklusive ICE-Zuschlag.
Sie	*Say yes, that's OK.*
Verkäufer	Vielen Dank, hier ist Ihre Fahrkarte und €2,50 zurück.
Sie	*Ask when the next train goes to Frankfurt.*
Verkäufer	Der nächste Zug fährt in 10 Minuten.
Sie	*Ask which platform it leaves from.*
Verkäufer	Von Gleis 14.
Sie	*Ask if you have to change.*
Verkäufer	Nein, der Zug ist direkt.
Sie	*Say thank you very much.*

Reading

Wann fährt der nächste Zug nach Heidelberg?
Study the timetable, then answer the
questions in relation to the given days
and times in the chart.

Hannover Hbf
→ **Heidelberg Hbf**

Fahrplanauszug – Angaben ohne Gewähr –

441 km

ab	Zug	Umsteigen	an	ab	Zug		an	Verkehrstage	
1.24	D 1599 🛏🍽						6.21	täglich	
5.21	ICE 997 ✕	Frankfurt(M)	7.43	7.51	IR 2473	🍴	8.43	Mo - Sa	01
6.12	IR 2475						10.43	Mo - Sa	01
6.50	ICE 571 ✕						9.51	Mo - Sa	01
7.24	ICE 791 ✕	Frankfurt(M)	9.43	9.51	IR 2475	🍴	10.43	täglich	
7.50	ICE 775 ✕	Mannheim Hbf	10.42	10.54	IC 119	✕	11.05	täglich	
8.12	IR 2477 🍴						12.43	täglich	
8.50	ICE 573 ✕						11.51	täglich	
9.23	ICE 793 ✕	Frankfurt(M)	11.43	11.51	IR 2477	🍴	12.43	täglich	
9.50	ICE 873 ✕	Frankfurt(M)	12.01	12.06	ICE 73	✕		täglich	
		Mannheim Hbf	12.42	12.54	IC 513	✕	13.05		
10.12	IR 2479 🍴	Frankfurt(M)	13.38	13.51	IR 2101	🍴	14.43	täglich	
10.50	ICE 575 ✕						13.51	täglich	
11.18	ICE 971 ✕	Frankfurt(M)	13.38	13.51	IR 2101	🍴	14.43	täglich	02
11.50	ICE 71 ✕	Mannheim Hbf	14.42	14.54	IC 613	✕	15.05	täglich	

	Montag um 10.00 Uhr	Donnerstag um 09.30	Sonntag um 06.30 Uhr
1 Wann fährt der nächste Zug nach Heidelberg, bitte?	*Der nächste Zug fährt um 10.12 Uhr.*		
2 Muss ich umsteigen?	*Ja, Sie müssen in Frankfurt umsteigen.*		
3 Kann ich im Zug etwas zum essen bekommen?	*Ja, es gibt einen Speisewagen (dining car).*		
4 Und wann kommt der Zug in Heidelberg an?	*Er kommt um 14.43 Uhr in Heidelberg an.*		

Go further

1 12.04 **Listen to four people talking about going to work and school. Connect the items in columns 1, 2 and 3 so they match what is said in the audio.**

Beispiel   Person 1 → **mit dem Fahrrad** → **20 Minuten**

Person	Wie fahren sie?	Wie lange brauchen sie?
Person 1	mit dem Auto	10 Minuten
Person 2	mit dem Fahrrad	50 Minuten
Person 3	geht zu Fuß	eine Stunde
Person 4	U-Bahn	20 Minuten

2 **Now read the interviews. Then answer these questions.**

Frauke Gerhard (27, Studentin)

‚Also, ich fahre immer mit dem Fahrrad zur Universität. Das geht schnell, ist gesund und außerdem gut für die Umwelt. Von meinem Haus bis zur Uni brauche ich ungefähr 20 Minuten. Im Winter fahre ich manchmal mit dem Bus. Ich habe einen Führerschein, aber ich fahre nur selten mit dem Auto.'

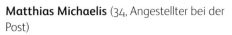

Matthias Michaelis (34, Angestellter bei der Post)

‚Ich fahre meistens mit dem Bus zum Bahnhof. Dann muss ich umsteigen. Vom Bahnhof nehme ich die U-Bahn zur Arbeit. Ich habe eine Monatskarte. Bus und Bahn sind nicht so teuer und in der U-Bahn kann ich auch lesen. Die Fahrt dauert ungefähr 50 Minuten.'

Günther Pfalz (38, Elektriker)

‚Ich fahre immer mit dem Auto. Da kann ich Radio hören, im Winter ist es warm und es geht schnell. Die Verbindung mit Bus und Bahn ist nicht gut. Da brauche ich zwei Stunden. Mit dem Auto dauert es aber nur eine Stunde.'

Andreas (14, Schüler)

‚Meine Schule ist nicht weit, ich kann zu Fuß gehen. Meistens hole ich einen Freund ab und dann gehen wir zusammen. Ich brauche nur 10 Minuten. Im Winter fährt mich manchmal mein Vater mit dem Auto.'

die Umwelt	environment
ungefähr	approximately, about
im Winter	in winter
der Führerschein (-e)	driving licence
umlsteigen	to change (a train, bus, etc.)
die Monatskarte (-n)	monthly ticket
die Fahrt (-en)	journey
die Verbindung (-en)	connection, link
dauern	to last

a Wie fährt Frauke zur Universität? _Sie fährt mit dem Auto._

b Wie lange braucht sie bis zur Uni? _____

c Wie fährt Herr Michaelis zum Bahnhof? _____

d Was macht er in der U-Bahn? _____

e Was sagt Herr Pfalz über die Verbindung mit Bus und Bahn?

_____

f Wie lange fährt er mit dem Auto zur Arbeit?

_____

g Wie kommt Andreas normalerweise zur Schule?

_____

Writing

Und wie fahren Sie zur Arbeit, zur Universität etc.? Write a short
paragraph about how *you* travel and use the examples as a model.

Test yourself

1 **What are the genders for the nouns in each line? Choose *m* for
masculine, *f* for feminine or *nt* for neuter nouns in the brackets.**

a Bus, Zug, Bahnhof, Flughafen/Airport ( )

b U-Bahn, Straßenbahn, Straße, Fahrkarte ( )

c Fahrrad, Taxi, Motorrad, Auto ( )

d Hotel, Fußballstadion, Stadtzentrum, Café ( )

e Kirche, Touristeninformation, Universität, U-Bahnstation, Arbeit ( )

2 **Wie heißt es richtig? Verbinden Sie.** Would you use **zur** or **zum** to
ask for the following places? The genders are given in exercise 1.

a Wie komme ich _____ Flughafen?

b Wie komme ich _____ Gedächtniskirche?

c Wie komme ich _____ Hotel Ramadan?

d Wie komme ich _____ Bahnhof?

e Wie komme ich _____ Universität?

f Wie komme ich _____ Café Extrablatt?

3 **Üben Sie den Dativ: dem oder der, zum oder zur? Ergänzen Sie.**

   a Peter lebt sehr gesund: Er fährt jeden Tag mit d ____ Fahrrad z ____ Universität.

   b In Berlin kann man schlecht parken. Frau Braun fährt immer mit d ____ U-Bahn z ____ Arbeit.

   c Herr Krause hat heute wenig Zeit und fährt mit d ____ Taxi z ____ Bahnhof.

   d Mit d ____ Zug ist man in drei Stunden in München.

   e In München kann man noch mit d ____ Straßenbahn fahren.

4 **Was passt zusammen?** Put these sentences in order to create a dialogue between Herr Marktgraf and a ticket seller at the Deutsche Bahn. Start with c. Note that **Gern geschehen** means You are welcome.

Herr Marktgraf	Verkäufer
a Vielen Dank. _____	**1** Von Gleis 18.
b Und von welchem Gleis fährt er? _____	**2** Hier bitte. Das macht €70.
c Ich möchte eine Fahrkarte nach Köln. _____	**3** Nein, Sie müssen nicht umsteigen.
d Und wann fährt der nächste Zug? _____	**4** Gern geschehen. Gute Fahrt!
e Hin und zurück. _____	**5** Einfach oder hin und zurück?
f Muss ich umsteigen? _____	**6** In einer Viertelstunde.

SELF CHECK

I CAN. . .
⚪ . . . ask for and buy a train ticket.
⚪ . . . say how I travel to work or university.
⚪ . . . ask how to get to the train station, the airport and other places.
⚪ . . . name at least three prepositions followed by the dative case.

Was hast du am Wochenende gemacht?

What did you do at the weekend?

In this unit you will learn how to:
▶ *say what happened at the weekend.*
▶ *talk about recent events.*
▶ *describe purchases.*
▶ *use the present perfect tense.*
▶ *use some adjectival endings.*

CEFR: *Can keep up with animated conversation between native speakers (B2); Can describe past activities (A2); Can scan longer texts to locate information (B1); Can describe an event (B1)*

The weekend, going clubbing

For most Germans, Austrians and Swiss people **das Wochenende** (*the weekend*) is a time to enjoy themselves. This could mean spending time with **Freunden und Familie** (*friends and family*), pursuing a hobby, doing a sport, or doing nothing and relaxing. According to a recent **Umfrage** (*survey*), Germans feel most **glücklich und zufrieden** (*happy and content*) with their lives at weekends.

For many young people the weekend is the best time for partying and going clubbing. German licensing laws are traditionally quite liberal and **Kneipen** (*pubs*), **Bars** (*bars*) and **Clubs** (*clubs*) generally stay open until the early hours. All major **Städte** (*cities*) offer a great choice of nightclubs with the hottest club scene said to be in Berlin.

 What are the German words for *pubs*, *survey* and *well-known*? And what do the words **glücklich und zufrieden** mean?

Vocabulary builder

WEEKEND ACTIVITIES

 1 13.01 **Was haben die Leute am Wochenende gemacht? Welches Bild passt? Read the sentences and look at the pictures which indicate what these people did at the weekend. Listen and match the sentences you hear to the pictures. Then listen, check your answers and repeat.**

1 Die Leute haben einen Ausflug gemacht.
2 Frau Meier hat im Krankenhaus gearbeitet.
3 Sandra hat für ihr Examen gelernt.
4 Frau Nowitzki hat auf dem Markt Blumen gekauft.
5 Frau Weber hat viel fotografiert.
6 Ronni hat im Stadtpark Fußball gespielt.

a

b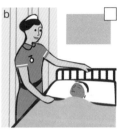

c

d

e

f

NEW WORDS

der Ausflug (¨e)	*excursion*
das Krankenhaus (¨er)	*hospital*
die Blume (-n)	*flower*

To talk about past events in German for most verbs you use **haben** + what is called the *past participle* of the verb. The past participle of a regular verb is normally formed by adding **ge-** in front of the verb and having **t** at the end: **gemacht**, **gekauft**, **gespielt** etc.

 NEW EXPRESSIONS

Look at the expressions that are used in the next listening and reading sections. Note their meanings.

Listening

müde	*tired*
noch	*still*
gerade	*just (with time)*
gestern	*yesterday*
Wir haben viel Spaß	*We (have) had a lot*
gehabt	*of fun*
bezahlen	*to pay*
romantisch	*romantic*
wie früher	*as in the old days*

Reading

die Platte (-n)	*record, vinyl*
einfach	*simple, simply*
toll	*fantastic, great*
die Stimme (-n)	*voice*
das Hemd (-en)	*shirt*
das Kaufhaus (¨er)	*department store*
der Wecker (-)	*alarm clock*
Er kann morgens	*He finds it difficult*
schlecht aufstehen.	*to get up in the morning.*
laut	*loud, noisy*

 # Listening

1 **13.02** **Ulrike and Angela erzählen, was sie am Wochenende gemacht haben. Hören Sie die Gespräche.** Listen to the audio and answer the question.

  a What day's activities are the women talking about?

  _____

2 **13.02** **Listen to the audio again. Identify who says the following sentences, Ulrike or Angela.**

Wer sagt was?	Ulrike (✓)	Angela (✓)
a Am Morgen war ich in der Stadt und habe eingekauft.	☐	☐
b Am Abend haben Bernd und ich gekocht.	☐	☐
c Wir haben viel Spaß gehabt.	☐	☐
d Wir haben klassische Musik gehört.	☐	☐
e Ich habe gestern Morgen einen neuen Computer gekauft.	☐	☐
f Am Nachmittag habe ich Britta und Georg besucht.	☐	☐
g Ich habe den ganzen Tag mit dem Computer gespielt.	☐	☐
h Am Abend waren wir dann zusammen in der neuen ‚Mondschein Bar' und haben bis drei Uhr getanzt.	☐	☐
i Ich habe auch im Internet gesurft.	☐	☐

Reading

1 13.03 **Was haben Sie denn auf dem Flohmarkt gekauft?**
Read the newspaper article about fleamarkets and answer
the question. Then listen to the interviews and read to check
pronunciation of new words.

a Who did the *Tagesanzeiger* newspaper interview? _____

Flohmärkte sind interessant!

**Flohmärkte sind im Moment sehr populär. Ob alt oder jung, arm
oder reich, altmodisch oder trendy – jeden Samstagmorgen
gehen Tausende auf den Flohmarkt. Der *Tagesanzeiger* wollte
wissen, was den Flohmarkt so interessant macht und was die
Leute kaufen. Wir haben letztes Wochenende vier Besucher
interviewt.**

Renate und Bernd Schmidt, 42 und 47

‚Wir haben eine alte Platte von den Rolling Stones gekauft. Die
Rolling Stones sind einfach super, unsere Lieblingsband. Mick Jagger
hat eine fantastische Stimme. Wir haben die Platte zwei Jahre
gesucht. €17,50 ist nicht billig, aber dafür ist die Platte einfach toll.'

Heinz Günther, 62

‚Ich habe ein interessantes Buch über Lateinamerika gekauft. Ich
reise gern und möchte diesen Sommer nach Mexiko fahren. Letztes
Jahr habe ich schon Peru besucht. Das Buch hat informative Texte
und viele schöne Fotos.'

Annett Wunderlich, 24

‚Ich habe ein neues Hemd gekauft. Für €7,50, aus London. Im
Kaufhaus zahle ich €15 oder mehr. Es sieht sehr cool aus, oder? Man
kann tolle Sachen auf dem Flohmarkt finden, fast alles.'

Christine Brandt und Werner Eickes, 20 und 30

‚Wir haben einen alten, mechanischen Wecker gekauft. Mein Mann
hat ein großes Problem: Er kann morgens schlecht aufstehen. Ich
glaube, der Wecker hier ist so laut, den muss man hören. Und wir
haben nur €2,50 bezahlt.'

2 Answer the questions about the interviews.

a Was haben Renate und Bernd Schmidt gekauft? _____

b Wohin fährt Herr Günther diesen Sommer und was macht er gern?
_____

c Was hat Annett gekauft und wie viel hat sie bezahlt? _____

d Welches Problem hat Herr Eickes? _____

Language discovery

1 Look at these sentences from the Listening section. Can you figure out in which position haben and the past participle (gemacht, gehabt, gekauft etc.) are in a sentence?

a Was hast du denn gestern gemacht?

b Wir haben viel Spaß gehabt.

c Ich habe gestern Morgen einen neuen Computer gekauft.

d Ich habe gerade gefrühstückt.

e Bernd und ich haben gekocht.

2 Ergänzen Sie. Use the earlier newspaper article to help you complete these sentences with adjectives. Note the different endings.

a Bernd und Renate sagen, Mick Jagger hat eine _____ Stimme.

b Herr Günther hat ein _____ Buch über Südamerika gekauft.

c Annett sagt, man kann _____ Sachen auf dem Flohmarkt finden.

d Frau Brandt und Herr Eickes haben einen _____ , _____ Wecker gekauft.

Learn more

1 PRESENT PERFECT TENSE FOR REGULAR VERBS

When they talk about the past, Germans most often use the present perfect tense. The present perfect tense of regular verbs like **spielen** and **kaufen** is formed by using **haben** with what is known as the past participle. This is very similar to the present perfect tense in English:

Ich habe viel gelernt.   *I've learned a lot.*

Usage

However, you need to know that whereas in English the present perfect tense is usually used when an event is still connected fairly closely with the present (*I have just ...*), it can also be used in German when speaking about events that have happened a long time ago:

Letztes Jahr habe ich mein Englisch-Examen gemacht.	*Last year I did my exam in English.*
1492 hat Kolumbus Amerika entdeckt.	*In 1492 Columbus discovered America.*

Formation

The present perfect tense is formed by using the appropriate form of **haben** with the past participle. To form the past participle of regular verbs you take the stem of the verb (e.g. **spiel-, kauf-),** add **ge-** at the beginning and **-t** at the end:

spiel-en	**ge**-spiel-**t**
kauf-en	**ge**-kauf-**t**

If the stem ends in **-t**, then an extra **-e** is added before the **-t**:

arbeit-en	**ge**-arbeit-**et**

Regular verbs like these are sometimes called 'weak' verbs. In German, the past participle normally goes to the end of the sentence:

Ich habe Tennis *gespielt.*	*I have played/played tennis.*
Ich habe ein Auto *gekauft.*	*I have bought/bought a car.*

Remember!

▶ Separable verbs put the **-ge-** between the prefix and the stem.

einkaufen	ein**ge**kauft

▶ No **ge-** is added before verbs with the following prefixes:

Prefix	Examples
be-	**be**zahlen – **be**zahl**t** (*to pay*)
er-	**er**zählen – **er**zähl**t** (*to tell a story*)
ent-	**ent**decken – **ent**deck**t** (*to discover*)
ver-	**ver**kaufen – **ver**kauf**t** (*to sell*)
zer-	**zer**stören – **zer**stör**t** (*to destroy*)

▶ There is also no **ge-** added with verbs ending with **-ieren.**

studieren	studier**t**

The verb *haben*

Here is a reminder of the forms of **haben** you might need when forming the present perfect tense.

ich habe	wir haben
du hast	ihr habt
Sie haben	Sie haben
er/sie/es hat	sie haben

Note that the past participle of **haben** is **gehabt**:

Ich habe viel Spaß gehabt.   *I have had/had a lot of fun.*

There will be more on the present perfect tense in Unit 14.

2 WAR *(WAS) AND* WAREN *(WERE)*

War and **waren** are the words most commonly used in German to say *was* or *were*:

Wo war Jochen gestern?   *Where was Jochen yesterday?*

Wir waren auf dem Markt.   *We were at the market.*

The full forms are:

ich war	wir waren
du warst	ihr wart
Sie waren	Sie waren
er/sie/es war	sie waren

3 ADJECTIVAL ENDINGS IN THE ACCUSATIVE CASE

Any adjective which comes between the indefinite article **ein** and a noun has to be given an ending, depending on the gender and case of the noun. For example, when you say what someone has got or buys, you need the accusative case. These endings are as follows:

Gender	Word	Ending	Example
masc.	der Wecker	-en	Werner hat **einen** mechanisch**en** Wecker gekauft.
fem.	die Platte	-e	Renate kauft **eine** alt**e** Platte.
neut.	das Buch	-es	Heinz kauft **ein** interessant**es** Buch.

Note, the above endings are used not only after **ein** but also after **kein**, **mein**, **dein**, etc.

Gender	Ending	Example
masc.	-en	Gibt es hier **keinen** interessant**en** Flohmarkt?
fem.	-e	Wie findest du **deine** neu**e** Lampe?
neut.	-es	Hast du **mein** alt**es** Hemd gesehen?

Note that in the plural, the endings differ. After words like **kein**, **mein**, **dein** etc. you add **-en** to the adjective:

Ich habe **meine** alt**en** CDs verkauft.

Ich habe **keine** neu**en** Bücher gekauft.

In the plural, if there is no definite article, the ending is **-e**.

Er hat neu**e** Hemden gekauft.

Auf dem Flohmarkt kauft man toll**e** Sachen.

No endings are added to the adjective when it does not occur in front of the noun:

Ist dein Hemd **neu**?

Dieser Flohmarkt ist wirklich sehr **interessant**.

Practice

1 Wie heißen die Partizipien? Write down the past participles of these verbs.

a spielen _gespielt_

b tanzen _____

c machen _____

d frühstücken _____

e kosten _____

f kochen _____

g telefonieren _____

h bezahlen _____

i besuchen _____

j einkaufen _____

2 Welches Wort passt? Reuse the past participles from **Übung 1** to complete these sentences.

a Das Smartphone hat €250 _gekostet_ .

b Sie haben in der Disco bis fünf Uhr am Morgen _____ .

c Sie hat Freunde _____ .

d Er hat im Supermarkt _____ .

e Er hat mit seiner Visakarte _____ .

f Letztes Wochenende hat er vegetarisch _____ .

g Hannah hat eine Stunde mit ihrer Freundin in New York _____ .

3 Üben Sie Adjektivendungen. Practise adjective endings. The genders are given in brackets.

a Er braucht einen neu__ Computer. (m)

b Sie hat ein toll__ Auto. (nt)

c Ich möchte eine groß__ Flasche Mineralwasser. (f)

d Peter hat einen interessant___ Beruf. (m)

e Hast du ein schön___ Wochenende gehabt? (nt)

f Sie haben alt___ Freunde besucht. (pl.)

4 **Wie heißt das Gegenteil?** What is the opposite of these words?

teuer – neu – altmodisch – schwer – arm – groß – langweilig – schlecht

a gut – _schlecht_

b klein – _____

c billig – _____

d interessant – _____

e alt – _____

f reich – _____

g leicht – _____

h modisch – _____

Pronunciation

13.04 **Listen to the pronunciation of the letter I in these words.**

leben	lernen	ledig	Lehre
helfen	wollen	vielleicht	wirklich
Enkel	Onkel	manchmal	kühl

The German I is closer to the first I in *little* as pronounced in standard British English. Try to avoid using the so-called dark I (the second I in little) in German.

How would you pronounce these words?

Schlüssel, selten, Milch

Writing

Was hat Bettina am Wochenende gemacht? Here are some details about Bettina's weekend. Write out a full version of what she did on Saturday/Sunday in the morning, in the afternoon and in the evening.

> *Am Samstagmorgen hat Bettina eingekauft. Danach hat sie ... Am Nachmittag hat sie ... Am Abend ...*

Samstag		Sonntag	
10:00	einkaufen; ein Paket abholen	**7:30**	Ausflug machen
15:00	Georg im Krankenhaus besuchen	**15:30**	im Garten arbeiten
19:00	Schach spielen mit Pia – Nudeln mit Pesto kochen	**20:00**	mit Christina telefonieren; für das Deutsch-Examen lernen

Go further

 1 FLOHMÄRKTE *(FLEAMARKETS)*

Markets selling antiques and second-hand goods are very popular in Germany. The **Flohmarkt am Tiergarten**, on the **Straße des 17. Juni**, is a must-see if you are in Berlin. Look out for leaflets advertising markets in smaller towns and even in remote villages. You'll find details of big city markets in magazines like *Zitty*.

Here's a typical extract from the **Flohmarkt** section of *Zitty*. See how much you can understand. Try to guess as much as you can from the context before you look at the vocabulary list.

Flohmarkt am Tiergarten Straße des 17. Juni,
Tel: 26 55 00 96 Sa/So 10 – 17 Uhr

Einer der meistbesuchten Flohmärkte in Berlin, der auch viele Touristen anzieht. Dementsprechend liegen die Preise etwas höher als bei anderen Locations. Doch wer ein bisschen tiefer schürft, wird auch hier ein Schnäppchen machen können. Es gibt Platten und CDs der verschiedensten Musikrichtungen, aber auch Möbel. Direkt angeschlossen ist ein Kunsthandwerkermarkt.

 NEW WORDS

anziehen	*to attract*
dementsprechend	*accordingly*
liegen	*to lie*

etwas höher als	*somewhat higher than*
doch	*however*
tief	*deep*
schürfen	*to dig, to scratch*
das Schnäppchen (-)	*bargain*
verschieden	*different/varied*
die Richtung (-en)	*direction/trend*
das Möbel (-)	*furniture*
angeschlossen	*adjoining, adjoined*
der Kunsthandwerkermarkt (¨e)	*art and craft market*

2 Richtig oder falsch?

a Viele Leute besuchen den Flohmarkt. _____

b Der Flohmarkt ist sehr billig. _____

c Es gibt nur Platten und CDs. _____

d Ein Kunsthandwerkermarkt ist ganz in der Nähe. _____

 Test yourself

1 Frau Adorno arbeitet bei einer Marketingfirma. Dort gibt es immer viel zu tun. Was hat sie am Dienstag gemacht? Read what Frau Adorno did on Tuesday. Write out what she did.

DIENSTAG	
8:30	ein Meeting mit Dr. Paul
10:00	mit Frau Martini telefonieren
10:30	die Firma Schmidt + Consultants besuchen
12:45	Mittagspause machen
15:00	Texte diktieren und Tickets für die Reise nach Rom buchen
17:00	einen schönen Mantel (coat) kaufen
18:30	mit Michael Badminton spielen

> Um 8 Uhr 30 hat sie ein Meeting mit Dr.
> Paul gehabt.
> Um 10 Uhr hat sie ...

2 Wie heißt es richtig? Identify the correct form of **waren.**

a Ich _____ gestern in einem Musical.

b Wo _____ du am Wochenende?

c _____ Sie schon einmal in Berlin?

d Er _____ am Dienstag in einem türkischen Restaurant.

e _____ ihr gestern einkaufen?

f Wir _____ um acht Uhr wieder im Hotel.

3 Was wir am Samstag auf dem Flohmarkt gekauft haben. Identify the missing endings on the adjectives. Check the genders of any nouns you don't know in a dictionary.

a ein alt_es_ Kaffeekännchen

b einen elektrisch_en_ Wecker

c eine cool_e_ Sonnenbrille

d ein alt___ Radio

e eine gut___ Jacke

f ein modisch___ Hemd

g eine fantastisch___ Lampe

h einen warm___ Mantel

i eine neu___ CD

j ein alt___ Fahrrad

k ein neu___ Handy

SELF CHECK

	I CAN...
●	... tell someone what I did at the weekend and talk about the past.
●	... describe purchases that I have made.
●	... use some verbs in the present perfect tense.
●	... work out what endings to use on adjectives in the accusative case after **ein, eine, einen.**

Wir sind ins Grüne gefahren.

We went into the countryside.

In this unit you will learn how to:
▶ *talk further about recent events.*
▶ *talk about the more distant past.*
▶ *use more words in the present perfect tense.*
▶ *communicate more about the past.*

CEFR: *Can understand the main point of radio programmes (B1); Can connect phrases to describe experiences (B1); Can describe a sequence of events (B1); Can write personal letters describing experiences (B1)*

Exploring the countryside

Germany, Austria and Switzerland are well known for their **schöne Landschaften** (*beautiful landscape*) and the latter two for their spectacular **Bergregionen** (*mountain regions*).

People of all ages take advantage of the beautiful surroundings and go **wandern** (*hiking*), either for **einen Ausflug** (*an excursion*) or make arrangements for a longer **Wanderurlaub** (*hiking holiday*).

There is an extensive network of **Wanderwege** (*hiking paths*) throughout Austria which caters for all abilities, ranging from short distances to **Weitwanderwege** (*long distance hiking paths*) covering hundreds of kilometres. If you get **hungrig** (*hungry*) or **durstig** (*thirsty*) on the way be assured that a **Gasthaus** or **Gasthof** (*inn*) is never far away. For simple, hearty food visit a **Jausenstation** or **Jausenhütte** (*snack bar/inn*) as some of these places are called in the mountains.

 What are the German words for *excursion neighbours, thirsty* and *hungry*? And what do Wanderwege and Wanderurlaub mean?

Vocabulary builder

14.01 A family of four decided to go on an excursion into the countryside. Read the sentences. Then listen and look at the pictures. Match the sentences to the pictures. Listen again and repeat the sentences.

1 Sie haben im Zug geschlafen.
2 Um 17.00 Uhr haben sie den Zug genommen.
3 Sie haben gut gegessen und getrunken.
4 Sie sind lange spazieren gegangen.
5 Sie sind mit dem Zug gefahren.
6 Sie sind um halb sieben aufgestanden.
7 Um ein Uhr sind sie sehr müde gewesen.
8 Sie haben gesungen.

a

b

c

d

e

f

g

h

 MORE NEW WORDS

spazieren gehen	*to go for a walk*
müde	*tired*

As you can see in the examples, some verbs form their present perfect in an irregular way and their past participles often have a vowel change and end in **–en**. A few verbs, like **gehen** or **fahren**, need **sein** rather than **haben** in the present perfect.

 NEW EXPRESSIONS

Look at the expressions that are used in the reading. Note their meanings.

gelernter Elektriker	*(a) qualified electrician*
das Unterhemd (-en)	*vest, undershirt*
bislang	*so far*
vorlbereiten	*to prepare*
der Terminkalender (-)	*diary*
bleiben	*to stay*
der Anzug (¨e)	*suit*

Reading

1 **Eine anstrengende Woche.** *A tiring week.* Read the text about the German pop singer Peter Wichtig and answer the question. Look up any words you don't know.

a In what order did Peter do these things? Number the activities.

___ saw a clip of his new video   ___ visited Florida   ___ visited New York

___ sang on MTV   ___ went to Salzburg   ___ went to the casino

---

DAS PORTRÄT:
Peter Wichtig

Peter Wichtig, 34, gelernter Elektriker, ist der Sänger der deutschen Rockband ‚Die grünen Unterhemden'. Bislang hat die Band zwei goldene Schallplatten bekommen. Im Moment bereitet er mit seiner Band eine große Tournee vor. Wir haben ihn in seinem Studio getroffen und mit ihm über das Leben eines Rockstars gesprochen und ihn gefragt: ‚Was haben Sie letzte Woche gemacht?'

.....‚Im Moment arbeite ich sehr viel. Ich bin praktisch kaum zu Hause gewesen. Mein Terminkalender ist total voll. Also, am Montag bin ich nach New York geflogen. Dort habe ich einige Produzenten getroffen. Am Abend war ich auf einer Party bei meinem alten Freund Robert (de Niro) und habe Kaviar gegessen und Champagner getrunken. Ich bin nur einen Tag in New York geblieben. Es war einfach zu kalt dort.

..... Dienstag und Mittwoch bin ich in Florida gewesen und bin im Meer geschwommen. Das war wunderbar. Außerdem habe ich einige Interviews gegeben und auch ein paar neue italienische Anzüge gekauft. Vom besten Designer natürlich. Ja, ich liebe Florida. Ich möchte mir dort gern eine Villa kaufen.

..... Donnerstag bin ich nach Deutschland zurückgekommen: Am Abend habe ich in einer Fernsehshow für MTV gesungen. Am Freitag habe ich wieder Interviews gegeben und bin dann nach Salzburg gefahren, wo ich ein kleines Haus habe und bin abends ins Kasino gegangen. Am Wochenende bin ich Ski gelaufen und habe den Video-Clip für meinen neuen Song gesehen. Das Lied heißt: *Ich kann dich nicht vergessen.* Sie können es bald kaufen, es ist fantastisch. Es kommt in einer Woche auf den Markt.'

---

2 Was ist hier falsch? Korrigieren Sie, bitte.

a Peter Wichtig ist nach Sibirien geflogen. _____

b Auf einer Party hat er Hamburger gegessen und Dosenbier getrunken. _____

c Er hat Robert Redford getroffen. _____

d In Florida ist er im Hotel-Swimmingpool geschwommen. _____

e Er hat neue Socken gekauft. _____

f Am Freitag ist er ins Kino gegangen. _____

g Am Wochenende ist er im Park spazieren gegangen. _____

h Das neue Lied heißt: Ich habe dich vergessen. _____

Language discovery

1 Which verbs in the text take sein and which take haben? Make a list. Notice what kinds of verbs go with sein.

sein	haben

2 Wie heißt es richtig? Identify the missing information. All verbs appear in the text. Notice how the past participle is formed for the missing verbs.

Infinitive	Past participle	Infinitive	Past participle
a trinken	*getrunken*	e gehen	_____
b _____	getroffen	f fahren	_____
c essen	_____	g _____	geflogen
d sprechen	_____	h _____	geblieben

Learn more

1 THE PRESENT PERFECT OF IRREGULAR VERBS

Irregular verbs form their past participles with a **ge-** at the beginning and an **-en**, rather than a **-t**, at the end:

ess-en (*to eat*) **ge-gess-en** (*eaten*)

geb-en (*to give*) **ge-geb-en** (*given*)

seh-en (*to see*) **ge-seh-en** (*seen*)

Many of these verbs also change their stem:

trink-en (*to drink*) **ge-trunk-en** (*drunk*)

schreib-en (*to write*) **ge-schrieb-en** (*written*)

sprech-en (*to speak*) **ge-sproch-en** (*spoken*)

For a list of common irregular verbs, often also called strong verbs, see the end of the book.

PRESENT PERFECT VERBS WITH SEIN

Some irregular verbs – often indicating movement or coming and going – form their perfect tense with **sein** rather than **haben**. The most important ones that you have met so far are:

Verb	Example
gehen	Ich **bin gestern auf den Markt gegangen.**
kommen	Tom **ist erst um ein Uhr morgens nach Hause gekommen.**
fahren	Ich **bin im Oktober nach Italien gefahren.**
aufstehen	Sie **ist um halb acht aufgestanden.**

The past participle of **sein** is quite irregular. Look at the form below:

Ich bin gestern sehr müde gewesen.* *I was very tired yesterday.*

*Note that it is very common to say **Ich war ...** instead of **Ich bin ... gewesen**.

Look at section 3 for further details on verbs taking **sein**.

REMEMBER!

▶ *Separable verbs put the* ***-ge-*** *where the verb separates:*

aufstehen - auf**ge**standen

▶ *As mentioned in the previous unit, verbs beginning with **be-, ent-, er-, ver-,** or **zer-** do NOT add a **ge-** in the past participle. This also applies to verbs beginning with **emp-**:*

Prefix	Example
emp-	**emp**fehlen – **emp**fohlen (to recommend)

2 OVERVIEW OF THE PRESENT PERFECT TENSE

In German the present perfect tense is most often used when people are describing past events informally, especially when they are speaking. Here is a summary of the different forms.

Regular verbs

Regular verbs like **kaufen** and **spielen** form the present perfect tense with **haben** + past participle. These past participles normally begin with **ge-** and end in **-t** and do not change their stems:

machen	**ge**mach**t**
spielen	**ge**spiel**t**

Irregular verbs

The past participles of verbs like **fahren**, **gehen**, **nehmen** and **schreiben** normally begin with **ge-** and end in **-en**. They often change their stems, too.

fahren	ge**fahr**en
gehen	ge**gang**en
nehmen	ge**n**ommen
schreiben	ge**schrieb**en

3 VERBS THAT TAKE SEIN

Although most irregular verbs form the present perfect tense with **haben**, there are also some verbs which use **sein**. The most important ones are:

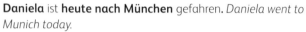

▶ *verbs indicating movement (e.g. coming and going) such as:*

fahren	**fliegen**
gehen	**kommen**

Daniela ist **heute nach München** gefahren. *Daniela went to Munich today.*

▶ verbs indicating a change of state such as:

sterben (*to die*)	**wachsen** (*to grow*)

Michael Jackson ist **2009** gestorben. *Michael Jackson died in 2009.*

▶ a few other verbs, such as **bleiben** (*to stay*)

Wir sind **den ganzen Tag zu Hause** geblieben.	*We stayed at home all day.*

Mixed verbs

Some verbs, when forming their past participles, combine the features of both regular and irregular verbs (hence the name 'mixed verbs'). These past participles end in **-t** like regular verbs, but also change their stem like many irregular verbs.

kennen	**gekannt**
bringen	**gebracht**

Separable verbs

The past participles of separable verbs add the **-ge-** where the verbs separate:

aufhören	**aufgehört**
aufstehen	**aufgestanden**

HABEN AND SEIN

Haben (*to have*) and **sein** (*to be*): these two past participles are used so frequently that they need to be listed separately:

haben	**gehabt**
sein	**gewesen**

NO GE- IN FRONT

Remember that verbs beginning with **be-**, **ent-**, **emp-**, **er-**, **ver-** and **zer-** do not add **ge-** to their past participles:

Prefix	Example
be-	**be**kommen – **be**kommen (*to get*)
ent-	**ent**lassen – **ent**lassen (*to dismiss*)
emp-	**emp**fehlen – **emp**fohlen (*to recommend*)
er-	**er**halten – **er**halten (*to receive*)
ver-	**ver**stehen – **ver**standen (*to understand*)
zer-	**zer**brechen – **zer**brochen (*to break*)

Practice

1 Wie heißen die Partizipien? Write down the past participles of
   these verbs:

a *sehen* *gesehen*

b *geben* _____

c *trinken* _____

d *singen* _____

e *treffen* _____

f *nehmen* _____

g *kommen* _____

h *gehen* _____

i *fahren* _____

j *aufstehen* _____

2 Was fehlt? Identify the correct form of either **haben** or **sein**.

a Am Wochenende _bin_ ich nach Köln gefahren.

b Er _____ in München sehr viel Bier getrunken.

c _____ Sie schon den neuen Film mit Russell Crowe gesehen?

d Am Donnerstag _____ Birgit ins Theater gegangen.

e _____ du schon einmal in Deutschland gewesen?

f Am Sonntag _____ Thomas seine Großeltern besucht.

g Gestern _____ ich einen alten Freund getroffen.

h Oh, das _____ ich vergessen.

3 Das hat Steffi gemacht. Complete the sentences with the correct
   past participle and the appropriate form of **haben** or **sein**.

a Ich _____ heute um sieben Uhr _____ . (aufstehen)

b Zum Frühstück _____ ich Toast _____ . (essen)

c Ich _____ um acht Uhr aus dem Haus _____ . (gehen)

d Ich _____ mit dem Fahrrad zur Arbeit _____ . (fahren)

e Nach der Arbeit _____ ich eine Freundin _____ . (treffen)

f Wir _____ einen Film auf Englisch _____ (sehen),
   aber ich _____ nicht alles _____ . (verstehen)

g Ich _____ den Film nicht _____ . (kennen)

 Speaking

Practise talking about what you did last week. Here are some ideas
for what to say.

When	What I did
Gestern	**habe ich (lange/viel/im Garten) gearbeitet.**
	habe ich Fußball/Tennis/Golf gespielt.
	habe ich meine Eltern/Freunde besucht.

Am Montag/Am Dienstag, etc.	bin ich ins Kino/ins Theater/in die Oper/in die Kirche gegangen. bin ich im Park spazieren gegangen.
Am Montagmorgen	bin ich nach Brighton/Paris gefahren.
Am Mittwochabend, etc.	habe ich ferngesehen.
Letzte Woche/Letztes Wochenende	habe ich einen langweiligen Film/eine englische Band/ein interessantes Theaterstück gesehen.

Achtung! Remember that the preposition **in** is followed by the accusative if movement is indicated, or by the dative case if the focus is more on location and position.

Ich bin **ins** Kino gegangen.   Ich war **im** Kino.

Writing

Eine Brieffreundin in Deutschland möchte wissen, was Sie letzte Woche oder letztes Wochenende gemacht haben. Bitte schreiben Sie ihr. You may find it helpful to refer to the expressions in the previous Speaking activity when completing this exercise.

Liebe Petra,

wie geht es dir? Ich hoffe, gut.
Also, du möchtest wissen, was ich _____ gemacht habe.
Kein Problem.

Also,

_____

_____

Ich freue mich schon auf deinen nächsten Brief.

Viele Grüße

dein/deine

_____

 Listening

14.02 **1 Mehr über Peter Wichtig. Peter war beim Radio-Sender OK München und hat ein Interview gegeben. Hören Sie bitte das Interview und beantworten Sie die Fragen.**

   a Seit wann macht er Musik? _____

   b Was war sein erster Hit? _____

   c Wie viele CDs hat er gemacht? _____

   d Wer schreibt seine Songs? _____

   e Was macht er in seiner Freizeit? _____

Reading and writing

Heinrich Böll: Sein Lebenslauf. Here is a list of some of the main events in the life of the German author, Heinrich Böll. Write a report on his life, using the information provided. You will need to know the following verb forms:

heiraten (*to get married*) → **geheiratet**
beginnen (*to begin*) → **begonnen**
erscheinen (*to appear*) → **erschienen***
bekommen (*to get*) → **bekommen**
sterben (*to die*) → **gestorben***

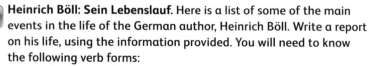

Der Lebenslauf des deutschen Schriftstellers Heinrich Böll
1917 am 21. Dezember in Köln geboren
1924–28 besucht die Volksschule in Köln-Raderthal
1928–37 besucht das Kaiser-Wilhelm-Gymnasium in Köln
1937 macht das Abitur
1937 beginnt in Bonn eine Buchhandelslehre
1939 studiert Germanistik an der Universität Köln
1939–45 ist Soldat im Zweiten Weltkrieg
1942 heiratet Annemarie Zech
1946–49 schreibt Kurzgeschichten in Zeitschriften
1949 sein erstes Buch erscheint (*Der Zug war pünktlich*)
1949–85 schreibt viele literarische Werke
1972 bekommt den Nobelpreis für Literatur
1985 stirbt am 16. Juni in Hürtgenwald/Eifel

der Schriftsteller (-)	*author*
die Volksschule (-n)	*old word for primary school*
das Abitur	*A-levels, High School Diploma*
der Buchhandel	*book trade*
die Lehre (-n)	*apprenticeship*
der Soldat (-en)	*soldier*
der Weltkrieg (-e)	*World War*
die Kurzgeschichte (-n)	*short story*
die Zeitschrift (-en)	*journal*
erscheinen*	*to appear*
das Werk (-e)	*work*
von ... bis ...	*from ... until ...*

* These verbs form their past tense with **sein**.

> Heinrich Böll ist am 21. Dezember 1917 in Köln geboren. Von 1924 bis 1928 hat er die Volksschule in Köln-Raderthal besucht. Von 1928 bis 1937 hat er ...

Go further

The word früher, meaning earlier, previously or in former times, is what you use in German to say what people used to do.

Früher haben Klaus und Doris nur klassische Musik gehört.
Klaus and Doris used to only listen to classical music.

1 **Herr Huber wird 65 Jahre alt. Lesen Sie über das Leben von Herrn Huber und beantworten Sie die Fragen.**

> **Vor 65 Jahren** war er ein Baby und hat keine Haare gehabt. Er hat lange geschlafen, aber er hat auch oft laut geschrien.
>
> **Vor 40 Jahren** hat er in München Betriebswirtschaftslehre (BWL) studiert. Damals hat er lange Haare gehabt. Er hat auch ziemlich stark geraucht und Rockmusik gehört.

Vor 30 Jahren hat er bei der Dresdner Bank gearbeitet. Zu der Zeit hat er kurze Haare gehabt. Er hat geheiratet und ein Haus gebaut. Er hat bald viel Stress gehabt und dann begonnen, zu viel zu essen und zu viel Alkohol zu trinken.

Vor 20 Jahren war er schwer krank. Er hat aufgehört zu rauchen und zu trinken. Er hat wieder Sport getrieben, ist dreimal in der Woche schwimmen gegangen und hat viel trainiert.

Vor 10 Jahren hat er graue Haare gehabt. Er war aber wieder gesund und hat viel Spaß am Leben gehabt.

Vor 5 Jahren ist er dann in den Ruhestand getreten, ist viel gereist und hat viel von der Welt gesehen. Er hat interessante Fotos gemacht und hat andere Sprachen gelernt.

Heute ist er Rentner und hat lange, weiße Haare. Er liest wieder viel, vor allem Heinrich Böll, hört manchmal Rockmusik und ist sehr glücklich.

 NEW WORDS

vor einem Jahr	*a year ago*
vor zwei/zehn/zwanzig Jahren	*two/ten/twenty years ago*
schreien	*to yell, to scream*
damals	*then, at that time*
stark rauchen	*to smoke heavily*
bauen (gebaut)	*to build (built)*
gesund	*healthy*
Spaß am Leben	*enjoyment of life*
in den Ruhestand treten	*to retire/go into retirement*
Rentner/in	*male/female pensioner*
vor allem	*above all*
glücklich	*happy*

2 Richtig oder falsch?

a Vor 40 Jahren hat er in Marburg Biologie studiert. _____

b Damals hat er lange Haare gehabt und hat auch stark geraucht. _____

c Vor 30 Jahren hat er bei Siemens gearbeitet. _____

d Damals hat er begonnen, zu viel Alkohol zu trinken. _____

e Vor 10 Jahren war er sehr krank. _____

f Vor 10 Jahren hat er auch keinen Spaß am Leben gehabt. _____

g Heute arbeitet er nicht mehr und ist sehr glücklich. _____

 3 14.03 **Vor 25 Jahren sind sie zusammen in die Schule gegangen und jetzt treffen sie sich und reden über die alten Zeiten**. Listen to these people comparing past times with the present, then fill in the two grids.

a Was haben die Leute früher gemacht?

Person	Haare	Trinken	Musik	Freizeit
Bernd	_____	hat viel Cognac getrunken	_____	hat in einer Band gespielt
Dieter	hat lange Haare gehabt	_____	_____	_____

b Und was machen die Leute heute?

Person	Haare	Trinken	Musik	Freizeit
Bernd	_____	_____	_____	_____
Dieter	_____	hört klassische Musik	_____	_____

4 **Und was haben Sie früher gemacht?** Now it's your turn. Think of four things that you did in the past and compare them to the present. Say sentences about them aloud. Use the previous exercises as a guide.

Beispiel Früher habe ich in Liverpool gewohnt, aber heute wohne ich in London.

Früher habe ich viel Michael Jackson gehört, heute höre ich ...

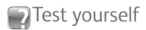# Test yourself

1 **Schreiben Sie die Sätze im Perfekt. Ergänzen Sie. Complete the sentences with the correct past participle.**

a Werner Lübke ist letzten Freitag nach Zürich _____ (fliegen).

b Dort hat er seine Freundin Dagmar _____ (besuchen).

c Dagmar hat ihn vom Flughafen _____ (abholen).

d Freitagabend sind sie ins Kino _____ (gehen).

e Sie haben einen sehr guten Film _____ (sehen).

f Samstag haben sie lange _____ (schlafen).

2 **Sein oder haben? Die Geschichte geht weiter ...**

a Erst um 10.30 Uhr ____ Werner und Dagmar aufgestanden.

b Um 11 Uhr ____ sie dann gefrühstückt.

c Sie ____ frische Brötchen gegessen.

d Dazu ____ sie zwei Tassen Kaffee getrunken.

e Und um 11.30 Uhr ____ sie dann im Stadtzentrum spazieren gegangen.

f Sie ____ mehrere neue Kleidungsstücke gekauft.

3 **Which of the past participles fits best?**

> empfohlen – verstanden – vergessen – ~~bezahlt~~ – erhalten – besucht

a Herr Dietrich hat mit seiner Kreditkarte *bezahlt* .

b Entschuldigen Sie bitte, aber ich habe das nicht _____.

c Carola hat meinen Namen _____.

d Gestern haben wir Frau Hermann im Krankenhaus _____.

e Der Kellner hat uns die Gemüsesuppe _____.

f Heinrich Böll hat 1972 den Nobelpreis _____.

SELF CHECK

I CAN. . .

●	. . . talk further about the past.
●	. . . say how things have changed compared with how they used to be.
●	. . . distinguish between regular and irregular verbs in the present perfect tense.
●	. . . understand which verbs take **sein** and which take **haben** in the present perfect tense.

15 Wohnen in Deutschland
Living in Germany

In this unit you will learn how to:
▶ *talk about different kinds of housing.*
▶ *name the various rooms in a house or flat.*
▶ *make comparisons.*
▶ *further use the dative case.*
▶ *use the comparative.*
▶ *use possessive adjectives.*

CEFR: *Can understand short personal letters (A2); Can handle short social exchanges (A2); Can write a short simple letter (A2); Can identify the main conclusions in argumentative texts (B1)*

Mieten oder kaufen? *Rent or buy?*

In Germany more people **mieten** (*rent*) their homes than in most other European countries. Only about 45% of homes in the western **Bundesländer** (*states / lander*) and about 35% in the eastern **Bundesländer** are owner-occupied, although these figures are steadily rising.

The majority of people live in **Wohnungen** (*apartments*) rather than individual **Häuser** (*houses*), and apartments tend to be quite spacious, especially in older buildings, or **Altbauwohnungen**.

Apartments are normally **unmöbliert** (*unfurnished*). **Mieten** (*rents*) are highest in big cities such as Munich, Frankfurt and Hamburg; they are significantly **billiger** (*cheaper*) in **Kleinstädten** (*small towns*) and the countryside and as well as in cities in **Ostdeutschland** (*eastern Germany*) and, perhaps surprisingly, in Berlin.

What are the German words for *rents*, *apartments* and *houses*? And what does unmöbliert mean?

Vocabulary builder

PLACES TO LIVE

☐

a

☐
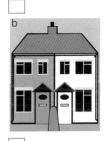
b

☐
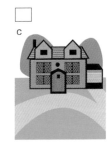
c

☐

d

☐
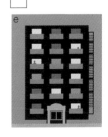
e

 1 **15.01 Wie heißt das? Listen and match the German words with the pictures. Then listen and repeat.**

1 Reihenhaus
2 Einfamilienhaus
3 Studentenwohnheim
4 Zweifamilienhaus
5 Hochhaus

 2 **15.02 Now listen to some more places to live. Listen and match the English and German expressions. Then practise pronunciation by listening and repeating.**

a **die Wohnung** (-en) _____   1 *a flat share*

b **das Zweifamilienhaus** (¨er) _____   2 *a detached house*

c **das Reihenhaus** (¨er) _____   3 *a student hostel*

d **das Einfamilienhaus** (¨er) _____   4 *a multi-storey building/tower block*

e	**das Studentenwohnheim (-e)** _____	**5**	_a terraced house_
f	**das Hochhaus (¨er)** _____	**6**	_a flat_
g	**die Altbauwohnung (-en)** _____	**7**	_a flat in an old building_
h	**die Wohngemeinschaft (-en)** _____	**8**	_a semi-detached house_

AT HOME

1 **15.03** Look at the floor plan and note the words for the various rooms of a flat. Then listen and repeat the rooms as they are listed from left to right.

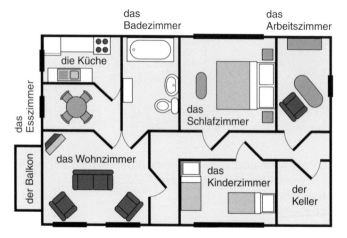

das Badezimmer
das Arbeitszimmer
die Küche
das Esszimmer
der Balkon
das Schlafzimmer
das Wohnzimmer
das Kinderzimmer
der Keller

2 **Wie heißen die Zimmer?** Read the explanation and identify the correct word.

a _das Schlafzimmer_ : dort schläft man

b _____ : ein Zimmer für Kinder

c _____ : dort kocht man

d _____ : dort kann man sich waschen

e _____ : dort wohnt man, liest, sieht fern etc.

f _____ : dort kann man im Sommer sitzen

g _____ : dort kann man lernen, am Computer arbeiten

3 15.04 Herr und Frau Wichmann are moving house. The removal men want to know where all the furniture and other items go. Was kommt ins Wohnzimmer, ins Kinderzimmer, ins Arbeitszimmer, in die Küche, in den Keller? (etc.) Tell them where to put each icon. Then listen and repeat to check your answers.

Beispiele   Der Computer kommt ins Arbeitszimmer.
Der Tennisschläger kommt in den Keller.

1 der Computer
2 der Tennisschläger
3 der Schrank
4 das Bett
5 der DVD-Player
6 der Küchentisch
7 die Pflanze
8 die Waschmaschine
9 der Kühlschrank
10 das Sofa
11 der Sessel
12 der Fernseher
13 das Bild
14 die Magazine
15 das Regal
16 die Bücher
17 der Topf
18 die Gummiente
19 die Teller

 NEW EXPRESSIONS

Look at the expressions that are used in the next interview and reading. Note their meanings.

Interview	
hell	*light, bright*
ruhig	*quiet*
der Blick (-e)	*view*
die Miete (-n)	*rent*
zufrieden	*happy/content*
der Nachbar (-n)	*neighbour*
nett	*nice*
teilen	*to share*
die Nebenkosten (pl.)	*bills*
darüber	*about it*
jemand	*someone*
auslziehen	*here: to move out*
Reading	
Leben Sie lieber …	*Do you prefer living …*
auf dem Land	*in the country*
bunt	*colourful*
offen	here: *open-minded*
kosmopolitisch	*cosmopolitan*
ziehen	here: *to move*
die Luft	*air*
die Entscheidung (-en)	*decision*
vermissen	*to miss*
entspannt	*relaxed*

Interview

 1 15.05 Vier Leute erzählen, wo sie wohnen. These four people are talking about where they live. Listen to the interviews and then match items in columns 1, 2, and 3 to show what is said in the text.

Wer?	Wo wohnen sie?	Wie ist es?
Person 1	in einer Wohngemeinschaft	hell und ruhig
Person 2	in einem Hochhaus	grün und ruhig
Person 3	in einem Einfamilienhaus	nicht zu teuer
Person 4	in einer Altbauwohnung	nett und interessant

2 Now read the text from the interviews and answer the questions.

1 Karl Potschnik, 57, Monteur bei VW

‚Ich wohne mit meiner Frau seit fünf Jahren in einem Hochhaus. Wir haben eine schöne Wohnung und einen wunderbaren Blick auf die Stadt, aber leider gibt es zu viele Graffiti. Die Miete ist nicht zu teuer, €375. Wir sind ganz zufrieden hier.'

2 Elisabeth Strutzak, 45, Angestellte bei der Post AG

‚Früher haben wir im Stadt zentrum gewohnt, aber vor zehn Jahren haben wir das Einfamilienhaus hier gekauft. Wir haben einen großen Garten. Es ist sehr grün und ruhig hier, die Nachbarn sind nett, nur für die Kinder ist es ein bisschen weit bis zur Schule.'

3 Matthias Michaelis, 24, Jura-Student

‚Ich wohne in einer Wohngemeinschaft mit drei anderen Studenten. Wir teilen die Miete und alle Nebenkosten. Manchmal gibt es natürlich Probleme, aber dann sprechen wir darüber. Ich wohne gern mit anderen Leuten zusammen. Es ist immer jemand da, mit dem man sprechen kann. Es ist nett und interessant.'

4 Jutta Heinrich, 73, Rentnerin

‚Ich wohne seit fünfzig Jahren in meiner Wohnung. Die Wohnung ist sehr hell und auch ruhig. Hundert Meter von hier bin ich auch geboren. Früher habe ich mit meinem Mann und den Kindern hier gewohnt. Aber mein Mann ist vor zehn Jahren gestorben und meine Kinder sind ausgezogen, und jetzt lebe ich allein.'

Richtig oder falsch? Korrigieren Sie die falschen Aussagen.

   a Herr Potschnik zahlt €375 Miete und ist nicht zufrieden. _____

   b Frau Strutzak wohnt gern in ihrem Einfamilienhaus und sagt, die Nachbarn sind sehr nett. _____

   c Matthias findet das Leben in seiner Wohngemeinschaft interessant. _____

   d Frau Heinrich lebt seit 73 Jahren in einer Altbauwohnung. _____

   e Ihr Mann ist vor zehn Jahren gestorben. _____

Reading

1 **15.06 Read the article and answer the question. Then listen to the audio to check pronunciation. What is the article about?**

  a why you should live in the city?
  b why you should live in the country?
  c the good and bad things about living in both?

STADT ODER LAND? PRO UND CONTRA

Unsere Städte werden immer größer, lauter, hektischer. Ist es nicht besser, auf dem Land zu leben? Wir haben zwei Personen gefragt: Leben Sie lieber auf dem Land oder in der Stadt? Und warum? Was ist besser?

Manfred Teutschek, 27, Student

,Auf dem Land wohnen? Nie wieder! Ich habe als Kind dort gelebt, es ist viel zu langweilig. Ich lebe gern in der Stadt. Das Leben ist interessanter, bunter als auf dem Land. Die Leute sind offener und man kann mehr machen. Aber manchmal ist es auch stressiger als auf dem Land, der viele Verkehr zum Beispiel und die Anonymität. Aber dann die vielen Theater, Clubs, Restaurants … Ich liebe es hier, denn es ist so kosmopolitisch.'

Esther Reimann, 45, Psychotherapeutin

,Wir haben 15 Jahre in Berlin gelebt und sind vor einem Jahr aufs Land gezogen. Es ist viel grüner hier, die Luft ist besser, die Leute sind freundlicher. Es war die richtige Entscheidung, ich vermisse die Stadt nicht. Zum Einkaufen brauche ich jetzt länger, denn ich muss mit dem Auto fahren, aber das Leben ist so viel entspannter hier.'

2 **Lesen Sie den Text *Stadt oder Land* noch einmal und setzen Sie die fehlenden Wörter ein.**

a Herr Teutschek findet die Leute in der Stadt offener als auf dem Land.

b Das Leben in der Stadt, sagt er, ist _____ und _____ .

c Manchmal ist es aber auch _____ als auf dem Land.

d Frau Reimann sagt, auf dem Land ist die Luft _____ und die Leute sind _____ .

e Zum Einkaufen braucht sie jetzt _____ .

f Aber das Leben ist viel _____ auf dem Land.

💡 Language discovery

1 **Look at these underlined words from the article. They are all adjectives in the comparative form, meaning *greener, longer, more interesting* etc. Which ending do they take?**

a Es ist viel <u>grüner</u> hier.

b Zum Einkaufen brauche ich jetzt <u>länger</u>.

c Das Leben ist <u>interessanter</u>, <u>bunter</u> als auf dem Land.

d Die Leute sind <u>offener</u>.

e Aber manchmal ist es auch <u>stressiger</u> als auf dem Land.

2 **Read the four interviews again and identify the missing words. Can you figure out in what case all the endings are?**

a Ich wohne mit _____ Frau seit fünf Jahren in _____ Hochhaus.

b Ich wohne in _____ Wohngemeinschaft mit drei anderen Studenten.

c Ich wohne seit fünfzig Jahren in _____ Wohnung.

d Früher habe ich mit _____ Mann und den Kindern hier gewohnt.

Learn more

1 COMPARATIVES

To make comparisons in English you simply add **-er** to short adjectives (e.g. *cheap*), or put **more** in front of longer ones (e.g. *interesting*):

This house is cheaper (than that one).
This book is more interesting (than that one).

Using adjectives in this way is called the comparative. In German normally only the **-er** form is used:

> Dieses Haus ist **billiger**.
> Dieses Buch ist **interessanter**.

Most adjectives of one syllable with an **a**, **o** or **u**, like **kalt** and **groß**, take an umlaut in the comparative form.

> Im Herbst ist es hier **kalt**.
> Im Winter ist es hier viel **kälter**.

> Unsere alte Wohnung war **groß**.
> Unsere neue Wohnung ist **größer**.

> Hier ist es schon im April ziemlich **warm**.
> Im Mai ist es **wärmer**.

The word **noch** (*here: even*) is often used with the comparative to provide emphasis.

> Klaus ist **jung**.
> Marion ist noch viel **jünger**.

A few adjectives, like **gut** and **hoch**, are irregular:

> Ich finde, dieses Auto ist **gut**.
> Aber dieses Auto ist noch **besser**.

> Das Matterhorn ist **hoch**.
> Der Mount Everest ist aber noch **höher**.

Another common word with irregular forms is **gern**:

Ich spiele gern Fußball.	*I like playing football.*
Aber ich spiele lieber Tennis.	*But I prefer playing tennis.*

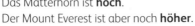

Some words, like **teuer** and **dunkel** (*dark*), often lose one **e** in the comparative form:

> In Frankfurt sind Wohnungen ziemlich **teuer**. In München sind sie aber **teurer**. Im Herbst ist es morgens **dunkel**. Im Winter ist es aber **dunkler**.

Note that the word for *than* is **als**:

> Auf dem Land ist die Luft besser **als** in der Stadt.
> Die Wohnungen in München sind teurer **als** die in Frankfurt.

2 POSSESSIVE ADJECTIVES

Words that indicate possession or who something belongs to are called possessive adjectives. Here is an overview of the *possessive adjectives* in German:

Possessive adjective	Example	Possessive adjective	Example
mein (*my*)	mein Freund, meine Mutter	unser (*our*)	unser Haus, unsere Wohnung
dein (*your*)	dein Auto, deine Schule	euer (*your*)	euer Vater, eure Mutter
Ihr (*your*)	Ihr Buch, Ihre Frau	Ihr (*your*)	Ihr Hotel, Ihre Wohnung
sein (*his*) ihr (*her*) sein (*its*)	sein Sohn, seine Tochter ihr Vater, ihre Mutter sein Essen, seine Milch	ihr (*their*)	ihr Sohn, ihre Tochter

Don't forget that possessive adjectives need various endings when used in structures with the accusative or dative case. (See also next section.)

3 DATIVE CASE ENDINGS

You have already seen that some prepositions (e.g. **mit** and **zu**) are always followed by dative case endings and that others (e.g. **in** and **auf**) are followed by the dative when the focus is on position or location.

You also know that in the dative case the endings on the definite articles change (**der** and **das** become **dem**, and **die** becomes **der**). Similar changes apply for the indefinite articles where the ending is **-em** for masculine and neuter nouns and **-er** for feminine nouns. This pattern also applies to the so-called possessive adjectives **mein**, **dein**, **sein**, etc.

masc. -(e)m	Bernd wohnt <u>mit</u> ein**em** Freund zusammen.
	Frau Krüger hat früher <u>mit</u> ihr**em** Mann hier gewohnt.
fem. -(e)r	Frau Heinrich lebt <u>in</u> ein**er** Altbauwohnung.
	Herr Thomas wohnt <u>mit</u> sein**er** Freundin zusammen.
neut. -(e)m	Jutta wohnt <u>in</u> ein**em** Hochhaus.
	Dieter Schneider lebt <u>mit</u> sein**em** Kind in Hamburg.
pl . -(e)n … -n*	Ich wohne <u>mit</u> mein**en** Freund**en** zusammen.
	Kirsten wohnt <u>mit</u> ihr**en** Kinder**n** in Köln.
	Rainer wohnt <u>seit</u> viel**en** Jahre**n** in Spanien.

*Note that, in the dative plural, not only the article or possessive adjective ends in **-(e)n**, but that, where possible, an **-n** is also added to the noun.

The dative can occur more than once in a sentence:

> Herr Thomas wohnt mit sein**er** Frau und sein**en** zwei Kinder**n** in ein**em** Einfamilienhaus.

Remember! Use the dative case:
▶ after ***an***, ***auf***, ***in*** when the focus is on position or location:
Wir haben **auf dem** Markt ein interessantes Buch gekauft.

▶ always after ***aus***, ***bei***, ***mit***, ***nach***, ***seit***, ***von***, ***zu***:
Ich fahre immer ***mit dem*** Fahrrad zur Schule.

Practice

 1 Contradict these false claims.

Beispiel   Birmingham ist größer als New York.
So ein Quatsch! Birmingham ist kleiner als New York.

So ein Quatsch! *What nonsense/rubbish!*

a Die Akropolis ist jünger als der Eiffelturm.
b In Deutschland ist es wärmer als in Südafrika.
c Das Essen im ‚Gourmet-Restaurant' ist schlechter als in der Mensa.
d Der Toyota Prius ist teurer als der Porsche.
e Tokio ist kleiner als Paris.
f Berlin ist langweiliger als Stuttgart.

2 Choose the most appropriate possessive adjective.

a Herr Kunstmann, ist das _____ Haus? (dein / Ihr)
b Das ist das Zimmer von Tina. Das ist _____ Zimmer. (sein / ihr)
c Das sind Peters Schuhe. Das sind _____ Schuhe. (seine / ihre)
d Das ist die neue Wohnung von Pia and Volker. Das ist _____ neue Wohnung. (unsere / ihre)
e Sind das deine Pflanzen? Nein, das sind nicht _____ Pflanzen. (meine / Ihre)
f Ist das eure Waschmaschine? Ja, das ist _____ Waschmaschine. (unsere / eure)
g Kennst du den Onkel von Sabrina? Ja, ich kenne _____ Onkel. (seinen / ihren)

3 Wie heißt es richtig? Identify the correct dative case endings.

a Frau Demitrez wohnt in ein___ Reihenhaus.
b Petra lebt seit drei Jahren in ein___ Wohngemeinschaft.
c Familie Schmidt wohnt in ein___ Hochhaus.
d Hans lebt in ein___ Studentenwohnheim.
e Lukas wohnt mit sein___ Freundin zusammen.
f Susanne lebt mit ihr___ Sohn in Berlin.
g Sie sind mit ihr___ Kinder___ in die USA gefahren.

 # Pronunciation

15.07 The ch sound in German is often difficult for English speakers who tend to close their throats and pronounce a k. In fact, if you keep your throat open and let the air continue to flow, you will make the right sound.

The pronunciation of **ch** depends on the kind of vowel in front of it. Listen to the audio and spot the differences.

ich	Rechnung	Töchter	Bücher	Mädchen	Milch
mache	Sprache	einfach	kochen	Tochter	Buch

When the **ch** is followed by an **s**, it is pronounced as a **k**:

Sachsen   **sechs**   **Fuchs**

How would you pronounce these words?

Nichte   **Dach**   **Märchen**   **Lachs**

 Reading

1   Herr und Frau Martini haben sehr lange eine neue Wohnung
    gesucht und endlich eine schöne Wohnung gefunden. Lesen Sie
    Ihre E-Mail. Beantworten Sie dann die Fragen.

Von: Marlies Martini
Gesendet: Mittwoch, 23. August
An: Imra Möller
Betreff: Wir haben eine neue Wohnung!

Liebe Imra,

danke für deine nette E-Mail. Endlich, endlich haben wir eine neue
Wohnung. Du weißt, wir haben fast sechs Monate gesucht. Bernd,
Sven und ich sind jetzt natürlich sehr glücklich, denn endlich
haben wir mehr Platz.

Es ist nämlich eine sehr große Wohnung und sie liegt relativ zentral,
in der Nähe vom Stadtpark. Die Umgebung ist ruhig und sehr grün,
aber leider ist es bis zum nächsten Supermarkt ein bisschen weit.

Wir haben vier Zimmer, ein Wohnzimmer, ein Schlafzimmer und ein
Kinderzimmer für Sven und dann sogar ein kleines Arbeitszimmer
und eine große Küche und ein Badezimmer. Die Zimmer sind groß
und hell. Aber leider haben wir keinen Garten.

Die Miete ist nicht so teuer, €465, natürlich plus Nebenkosten, also
plus Wasser, Strom und Gas. Das ist ziemlich günstig.

Die Verkehrsverbindungen sind sehr gut, denn bis zur U-Bahn
sind es nur fünf Minuten und mit der U-Bahn brauche ich dann
nur noch 10 Minuten bis zur Arbeit. Im Sommer kann ich mit dem
Fahrrad zur Arbeit fahren: ein gutes Fitness-Programm.

Und wie geht es dir? Und deinem Mann und den Kindern? Hat
Peter schon einen neuen Job gefunden?

Grüß alle herzlich und ich hoffe, es geht euch gut.

Deine Marlies

2 Beantworten Sie die folgenden Fragen.

a Wie lange haben sie gesucht?
b Wie viele Zimmer hat die Wohnung?
c Wie hoch ist die Miete?
d Wo liegt die Wohnung?
e Wie sind die Verkehrsverbindungen?

NEW WORDS

der Platz (¨e)	*here:space*
die Umgebung (sing.)	*surroundings (pl.)*
der Strom	*electricity*
günstig	*reasonable (price)/cheap*
die Verkehrsverbindungen (pl.)	*transport (links)*
relativ	*relatively*

3 Was für Vorteile und Nachteile hat die neue Wohnung? Make a list of five more advantages and two more disadvantages of Herr and Frau Martini's new flat.

Vorteile (+)	Nachteile (–)
Sie haben jetzt mehr Platz.	– Bis zum nächsten Supermarkt ist es ein bisschen weit.
–	–
–	–
–	
–	
–	

Speaking

1 15.08 Take on the role of Marlies Martini and answer the questions. Work out your replies, then answer the questions as you hear them on the audio. Then compare your answers with the audio.

a Wohnen Sie in einem Haus oder in einer Wohnung?
b Wie viele Zimmer hat die Wohnung?
c Wie sind die Zimmer?
d Haben Sie einen Garten?

e Ist die Miete oder die Hypothek teuer?
f Wie ist die Umgebung?
g Haben Sie gute Verkehrsverbindungen?
h Wie lange fahren Sie zur Arbeit?
i Fahren Sie mit dem Auto, mit dem Bus oder mit der U-Bahn?

2 **Now go through the questions again, this time answer for yourself. Change Wohnung to Haus and zur Arbeit to zur Universität or in die Stadt as appropriate. Note that morgage is** *die Hypothek.*

 # Writing

Wohnungstausch (*flat swap*): Eine deutsche Familie aus Hamburg möchte im Sommer einen Wohnungstausch machen. Schreiben Sie eine E-Mail an Frau Löschmann und beschreiben Sie Ihre Wohnung.

Frau Löschmanns Fragen:

a Wo liegt Ihre Wohnung? Zentral? Außerhalb?
b Liegt sie ruhig oder nicht so ruhig?
c Wie weit ist es bis zum Supermarkt?
d Wie sind die Verkehrsverbindungen?
e Wie viele Schlafzimmer hat die Wohnung?
f Und wie viele Badezimmer?
g Ist die Küche groß oder ziemlich klein?
h Haben Sie einen Fernseher? Wenn ja, kann man auch deutsche Programme bekommen?
i Haben Sie einen Garten oder einen Balkon?
j Gibt es in der Nähe einen Park?
Schreiben Sie mehr, wenn Sie wollen!

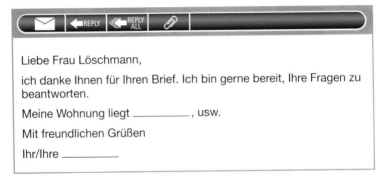

Liebe Frau Löschmann,

ich danke Ihnen für Ihren Brief. Ich bin gerne bereit, Ihre Fragen zu beantworten.

Meine Wohnung liegt _____ , usw.

Mit freundlichen Grüßen

Ihr/Ihre _____

NEW WORDS

der Tausch	*swap, exchange*
außerhalb	*outside*
weit	*far*
ziemlich	*rather, quite*
bereit	*ready, prepared*

Go further

TALKING ABOUT WHERE YOU LIVE

1 **15.09 Look at the expressions for talking about where you live as you listen and repeat.**

Ich wohne / Wir wohnen …	in einem Reihenhaus/in einer Wohnung/in einem Studentenwohnheim etc.
Die Wohnung / Das Haus hat …	2/3/4 Zimmer.
Die Wohnung …	relativ zentral.
	ziemlich weit außerhalb.
Die Zimmer sind relativ / sehr …	klein/groß/laut/hell/etc.
Wir haben …	viele/wenige/alte/neue/moderne/ antike Möbel.
Die Umgebung ist nicht so/ziemlich …	grün/ruhig/laut/etc.
Die Verkehrsverbindungen	sind … gut/schlecht.

2 **Wie heißt das Gegenteil? Look at the words and match them with their opposites.**

~~außerhalb~~ – antik – teuer – neu – klein – laut – dunkel – interessant

a zentral – *außerhalb*

b groß – _____

c hell – _____

d langweilig – _____

e billig – _____

f alt – _____

g modern – _____

h ruhig – _____

Test yourself

1 Wie heißt der Komparativ?

a klein – **kleiner**

b groß – _____

c alt – _____

d laut – _____

e gut – _____

f teuer – _____

g hoch – _____

h billig – _____

i interessant – _____

j stressig – _____

2 Mein, dein, sein etc.? Which possessive adjective fits best?

Beispiel: Das ist die Tasche von Rebecca. Das ist ihre Tasche.

a Das ist das Bild von Thomas. Das ist _____ Bild.

b Das ist das Magazin von Stefanie. Das ist _____ Magazin.

c Ist das deine Lampe? Ja, das ist_____ Lampe.

d Sind das eure Bücher? Nein, das sind nicht _____ Bücher.

e Frau Sandmann, ist das Ihr Handy? Oh ja, das ist _____ Handy.

f Sind das die CDs von Tim and Katja? Ja, das sind _____ CDs.

3 Philipp is describing his housing situation. Identify the missing dative endings.

a Ich wohne in ein___ 4-Zimmer-Wohnung.

b Ich lebe mit mein___ Bruder und mein___ Eltern zusammen.

c In mein___ Zimmer steht mein Bett, mein Schreibtisch und mein Laptop.

d Von unser___ Wohnzimmer haben wir einen tollen Blick auf die Stadt.

e Wir haben keinen Garten, aber wir sitzen oft auf unser___ Balkon.

f Zur Schule fahre ich meistens mit mein___ Fahrrad.

g Mein Bruder ist älter als ich und er fährt mit sein___ Auto zur Arbeit.

SELF CHECK

I CAN. . .

○	. . . talk about different types of housing and locations.
○	. . . describe my home.
○	. . . make comparisons.
○	. . . use the correct endings for the dative case.

16
Welches Hotel nehmen wir?

Which hotel shall we take?

In this unit you will learn how to:
▶ *book a hotel room.*
▶ *compare different hotels.*
▶ *describe the location of buildings.*
▶ *use the superlative.*
▶ *use more prepositions (+ acc./dat.).*

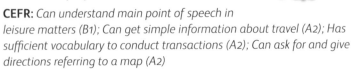

CEFR: *Can understand main point of speech in leisure matters (B1); Can get simple information about travel (A2); Has sufficient vocabulary to conduct transactions (A2); Can ask for and give directions referring to a map (A2)*

Touristeninformation

Tourism in German-speaking countries is highly organised. Almost every town has its own **Touristeninformation** (*tourist information*), sometimes called **Fremdenverkehrsamt** and many of their services are now available online.

Hotels (*hotels*) in Germany come in all **Preisklassen** (*price ranges*) and **Ausstattungen** (*designs*). So you can expect to find top international **Hotelketten** (*hotel chains*), such as Hilton or Ramada. But you will also discover smaller hotels, which are memorable for their **Individualität** (*individuality*) and convenient locations.

As an alternative to hotels there are **Pensionen** (*B&Bs*) and **Ferienwohnungen** (*holiday flats*). You will also find about 600 **Jugendherbergen** (*youth hostels*) all over Germany.

 What words in the text mean *B&Bs, youth hostels* and *holiday flats*? And what do Hotelketten and Preisklassen mean?

Vocabulary builder

IM HOTEL

1 **16.01** **Make yourself familiar with the German words for these hotel words. Listen and number the items in the order you hear them. Then listen and repeat.**

a Einzelzimmer _____
b Doppelzimmer _____
c Bad _____
d Dusche _____
e Schlüssel _____

TALKING ABOUT LOCATION

16.02 The following prepositions can help you to express where something is situated. Listen and match the English words to the German expressions. Then repeat the words to practise pronunciation.

a **in** _____   **1** *between*
b **an** _____   **2** *under*
c **auf** _____   **3** *on (to)*
d **hinter** _____   **4** *in front of*
e **neben** _____   **5** *over*
f **über** _____   **6** *at*
g **unter** _____   **7** *next to*
h **vor** _____   **8** *in (to)*
i **zwischen** _____   **9** *behind*

NEW EXPRESSIONS

Look at the expressions that are used in the next conversations and a map reading activity. Note their meanings.

Conversation 1

Haben Sie ein Zimmer frei?	*Have you got a room?*
die Antiquitätenmesse (-n)	*antiques fair*
Ist das Zimmer ruhig?	*Is the room quiet?*
Das Zimmer liegt zum Park.	*The room faces /looks out onto the park.*
Bitte tragen Sie sich ein.	*Please fill in your details.*
Um wie viel Uhr gibt es Frühstück?	*What time is breakfast?*
zwischen	*between*
Ich wünsche Ihnen einen angenehmen Aufenthalt.	*I wish you a pleasant stay.*

Map-reading activity

geradeaus	*straight on*
gehen Sie links/rechts	*go to the left/right*
wieder links/rechts	*(turn) left/right again*
auf der linken Seite	*on the left-hand side*
auf der rechten Seite	*on the right-hand side*
Da finden Sie …	*There you'll find …*

Conversations

1 16.03 Hören Sie jetzt den Dialog und beantworten Sie dann die Frage. *What day of the week does the conversation take place?*

Herr Oetken	Guten Tag. Haben Sie ein Zimmer frei?
Empfangsdame	Ja, ein Einzelzimmer oder ein Doppelzimmer?
Herr Oetken	Ich möchte ein Doppelzimmer für zwei Personen, bitte.
Empfangsdame	Und für wie lange?
Herr Oetken	Für zwei Nächte.
Empfangsdame	Für zwei Nächte. Von heute, Montag bis Mittwoch?
Herr Oetken	Ja. Von Montag bis Mittwoch. Meine Frau und ich möchten nämlich auf die Antiquitätenmesse gehen.
Empfangsdame	Das ist bestimmt interessant. Möchten Sie ein Zimmer mit Bad oder mit Dusche?
Herr Oetken	Mit Bad, bitte.

Empfangsdame	Da habe ich Zimmer Nr. 14 zu €77,50.
Herr Oetken	Ist das Zimmer ruhig?
Empfangsdame	Ja, das Zimmer liegt zum Park. Es ist sehr ruhig.
Herr Oetken	Gut. Dann nehme ich das Zimmer.
Empfangsdame	So. Hier ist der Schlüssel. Bitte tragen Sie sich ein.
Herr Oetken	Um wie viel Uhr gibt es Frühstück?
Empfangsdame	Zwischen sieben und zehn Uhr.
Herr Oetken	Vielen Dank.
Empfangsdame	Ich wünsche Ihnen einen angenehmen Aufenthalt.

2 **Richtig oder falsch? Korrigieren Sie die falschen Aussagen.**

a Herr Oetken nimmt ein Einzelzimmer. _____

b Er bleibt zwei Nächte. _____

c Er möchte mit seiner Sekretärin auf eine Antiquitätenmesse gehen. _____

d Herr Oetken nimmt ein Zimmer mit Dusche. _____

e Das Zimmer kostet €67,50. _____

f Frühstück gibt es bis 10 Uhr. _____

If you want to say that something is *the cheapest*, *the furthest* or *the most comfortable*, the common way in German is to say **am billigsten**, **am weitesten** or **am komfortabelsten**.

3 16.04 **Hören Sie den Dialog und beantworten Sie die Fragen. What is the woman looking for?** _____

Frau Johannsen	Guten Tag, ich suche ein Hotelzimmer für zwei Tage. Haben Sie etwas frei?
Frau Izmir	Im Moment ist es ein bisschen schwierig, einen Augenblick – ja, ich habe hier drei Hotels gefunden: das Hotel Offenbach, das Hotel Atlanta und die Pension Schneider.
Frau Johannsen	Welches Hotel liegt denn am zentralsten?
Frau Izmir	Am zentralsten liegt das Hotel Offenbach, nur fünf Minuten vom Zentrum.

Frau Johannsen	Und am weitesten?
Frau Izmir	Am weitesten entfernt ist das Hotel Atlanta, etwa eine halbe Stunde.
Frau Johannsen	Und preislich, welches Hotel ist am billigsten?
Frau Izmir	Am billigsten ist die Pension Schneider, das Einzelzimmer für €67,50. Ein Einzelzimmer im Hotel Offenbach kostet €90 und im Hotel Atlanta ist es am teuersten: €130.
Frau Johannsen	Und welches Hotel ist am komfortabelsten?
Frau Izmir	Am komfortabelsten ist das Hotel Atlanta, mit SwimmingPool und Park. Das ist sehr schön.
Frau Johannsen	Ich glaube, ich nehme das Hotel Offenbach. Kann ich gleich bei Ihnen buchen?
Frau Izmir	Ja, kein Problem.

4 **Welche Informationen fehlen hier? Lesen Sie den Dialog noch einmal und finden Sie die fehlenden Informationen.** *Read the dialogue again and identify the missing information.*

Hotel/Pension	Zimmer	Preis für Einzelzimmer	Entfernung	Pluspunkte
Offenbach	80	_____	_____	sehr zentral, gute Bar
Atlanta	120	€ 130	_____	_____
Schneider	28	_____	20 Minuten vom Zentrum	nette Atmosphäre, ruhig

Language discovery

Read the last dialogue again and identify the missing words in these sentences. Can you figure out what endings the adjectives take in German when conveying the idea of cheapest, furthest, most comfortable etc.? And what other little word is used?

   a Welches Hotel liegt denn am _____ ?
   b Am _____ liegt das Hotel Offenbach.
   c Und preislich, welches Hotel ist am _____ ?
   d Am _____ ist das Pension Schneider.
   e Und _____ weitesten?
   f Am _____ entfernt ist das Hotel Atlanta.
   g Und welches ist _____ _____ ?
   h Am _____ ist das Hotel Atlanta.

Learn more

1 THE SUPERLATIVE

In English when you want to single out one item from among a group as being the cheapest or most interesting of all, you add **-(e)st** to a short adjective or put **most** in front of a longer one:

> This house is the cheapest.
> This book is the most interesting.

This form is called *the superlative*. In German it goes as follows:

> Dieses Haus ist am billigsten.
> Dieses Buch ist am interessantesten.

As you can see, the word **am** is added and the ending is **-(e)sten**. Adjectives with an **a**, **o** or **u** which take an umlaut in the comparative form, also need one in the superlative:

Adjective	Comparative	Superlative
groß	größer	am größten
alt	älter	am ältesten
jung	jünger	am jüngsten

Here are some of the most important irregular forms:

Adjective	Comparative	Superlative
hoch	höher	am höchsten
gut	besser	am besten
gern	lieber	am liebsten
viel	mehr	am meisten

Adjectives which lose an e in the comparative form, like **teuer** and **dunkel**, usually take one in the superlative:

Adjective	Comparative	Superlative
teuer	teurer	am teuersten
dunkel	dunkler	am dunkelsten

2 PREPOSITIONS WITH THE ACCUSATIVE OR DATIVE

When position or location is indicated, some prepositions need either the accusative or the dative case, depending on whether the focus is on movement or on location. Including **in** and **auf**, which you have already met, these prepositions are:

an, auf, hinter, in, neben, über, unter, vor, zwischen

Here are a few examples:

Accusative:	**Wohin?** *(Where to?)*
Wir gehen …	**an den** Tisch.
	auf den Marktplatz.
	vor die Tür.
	ins Kino.
	hinter das Hotel.
Dative:	**Wo?** *(Where?)*
Wir sitzen …	**am** Tisch.
	auf dem Marktplatz.
	vor der Tür.
	im Kino.
	hinter dem Hotel.

Note that there are several pairs of verbs that are used to indicate movement on the one hand and location on the other. The main verbs of this kind are:

legen	*to lay, to place (in a lying position)*
liegen	*to lie, to be*
stellen	*to put, to place (in a standing position)*
stehen	*to stand, to be*
hängen	*to hang, to place (in a hanging position)*
hängen	*to hang, to be*

In English the verbs *to put* and *to be* are frequently used to cover these functions, but German generally prefers to be more precise.

Er legt das Handy ins Regal.	*He's putting the video onto the shelf.*
Das Handy liegt im Regal.	*The video is on the shelf.*
Wir stellen die Vase auf den Tisch.	*We're putting the vase onto the table.*
Die Vase steht auf dem Tisch.	*The vase is on the table.*
Susanne hängt das Picasso-Poster an die Wand.	*Susanne is hanging/putting the Picasso poster onto the wall.*
Das Picasso-Poster hängt an der Wand.	*The Picasso poster is (hanging) on the wall.*

Practice

1 Welche Antwort passt zu welcher Frage?

a Haben Sie ein Zimmer frei? _____

b Haben Sie ein Doppelzimmer frei? _____

c Ein Zimmer mit Bad oder Dusche? _____

d Was kostet das Zimmer? _____

e Ist das Zimmer ruhig? _____

f Von heute bis Freitag? _____

g Wann gibt es Frühstück? _____

1 Zwischen halb sieben und neun.

2 Ja, genau. Bis Freitag.

3 Ja, für wie viele Tage?

4 Tut mir leid, wir haben nur noch Einzelzimmer.

5 Ein Zimmer mit Dusche.

6 €80, inklusive Frühstück.

7 Nein, leider nicht. Es liegt zur Straße.

2 Ergänzen Sie den Superlativ. Read Conversation 2 again and answer the questions.

a Das Hotel Offenbach ist größer als die Pension Schneider, aber das Atlanta-Hotel ist _____ _____ .

b Das Hotel Offenbach ist billiger als das Hotel Atlanta, aber die Pension Schneider ist _____ _____ .

c Die Pension Schneider liegt zentraler als das Hotel Atlanta, aber das Hotel Offenbach liegt _____ _____ .

d Die Pension Schneider ist ruhiger als das Hotel Offenbach, aber das Atlanta-Hotel ist _____ _____ .

3 Wo ist was? Look at the map and choose the appropriate prepositions to complete the following sentences.

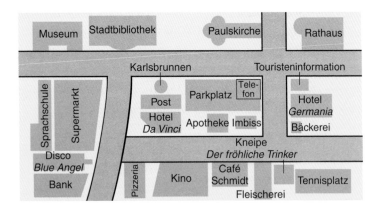

gegenüber   neben   gegenüber   zwischen   hinter   neben

a Das Kino ist gegenüber dem Hotel Da Vinci.
b Die Paulskirche ist rechts _____ der Stadtbibliothek.
c Das Museum liegt _____ der Sprachschule.
d Das Hotel Germania liegt _____ der Touristeninformation und
   der Bäckerei.
e Der Parkplatz liegt _____ der Apotheke.
f Das Café Schmidt ist _____ der Fleischerei.

4 **16.05 Herr Prinzmann arbeitet in der Touristeninformation in
Greifshagen. Was antwortet er auf die Fragen?** First match his
answers to the questions and then check your answers on the audio.

Touristen fragen

a Wo ist denn hier das
   Stadtmuseum? _____

b Kann man hier italienisch
   essen? _____

c Gibt es in der Nähe eine
   öffentliche
   Telefonzelle? _____

d Wo ist denn das
   Rathaus? _____

Herr Prinzmann antwortet

1 Direkt hier gegenüber.

2 Ja, fahren Sie geradeaus, dann
   die erste links, gegenüber dem
   ‚Da Vinci'.

3 Fahren Sie geradeaus, dann
   links und immer geradeaus.
   Auf der linken Seite ist die
   Pizzeria Mario.

4 Gehen Sie links, nehmen Sie die
   erste Straße rechts. Es liegt
   zwischen der Fleischerei und
   dem Kino.

e Wo ist denn hier ein Parkplatz? _____

f Gibt es hier in der Nähe ein Café? _____

g Ich habe gehört, es gibt hier eine tolle Disco. _____

5 Direkt hier gegenüber.

6 Ja, natürlich. Hier gegenüber, auf dem Parkplatz.

7 Gehen Sie immer geradeaus. Es ist auf der rechten Seite neben der Bibliothek.

 Speaking

1 16.06 **Book a hotel room using the prompts in the picture. Check your answers on the audio.**

 3 Nächte

Gast	Guten Tag. Haben Sie ein **a** _____?
Empfangsdame	Ein Einzelzimmer oder ein Doppelzimmer?
Gast	**b** _____
Empfangsdame	Und für wie viele Nächte?
Gast	**c** _____
Empfangsdame	Möchten Sie ein Zimmer mit Bad oder Dusche?
Gast	**d** _____
Empfangsdame	Gut. Zimmer 14. Bitte tragen Sie sich hier ein.
Gast	**e** _____
Empfangsdame	Zwischen halb sieben und halb neun. Ich wünsche Ihnen einen angenehmen Aufenthalt.

 2 16.07 **Übernehmen Sie die Rolle von Herrn Prinzmann. Schreiben Sie zuerst Ihre Antworten. Beantworten Sie dann die Fragen auf der Audioaufnahme. Note that fountain is der Brunnen and der Imbiss is hot-dog stall.**

Empfangsdame	Zwischen halb sieben und halb neun. Ich wünsche Ihnen einen angenehmen Aufenthalt.
Touristin	Guten Tag. Wo ist denn hier die Bibliothek?
Sie	Go straight ahead. The library is on the right-hand side, next to the museum.
Touristin	Und gibt es hier auch eine Post?
Sie	Yes, of course. Go straight on and take the first street to your left. The post office is behind the fountain.
Touristin	Gibt es hier in der Altstadt eine Apotheke?
Sie	Yes, of course. Go to the left, then turn right. The pharmacy is between the hot-dog stall and the hotel 'Da Vinci'.
Touristin	Und haben Sie hier auch einen Supermarkt?
Sie	Go straight on. The supermarket is opposite the museum.
Touristin	Vielen Dank. Kann man denn hier abends auch irgendwo ein gutes Bier trinken?
Sie	Of course. Go to the left, then left again. There you'll find a pub on the left-hand side, next to the bakery. The pub is very good.

? Test yourself

1 **Wo sind die Möbel jetzt? Do you remember Mr and Mrs Wichmann (from Unit 15) moving house? Their furniture is now where the removal men put it. Work out where the items are, following the examples:**

   a Das Regal haben sie neben den Fernseher gestellt.

   Das Regal steht jetzt neben dem Fernseher.

   b Das Picasso-Poster haben sie über das Sofa gehängt.

   Das Picasso-Poster hängt jetzt über dem Sofa.

   c Die Waschmaschine haben sie in den Keller gestellt.

   _____

   d Das Foto von Oma Lisbeth haben sie ins Esszimmer gehängt.

   _____

   e Die CDs haben sie ins Regal gestellt.

   _____

   f Die Pflanze haben sie auf den Balkon gestellt.

   _____

g Das Poster von Lionel Messi haben sie ins Kinderzimmer gehängt.

_____

h Das Sofa haben sie zwischen das Regal und den Tisch gestellt.

_____

2 Ergänzen Sie die Komparativformen und Superlativformen.

Adjecktiv	Komparativ	Superlativ
a _____	wärmer	_____
b kalt	_____	am kältesten
c interessant	_____	_____
d billig	_____	_____
e hoch	_____	_____
f teuer	_____	_____
g _____	lieber	_____
h gut	_____	_____

3 Bilden Sie den Komparativ und Superlativ.

Beispiel **hoch:** das Matterhorn, der Kilimandscharo, der Mount Everest

Der Kilimandscharo ist höher als das Matterhorn, aber der Mount Everest ist am höchsten.

a lang: der Rhein, der Nil, der Amazonas
b groß: Deutschland, Kanada, Russland
c alt: das Empire State Building, der Tower of London, das Colosseum
d hart: Silber, Gold, Granit
e teuer: der BMW M6, der Ferrari F430, der Volkswagen Passat

SELF CHECK

	I CAN. . .
○	. . . book a hotel room.
○	. . . compare and contrast the price and location of various hotels.
○	. . . describe where something is located.
○	. . . use comparative and superlative adjectives.
○	. . . name some prepositions which need either the accusative or the dative case.

17 *Ist Mode wichtig?*
Is fashion important?

In this unit you will learn how to:
▶ *describe items of personal appearance.*
▶ *say what clothes you like wearing.*
▶ *use adjectival endings after indefinite articles.*
▶ *use etwas and nichts.*

CEFR: *Can use simple descriptive language to make statements and compare things (A2); Can make and respond to suggestions (A2); Can write a simple connected text (B1); Can develop an argument (B1); Can identify implied and stated opinions (B2)*

Mode *Fashion*

Although Germany doesn't have the same reputation for fashion as France or Italy, it does lay claim to some internationally renowned **Modedesigner** (*fashion designers*), including Jil Sander, Karl Lagerfeld and Wolfgang Joop.

Germany is also home to a number of well-known **Modemarken** (*fashion labels*) such as Boss, Strenesse and Gary Weber. The two **Sportartikelhersteller** (*sports clothing manufacturers*) Adidas and Puma were founded by the Dassler brothers in **Bayern** (*Bavaria*) in the late 1940s.

Die Modeindustrie (*fashion industry*) is an important industry in Germany, employing thousands of people. Since re-unification, the centre for fashion has moved to Berlin, which also hosts Germany's most important **Modenshow** (*fashion show*), the Berlin Fashion Week.

You can buy **Kleidung** (*clothes*) in a **Modegeschäft** (*fashion shop*), in a **Boutique** (*boutique*) or a **Kaufhaus** (*department store*).

What are the German words for *clothes, skirt, blouse* and *department store*? And what do Modeindustrie, Modegeschäft and Modemarken mean?

Vocabulary builder

 17.01 Listen and match the English words to the German colour expressions. Then listen and repeat.

a blau _____
b braun _____
c grau _____
d grün _____
e rot _____
f schwarz _____
g weiß _____
h gelb _____
i dunkel _____
j hell _____

1 *green*
2 *yellow*
3 *black*
4 *brown*
5 *light*
6 *grey*
7 *blue*
8 *red*
9 *dark*
10 *white*

CLOTHING

1 17.02 Listen and read the items each person is wearing. Then listen and repeat the words.

das Hemd
die Krawatte (rot)
der Anzug (blau)
der Mantel (grau)
die Hose
(rot)
(braun)
die Schuhe (schwarz)
(blau)
das T-Shirt (weiß)
die Turnschuhe (weiß)

die Bluse (gelb)
die Jacke (braun)
der Gürtel
der Rock (braun)
die Strumpfhose (gelb)
die Mütze (gelb)
(grün)
die Jeans (schwarz)
(gelb)

2 **Richtig oder falsch?** Decide if the descriptions of the four people are true or not. Correct the wrong descriptions.

Beispiel Der Mann trägt einen braunen Anzug und eine gelbe Krawatte.

Falsch. Der Mann trägt einen blauen Anzug und eine rote Krawatte.

a Außerdem trägt er ein weißes Hemd, einen grauen Mantel und schwarze Schuhe. _____

b Die Frau trägt eine gelbe Bluse und eine braune Jacke. _____

c Außerdem trägt sie einen blauen Rock, eine weiße Strumpfhose und weiße Schuhe. _____

d Das Mädchen trägt eine blaue Jeans, ein weißes T-Shirt, eine rote Baseball-Mütze und weiße Turnschuhe. _____

e Der Junge trägt eine blaue Jeans, ein gelbes T-Shirt, eine grüne Baseball-Mütze und grüne Turnschuhe. _____

Note that in English both *trousers* and *jeans* are plural, but in German **Hose** and **Jeans** are singular:

Ich habe heute **eine** neue **Hose** gekauft.

Wo **ist** meine alte **Jeans**?

Remember that the adjective endings after **einen/eine/ein** are: **-en** for masculine nouns (**einen braunen Anzug**), **-e** for feminine nouns (**eine braune Jacke**) and **–es** for neuter nouns (**ein weißes T-Shirt**).

3 **Was passt am besten? Ergänzen Sie.**

Rock   Mantel   Sachen   Anzug   Hemd

a Im Büro tragen viele Männer einen _____.

b Wenn es kalt ist, trägt man meistens einen _____.

c Eine Frau trägt eine Bluse, ein Mann trägt ein _____.

d Zu Hause trägt man oft bequeme _____.

e Viele Frauen tragen jetzt lieber eine Hose als einen _____.

NEW EXPRESSIONS

Look at the expressions that are used in the next interview and reading.
Note their meanings.

Interview

die Mode (-n)	*fashion*
sollen	*(here) are supposed to*
der Ausdruck (¨e)	*expression*
die Fünfzigerjahre (pl.)	*the Fifties*
anlziehen	*to put on*
der Mensch (-en)	*person*
bedeuten	*to mean*
tragen	*to wear*
bequem	*comfortable*
auslsehen	*to look, appear*
die Sachen	*things*
die Frisur (-en)	*hairstyle*

Reading

die Einladung (-en)	*invitation*
der Knoblauch	*garlic*
feiern	*to celebrate*
hässlich	*ugly*
schrecklich	*awful, terrible*
je ... desto	*the more ... the more*
das Dosenbier (-e)	*canned beer*

Interview

1 17.03 **Listen and read. Then answer the question.**
**Für welche Person ist Mode wichtig (✓) und für wen ist sie
unwichtig (x)?**

	[✓]	[x]
Bettina Haferkamp	☐	☐
Johann Kurz	☐	☐
Boris Brecht	☐	☐
Ulrike Maziere	☐	☐

Bettina Haferkamp, 52, Lehrerin

‚Jedes Jahr gibt es etwas Neues. Dieses Jahr kurze Röcke, nächstes Jahr lange Röcke. Die Leute sollen immer etwas Neues kaufen. Ich ziehe nur an, was ich mag. Am liebsten trage ich bequeme Sachen.'

Johann Kurz, 38, Journalist

‚Ich finde, Mode ist ein wichtiger Ausdruck unserer Zeit. Sie zeigt, was Leute denken und fühlen. Zum Beispiel die Mode in den Fünfzigerjahren oder die Punk-Mode. Heute kann man doch anziehen, was man möchte. Das finde ich gut.'

Boris Brecht, 28, arbeitslos, Rock Musiker

‚Ich bin ein individueller Mensch. Schwarze Sachen finde ich am besten. Ich kaufe viel auf dem Flohmarkt oder in Secondhandshops ein. Modetrends finde ich langweilig.'

Ulrike Maziere, 20, Kosmetikerin

‚Mode bedeutet viel für mich. Ich bin ein sportlicher Typ und trage gern schöne Sachen. Ich möchte gut aussehen. Eine modische Frisur, ein modernes Outfit - das ist sehr wichtig für mich.'

2 **Wie steht das im Text? Read the text again and find the expressions which convey a similar meaning.**

a Ich bin sportlich. _Ich bin ein sportlicher Typ_____.

b Mode zeigt, was Leute denken. _____

c Die Leute sollen mehr Geld ausgeben. _____

d Schwarz finde ich am besten. _____

e Ich trage nur, was ich mag. _____

f Mode ist sehr wichtig. _____

3 **Was sagen die Leute pro Mode und contra Mode? List three more pros and one more con of fashion according to the four people in the interview.**

Pro (+)	Contra (-)
Mode ist ein Ausdruck unserer Zeit.	Die Leute sollen immer etwas Neues kaufen.
–	–
–	
–	

Reading

1 17.04 **Read the invitation to a party and answer the question. Then listen and read to check pronunciation.**

   a Why are the people having the party? _____

Einladung zur Bad-Taste-Party

Liebe Freunde,

wie jedes Jahr feiern wir diesen Juni wieder unsere Geburtstage mit einer großen Party. Und wie jedes Jahr haben wir auch ein besonderes Motto. Nein, dieses Mal ist es nicht Dracula (war das letztes Jahr nicht fantastisch? All der Tomaten-Ketchup und der viele Knoblauch!).

Das Motto für dieses Jahr heißt: Bad-Taste. Wer kein Englisch kann: das bedeutet 'schlechter Geschmack'.

Also: Holt die alten Hemden, Blusen, Röcke, Sonnenbrillen aus dem Schrank. Je hässlicher, schrecklicher, älter – desto besser.

Und wir haben auch einen tollen Preis für die Person, die am schlechtesten, am hässlichsten aussieht.

Also – seid kreativ!

Und natürlich gibt es wie immer auch tolle Musik zum Tanzen.

Also, bis zum 24.

Jutta und Christian

PS: Bringt etwas zum Trinken mit! Dosenbier von Aldi, Lambrusco, Liebfraumilch?

---

2 **Richtig oder falsch? Wie heißen die richtigen Antworten?**

   a Jutta und Christian machen jeden Monat eine Party. _____

   b Das Motto für die letzte Party war Dracula. _____

   c 'Bad taste' heißt auf Deutsch 'schlechter Geschmack'. _____

   d Die Person, die am schönsten aussieht, bekommt einen Preis.
   _____

   e Die Gäste bringen etwas zum Essen mit. _____

💡 Language discovery

1 **Look at these two sentences from the interview. Can you figure out what etwas Neues means in English?**

   a Jedes Jahr gibt esetwas Neues.

   b Die Leute sollen immer etwas Neues kaufen.

2 **Read the four interviews again and identify the missing adjective endings. All examples are in the nominative case. What are the required endings if an adjective is used before masculine, feminine and neuter nouns?**

   a Ich bin ein individuell___ Mensch. (m)

   b Ich bin ein sportlich___ Typ. (m)

   c Ich finde, Mode ist einwichtig___ Ausdruck unserer Zeit. (m)

   d Eine modisch___ Frisur ... (f)

   e Ein modern___ Outfit ... (nt)

Learn more

1 ETWAS, WAS / ALLES, WAS / NICHTS

If you want to say *something new, something cheap, something interesting*, etc. in German, you use **etwas** + adjective + **-es**:

   etwas Neues, etwas Billiges, etwas Interessantes

The equivalents to *something that* and *everything that* are **etwas**, **was** and **alles**, **was**:

Gibt es etwas, was Sie nicht gerne anziehen?	*Is there something that you don't like wearing?*
Ich trage alles, was bequem ist.	*I wear everything that is comfortable.*

Sometimes you can leave out the word *that* in English – *Is there something you don't like wearing?* In German you always have to keep the word **was**. There is usually a comma before the word was.

The same pattern applies to **nichts** *nothing/anything*:

   nichts Neues, nichts Billiges, nichts Interessantes

Note that you need a capital letter for the word after **etwas** and **nichts**.

2 ADJECTIVE ENDINGS AFTER THE INDEFINITE ARTICLE

So far we have dealt with the endings in the accusative case after the indefinite article (**ein, eine**, etc.), **kein** or the possessive adjectives (**mein, dein, Ihr**, etc.). Here are the adjective endings you need for the accusative case after the indefinite articles:

Adjective endings accusative		
masc.	-en	Werner hat einen mechanisch**en** Wecker gekauft.
fem.	-e	Renate hat meine alt**e** Waschmaschine gekauft.
neut.	-es	Annett hat ein neu**es** Hemd gekauft.

The nominative case is used to refer to the subject of the sentence and it is also used after the verb **sein** (*to be*). Here are the adjective endings you need for the nominative case after the indefinite articles. These endings are the same as for the accusative, except for the masculine nouns.

Adjective endings nominative		
masc.	-en	Das ist ein billig**er** Rock.
fem.	-e	Das ist eine modisch**e** Frisur.
neut.	-es	Das ist kein modern**es** Outfit.

If a possessive adjective or **kein** precedes the adjective in the nominative and accusative plural, the endings are **–en**. Without a possessive or **kein**, the ending is –e:

Plural adjective endings nominative/accusative		
nom.	-en	Das sind meine neu**en** CDs.
	-e	Das sind schön**e** Schuhe.
acc.	-en	Habt ihr keine neu**en** CDs gekauft?
	-e	Er trägt schön**e** Schuhe.

Endings are only required when the adjective is placed in front of a noun. As you know, certain prepositions, like **mit** and **von**, are followed by the dative case. Here are the adjective endings you need for the dative case after the indefinite articles. You will be relieved to see all forms end in **-en**. Remember, in the dative you add an additional **-n** to the plural noun wherever possible.

Adjective endings dative		
masc.	-en	Werner trägt ein weißes Hemd mit einem schwarz**en** Anzug.
fem.	-en	Anna trägt einen braunen Rock mit einer gelb**en** Bluse.
neut.	-en	Florian trägt eine rote Jacke mit einem blau**en** Hemd.
pl.	-en	Er trägt seinen Anzug mit seinen schwarz**en** Schuhen.
	-en	Er trägt einen Anzug mit schwarz**en** Schuhen.

Martin trägt ein blaues Hemd mit einer dunkelblauen Hose, einem schwarzen Mantel und schwarzen Schuhen.

If you are listing a number of items, then the preposition determines the case, not only of the first item but also of the following items as well:

As you can see, in this example all three items listed after **mit** require dative case endings.

 Practice

1 Match the German sentences with the English translations.

a Das ist etwas Neues.
b Das bedeutet nichts Gutes.
c Es ist nichts Gefährliches.
d Da ist etwas Wahres dran.
e Mach nichts Dummes.

1 It's nothing dangerous.
2 There's some truth in this.
3 Don't do anything stupid.
4 That's something new.
5 This doesn't mean anything good.

2 Wie heißt es richtig? Üben Sie Adjektivendungen im Nominativ.

a Die Idee ist gut. → *Das ist eine gute Idee* _____ .

b Der Film war langweilig. → *Das war ein* _____ *Film* .

c Der Kaffee ist stark. → *Das ist ein* _____ *Kaffee* .

d Das Buch ist interessant. → _____

e Das Problem ist schwierig. → _____

f Der Computer ist neu. → _____

g Die Leute sind unfreundlich. → _____

h Das Hotel ist billig. → _____

i Die Frage ist kompliziert. → _____

3 Wie heißen die Endungen? Ergänzen Sie die Endungen im Dativ.

a Die Frau trägt eine gelbe Bluse mit einer dunkelbraun__ Jacke und ein__ braun__ Rock.

b Außerdem trägt sie braune Strümpfe mit braun__ Schuh__.

c Das Mädchen trägt eine blaue Jeans mit ein__ weiß__ T-Shirt, ein__ rot__ Baseball-Mütze und weiß__ Turnschuh__.

d Der Junge trägt eine schwarze Jeans mit ein__ grün__ T-Shirt, ein__ gelb__ Baseball-Mütze und gelb__ Turnschuh__.

e Der Mann trägt einen dunkelblauen Anzug mit ein__ rot__ Krawatte.

f Außerdem trägt er ein weißes Hemd mit ein__ grau__ Mantel und schwarz__ Schuh__.

Pronunciation

17.05 At the end of a word the letter **g** in German is pronounced more like an English *k*:

Tag   Ausflug   Anzug   mag

At the end of a word **ig** is pronounced like **ich**:

billig   ruhig   zwanzig   langweilig   Honig

As soon as the **g** is no longer at the end of the word or syllable it is pronounced as a **g**:

Tage   Ausflüge   Anzüge   mögen

How would you pronounce these words?
sag, sagen, fünfzig, ledig

 # Speaking

17.06 You are in a department store and are looking for a jacket. A sales assistant helps you. Prepare your responses, using the English prompts to guide you. Then, using the audio, play your role in German.

Verkäufer	Guten Tag. Wie kann ich Ihnen helfen?
Sie	*Return his greeting and say that you are looking for a new jacket.*
Verkäufer	So, eine neue Jacke suchen Sie? Und welche Farbe? Schwarz? Grau?
Sie	*Say you'd like a grey jacket – for a party.*
Verkäufer	So, bitte schön. Hier haben wir graue Jacken.
Sie	*Say you're looking for something fashionable.*
Verkäufer	Tja, wenn es um Mode geht – dann haben wir hier Jacken von Armani und Versace.
Sie	*Say fine, but Italian jackets are very expensive.*
Verkäufer	Ja, das stimmt. Aber die Qualität ist auch sehr gut.
Sie	*Agree with him and say that it is also a very fashionable party in New York.*
Verkäufer	Dann nehmen Sie doch am besten eine Jacke von Armani.

Listening

17.07 Frau Martens ist Verkäuferin in einem Kaufhaus. Was denkt sie über Mode? Hören Sie, was sie sagt. Was stimmt? Frau Martens works in a department store. Work out what she says.

a Sie sagt, Verkäuferin ist ein (interessanter / anstrengender) Beruf.

b Die Arbeit im Haushalt ist (langweilig / anstrengend).

c Ihr Sohn findet Computerspiele (interessant / langweilig).

d Sie findet, sie ist ein (modischer / kein modischer) Typ.

e Die Töchter von Frau Martens finden Mode (wichtig / unwichtig).

f Kunden sind (immer freundlich / manchmal unfreundlich / oft unfreundlich).

NEW WORDS

bei der Arbeit	*at work*
zu Hause	*at home*
die Lieblingsfarbe (-n)	*favourite colour*

 # Writing

Beantworten Sie die Fragen. Write out your answers to the clothing survey questions. Then write a paragraph about what you like to wear.

a Was tragen Sie normalerweise bei der Arbeit / an der Universität?

b Was tragen Sie am liebsten zu Hause?

c Was tragen Sie gern, was tragen Sie nicht gern?

d Haben Sie eine Lieblingsfarbe?

e Ist Mode wichtig für Sie?

f Sie gehen zu einer Bad-Taste-Party. Was ziehen Sie an?

a Bei der Arbeit trage ich normalerweise eine Jeans und ein weißes Hemd.
b Zu Hause ...

Go further

1   **17.08 Review the expressions for talking about what you wear. Listen and repeat.**

Bei der Arbeit …	trage ich meistens einen Rock mit einer Bluse, einen Anzug, ein weißes Hemd etc.
Bei der Arbeit muss ich …	eine grüne/blaue Uniform tragen.
An der Universität …	trage ich gern eine Jeans mit einem weißen Hemd/einem dunklen Pullover.
Zu Hause …	trage ich am liebsten bequeme Kleidung.
Ich mag …	helle/dunkle Farben, bequeme Kleidung.
Ich trage nicht gern …	Jeans, Röcke, Blusen, Krawatten etc.

2   **17.09 Was für Kleidung tragen die Leute? Richard Naumann stellt die Fragen. Hören Sie zu und ergänzen Sie die Tabelle.**

	bei der Arbeit	zu Hause	was sie gern tragen	was sie nicht gern tragen
Dialog 1 Mareike Brauer				
Dialog 2 Günther Scholz				

Test yourself

1   **Use the adjectives in brackets to convey the meaning of something/nothing interesting, new etc.**

Hast du etwas Interessantes gemacht?

Beispiel Hast du etwas _____ gemacht? (interessant)

a   Hast du etwas _____ gekauft? (neu)

b   Ich trage gern etwas _____ . (modisch)

c   Hast du nichts _____ gefunden? (billig)

d   Susann trägt immer etwas _____ . (elegant)

e   Nils trägt gern etwas _____ . (sportlich)

f   Oh, ich habe etwas _____ .gemacht. (dumm)

g   Das ist nichts _____ . (wichtig)

2 **The nouns in each line all have the same gender. Choose** *m* **for masculine,** *f* **for feminine or** *nt* **for neuter nouns.**

   a Anzug, Mantel, Rock, Schuh ( )

   b Jacke, Hose, Mütze, Bluse ( )

   c Krawatte, Uniform, Kleidung, Frisur ( )

   d Gürtel, Ausdruck, Typ, Mensch ( )

   e Hemd, T-Shirt, Outfit, Kaufhaus ( )

3 **Endungen. Ergänzen Sie, bitte.**

   a **Verkäuferin** Ich arbeite in ein__ groß__ Kaufhaus in München. Bei der Arbeit trage ich ein__ schwarz__ Rock und ein__ weiß__ Bluse. Im Winter trage ich zu mein__ schwarz__ Rock auch ein__ schwarz__ Jacke.

   b **Student** Im Moment arbeite ich bei Burger King und muss ein__ hässlich__ Uniform tragen. An der Uni trage ich aber immer ein__ blau__ Levi-Jeans mit ein__ modisch__ T-Shirt. Mir gefallen am besten amerikanisch__ oder britisch__ T-Shirts. Alt__ Sachen vom Flohmarkt gefallen mir manchmal auch.

SELF CHECK

	I CAN. . .
◯	. . . talk about clothing and give my opinion on fashion.
◯	. . . say what clothes I wear for work and for relaxing.
◯	. . . use **etwas** and **nichts**.
◯	. . . use the correct endings for adjectives after indefinite articles.

18 Und was kann man ihnen schenken?

And what can we give them?

In this unit you will learn how to:
▶ *read invitations to various events.*
▶ *say what is given to whom.*
▶ *ask for help and advice.*
▶ *use indirect objects.*
▶ *use the dative case in various ways.*
▶ *use adjectival endings after definite articles.*

CEFR: *Can understand personal notes and letters (B1); Can express feelings and opinions (B1); Can ask others to give their views (B1); Can keep up with an animated conversation (B2)*

Feiern Celebrating

Special occasions are generally celebrated with enthusiasm in Germany. Families make great efforts to get together for **Geburtstage** *(birthdays)*, **Taufen** *(baptisms)*, **Hochzeiten** *(weddings)* and other **Familienfeiern** *(family celebrations)*; some people travel long distances to be present.

Weihnachten *(Christmas)* is celebrated in the traditional way. **Geschenke** *(presents)* are usually exchanged **am Heiligabend** *(on Christmas Eve)*. **Weihnachtsmärkte** *(Christmas markets)* throughout Germany provide seasonal decorations, food and drink. The **Christkindlmarkt** in **Nürnberg** *(Nuremberg)* is perhaps the most famous of these markets.

Silvester *(New Year's Eve)* is celebrated with fireworks and **Sekt** (a champagne-like fizzy wine). **Neujahr** *(New Year's Day)* is **ein Feiertag** *(a public holiday)* in Germany – some people need this in order to get over their **Kater** *(hangover)*.

 What are the German words for birthdays, weddings, Christmas and presents? And what do Silvester, Neujahr and Kater mean?

Vocabulary builder

1 18.01 **Lesen Sie die Einladungen auf den nächsten Seiten und finden Sie die deutschen Wörter. Match the words then listen to check your answers. Then listen again and read to check pronunciation.**

   a birthday party: **die** _____

   b wedding: **die** _____

   c barbecue: **die** _____

   d house-warming party: **die** _____

Susanne Fröhlich   Michael Hartmann

Wir heiraten am Samstag, dem 8. Mai, um 14.30 Uhr in der Elisabethkirche, Marburg.
Zu unserer Hochzeit laden wir Sie herzlichst ein.

Ahornweg 31
35043 Marburg

Hauptstraße 48
35683 Dillenburg

Peter wird nächsten Samstag

8

Jahre alt.

Das möchten wir natürlich feiern – mit einer ganz tollen Geburtstagsparty, mit Kuchen und vielen Spielen.

Wir fangen um 15.00 Uhr an. Bringt auch eure Eltern mit.

Die Adresse: Familie Schäfer, Am Bergkampe 4

Lange haben wir gesucht und endlich unser ‚Schloss' gefunden.
Darum möchten wir euch, liebe Bärbel, lieber Georg, zu unserer

HAUSEINWEIHUNGSFEIER
am 30. November, um 20.00 Uhr einladen.

Unsere neue Adresse: 90482 Nürnberg,
Waldstraße 25.
Unsere neue Telefonnummer: 378459
Viele Grüße
Uschi und Matthias
Hasenberg

Mareike und Jörg Schwichter
Krummer Weg 12
24939 Flensburg
Tel. 55 32 17

Liebe Susanne, lieber Gerd,

bevor der Winter kommt, möchten wir noch einmal eine Grillparty in unserem Garten machen.

Der Termin: der letzte Samstag im Monat, der 27. September, ab 19.00 Uhr.

Könnt ihr kommen?

Natürlich gibt es nicht nur Fleisch, sondern wir haben auch Essen für Vegetarier.

Bringt doch bitte einen Salat mit. Alles andere haben wir.

Alles Gute

eure Schwichters

P.S. Wie war es denn in Spanien? Habt ihr viel Spaß gehabt?

2 18.02 **Now listen and match the English words to the German words used in the invitations.**

a heiraten _____
b einlladen _____
c feiern _____
d das Schloss (¨er) _____
e die Feier (-n) _____
f der Vegetarier (-)/-in (-innen) _____

1 *to celebrate*
2 *celebration*
3 *castle*
4 *vegetarian*
5 *to marry*
6 *to invite*

3 Richtig oder falsch? Korrigieren Sie die falschen Aussagen.

a Susanne und Michael heiraten am 28. Mai in Marbach.
   _____

b Familie Schäfer feiert nächsten Samstag Peters achten Geburtstag.
   _____

c Uschi und Matthias haben ihren idealen Garten gefunden.
   _____

d Susanne und Gerd wollen eine Bad-Taste-Party machen.
   _____

e Vegetarier müssen ihr Essen mitbringen. _____

NEW EXPRESSIONS

Look at the expressions that are used in the next reading and conversation. Note their meanings.

Reading

der Führerschein (-e)	*driving licence*
der Luftballon (-s *or* -e)	*balloon*
das Poster (-)	*poster*
mitlbringen	*to bring something along*

Conversation

wem	*(to) whom*
empfehlen	*to recommend*
gefallen (+ dative)	*to like, lit 'to please'*
der Schal (-s)	*scarf*
bezaubernd	*enchanting*
die Tasche (-n)	*bag*
die Seide (no pl.)	*silk*
aus echter Seide	*made of real silk*
die Haarfarbe (-n)	*hair colour*
die Kasse (-n)	*cash desk*

Reading

1  18.03 **Und was kann man schenken?**
Read how giving something to
someone is expressed in German. Then
answer the question.
What item is NOT suggested as a gift?
a flowers   b alcohol
c CDs   d a balloon

Max hat Geburtstag. Er mag alles,
was aus Frankreich kommt. Martin
hat seinem Freund ein Geschenk
mitgebracht. Er schenkt ihm eine
Flasche Kognak.

Martinas Kollegin Astrid hat ihren
Führerschein gemacht. Jetzt kann sie
allein Auto fahren. Martina bringt Astrid
ein Geschenk mit. Sie bringt ihr
Blumen mit.

Ronald hat Geburtstag. Kirsten und
Peter haben ihrem Enkelsohn einen
Luftballon mitgebracht. Sie schenken
ihm einen Luftballon.

Hanna und Carsten machen eine
Hauseinweihungsfeier. Susanne und
Michael haben ihren Freunden ein
Geschenk mitgebracht. Sie schenken
ihnen ein Poster.

2 Richtig oder falsch? Korrigieren Sie die
falschen Aussagen.

a Max hat Geburtstag. Er ist ein
England-Fan. _____

b Astrid bekommt Blumen, denn sie hat ihren Führerschein gemacht.

_____

c Ronald ist der Enkelsohn von Kirsten und Peter. _____

d Hanna und Carsten machen eine Grillparty. _____

Conversation

1 18.04 **Im Geschäft 'Alles für die Frau'. Hören Sie sich den Dialog an und beantworten Sie die Fragen.**

What does Herr Kern want to buy? _____

Herr Kern	Guten Tag. Können Sie mir helfen?
Verkäuferin	Ja, natürlich.
Herr Kern	Ich suche ein Geschenk für meine Frau. Können Sie mir etwas empfehlen?
Verkäuferin	Hier haben wir zum Beispiel das neue Parfüm von L'Oreal 'Ägyptischer Mond' oder das bezaubernde 'Ninette'. Beide kosten nur €49,99.
Herr Kern	Mmh, Parfüm ... das ist immer schwierig. Was gibt es denn sonst noch?
Verkäuferin	Nun, wir haben hier zum Beispiel diese wunderbaren Damentaschen im Angebot.
Herr Kern	Sie meinen die braunen Taschen hier?
Verkäuferin	Gefallen sie Ihnen?
Herr Kern	Nun ja, die kleine Tasche hier ist schön, aber meine Frau hat schon eine.
Verkäuferin	Wie ist es denn mit einem Schal? Diese hier sind alle aus echter Seide. Beste Qualität.
Herr Kern	Der weiße Schal gefällt mir nicht. Der sieht ein bisschen zu altmodisch aus. Aber der rote hier gefällt mir. Und der blaue ist auch sehr schön.
Verkäuferin	Nun, welche Haarfarbe hat denn Ihre Frau?
Herr Kern	Blond.
Verkäuferin	Dann nehmen Sie lieber den blauen Schal. Das sieht besser aus.
Herr Kern	Wenn Sie meinen. Vielen Dank für Ihre Hilfe.
Verkäuferin	Gern geschehen. Bitte zahlen Sie da drüben an der Kasse.

2 Read the text and answer the questions.

a Wem möchte Herr Kern etwas schenken? _____

b Wie teuer sind die Parfüms? _____

c Warum nimmt er keine Tasche? _____

d Wie sieht der weiße Schal aus? _____

e Welchen Schal nimmt er? _____

 Language discovery

1 **Look at the conversation again and identify the missing adjective endings. These endings are needed after the definite article in the nominative. Do they differ from the endings after the indefinite article (ein, eine, ein) you've met in the previous unit?**

a Der weiß ___ Schal gefällt mir nicht. (m)

b Aber der rot ___ hier gefällt mir. (m)

c Und der blau ___ ist auch sehr schön. (m)

d Nun ja, die klein ___ Tasche hier ist schön. (f)

e Das ist das neu ___ Perfüm. (nt)

2 **Read the dialogue again and identify the missing words. What are the German equivalents of *him*, *her* and *them*? Can you figure out what case is used when giving something *to someone*?**

a Martin hat seinem Freund ein Geschenk mitgebracht. Er schenkt _____ eine Flasche Kognak.

b Martina bringt Astrid ein Geschenk mit. Sie bringt _____ Blumen mit.

c Kirsten und Peter haben ihrem Enkelsohn einen Luftballon mitgebracht. Sie schenken _____ einen Luftballon.

d Susanne und Michael haben ihren Freunden ein Geschenk mitgebracht. Sie schenken _____ ein Poster.

Learn more

1 ADJECTIVE ENDINGS AFTER THE DEFINITE ARTICLE

In the previous unit you saw how adjective endings work after indefinite articles (**ein**, **eine** etc.). When used after definite articles (**der**, **die**, **das** etc.) the following endings are required:

In the nominative singular all adjectives take an **-e**, regardless of their gender:

Der rot**e** Schal ist schön. (m)

Die klein**e** Tasche gefällt mir. (f)

Das neu**e** Buch ist fantastisch. (nt)

In the accusative singular all feminine and neuter forms take an **–e**, and the masculine **–en**:

Ich kaufe den rot**en** Schal. (m)

Ich möchte die braun**e** Tasche. (f)

Ich lese das neu**e** Buch von Follett. (nt)

All forms in the dative take **–en**, as do all plural forms. Here is a summary of the adjective endings after the definite article:

Nominative	
masc.	Der neu**e** Film mit de Niro ist sehr gut.
fem.	Die neu**e** CD von Jennifer Lopez ist fantastisch.
neut.	Ist das neu**e** Buch von Dan Brown wirklich gut?
pl.	Die neu**en** Modelle von BMW sind sehr modern.
Accusative	
masc.	Hast du den neu**en** Film mit de Niro gesehen?
fem.	Hast du schon die neu**e** CD von Jennifer Lopez gehört?
neut.	Hast du das neu**e** Buch von Dan Brown gelesen?
pl.	Hast du schon die neu**en** Modelle von BMW gesehen?
Dative	
masc.	In dem neu**en** Film spielt auch Kate Winslet.
fem.	Er hat mit der alt**en** Band von Herbie Hancock gespielt.
neut.	In dem neu**en** Buch gibt es ein Happy-End.
pl.	Er ist mit den neu**en** Modellen von BMW gefahren.

2 DIRECT AND INDIRECT OBJECTS

You already know that the dative case is used after certain prepositions. It is also used to indicate *to whom* something is being given or done. This part of the sentence is often referred to as the *indirect object*.

We now need to distinguish between *direct* and *indirect objects*. In the sentence:

Frau Semmelbein schenkt ihrem Sohn einen Hund.

Einen Hund is said to be the *direct object* of the verb **schenken** because it is *directly* associated with the act of giving, and **ihrem Sohn** is said to be the *indirect object* because it indicates *to whom* the object was given.

In German, the *direct object* requires the *accusative case* and the *indirect object* the *dative case*.

The *direct object* or the *indirect object* can also come in first place:

Einen Hund schenkt Frau Semmelbein ihrem Sohn.

Ihrem Sohn schenkt Frau Semmelbein einen Hund.

The basic meaning of these sentences remains the same; there is merely a change of emphasis. Note that in these examples the verb stays in the same place: as second element in the sentence.

3 PERSONAL PRONOUNS IN THE DATIVE

Words like **ihm** (*(to) him*) and **ihr** (*(to) her*) are called *indirect object pronouns*.

Wir schenken **ihm** eine CD.	***We're giving** him **a CD.***
Wir schenken **ihr** ein Buch.	***We're giving** her **a book.***

You have actually met some of these pronouns before in expressions such as

Wie geht es **Ihnen**?	*(lit.) **How is it going** to you?*
Danke, **mir** geht's gut.	*(lit.) To me **it goes well.***

Here is an overview of the personal pronouns in the dative case:

Singular		
ich →	mir	**Mir** geht's gut.
du →	dir	Wie geht's **dir**?
Sie →	Ihnen	Hoffentlich geht's **Ihnen** morgen besser.
er (masc.) →	ihm	**Ihm** geht's heute nicht so gut.
sie (fem.) →	ihr	**Ihr** geht's jetzt viel besser.
es (neut.) →	ihm	**Ihm** (dem Kind) geht's leider nicht so gut.
Plural		
wir →	uns	**Uns** geht's sehr gut.
ihr →	euch	Wie geht's **euch**?
Sie →	Ihnen	Wir wünschen **Ihnen** allen eine gute Reise.
sie →	ihnen	**Ihnen** geht's wirklich sehr gut.

4 THE DATIVE CASE

Here is a summary of the three main uses of the dative case:

▶ *After certain prepositions. Use it after **an**, **auf**, **hinter**, **in**, **neben**, **über**, **unter**, **vor**, **zwischen** when the focus is on position or location.*

Wir haben **auf dem** Markt ein interessantes Buch gekauft.

▶ Use it always after **aus, bei, mit, nach, seit, von, zu.**

Ich fahre immer **mit dem** Fahrrad **zur** Schule.

▶ *To indicate to whom something is being given, done, etc. In other words to indicate the indirect object.*

Ich schenke **meinem** Freund einen neuen CD-Spieler zum Geburtstag.

▶ With verbs such as **helfen**, **empfehlen** and **gefallen**.

Sie hilft **der Frau.** → Sie hilft **ihr.**

Das Auto gefällt **dem Mann**. → Das Auto gefällt **ihm.**

Furthermore, it occurs in some expressions where often the meaning of *to* is expressed:

Können Sie mir sagen, wie spät es ist?

Can you say to me (i.e. tell me) ...?

Können Sie mir etwas empfehlen?

Can you recommend something to me?

Practice

1 **Find the correct endings for the following adjectives. All the sentences use the definite article and are in the nominative case.**
   a Die grün __ Jacke ist toll.
   b Der rot __ Schal sieht sehr gut aus.
   c Der neu __ Film mit George Clooney ist ein bisschen langweilig.
   d Das schwarz __ Hemd sieht sehr trendy aus.
   e Das kalt __ Bier hat gut geschmeckt.
   f Die neu __ Songs von Rihanna sind fantastisch.

2 **Identify the direct object (DI) and indirect object (IO) in these sentences.**
   a Sie kauft den Kindern ( ) ein Eis ( ).
   b Magda bringt ihrer Mutter ( ) Blumen ( ) mit.
   c Hast du dem Verkäufer ( ) schon das Geld ( ) gegeben?
   d Kannst du mir ( ) bitte eine Flasche Wasser ( ) mitbringen?
   e Sie haben ihrem Sohn ( ) ein Auto ( ) gekauft.
   f Petra hat den Leuten ( ) ihre neue Wohnung ( ) gezeigt.

3 **Ihr, ihm oder ihnen? Setzen Sie die fehlenden Wörter ein.**
   a Lena hat Geburtstag. Marcus schenkt __ eine CD.
   b Frank macht eine Party. Susi bringt __ eine Flasche Sekt mit.
   c Steffi und Caroline haben Hunger. Ihre Mutter kauft __ Pommes frites.
   d Svenja fährt nach Österreich. Ihr Bruder gibt __ einen guten Reiseführer.

e Christina und Robert heiraten. Herr Standke schenkt ___ ein schönes Bild.

f Herr Fabian wird 65. Seine Kollegen haben ___ eine Geburtagskarte geschrieben.

Speaking

 18.05 Und jetzt Sie! Sie sind in einer Buchhandlung und suchen ein Buch über New York. Ein Verkäufer hilft Ihnen. Bereiten Sie Ihre Antworten vor und spielen Sie dann die Rolle auf der Audioaufnahme. To say You don't like it, it's **Er gefällt mir nicht. If you want to say that** You like that one, it's **Das gefällt mir.**

Verkäufer	Guten Tag.
Sie	*Return his greetings and ask if he can help you.*
Verkäufer	Ja, natürlich. Was kann ich denn für Sie tun?
Sie	*Say you are looking for a book about New York. Could he recommend something?*
Verkäufer	Ja, hier haben wir zum Beispiel den neuen Reiseführer von Merian. Sehen Sie einmal. Gefällt er Ihnen?
Sie	*Say no. You don't like it.*
Verkäufer	Hier ist das neue New York Buch von Hans Fischer.
Sie	*Say you like that one. Ask how much it costs.*
Verkäufer	€12,40.
Sie	*Say you'll take that book. Ask if they've got the new book by Dan Brown.*
Verkäufer	Ja, natürlich. Ich hole es Ihnen.
Sie	*Say thank you and ask where the cash desk is.*
Verkäufer	Gern geschehen. Die ist gleich hier vorne. Auf Wiedersehen.

Listening

 18.06 Was bringen wir der Familie mit? Saskia und ihre Schwester Sys waren für drei Wochen in New York. Morgen fahren sie nach Deutschland zurück. Große Panik: Sie müssen noch Geschenke für ihre Familie kaufen! Hören Sie zu: Was schenken sie ihrer Mutter, ihrem Vater, der Großmutter, Tante Heide und Onkel Georg? Warum?

Die Geschenke: eine kleine Freiheitsstatue, ein U-Bahn-Plan, ein Bademantel, Turnschuhe, eine Baseball-Mütze.

Wem?	Was bringen sie mit?	Warum?
Mutter	Sie bringen ihr eine kleine Freiheitsstatue mit.	Sie mag solche Sachen.
Vater	Sie bringen ihm ...	_____ ?
Oma	_____ ?	_____ ?
Tante Heidi	_____ ?	_____ ?
Onkel Georg	_____ ?	_____ ?

NEW WORDS

aufregend	*exciting*
die Freiheitsstatue	*Statue of Liberty*
solche Sachen	*such things*
sammeln	*to collect*
der Bademantel (¨)	*bathrobe*

Go further

1 18.07 Note these useful expressions with the dative for shopping for gifts as you listen and repeat.

Können Sie mir helfen?	*Can you help me?*
Könnten Sie mir etwas empfehlen?	*Could you recommend something for me?*
Gefällt Ihnen / dir das T-Shirt?	*Do you like the T-shirt?*
Gefallen Ihnen / dir die Hemden?	*Do you like the shirts?*
Können Sie mir sagen, wie spät es ist?	*Can you tell me what the time is?*
Wie geht es Ihnen / dir?	*How are you?*

2 Welche Antwort passt zu welcher Frage?

   a Können Sie mir helfen?   **1** Es gefällt mir nicht. Es ist zu teuer.

   b Gefällt Ihnen das Hotel?   **2** Ihm geht es nicht so gut.

c Können Sie mir ein Buch für meine Tochter empfehlen?

d Gefällt dir Berlin?

e Wie geht es Frau Hansen?

f Können Sie mir sagen, wie spät es ist?

g Wie geht es Sven?

h Gefallen dir die Bilder?

3 Sie gefallen mir nicht. Sie sind schrecklich.

4 Natürlich helfe ich Ihnen.

5 Das kann ich Ihnen sagen, fünf nach vier.

6 Ja, es ist eine tolle Stadt.

7 Ihr geht es wieder besser.

8 Ich empfehle Ihnen ‚Winnie Puuh'.

🔘 Test yourself

1 **Wer bekommt was? Markus is giving up his student flat to study in the US and has decided to give some of his things to friends or relatives. Identify the missing adjective endings.**

   a Den teur___ CD-Spieler schenkt er seinem Freund Tim.

   b Er gibt die schwarz___ Katze seiner Oma.

   c Das interessant___ Buch über Afrika schenkt er seinem Onkel.

   d Seiner Freundin Susi gibt er den neu___ Computer.

   e Das alt___ Handy gibt er seiner Schwester.

   f Die toll___ Fußballbilder schenkt er seinem Freund Lukas.

   g Die alt___ CDs verkauft er auf dem Flohmarkt.

2 **Was kann man den Personen schenken? What could you give these people as a present? Choose an appropriate gift from the list below.**

   a Herr Koch, 65, liebt klassische Musik. *Man kann ihm eine CD von Maria Callas schenken.*

   b Gisela Anders, 25, geht gern ins Kino, findet Indien toll. _____

   c Gerd Schmücke, 40, ist ein großer Fußballfan, joggt viel.

   _____

   d Heinz und Martha Schmidt, 53 und 50, essen und trinken gern.

   _____

   e Heide, 12, liest gern, mag die Natur. _____

   f Peter, 15, arbeitet viel am Computer. _____

   1 eine Flasche Wein

   2 ein Computerspiel

   3 ein Buch über Indien

   4 eine CD von Maria Callas

   5 Turnschuhe

   6 ein Buch über Blumen und Pflanzen

SELF CHECK

I CAN. . .

- ○ . . . understand event invitations.
- ○ . . . say what to give people and why.
- ○ . . . ask for help and recommendations.
- ○ . . . use indirect objects.
- ○ . . . name the three ways in which the dative case is used.
- ○ . . . use the correct adjective endings with the definite article.

19 Gesundheit
Health

In this unit you will learn how to
▶ *discuss health.*
▶ *name parts of the body.*
▶ *report on aches and pains.*
▶ *use modal verbs.*
▶ *use* wenn + *verb at end of clause.*

CEFR: *Can identify speaker viewpoints and attitudes (B2); Can read articles concerned with attitudes or viewpoints (B2); Can explain a problem (B2); Can give reasons and explanations for opinions (B1)*

German health care

In some countries you go to a **Allgemeinarzt** (*GP*) first for almost any **Beschwerden** (*complaints*) and then get referred on to a **Facharzt** (*specialist*) if necessary.

In Germany you tend to choose a doctor appropriate for a given condition. You take along a **Krankenversichertenkarte** (*health insurance card*) and get the doctor to sign a form. You also pay a small **Gebühr** (*fee*) every three months. Your **Krankenkasse** (*health insurance fund*) then makes a payment on your behalf.

The **Allgemeine Ortskrankenkasse** (AOK) provides statutory health care for large numbers of people who are not **privatversichert** (*insured privately*) or not with their firm's insurance scheme.

A UK resident travelling to German-speaking countries will be insured for most **Notfallbehandlungen** (*emergency treatment*) if they take their **Europäische Krankenversicherungskarte** (*European Health Insurance Card*) with them. US residents should obtain adequate **Krankenversicherung** (*health insurance*) before commencing their journey.

For minor problems visit **eine Apotheke** (*a pharmacy/drugstore*) and ask the **Apotheker** (*pharmacist*) for advice.

What are the German words for GP, specialist, pharmacy and pharmacist? And what does eine Notfallbehandlung mean?

Vocabulary builder

KÖRPERTEILE *BODY PARTS*

 1 19.01 **Note the German words for various parts of the body. Listen and identify the article for each one. Then listen and repeat. You will also hear the plural form.**

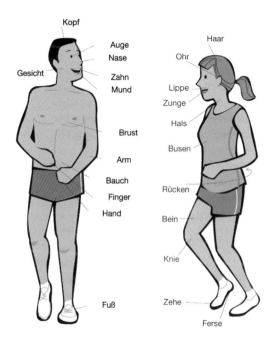

Kopf
Auge
Nase
Gesicht
Zahn
Mund

Haar
Ohr
Lippe
Zunge
Hals

Brust
Arm
Bauch
Finger
Hand

Busen
Rücken
Bein
Knie

Fuß
Zehe
Ferse

WAS TUT HIER WEH?

 1 19.02 **Listen and match the English words to the German expressions for talking about aches and pains. Then listen and repeat.**

a weh ǀ tun _____
b Mein Kopf tut weh. _____
c Meine Augen tun weh. _____
d die Grippe _____
e der Schmerz (-en) _____
f Kopfschmerzen _____
g der Kater (-) _____

1 *pain*
2 *flu*
3 *hangover*
4 *headache*
5 *My eyes are aching/hurt.*
6 *to hurt/ache*
7 *My head hurts/aches.*

2 Welche Sätze passen zu welchem Bild? Ordnen Sie bitte zu.
Match the sentences with the pictures.

a  b

c  d

e  f

g  h

1 Die Augen tun weh. Sie hat 10 Stunden am Computer gearbeitet.
_____

2 Sein Rücken tut weh. Er hat im Garten gearbeitet. _____

3 Der Hals tut weh. Er ist dick. _____

4 Sie hat eine Grippe: Kopfschmerzen und Fieber. _____

5 Der Zahn tut weh. Er muss zum Zahnarzt. _____

6 Er ist topfit. Er hat keine Schmerzen. _____

7 Ihr Arm tut weh. Sie hat zu viel Tennis gespielt. _____

8 Ihr Kopf tut weh. Sie hat zu viel Wein getrunken. Sie hat einen Kater.
_____

Wie kann man es anders sagen? Note the two ways you can talk about aches and pains in German:

Mein Zahn tut weh. →	Ich habe Zahnschmerzen.
Sein Rücken tut weh. →	Er hat Rückenschmerzen.
Ihr Hals tut weh. →	Sie hat Halsschmerzen.
Meine Ohren tun weh. →	Ich habe Ohrenschmerzen.

Note that **Schmerzen** is normally used in the plural.

 NEW EXPRESSIONS

Look at the expressions that are used in the next reading and conversation. Note their meanings.

Reading

regelmäßig	*regularly*
rauchen	*to smoke*
krank	*ill, sick*
der Urlaub (-e)	*holiday*
das Gewicht (-e)	*weight*
Sport treiben	*to do sports*
das Fett (-e)	*fat*
der Rücken (-)	*back*
das Tauchen (no pl.)	*diving*

Conversation

Was fehlt Ihnen?	*What's the matter with you?*
fast	*almost*
Es wird immer schlimmer	*It's getting worse.*
verspannt	*seized up, in spasm*
nichts Schlimmes	*here: nothing serious*
verschreiben	*to prescribe*
gegen die Schmerzen	*for your (lit. the) pain*
Gern geschehen.	*You're welcome.*
Gute Besserung!	*Get well (soon)!*

In unit 11 you met the modal verbs **können** and **müssen**. There are three more modals which all appear in the following text: **dürfen** (*may/to be allowed to*), **sollen** (*should*) and **wollen** (*to want to*). Note that they are quite irregular: *I want* is **ich will**, *I should* **ich soll** and *I may* **ich darf**. The equivalent of *I must not* is **ich darf nicht**.

Reading

1 Vier Leute erzählen, ob sie genug für ihre Gesundheit tun. Lesen Sie die folgenden Texte und beantworten Sie dann die Frage.

Which person has health problems? _____

Tun Sie genug für Ihre Gesundheit?

Gabriela Tomascek, 21, Designerin

‚Ich denke, es ist gesund, wenn man regelmäßig Sport macht. Ich spiele Fußball, Handball, ein bisschen Tennis. Ich rauche nicht, trinke sehr wenig Alkohol. Außerdem esse ich gesund, viel Salat und Obst. Ja, ich denke ich tue genug. Ich fühle mich sehr fit und bin nur selten krank. Nächstes Jahr will ich vielleicht einen Fitnessurlaub machen.'

Michael Warnke, 45, Computer-Programmierer

‚Ich habe Probleme mit dem Herzen und meinem Gewicht. Der Arzt sagt, es ist ungesund, wenn man raucht. Ich darf nicht mehr rauchen und soll auch weniger Fett essen. Außerdem soll ich auch mehr Sport treiben, denn ich sitze den ganzen Tag am Computer. Im Moment jogge ich abends, aber am Wochenende will ich auch mehr mit dem Rad fahren.'

Marianne Feuermann, 49, Bankkauffrau

‚Ich habe im Moment Rückenprobleme und soll viel schwimmen gehen. Meistens schwimme ich vier- bis fünfmal pro Woche. Früher habe ich oft Volleyball gespielt. Meine Ärztin hat mir gesagt, ich darf nicht mehr Volleyball spielen. Ich darf leider auch nicht mehr Ski fahren. Wenn es mir wieder besser geht, will ich wieder mehr Sport treiben und wieder aktiver leben.'

Egbert Schmidt-Tizian, 53, Verkäufer

‚Meine Frau ist eine Sport-Fanatikerin. Im Sommer Windsurfen und Tauchen im Roten Meer, im Winter Ski fahren in den Alpen und ich muss immer mit. Mein Arzt hat schon gesagt, ich soll nicht mehr so viel Sport machen, denn das ist nicht gut für mich. Ich glaube, ich tue zu viel im Moment. Ich will mehr relaxen. Ich brauche mehr Freizeit.'

2 Answer the questions.

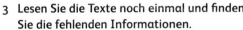

a Wer joggt abends? _____

b Wer möchte mehr relaxen? _____

c Wer hat früher Volleyball gespielt?

_____

d Wer lebt sehr gesund? _____

e Wer treibt viel Sport? _____

f Wer darf nicht mehr Ski fahren?

_____

3 Lesen Sie die Texte noch einmal und finden Sie die fehlenden Informationen.

	Was tun sie im Moment?	Was dürfen sie nicht tun?	Was sollen sie tun?	Was wollen sie tun?
Gabriela	_____	X	X	will vielleicht einen Fitnessurlaub machen
Michael	_____	darf nicht mehr rauchen	_____	_____
Marianne	geht vier- bis fünfmal in der Woche schwimmen	_____	_____	_____
Egbert	_____	X	soll nicht mehr so viel Sport machen	_____

Conversation

1 19.03 Frau Philipp ist bei ihrer Ärztin. Hören Sie zu and beantworten Sie die Frage.

a Why is Frau Philipp at the doctor? _____

Dr. Scior	Guten Tag, Frau Philipp, was kann ich für Sie tun? Was fehlt Ihnen?
Frau Philipp	Frau Scior, ich habe ziemlich starke Rückenschmerzen.
Dr. Scior	Oh, das tut mir leid. Wie lange haben Sie die Schmerzen denn schon?
Frau Philipp	Fast vier Wochen, aber es wird immer schlimmer.
Dr. Scior	Arbeiten Sie denn viel am Schreibtisch?

Frau Philipp	Ja, wir haben ein neues Computersystem, und jetzt arbeite ich fast die ganze Zeit am Computer.
Dr. Scior	Kann ich bitte einmal sehen ... Also, der Rücken ist sehr verspannt. Treiben Sie denn Sport?
Frau Philipp	Nicht sehr viel. Im Moment spiele ich nur ein bisschen Volleyball.
Dr. Scior	Also Frau Philipp, ich glaube, es ist nichts Schlimmes. Ich verschreibe Ihnen 10 Massagen und auch etwas gegen die Schmerzen. Und Sie dürfen in den nächsten Wochen nicht Volleyball spielen, gehen Sie lieber zum Schwimmen.
Frau Philipp	Kann ich denn sonst noch etwas tun?
Dr. Scior	Ja, Sie müssen bei der Arbeit bequem sitzen und der Schreibtisch muss die richtige Höhe haben. Das ist sehr wichtig.
Frau Philipp	Gut, vielen Dank.
Dr. Scior	Gern geschehen. Und gute Besserung, Frau Philipp.

2 **Richtig oder falsch? Was ist richtig?**

   a Frau Philipp hat Rückenschmerzen. _____
   b Die Schmerzen hat sie schon seit sechs Wochen. _____
   c Sie arbeitet viel am Computer. _____
   d Die Ärztin verschreibt ihr 10 Massagen. _____
   e Frau Philipp darf nicht mehr schwimmen. _____
   f Die Ärztin sagt, es ist sehr gefährlich. _____

Language discovery

1 **Read the dialogue again and identify the correct form of either dürfen, sollen or wollen. Which of these verbs have a vowel change when used with ich?**

   a Nächstes Jahr _____ ich vielleicht einen Fitnessurlaub machen.
   b Ich _____ nicht mehr rauchen und _____ auch weniger Fett essen.
   c Außerdem _____ ich auch mehr Sport treiben
   d Meine Ärztin hat mir gesagt, ich _____ nicht mehr Volleyball spielen.
   e Ich _____ mehr relaxen.

2 Look at the following sentences. Can you figure out where the verb is placed (**macht, raucht, geht**) in clauses introduced by **wenn**?

   a Ich denke, es ist gesund, wenn man regelmäßig Sport macht.

   b Der Arzt sagt, es ist ungesund, wenn man raucht.

   c Wenn es mir wieder besser geht, will ich wieder mehr Sport treiben.

Learn more

1 MODAL VERBS

In Unit 11 you met the modal verbs **können** and **müssen**. There are three more modal verbs:

▶ **wollen** (*to want*)

Ich will nächstes Jahr in die Schweiz fahren.	*I want to go to Switzerland next year.*

▶ **dürfen** (*may/to be allowed to*)

Darf ich noch Volleyball spielen?	*Am I still allowed to play volleyball?*
Ich darf nicht mehr rauchen.	*I'm not allowed to smoke any more.*

▶ **sollen** (*should/ought to*)

Mein Arzt sagt, ich soll weniger Fett essen.	*My doctor says I should eat less fat.*

Like **können** and **müssen**, these other modal verbs are quite irregular. Here is a grid showing their present tense forms.

	dürfen (may)	können (can)	müssen (must)	wollen (want [to])	sollen (should)
ich*	darf	kann	muss	will	soll
du	darfst	kannst	musst	willst	sollst
Sie	dürfen	können	müssen	wollen	sollen
er/sie/es*	darf	kann	muss	will	soll
wir	dürfen	können	müssen	wollen	sollen
ihr	dürft	könnt	müsst	wollt	sollt
Sie	dürfen	können	müssen	wollen	sollen
sie	dürfen	können	müssen	wollen	sollen

*Note that with modal verbs the **ich** and **er/sie/es** forms are the same. They therefore do not have the endings (**-e** for **ich** and **-t** for **er/sie/es**) that are used with most other verbs in the present tense.

Modal verbs are occasionally used on their own:

Ich kann sehr gut Englisch.   *I can speak English very well.*

Wir wollen morgen nach   *We want to go to Munich*
München.   *tomorrow.*

But they nearly always need a second verb and this is sent to the end of the sentence or clause:

	Modal		**Second verb**
Hier	**darf****	man leider nicht	**parken.**
Jetzt	**müssen**	wir nach Hause	**gehen.**
Wir	**wollen**	morgen nach Berlin	**fliegen.**

Note that if you want to say *can't* or *mustn't* in German, you often use **dürfen + nicht/kein, e.g.

Hier dürfen Sie nicht parken.   *You can't park here.*

Du darfst keinen Alkohol trinken.   *You mustn't drink any alcohol.*

2 USING *WENN*

If you wanted to say that you think it is healthy if one runs regularly or you think it is unhealthy if one eats too many hamburgers, you would form sentences with **wenn** (*when/if*) in German:

Ich denke, es ist gesund, **wenn** man regelmäßig **joggt**.

Ich finde, es ist ungesund, **wenn** man viele Hamburger **isst**.

A comma is needed in order to separate the wenn clause from the rest of the sentence.

Wenn can mean *if* or *when* and it sends the verb to the end of the **wenn** clause:

Mir gefällt es, **wenn** die Sonne *scheint*.

Mir gefällt es, **wenn** es im Herbst windig *ist*.

Note that when you put **wenn** at the beginning of a sentence, the second clause of the sentence starts with a verb:

Wenn es morgen Nachmittag *regnet*, **gehe** ich ins Kino.

Wenn ich nicht zu viel Arbeit *habe*, **kann** ich ins Café gehen.

Wenn meine Freundin mitkommen *kann*, **möchte** ich nach Wien fahren.

The **wenn** clause needs a comma either at the beginning or at the end, as in the examples given above.

Practice

1 **Was passt am besten? Complete the sentences with the most suitable modal verb: sollen, wollen, dürfen.**

a Herr Kaspar ist zu dick. Die Ärztin sagt, er ____ weniger essen.

b Frau Meier liebt Italien. Sie ____ nächstes Jahr nach Neapel fahren.

c Peter ist morgens immer müde. Seine Mutter sagt, er ____ früher ins Bett gehen.

d Beate Sabowski hat Herzprobleme. Der Arzt sagt, sie ____ nicht mehr rauchen.

e Kinder unter 16 Jahren ____ den Film nicht sehen.

f Man ____ nicht zu viel Kaffee trinken.

g Im Sommer fahre ich nach Argentinien. Vorher ____ ich ein wenig Spanisch lernen.

 2 **Ordnen Sie zu. First decide what you consider to be healthy and unhealthy. Then talk about your opinions using wenn with these examples.**

viele Hamburger essen	ein Glas Rotwein pro Tag trinken
regelmäßig joggen	Fahrrad fahren
Salat essen	jeden Tag vier Flaschen Bier trinken
fernsehen und Kartoffelchips essen	fünf Stunden ohne Pause vor dem Computer sitzen
zweimal in der Woche schwimmen gehen	lange spazieren gehen

gesund	ungesund
• _regelmäßig joggen_	• _viele Hamburger essen_
• _____	• _____
• _____	• _____
• _____	• _____
• _____	
• _____	

Beispiel Ich denke, es ist gesund, wenn man regelmäßig joggt.

 Pronunciation

19.04 At the end of a word or syllable the letter **b** in German is pronounced more like an English **p**:

> **gib hab Urlaub halb abholen Obst**

When the **b** is no longer at the end of the word or syllable it is pronounced as an English *b*:

> **geben haben Urlaube halbe**

How would you pronounce these words? **ob**, **Ober**, **Herbst**, **schreibt**, **schreiben**.

Speaking

19.05 Spielen Sie die Rolle der Patientin / des Patienten. Bereiten Sie Ihre Antworten vor. Überprüfen Sie dann Ihre Antworten auf der Audioaufnahme.

Dr. Amm	Guten Tag. Wie kann ich Ihnen helfen? Was fehlt Ihnen?
Patient/in	*Say that you've got a sore throat.*
Dr. Amm	Oh, das tut mir leid. Wie lange haben Sie die Schmerzen denn schon?
Patient/in	*Tell him for about three days and that it's getting worse.*
Dr. Amm	Was sind Sie von Beruf, wenn ich fragen darf?
Patient/in	*Say that you're a teacher.*
Dr. Amm	Ach so! Lehrer haben oft Probleme mit dem Hals. In der Klasse müssen Sie oft zu viel sprechen, das ist nicht gut für den Hals.
Patient/in	*Say yes, but what should you do?*
Dr. Amm	Also, ich verschreibe Ihnen Tabletten. Essen Sie auch viel Eis und trinken Sie viel Wasser. Fahren Sie bald in Urlaub?
Patient/in	*Say yes, next week you're flying to Florida.*
Dr. Amm	Gut, dann müssen Sie versuchen, ein bisschen zu relaxen. Und Sie dürfen nicht zu viel sprechen!
Patient/in	*Say all right and thanks very much.*
Dr. Amm	Gern geschehen. Und gute Besserung.

Writing

Schreiben Sie Ihre Meinung. Answer the questions and write down what you personally think. Of course, opinions may differ on the answers!

Beispiel Ist es gesund, wenn man 12 Stunden pro Tag vor dem Computer sitzt?

Nein, es ist nicht gesund, wenn man 12 Stunden pro Tag vor dem Computer sitzt.

a Ist es gut, wenn man manchmal einen Schnaps trinkt?
b Ist es schlecht, wenn man zu viel Fernsehen sieht?
c Ist man altmodisch, wenn man keine Jeans trägt?
d Ist es ungesund, wenn man jeden Tag fünf Tassen Kaffee trinkt?
e Ist es gesund, wenn man viermal pro Woche ins Fitnesscenter geht?

Go further

 19.06 Here are a few useful expressions for talking about what kind of pains you have and how long you have had them; also for asking what you have to do and what you can and can't do. Listen and repeat the expressions.

 NEW VOCABULARY

die Tablette (-n)	*tablet, pill*
die Tropfen (pl)	*drops*

Saying how you feel	
Ich habe ...	**Magenschmerzen/Kopfschmerzen etc.**
Ich habe die Schmerzen ...	**seit zwei Tagen/seit einer Woche/seit einem Monat etc.**
Kann ich/Darf ich ...	**zur Arbeit gehen/aus dem Haus gehen/ ... etc.?**

Saying how you feel	
Muss ich ...	im Bett bleiben/ins Krankenhaus/ etc.?
Wie oft muss ich ...	die Tabletten nehmen /die Tropfen nehmen/ etc.?
Was kann ich/darf ich/darf ich nicht /soll ich ...	essen/trinken/machen/ etc.?

1 **Sagen Sie's auf Deutsch! How would you say the following expressions in German?**

   a I've got a headache.

   b I've had back pain for one week.

   c I've had stomach pain for two days.

   d How often must I take the pills?

   e Must I stay at home?

   f What should I eat?

Test yourself

1 **Ergänzen Sie, bitte.**

   a Mein Arzt sagt, ich **soll** mehr schwimmen gehen. (sollen)

   b Was _____ ich machen? (sollen)

   c Nächsten Monat _____ er mit einem Tanzkurs anfangen. (wollen)

   d Stefan und Andrea _____ im Sommer heiraten. (wollen)

   e _____ du eigentlich wieder Volleyball spielen? (dürfen)

   f Hier _____ man nicht rauchen. (dürfen)

   g Kinder unter 16 Jahren _____ den Film nicht sehen. (dürfen)

2 **Join the pairs of sentences together, using wenn.**

   Beispiel Du willst länger schlafen? Dann musst du früher ins Bett gehen.

Wenn du länger schlafen willst, musst du früher ins Bett gehen.

a Du möchtest Englisch lernen? Dann
   musst du in eine Sprachschule gehen.
b Bodo möchte ein altes Buch über Deutschland finden? Dann muss
   er bei Amazon suchen.
c Ihr wollt nächste Woche nach New York fliegen? Dann müsst ihr
   bald eure Tickets buchen.
d Sie haben Rückenschmerzen? Dann müssen Sie zum Arzt gehen.
e Marcus möchte ein Jahr in Madrid leben? Dann muss er vorher
   Spanisch lernen.
f Du hast Hunger? Dann musst du etwas essen.

SELF CHECK

I CAN...

... say what I consider to be healthy and unhealthy.

... name parts of the body.

... say what aches and pains I have.

... use modal verbs correctly.

... use structures with **wenn**.

20 Wetter und Urlaub
Weather and holidays

In this unit you will learn how to:
▶ *report on weather conditions.*
▶ *talk about past holidays.*
▶ *use prepositions relating to places.*
▶ *use the simple past tense of* haben *and* sein.
▶ *use the simple past tense of modal verbs.*

CEFR: *Can understand extended speech while listening (B2); Can understand current affairs programmes (B2); Can orally present clear, detailed descriptions (B2); Can narrate a story (B1); Can write about past events (A2)*

German holidays

Many Germans nowadays are entitled to six weeks' paid **Urlaub** (*holiday*) a year. They also enjoy numerous **Feiertage** (*public holidays*), most of which are religious in origin. The total number of **Feiertage** differs from **Bundesland** to **Bundesland**, but it tends to be among the highest in Europe. German reunification is celebrated on 3 October with the **Tag der deutschen Einheit** (*Day of German Unity*).

Germans enjoy travelling and often call themselves die **Reiseweltmeister** (*world's travel champions*). Currently, no other nation spends more money on **Auslandsreisen** (*foreign travels*).

The favourite **Urlaubsziele** (*holiday destinations*) for Germans are **Spanien** (*Spain*) and **Italien**.

However, more than 30% of Germans spend their holiday in their own country. The most visited areas in Germany are **die Friesischen Inseln** (*Frisian Islands*), **die Ostseeküste** (*Baltic Sea coast*), **der Rhein** (*Rhine*), **der Schwarzwald** (*Black Forest*) and **die Bayerischen Alpen** (*Bavarian Alps*).

 What are the German words for holiday and public holidays? And what do die Ostseeküste, der Schwarzwald and die Bayerischen Alpen mean?

Vocabulary builder

 1 20.01 **Die vier Jahreszeiten. Listen to the four seasons and match the correct words with the pictures.**

a	**b**	**c**	**d**
der Winter	der Frühling	der Herbst	der Sommer

 2 20.02 **Wie ist das Wetter? Read the descriptions of today's weather conditions and match them to the appropriate sentences in the present perfect tense. Then listen and check your answers.**

a

Die Sonne. Heute scheint die Sonne. _____

b

Der Regen. Im Moment regnet es. _____

c

Der Schnee. Jetzt schneit es. _____

d

Der Wind. Es ist heute windig. _____

e

Der Nebel. Es ist morgens oft neblig. _____

f

Die Temperatur. Hier beträgt die Temperatur 24 Grad. _____

1 *Letzten Herbst hat es viel geregnet.*

2 *In London war es früher sehr neblig.*

3 *Im Winter hat es viel geschneit.*

4 *Im Herbst war es windig.*

5 *Die Temperatur hat 10 Grad betragen.*

6 *Gestern hat die Sonne geschienen.*

 3 **20.03 Hören Sie die folgenden zwei Interviews. Wo waren die Leute im Urlaub? In welcher Jahreszeit waren sie dort? Wie hoch waren die Temperaturen? Wie war das Wetter? Complete the grid.**

	Wo sie waren	Jahreszeit	Temperaturen	Wetter
Interview 1 *Bärbel Specht*				
Interview 2 *Jutta Weiß*				

 NEW EXPRESSIONS

Look at the expressions that are used in the next interview and conversation. Note their meanings.

Interview	
der Strandurlaub (-e)	*beach holiday*
tagsüber	*during the day*
liegen	*to lie (in the sun, etc.)*
wiederǀkommen	*to come again/back*
der Berg (-e)	*mountain*
die Ostsee	*the Baltic (Sea)*
beenden	*to finish*
der Traum (¨e)	*dream*
Conversation	
einzig	*(here) complete, absolute*
überhaupt nicht	*not at all*
deshalb	*therefore/so*
ärgerlich	*annoying*
passieren	*to happen*
der Hang (¨e)	*slope*
ausǀprobieren	*to try out*
gegen (+ acc.)	*against*
der Baum (¨e)	*tree*

Interview

 1 20.04 **Vier Leute erzählen, wo sie im Urlaub waren und was sie gemacht haben. Hören Sie zu und beantworten Sie dann die Fragen.**

a Was hat Wolfgang Schmidt abends gemacht? _____

b Konnte er nur spanisches Bier kaufen? _____

c Wie oft machen Sieglinde und Renate Bosch einen Skiurlaub? _____

d Wohin wollen sie nächstes Jahr im Urlaub fahren? _____

e Was für Wetter hatten Gerlinde Wagner und ihr Mann in Travemünde? _____

f Wollen sie nächstes Jahr wieder nach Travemünde fahren? _____

g Hat Peter Kemper schon einen Job gefunden? _____

h Was hat er vor zwei Jahren gemacht? _____

2 20.04 **Now read the interviews and listen to check pronunciation.**

Wolfgang Schmidt, 47

‚Ich bin auf Mallorca gewesen, ein richtiger Strandurlaub. Ich habe tagsüber lange in der Sonne gelegen und bin ein bisschen geschwommen. Abends habe ich gut gegessen und bin manchmal in die Hotel bar gegangen. Man konnte auch richtiges deutsches Bier kaufen. Wie zu Hause. Das hat mir gut gefallen. Nächstes Jahr möchte ich wiederkommen.‘

Sieglinde Bosch, 42

‚Im Winter machen meine Schwester und ich jedes Jahr einen Skiurlaub und fahren in die Berge. Dieses Jahr waren wir in Kitzbühel, in Österreich, fantastisch. Der Schnee war gut, die Pisten ausgezeichnet. Wir sind jeden Tag mehrere Stunden Ski gelaufen. Nach dem Urlaub haben wir uns total fit gefühlt. Nächstes Jahr wollen wir vielleicht mal in die Schweiz fahren.‘

Gerlinde Wagner, 64

‚Dieses Jahr sind mein Mann und ich an die Ostsee gefahren, nach Travemünde. Das Wetter war eine Katastrophe. Wir hatten meistens Regen. Außerdem war es sehr kalt und wir konnten nur selten schwimmen gehen. Und teuer war es auch. Nein, nie wieder an die Ostsee. Nächstes Jahr fliegen wir lieber in den Süden, nach Spanien oder Griechenland.‘

Peter Kemper, 25

‚Dieses Jahr habe ich keinen Urlaub gemacht. Ich habe gerade mein Studium beendet und suche jetzt einen Job. Das ist nicht einfach im Moment. Ich hoffe, nächstes Jahr habe ich mehr Geld. Dann würde ich gerne nach New York fliegen. Das ist mein Traum. Ich liebe große Städte. Am liebsten mache ich Städtereisen. Vor zwei Jahren bin ich nach Mexiko-City geflogen.‘

Conversation

1 20.05 **Hören Sie, was Susanne im Urlaub gemacht hat. Beantworten Sie dann die Frage.**
What could Susanne no longer do after her accident? _____

Peter	Hallo Susanne. Na, wie war dein Skiurlaub?
Susanne	Ach, Peter. Eine einzige Katastrophe.
Peter	Wieso, was ist denn passiert?
Susanne	Ach, die ersten Tage hatten wir viel zu wenig Schnee. Deshalb konnten wir überhaupt nicht Ski fahren.
Peter	Oh, das ist ja ärgerlich. Und dann?
Susanne	Dann hat es so viel geschneit, dann durften wir zwei Tage nicht auf die Piste. Der Schnee war zu hoch.
Peter	Und dann?
Susanne	Dann konnten wir fahren, es war ideales Wetter. Aber weißt du, was mir passiert ist? Ich wollte einen neuen Hang ausprobieren, aber er war zu schnell für mich. Tja, und dann bin ich gegen einen Baum gefahren.
Peter	Gegen einen Baum? Wie schrecklich. Und musstest du ins Krankenhaus?
Susanne	Ja. Meine Beine haben mir wehgetan, aber es war nichts Schlimmes. Ich musste nur drei Tage im Krankenhaus bleiben. Aber Ski fahren durfte ich dann nicht mehr. Ich konnte nur noch spazieren gehen.
Peter	Das tut mir leid. Und wie geht es dir jetzt?
Susanne	Jetzt geht es mir wieder gut. Aber nächstes Jahr, weißt du, da fahre ich im Winter lieber nach Teneriffa.

2 Sind die Aussagen richtig oder falsch?

a Ihr Urlaub war wunderbar. _____

b Die ersten Tage konnte sie nicht Ski fahren. _____

c Dann hat es sehr viel geschneit. _____

d Sie ist gegen einen anderen Skifahrer gefahren. _____

e Sie musste eine Woche im Krankenhaus bleiben. _____

f Jetzt geht es ihr wieder besser. _____

Language discovery

1 **Look at the underlined modal verbs from the conversation. They are all in the simple past tense. Can you figure out what endings are used in German to express the meanings of *I could*, *I had to*, *I wanted* and *I was not allowed to*?**

a Ich <u>konnte</u> nur noch spazieren gehen.

b Ich <u>musste</u> nur drei Tage im Krankenhaus bleiben.

c Ich <u>wollte</u> einen neuen Hang ausprobieren.

d Aber Ski fahren <u>durfte</u> ich dann nicht mehr.

2 **Read the four interviews again and identify the missing prepositions. Note the various words used.**

   a Dann würde ich gern _____ New York fliegen.

   b Vor zwei Jahren bin ich _____ Mexico-City geflogen.

   c Dieses Jahr waren wir _____ Kitzbühel, _____ Österreich.

   d Nächstes Jahr wollen wir vielleicht _____ die Schweiz fahren.

   e Ich bin _____ Mallorca gewesen.

   f Nein, nie wieder _____ die Ostsee.

Learn more

1 SIMPLE PAST TENSE: *SEIN, HABEN*

You have learned that Germans normally use the present perfect tense when talking about past events. However, as explained in Unit 13, **war/ waren**, meaning *was/were*, are often used as an alternative to the present perfect. You may have noticed a few examples in the texts above:

> Das Wetter **war** eine Katastrophe.

> Der Schnee **war** gut.

> Dieses Jahr **waren** wir in Kitzbühel.

The simple past tense forms of the verb **haben – hatte / hatten –** are also often used when referring to the past. Examples from this unit are:

> Die ersten Tage **hatten** wir viel zu wenig Schnee.

> Wir **hatten** meistens Regen.

There is really little or no difference in meaning between using the *simple past* or *present perfect*:

> Ich **war** letzten Sommer in Österreich.

> Ich **bin** letzten Sommer in Österreich **gewesen**.

> *I was in Austria last summer.*

> Peter **hatte** diesen Sommer kein Geld.

> Peter **hat** diesen Sommer kein Geld **gehabt**.

> *Peter had no money this summer.*

Here is a summary of **sein** and **haben** in the simple past and the present perfect tense:

	sein		haben	
	simple past	present perfect	simple past	present perfect
ich	**war**	bin gewesen	**hatte**	habe gehabt
du	**warst**	bist gewesen	**hattest**	hast gehabt
Sie	**waren**	sind gewesen	**hatten**	haben gehabt
er / sie / es	**war**	ist gewesen	**hatte**	hat gehabt
wir	**waren**	sind gewesen	**hatten**	haben gehabt
ihr	**wart**	seid gewesen	**hattet**	habt gehabt
Sie	**waren**	sind gewesen	**hatten**	haben gehabt
sie	**waren**	sind gewesen	**hatten**	haben gehabt

2 SIMPLE PAST TENSE: MODAL VERBS

Modal verbs, too, are often used in the simple past tense. Here are a few examples:

dürfen

> past tense meaning: *was/were allowed to*
>
> Als Kind **durfte** ich nur eine Stunde pro Tag fernsehen.
>
> *As a child I **was allowed to** watch TV for only one hour a day.*

können

> past tense meaning: *could, was/were able to*
>
> Im Winter **konnten** wir Ski laufen.
>
> *In winter we **were able to** go skiing.*

müssen

> past tense meaning: *had to*
>
> Bernd **musste** gestern um 6 Uhr aufstehen.
>
> *Bernd **had to** get up at 6 o'clock yesterday.*

sollen

> past tense meaning: *was/were supposed to*
>
> Ich **sollte** heute meine Eltern besuchen.
>
> *I **was supposed to** visit my parents today.*

wollen

> past tense meaning: *wanted to*
>
> Hans und Inge **wollten** ins Kino mitkommen.
>
> *Hans and Inge **wanted to** come to the cinema with us.*

Here is a summary of the modal verb forms in the simple past tense. Note the endings (**-te, -test, -ten, -tet**) added to the stem:

	dürfen*	**können***	**müssen***	**sollen**	**wollen**
ich	durfte	konnte	musste	sollte	wollte
du	durftest	konntest	musstest	solltest	wolltest
Sie	durften	konnten	mussten	sollten	wollten
er / sie / es	durfte	konnte	musste	sollte	wollte
wir	durften	konnten	mussten	sollten	wollten
ihr	durftet	konntet	musstet	solltet	wolltet
Sie	durften	konnten	mussten	sollten	wollten
sie	durften	konnten	mussten	sollten	wollten

Don't forget that the umlaut found in the infinitive forms of **dürfen**, **müssen** and **können** is not found in the simple past tense forms.

You will learn more about the simple past tense in Unit 22.

3 PREPOSITIONS AND PLACES

What prepositions do you use in German in connection with places? These examples provide you with an overview of which prepositions to use and when. Note that, as in English, a different preposition is often used depending on whether *you are going somewhere* or if *you are somewhere* (e.g. 'I am going *to* Berlin' and 'I am *in* Berlin').

Städte	Ich fahre **nach** Berlin.	Ich bin **in** Berlin.
Länder	Sie fährt **nach** Frankreich. Aber: Sie fährt **in** die Schweiz/**in** die Türkei. Sie fährt **in** die USA.	Sie ist **in** Frankreich. Aber: Sie ist **in** der Schweiz/**in** der Türkei. Sie ist **in** den USA.
Land	Sie sind **aufs** Land gefahren.	Sie waren **auf** dem Land.
Insel	Sie sind **nach** Mallorca geflogen.	Sie waren **auf** Mallorca.
Meere	Er fährt **ans** Meer/**an** die Ostsee/**an** den Atlantik.	Er ist **am** Meer/**an** der Ostsee/**am** Atlantik.
Berge	Sie fahren **in** die Berge. Sie steigen **auf** den Berg.	Sie sind **in** den Bergen. Sie sind **auf** dem Berg.

Remember that prepositions such as **in**, **auf** and **an** require the accusative case forms when movement is indicated (**Sie fährt in die Schweiz**), and the dative forms when the focus is on position (**Sie ist in der Schweiz**).

Practice

1 **Iain erzählt über seinen Urlaub. Setzen Sie die Verben in die Vergangenheitsform (simple past).**

   a Ich *war* dieses Jahr mit meiner Freundin in Griechenland. (sein)
   b Das Wetter _____ sehr gut. (sein)
   c Wir _____ viel Sonne. (haben)
   d Wir _____ auf einem Campingplatz. (sein)
   e Der Campingplatz _____ ein Restaurant und einen Laden. (haben)
   f Der Laden _____ eigentlich alles, was wir brauchten und wir _____ eine wunderbare Zeit. (haben/haben)

2 **Ergänzen Sie die Endungen.**

   a Ich konnt _____ leider nicht mit auf die Party gehen.
   b Wollt _____ du nicht letztes Jahr einen Yogakurs machen?
   c Die Kinder durft _____ am Samstag bis 10 Uhr aufbleiben.
   d Wann musst _____ ihr gestern nach Hause?
   e Schade, dass Sie nicht mitkommen konnt _____ .
   f Ich sollt _____ heute eigentlich nach Manchester fahren.
   g Er konnt _____ früher 10 Kilometer in 40 Minuten laufen.
   h Durft _____ du als Kind viel fernsehen?

3 **Welche Präposition fehlt?**

   a Carola macht eine Reise _____ Paris.
   b Bist du schon einmal _____ Österreich gewesen?
   c Fahrt ihr dieses Jahr wieder _____ die USA?
   d Am Wochenende fährt Herr Schmücke oft _____ Land.
   e Sebastian hat ein schönes Haus _____ Mallorca.
   f Magda läuft gern Ski und fährt oft _____ die Berge.
   g Familie Herrmann macht meistens Urlaub _____ der Ostsee.

Speaking

20.06 Sie kommen aus dem Urlaub zurück. Ein Kollege fragt Sie, wie Ihr Urlaub war. Bereiten Sie Ihre Antworten vor und beantworten Sie dann die Fragen auf der Audioaufnahme.

Kollege	Ach, da sind Sie wieder! Und wie war Ihr Urlaub?
Sie	*Tell him an absolute catastrophe.*
Kollege	Wieso, was ist denn passiert?
Sie	*Say that the first three days you had rain. So you couldn't therefore go for walks.*
Kollege	Oh, das ist ja ärgerlich. Und dann?
Sie	*Say that a friend and you drove into a tree with the car.*
Kollege	Gegen einen Baum? Wie schrecklich. Und mussten Sie ins Krankenhaus?
Sie	*Say yes, your legs hurt, but it was nothing bad.*
Kollege	Und wie lange mussten Sie im Krankenhaus bleiben?
Sie	*Say only two days, but you then had to go home.*
Kollege	Das tut mir leid. Und wie geht es Ihnen jetzt?
Sie	*Say that you're OK again now.*

 Listening

20.07 Der Wetterbericht im Radio Hören Sie zu. Welche Antwort stimmt?

a Nachts sind es (6 / 16) Grad.

b Tagsüber sind es im Südosten (21 / 22 / 23) Grad.

c Montag gibt es im Norden und Osten (Wolken und Regen / (Wolken, aber keinen Regen).

d Dienstag gibt es in ganz Deutschland (Sonne / Schauer).

e Am Mittwoch ist es (schlechter / besser).

 NEW WORDS

ablkühlen	*to cool down*
übrig	*remaining*
das Gebiet (-e)	*area, region*
die Aussicht (-en)	*prospect, outlook*

 Reading

1 **Die Deutschen machen oft Urlaub. Aber häufig fahren sie nur für ein paar Tage weg. Wohin fahren sie dann? Lesen Sie bitte den Text und beantworten Sie dann die Fragen.**

Trend: Kurztrip statt Strandurlaub

Lieber häufiger im Jahr für einige Tage wegfahren, als im Urlaub drei Wochen lang an einem Ferienort bleiben. 22 Millionen Deutsche finden Kurztrips (vor allem Städtereisen mit dem Bus) spannender als eine große Reise. Das Ergebnis einer Tourismus-Analyse vom letzten Jahr zeigt auch: Absoluter Renner bei den Zielen für Wochenendtrips ist immer noch Paris. Dann folgen Berlin, München, Wien und Hamburg.

Von je 100 Befragten, die in den letzten Jahren eine 2- bis 4tägige Städtereise unternommen haben, wählten als Reiseziel:

Paris	19
Berlin	17
München	12
Wien	10
Hamburg	10
London	10
Prag	8
Rom	6
Dresden	6
Amsterdam	5
Venedig	4
Köln	3
Budapest	2
Florenz	2
Kopenhagen	2
Istanbul	2

NEW WORDS

weg|fahren	to go away (somewhere)
spannend	exciting
der Ferienort (-e)	holiday resort
das Ergebnis (-se)	result
absoluter Renner	here: top seller
wählen	to choose, to elect
das Reiseziel (-e)	travel destination

Richtig oder falsch?

a Immer mehr Deutsche machen kurze Urlaube. _____

b 22 Millionen finden lange Urlaube besser. _____

c Die meisten Kurztrips sind mit dem Bus. _____

d Die meisten Städtereisenden fahren nach Paris. _____

e Es fahren mehr Leute nach Amsterdam als nach London. _____

 # Writing

An old friend wants to know what you did on your holiday. Rewrite the following story by adapting it to the first person singular (ich). Start each sentence with an item in bold type.

Sie waren **letztes Jahr** in Heidelberg im Urlaub. Sie haben **dort** in einer Jugendherberge gewohnt. Sie sind **abends** in eine Karaoke-Kneipe gegangen. Sie haben **in der Kneipe** ein Lied von Elvis Presley gesungen. Ein Produzent hat Sie **dort** gehört. Ihre Stimme hat **ihm** sehr gut gefallen. Sie sind **am nächsten Tag** mit ihm nach Berlin geflogen. Sie haben **in einem Studio** eine neue CD gemacht. Sie sind 10 Tage in **Berlin** geblieben. Sie haben **dann** im Fernsehen und im Radio gesungen. Sie wollen **nächstes Jahr** in Las Vegas singen.

Letztes Jahr war ich in Heidelberg im Urlaub. **Dort** habe ich..., etc.

 # Go further

 1 **20.08** **Listen to the expressions for talking about the weather and repeat.**

Talking about the weather	
In Madrid ist es ... In Madrid it's ...	**heiter, wolkig, bedeckt.** fine, cloudy, overcast.
In London gibt es ... In London there is / are ...	**Schauer, Gewitter, Schnee, Regen, Nebel.** showers, thunderstorms, snow, rain, fog.

2 Sehen Sie sich die Wetterkarte an und beantworten Sie die Fragen.

   a Wo ist es wärmer: in London oder in München?

   b Wie hoch sind die Temperaturen in Dublin?

   c Regnet es in Berlin?

   d Regnet es in Wien?

   e Wo gibt es in Europa Gewitter?

   f Wie ist das Wetter in Kairo?

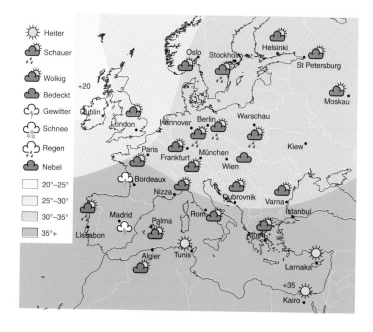

# Test yourself

1 Welche Endungen fehlen? Vorsicht – manchmal braucht man keine Endung.

a Letztes Jahr war ___ ich in Kanada.

b War ___ Sie schon einmal in Berlin?

c Louise war ___ gestern nicht da.

d War ___ ihr am Wochenende tanzen?

e Hat ___ du einen schönen Urlaub?

f Ich hat ___ gestern keine Zeit.

g Er war ___ gestern aus und hat ___ heute Morgen einen Kater.

2 Setzen Sie die Modalverben in die richtige Form.

a Eigentlich ___ (wollen) ich gestern Abend ins Kino gehen, aber ich ___ (müssen) lange arbeiten.

b Im Hotel ___ (können) wir noch nach Mitternacht etwas zu trinken bekommen.

c Frau Schmidt ___ (sollen) schon letzte Woche zum Arzt gehen, aber leider ___ (können) sie nicht.

d Früher ___ (dürfen) man in unserer Straße parken.

e ___ (müssen) Sie früher in der Schule Latein lernen?

3 Welche Präpositionen fehlen?

Liebe Inga,

na, wie geht's? Dieses Jahr sind wir nicht _____ Indien geflogen oder _____ die Berge gefahren. Nein, wir haben Urlaub _____ der Ostsee gemacht, _____ der Insel Rügen. Rügen liegt im Nordosten Deutschlands. Das Wetter war gut, wir sind viel _____ Meer geschwommen. Außerdem haben wir einen Ausflug _____ Berlin gemacht. Dort war es natürlich auch sehr interessant. So viel hat sich verändert. Wir sind _____ Pergamonmuseum gegangen und waren auch _____ Museum für Deutsche Geschichte.

Wie ist deine neue Wohnung? Ich hoffe, es geht dir gut.

Bis bald und grüß alle!

Deine Martina

SELF CHECK

I CAN. . .

⦿ . . . report on present and past weather conditions.

⦿ . . . talk about holidays that I have been on.

⦿ . . . use the correct prepositions with places and place names.

⦿ . . . use the simple past tense of modal verbs and **haben** and **sein**.

21

Telefonieren und die Geschäftswelt

Telephoning and the business world

In this unit you will learn how to:
▶ *make and answer phone calls.*
▶ *make and rearrange business appointments.*
▶ *say what belongs to whom.*
▶ *use various forms of the genitive case.*

CEF: *Can give reasons and explanations for plans (B2); Can follow talks of a professional nature (B2); Can understand texts about job-related topics (B1)*

Telephone and business etiquette

German speakers often answer the phone by saying their **Nachnamen/ Familiennamen** (*surname*): **Schmidt** or **Schmidt am Apparat**. Using **du** or first names **am Telefon** (*on the phone*) to someone you do not know is considered inappropriate. At the end of a formal **Telefongespräch** (*telephone conversation*) people usually say **Auf Wiederhören**, instead of **Auf Wiedersehen**.

Don't underestimate the importance of **Pünktlichkeit** (*punctuality*) in German culture. Arriving even five to ten minutes later for a **Meeting** (*meeting*) than the appointed time is perceived as **spät** (*late*).

When invited to a home, good quality **Schokolade** (*chocolate*), **ein Schal** (*a scarf*) for your **Gastgeberin** (*hostess*) or **ein Blumenstrauß** (*a bouquet of flowers*) are all acceptable **Geschenke** (*gifts*). However, avoid **rote Rosen** (*red roses*) as they symbolise romantic intentions.

 What are the German words for *punctuality*, *telephone conversation* and a *bouquet of flowers*? And what do people often say at the end of a telephone conversation?

Vocabulary builder

MAKING TELEPHONE CALLS

1 Look at the pictures and read the expressions used when speaking directly to a person.

a _____   b _____   c _____

2 Look at the pictures and read the expressions used when you want to speak to another person.

3 Match the expressions with the English translations.

a **Bist du es?** _____   1 *I'll fetch her.*

b **am Apparat** _____   2 *to connect, to put through*

c **Ich hole sie.** _____   3 *Is that you?*

d **verbinden** _____   4 *on the phone, speaking*

4 Welche Fragen und Begrüßungen sind formell, welche informell? Machen Sie eine Liste.

Informell	Formell
– Hallo, Bernd, bist du es?	– Guten Tag, Herr Preiß.
–	–
	–
	–

5 21.01 Hören Sie den Anrufbeantworter von Familie Schweighofer. Welche Wörter fehlen?

Guten Tag. ____ ist der telefonische Anrufbeantworter von Evelyn und Michael Schweighofer. Wir sind im Moment ____ nicht da. Sie können uns aber gerne nach dem Pfeifton eine ____ hinterlassen. Bitte sagen Sie uns Ihren ____ und Ihre ____ und wir ____ Sie dann so schnell wie möglich ____ .

NEW EXPRESSIONS

Look at the expressions that are used in the next conversation. Note their meanings.

Conversation 1

der Anrufbeantworter (-)	*answer machine*
eine Nachricht hinterlassen	*to leave a message*
zurück / rufen	*to call back*
der Raum (¨e)	*room, space*
der Texter (-)	*copy writer*
die Sekretärin (-nen)	*secretary*
daneben	*next to that*
der Grafiker (-)	*graphic artist*
der Chef (-s) / die Chefin (-nen)	*head, boss*

Conversation 2

die Messe (-n)	*trade fair*
der Termin (-e)	*appointment*
dringend	*urgent*
die Geschäftsreise (-)	*business trip*
absagen	*to cancel (an arrangement)*
einen Termin aus I machen	*to make an appointment*
der Terminkalender (-)	*diary*
Passt es Ihnen ...?	*Does it suit you ...?*
Das passt mir gut.	*It suits me very well.*

Conversations

1 21.02 **Frau Paul hat heute ihren ersten Tag in der Werbefirma, 'Pleinmann'. Herr Riha zeigt ihr die Firma. Lesen Sie, was er sagt und finden Sie heraus, wer in welchem Büro arbeitet. Schreiben Sie die Nummer auf. Hören Sie dann den Text.**

  a Hier vorne rechts ist der Raum des Designers, Bernd Buck. Er hat in New York studiert. Büro Nr. _6_

  b Daneben ist das Büro der Texter, Michaela und Günther. Beide sind fantastisch, manchmal ein bisschen temperamentvoll. Büro Nr. ____

  c Hier vorne links ist das Büro der Sekretärin, Frau Schüller. Sie ist wirklich sehr nett. Büro Nr. ____

  d Daneben ist das Büro des Grafikers, Herrn Meier-Martinez. Büro Nr. ____

  e Und ganz hinten links ist das Büro des Managers, Guido Kafka. Ein sehr intelligenter Mensch. Büro Nr. ____

  f Gegenüber ist das Zimmer der Chefin, Frau Conrad. Büro Nr. ____

3			4
2			5
1	Frau Paul und Herr Riha ●		6

2 **When she gets home, Frau Paul tries hard to remember the layout of the office. How did she do? Richtig oder falsch? Korrigieren Sie die falschen Aussagen.**

  a Vorne rechts war das Büro der Sekretärin. Nein, vorne rechts war das Büro des Designers.

  b Links vorne war das Büro des Designers. _____

  c Daneben war das Büro des Grafikers, Meier-Martinez.

  _____

  d Auf der rechten Seite in der Mitte war das Zimmer der Chefin, Frau Conrad. _____

e Und ganz hinten rechts war der Raum des Managers, Guido Kafka. _____

f Ganz hinten links war dann das Zimmer der Texter, Michaela und Günther. _____

3 **21.03 Frau Muth and Herr Schneider are trying to rearrange an appointment over the phone. Listen and answer the question.**

a Herr Schneider needs to rearrange the meeting because:

1 he's got another meeting

2 he's on a business trip

3 he is ill

4 **21.03 Hören Sie das Gespräch noch einmal und entscheiden Sie, ob die Aussagen richtig oder falsch sind. Lesen Sie dann den Text und überprüfen Sie Ihre Antworten.**

a Frau Muth hat im Moment viel zu tun. _____

b Herr Schneider hat am Anfang der Woche einen Termin mit ihr. _____

c Er fährt auf Urlaub in die USA. _____

d Am Donnerstag nächster Woche hat Frau Muth eine Launchparty. _____

e Sie machen einen Termin für Ende der Woche, für Freitag. _____

Herr Schneider	Guten Tag, Frau Muth. Hier ist Konrad Schneider von der Firma B.A.T-Grafiks.
Frau Muth	Ja, Herr Schneider. Wie geht es Ihnen?
Herr Schneider	Danke, ganz gut. Und Ihnen?
Frau Muth	Sehr gut. Danke. Im Moment haben wir sehr viel Arbeit, wegen der Messe im Februar.
Herr Schneider	Frau Muth, wir haben am Ende der Woche einen Termin. Es tut mir leid, aber ich muss ihn wegen einer dringenden Geschäftsreise in die USA absagen.
Frau Muth	Ja, natürlich. Das ist kein Problem. Sollen wir gleich einen neuen Termin ausmachen?
Herr Schneider	Ja, gerne. Ich hole meinen Terminkalender.
Frau Muth	Passt es Ihnen denn Anfang der nächsten Woche?

Herr Schneider	Am Anfang der Woche habe ich schon einige Termine. Besser ist es Mitte der Woche oder am Ende. Vielleicht am Donnerstag.
Frau Muth	Donnerstagvormittag ist es schlecht, wegen einer Launchparty für unser neues Produkt. Aber am Nachmittag, da geht es. Um 14.00 Uhr?
Herr Schneider	Das passt mir gut. Aber sind Sie sicher, trotz der Party am Vormittag?
Frau Muth	Kein Problem, Herr Schneider. Und wenn Sie Zeit haben, kommen Sie doch ein bisschen früher.

 Language discovery

1 **Read the first Conversation again and identify the missing words. What forms are used for masculine, feminine and plural nouns to say 'of the'? And what letter is added to masculine nouns?**

a Hier ist das Büro _____ Grafikers, Herrn Meier-Martinez. (m)
b Und ganz hinten ist das Büro _____ Managers, Guido Kafka. (m)
c Und vorne links ist das Büro _____ Sekretärin, Frau Schüller. (f)
d Gegenüber ist das Zimmer _____ Chefin, Frau Conrad. (f)
e Daneben ist das Büro _____ Texter, Michaela und Günther. (pl)

Learn more

1 GENITIVE CASE

This is the fourth and last of the cases in German, the so-called *genitive* case. You have probably already worked out from the examples that the genitive indicates some kind of possession or ownership. The definite article in the genitive can be roughly translated as *of the*. So, **das Büro der Sekretärin** is *the office of the secretary* – in other words, *the secretary's office*. Here is an overview of the genitive case using the definite article.

Gender	Noun with article	Genitive case example
masc.	der Designer	Hier rechts ist der Raum **des** Designer**s**.
fem.	die Sekretärin	Hier vorne links ist das Büro **der** Sekretärin.
neut.	das Büro	Herr Kafka ist der Manager **des** Büro**s**.
pl.	die Texter	Daneben ist das Büro **der** Texter.

Note that with masculine and neuter nouns the definite article is **des** and the noun also adds an **-(e)s**. With feminine and plural nouns the definite article is **der** and no additional endings are required.

You also need to know the genitive forms of the indefinite article. Fortunately, the pattern is very similar. It is **-(e)s** for masculine and neuter nouns and **-er** for feminine nouns. The same pattern also applies to the possessive adjectives (**mein**, **dein**, **Ihr**, etc.) and to **kein**.

Gender	Article	Genitive case example
masc.	ein**es** mein**es**	Was ist die Rolle ein**es** Mann**es** in der heutigen Welt? Das ist das Haus mein**es** Lehrer**s**.
fem.	ein**er** mein**er**	Herr Breitling ist Manager ein**er** Firma in München. Das ist der Computer mein**er** Kollegin.
neut.	ein**es** mein**es**	Das Leben ein**es** Kind**es** kann manchmal schwierig sein. Die Nebenkosten mein**es** Zimmer**s** sind sehr günstig.
pl.	-------- mein**er**	Darf ich die Mutter mein**er** Kinder vorstellen?

As you can see from the examples, nouns of one syllable (like **Mann** and **Kind**) tend to add **-es** in the genitive and not just **-s**:

die Rolle ein**es** Mann**es**
das Leben ein**es** Kind**es**

 Common expressions with the genitive

am Anfang der Woche	*at the beginning of the week*
Mitte der Woche	*in the middle of the week*
am Ende des Monats	*at the end of the month*
wegen einer Geschäftsreise	*because of a business trip*
trotz der Party	*in spite of the party*

2 ADJECTIVE ENDINGS IN THE GENITIVE

The adjective endings in the genitive case after the definite and indefinite article and possessive adjectives are **-en** for all genders and the plural.

Die Mutter meines neuen Freundes.	*The mother of my new (boy)friend.*
Der Vater seiner neuen Freundin.	*The father of his new (girl)friend.*
Das Büro unserer neuen Kollegen.	*The office of our new colleagues.*

3 PREPOSITIONS + GENITIVE

In this unit you met two prepositions that require the genitive: **wegen** (*because of*) and **trotz** (*despite, in spite of*). Here are some more of the most commonly used prepositions + genitive followed by a few examples:

(an)statt	*instead of*
exklusive	*exclusive of*
außerhalb	*outside of*
bezüglich	*concerning, with regard to*
inklusive	*inclusive of*
innerhalb	*inside of, within*
während	*during*

Bezüglich Ihres letzten Briefes	*Concerning your last letter*
Inklusive aller Nebenkosten	*Inclusive of all extra costs*
Innerhalb unseres kleinen Zimmers	*Inside our small room*
Während ihres langen Lebens	*During her long life*

4 WEAK NOUNS

You will have noticed that the word **Herr** has an **n** at the end in some of the examples. This is because **Herr** belongs to a group of nouns (called weak nouns) that add **-(e)n** in the accusative, dative and genitive cases:

Das ist Herr Schmidt.	Nominative
Kennen Sie Herrn Schmidt schon?	Accusative
Ich möchte mit Herrn Schmidt sprechen.	Dative

Other nouns that belong to this group include: **der Mensch**, **der Name**, **der Student**:

Bitte sagen Sie Ihren Name**n**.	Accusative
Kennen Sie diesen Mensch**en**?	Accusative
Können Sie diesem Student**en** helfen?	Dative

 Practice

1 **Ergänzen Sie. Some of the nouns don't require endings.**

   a Der Name *der* Firma ist Inter-Design.

   b Ich habe den Namen d＿＿ Designerin＿＿ vergessen.

   c Die Telefonnummer d＿＿ Kundin＿＿ ist 45 76 98.

   d Die Rechnung d＿＿ Hotel＿＿ war astronomisch.

e Die Reparatur d___ Computer___ hat drei Wochen gedauert.

f Mir gefällt die Farbe d___ neuen Firmenauto___ nicht.

g Die Anzahl d___ Leute___ ohne Arbeit beträgt etwa drei Millionen.

2 Was passt zusammen? Verbinden Sie die Satzteile.

a	Trotz des starken Windes	**1**	lernte er viele Fremdsprachen.
b	Wegen einer wichtigen Reise	**2**	konnten die Flugzeuge starten.
c	Während seines langen Lebens	**3**	verkaufte die Firma viele Autos.
d	Inklusive aller Nebenkosten	**4**	passt mir sehr gut.
e	Innerhalb des letzten Monats	**5**	beträgt die Miete €870 pro Monat.
f	Ein Termin am Anfang der Woche	**6**	muss ich den Termin absagen.

3 Setzen Sie die fehlenden Wörter ein. In der Mitte erscheint dann (fast) ein zwölftes Wort. Was ist es?

1. Guten Morgen. Schwarz am _____ .
2. Sagen Sie bitte, er soll _____ .
3. Sprechen Sie bitte nach dem _____ .
4. Ja, Herr Gruber ist in seinem Büro. Ich _____ .
5. Es tut mir leid. Aber diese Nummer ist _besetzt_ .
6. Möchten Sie eine Nachricht _____ ?
7. Freye, Firma Braun, _Anschluss_ 314.
8. Die _____ ist besetzt. Ich versuche es später noch einmal.
9. Darf ich bitte eine _____ hinterlassen?
10. Bitte sagen Sie uns Ihren _____ und Ihre Telefonnummer.
11. Möchten Sie ihr etwas _____ ?

NEW WORDS

besetzt	*busy*
der Anschluss ("e)	*here: extension*

 ## Pronunciation

21.04 In German the letter *a* is pronounced long in some words and short in others. Listen first to words that contain a short *a* and then to words that contain a long *a*:

an	machen	was	Dank	man
nach	Name	war	haben	sagen

You will probably find that you develop a feel for whether *a* should be long or short in a given word. How would you pronounce these words, all of which you have met in the course?

Hand, Nase, das, Grad, Tante, Hamburg

 ## Speaking

21.05 **Sie müssen einen Termin mit Frau Conrad von der Werbeagentur Pleinmann absagen. Schreiben Sie zuerst Ihre Antworten auf und beantworten Sie dann die Fragen auf der Audioaufnahme.**

Frau Schüller	Werbeagentur Pleinmann. Guten Tag.
Sie	*Say good day and that you would like to talk to Frau Conrad.*
Frau Schüller	Ja, einen Moment bitte. Ich verbinde.
Sie	*Say thank you very much.*
Frau Conrad	Conrad. Guten Tag.
Sie	*Say your name. Tell Frau Conrad that you have an appointment for the beginning of the week.*
Frau Conrad	Ja, das stimmt. Ja, am Montag, um 15.00 Uhr.
Sie	*Say that you are very sorry, but you have to cancel the appointment.*
Frau Conrad	Nun, das ist kein Problem. Wollen Sie gleich einen neuen Termin ausmachen?
Sie	*Say yes and ask if the end of the week suits her.*
Frau Conrad	Ja, das passt mir gut. Sagen wir Freitagmorgen, um 10.00 Uhr?
Sie	*Say you don't have any appointments for Friday morning. That suits you well. Say goodbye.*

Listening

1 21.06 In welchen Dialogen (1, 2 or 3) sagen die Leute die Sätze? Hören Sie bitte zu und kreuzen Sie an. Read the situations. Then listen and check the conversations in which each situation occurs.

	1	2	3
Sie ist beim Zahnarzt.	☐	☐	☐
Die Leitung ist besetzt.	☐	☐	☐
Er ist auf Geschäftsreise.	☐	☐	☐
Soll sie zurückrufen?	☐	☐	☐
Wollen Sie warten?	☐	☐	☐
Wollen Sie eine Nachricht hinterlassen?	☐	☐	☐
Er möchte mich morgen zurückrufen.	☐	☐	☐
Ich bin zu Hause.	☐	☐	☐
Ich rufe später noch mal an.	☐	☐	☐

2 21.06 Hören Sie die Dialoge noch einmal und beantworten Sie die Fragen.

a (Dialog 1) Was macht Frau Dr. Martens gerade? _____

b (Dialog 2) Wo ist Sandy und wann kommt sie wieder nach Hause? _____

c (Dialog 3) Wo ist Peter Fink und wann ist er wieder im Büro?

_____

NEW WORDS

Die Leitung ist besetzt.	_The line is busy/engaged._
die Geschäftsreise (-n)	_business trip_
jemandem etwas ausrichten	_to give a message to someone_

 Test yourself

1 Was passt zusammen?

a Ist Corinna da?

b Können Sie Herrn Grün etwas ausrichten?

c Spreche ich mit Frau Kemper?

d Können Sie Julia sagen, ich habe angerufen?

e Kann ich bitte mit Herrn Martin sprechen?

f Bist du es, Renate?

1 Natürlich kann ich ihm etwas ausrichten.

2 Einen Moment. Ich verbinde.

3 Tut mir leid, sie ist nicht zu Hause.

4 Natürlich bin ich es.

5 Ja, hier ist Kemper am Apparat.

6 Natürlich kann ich ihr das sagen.

2 Ordnen Sie bitte zu. Herr Kunz möchte mit Frau Nadolny sprechen. Was sagt Herr Kunz? Herr Kunz wants to talk to Frau Nadolny. The role of the secretary is in the correct order but Herr Kunz's role needs rearranging.

Sekretärin

a Firma Möllemann. Guten Tag! _____

b Es tut mir leid, Frau Nadolny ist gerade in einem Meeting. _____

c Das ist schwer zu sagen. Möchten Sie eine Nachricht hinterlassen? _____

d Natürlich. Was soll ich ihr ausrichten? _____

e Gut. Hat sie Ihre Nummer? _____

f Das ist vielleicht eine gute Idee. _____

g Und wie lange sind Sie heute im Büro? _____

h Ich richte es ihr aus, Herr Kunz. Vielen Dank und auf Wiederhören. _____

Herr Kunz

1 Guten Tag, Kunz. Ich möchte gern mit Frau Nadolny sprechen.

2 Wenn das möglich ist, gerne.

3 Können Sie ihr sagen, sie möchte mich bitte zurückrufen.

4 Auf Wiederhören.

5 Herr Kunz, Firma Bötticher, Anschluss 212.

6 Wie lange geht das Meeting denn?

7 Ich bin bis 16.00 Uhr an meinem Schreibtisch.

8 Ich denke schon, aber ich kann sie Ihnen noch mal geben.

3 Sagen Sie es anders. Practise the genitive case by rewriting the following sentences.

Beispiel Die Schwester von meinem neuen Freund ist sehr arrogant.
Die Schwester meines neuen Freundes ist sehr arrogant.

a Das Auto von meinem Bruder fährt sehr schnell.

b Der Computer von meiner Kollegin ist fantastisch.

c Die Firma von meinem alten Schulfreund war letztes Jahr sehr erfolgreich.

d Die Kollegen von meinem Mann sind alle schrecklich langweilig.

e Die Managerin von der exquisiten Boutique ,La dame' kommt aus Paris.

f Das Büro von unserem neuen Designer ist sehr schick.

g Der Laptop von meinem Sohn hat €500 gekostet.

h Das Geschenk von meinen Kollegen hat mir gut gefallen.

SELF CHECK

I CAN...

○ ... initiate and answer phone calls.

○ ... make and rearrange business appointments.

○ ... say what belongs to whom.

○ ... use the genitive case appropriately and correctly.

Stellenangebote und Lebensläufe
Job adverts and CVs

In this unit you will learn how to:
▶ *read job adverts.*
▶ *write a CV.*
▶ *use more verbs in the simple past tense.*
▶ *handle job applications.*

CEF: *Can adapt reading style and speed to different texts and purposes (B2); Can understand texts of job-related language (B1); Can understand specialized texts (B2); Can synthesize information from a number of sources (B2); Can write clear detailed descriptions (B2)*

Lebensläufe CVs

The tabular format illustrated in Peter Frankenthal's **Lebenslauf** (*CV*) in the Reading section is very widely used in Germany. It is common practice in German CVs to include the **Schule** (*school*) you went to and the **Abschlüsse** (*qualifications*) you gained.

The **Schulsystem** (*school system*) in Germany varies from **Bundesland** to **Bundesland**, but in general all pupils go to the **Grundschule** (*primary school*) when they are about six, and then four years later, according to their attainment/abilities, transfer to one of various types of schools, where they do different courses and attend for different lengths of time: the **Hauptschule**, a bit like the British Secondary Modern School, where courses lead to the **Hauptschulabschluss**; the **Realschule**, leading to the **Realschulabschluss**, a bit like the GCSE qualifications in Britain; and the **Gymnasium** or grammar school, leading to the **Abitur**, which is roughly comparable to A levels in the UK or the High School Diploma in the US.

What are the German words for *school, primary school, qualifications* and *CV*? And what is **das Abitur** comparable to?

Vocabulary builder

 22.01 Ordnen Sie zu. Wie heißen die Ausdrücke auf Englisch? Listen and match the English translations to the German words.

a Er braucht eine besondere Betreuung _____

b Arbeitszeit nach Vereinbarung _____

c Sie müssen Büroerfahrung haben _____

d Bewerbungen an _____

e Zum sofortigen Eintritt _____

f Wegen einer plötzlichen Vakanz _____

1 *You have to have office experience*

2 *Because of a sudden vacancy*

3 *To start immediately*

4 *He needs special care*

5 *Send your application to*

6 *Working hours by agreement*

 NEW EXPRESSIONS

Look at the expressions that are used in the next reading and conversation. Note their meanings.

Reading 1

die Kenntnis (-se)	*knowledge, skill(s)*
die Erfahrung (-en)	*experience*
die Bewerbung (-en)	*application*
die Kinderfrau (-en)	*nanny*
engagiert	*committed*
betreuen	*to look after, to care for*
versiert	*well versed*
der Redakteur (-) / die -in (nen)	*editor*
zwecklos	*pointless*
lebenslustig	*full of the joys of life*
die Hingabe	*devotion, dedication*
sofort	*immediately*
der Eintritt (-e)	*entrance, start*
rüstig	*sprightly*
der Frührentner (-) / die -rentnerin (nen)	*someone who has taken early retirement*
der Teilzeitjob (-s)	*part-time job*

Reading 2

der Werdegang ("e)	*development/career*
die Grundschule (-n)	*primary school*
der Realschulabschluss ("e)	*roughly equivalent to GCSE in the UK*
die Lehre (-n)	*apprenticeship*
der Bankkaufmann ("er)	*qualified bank clerk*
der Filialleiter (-) / die -in (nen)	*branch manager*
fließend	*fluent*

 # Readings

 1 **22.02 Here are five Stellenangebote (*job adverts*). Without looking at all the details, answer the question. Then listen to check pronunciation.**

a What kind of job is on offer in each advert?

1 _____ 2 _____ 3 _____ 4 _____

5 _____

1

> Student / Studentin für Bürotätigkeit 2–3 Tage pro Woche für unsere PR-Agentur gesucht. Sie müssen journalistisches Talent, sowie Büroerfahrung, PC- und Englischkenntnisse haben. Bewerbungen an: mail@joestpr.de oder anrufen bei Unternehmensberatung Joest
>
> Tel.: 08806/92300

2

Musiker-Eltern (Bayerische Staatsoper) suchen engagierte Kinderfrau, die zeitlich flexibel, 2–3 Vormittage und 2–3 Abende, Nähe Westpark, 2 Kinder, ab Mai betreut. Der Junge ist Diabetiker und braucht eine besondere Betreuung.

Tel.: 089/54379004

Fr. Heidt

3

Wegen einer plötzlichen Vakanz sucht das MALLORCA MAGAZIN, die deutsche Wochenzeitung auf Mallorca, möglichst per sofort versierten LOKALREDAKTEUR mit perfekten Spanischkenntnissen und mehrjähriger Berufserfahrung (andere Bewerbungen zwecklos). Eilangebote an: MALLORCA MAGAZIN, Redaktionsdirektion, Apartado de Correos 304, E- 07012 Palma de Mallorca, Fax: 003471/714533

4

Suche lebenslustigen Koch, ab April, für Café-Restaurant in Prenzlau/Brandenburg, der feine Fisch- und vegetarische Gerichte mit Hingabe kocht.

Bewerbung bitte unter Chiffre: ZS2073098 an SZ

5

Wir suchen zum sofortigen Eintritt rüstigen Rentner / Frührentner, auch weiblich, als Nachtportier. Arbeitszeit nach Vereinbarung. Bewerbungen bitte an: Hotel Mayer, Augsburger Str. 45, 82110 München-Germering. Tel.: 089/844071

2 **Welches Stellenangebot ist es? Lesen Sie die folgenden Sätze und finden Sie heraus, welcher Satz zu welchem Stellenangebot passt.**

a Man sucht jemanden ab April. Er muss Spaß am Leben haben. _4_

b Wenn Sie diesen Job annehmen, müssen Sie nachts arbeiten. ___

c Hier arbeiten Sie für ein deutschsprachiges Magazin, aber Sie müssen auch Spanisch sprechen. ___

d Bei diesem Job müssen Sie zwei Kinder betreuen. Die Eltern spielen bei der Bayerischen Staatsoper. ___

e Wenn Sie vegetarisch kochen können, gefällt Ihnen vielleicht dieser Job. ___

f Wenn Sie in einem südlichen europäischen Land arbeiten wollen, passt dieser Job vielleicht zu Ihnen. ___

g Wenn Sie Englisch sprechen, mit einem Computer arbeiten können und Studentin sind, ist dieser Teilzeitjob richtig für Sie. ___

3 **Wer bewirbt sich um welche Stelle? Match these people with the most suitable job in the advertisements.**

a Bernd Schulte, 63, ist noch sehr fit. Er möchte einen Teilzeitjob haben und vielleicht nachts arbeiten. ___

b Bettina Hartmann, 24, ist Studentin und muss nebenbei Geld verdienen. Sie spricht sehr gut Englisch und hat schon in verschiedenen Büros gearbeitet. ___

c Martina Wustermann, 35, hat jahrelang bei Lokalzeitungen als Redakteurin gearbeitet. Sie spricht mehrere Fremdsprachen (Englisch, Französisch, Spanisch) und möchte jetzt im Ausland arbeiten. ___

d Jochen Kinsky, 25, hat gerade eine Kochlehre beendet. Er ist Vegetarier und möchte für ein Restaurant in der Nähe von Berlin arbeiten. ___

e Silke Zehnder, 28, interessiert sich für Kinder. Sie möchte einen Teilzeitjob, der ihr Zeit für ihre Hobbys lässt. Sie geht auch gern mal ins Konzert. ___

Reading

1 22.03 **Lesen Sie den Lebenslauf von Peter Frankenthal und beantworten Sie die Frage. Then listen and check your pronunciation.**

a In what area does Peter work?

1 sales   **2** banking   **3** publishing

LEBENSLAUF

Name:	Peter Frankenthal
geboren:	29.07.1980 in Frankfurt/Main
Nationalität:	deutsch
Familienstand:	verheiratet, 2 Kinder
Wohnort:	Mainz

<u>Werdegang</u>

1986-1990	Grundschule in Frankfurt
1990-1996	Schiller-Schule in Offenbach
	Abschluss: Realschulabschluss
1996-1999	Bank lehre bei der Dresdner Bank in Offenbach
1999-2003	Bankkaufmann bei der Dresdner Bank in Offenbach
2003-2012	Bankkaufmann bei der Commerzbank, Frankfurt
	Besuch von Sprachkursen in Englisch und Französisch
seit 2012	Filialleiter Commerzbank in Mainz-Süd

<u>Besondere Kenntnisse</u>

Englisch und Französisch fließend

Sehr gute Computerkenntnisse

---

2 Richtig oder falsch? Korrigieren Sie die falschen Aussagen.

a Herr Frankenthal ist ledig. _____

b Er ist in Frankfurt geboren. _____

c In Frankfurt hat er auch seinen Realschulabschluss gemacht. _____

d Nach der Schule hat er gleich eine Lehre gemacht. _____

e Seinen ersten Job hatte er bei der Commerzbank. _____

f Von 2003 bis 2012 hat er wieder in Frankfurt gearbeitet. _____

g Seit 2012 ist er Filialleiter. _____

3 This time Peter has written out in full the details of his career. Read through his CV and then do the exercise.

Ich bin am 29. Juli 1980 in Frankfurt am Main geboren. Von 1986 bis 1990 ging ich in die Grundschule in Frankfurt. Danach wechselte ich auf die Schiller-Schule in Offenbach. 1996 machte ich dort den Realschulabschluss.

Von 1996 bis 1999 machte ich eine Banklehre bei der Dresdner Bank in Offenbach. Anschließend bekam ich eine feste Stellung als Bankkaufmann bei der gleichen Bank, wo ich dann bis 2003 arbeitete.

2003 wechselte ich auf die Commerzbank in Frankfurt, wo ich bis 2012 als Bankkaufmann tätig war. Von 2003 bis 2012 besuchte ich auch Sprachkurse in Englisch und Französisch.

Seit 2012 bin ich Filialleiter bei der Commerzbank in Mainz-Süd.

NEW WORDS

wechseln   *to change*

die feste Stellung (-en)   *permanent position, post*

4 Welche Wörter fehlen?

a Von 1986 bis 1990 ging Peter in die _____.

b 1996 machte er den _____.

c Dann machte er eine _____ bei der Dresdner Bank.

d Seit 2012 ist er _____ in Mainz-Süd.

Language discovery

Read Peter's written out CV again and identify the missing simple past tense forms of these verbs. Which of these words follow a regular pattern and have a -te ending and which ones are different?

a Von 1986 bis 1990 _____ ich in die Grundschule in Frankfurt. (gehen)

b Danach _____ ich auf die Schiller-Schule in Offenbach. (wechseln)

c 1996 _____ ich dort den Realschulabschluss. (machen)

d Anschließend _____ ich eine feste Stellung als Bankkaufmann. (bekommen)

e Bis 2003 _____ ich bei der gleichen Bank. (arbeiten)

f Von 2003 bis 2012 _____ ich auch Sprachkurse in Englisch und Französisch. (besuchen)

Learn more

1 THE SIMPLE PAST TENSE

The simple past form of verbs is commonly used in German when people *write* about the past, whereas the present perfect tense is used more for the *spoken* language.

In Unit 20 you met the simple past tense forms of **sein**, **haben** and of modal verbs, which can be used in both the spoken and the written language.

Here is an overview of how you form the simple past tense:

▶ Regular verbs add a **-t** plus the relevant ending to their stem.

▶ Irregular verbs usually change either their vowel or sometimes their whole stem and don't add endings in the **ich** and **er/sie/es** form.

	regular verbs		irregular verbs	
	mach-en	besuch-en	geh-en	bekomm-en
ich	mach**te**	besuch**te**	ging	bekam
du	mach**test**	besuch**test**	ging**st**	bekam**st**
Sie	mach**ten**	besuch**ten**	ging**en**	bekam**en**
er/sie/es	mach**te**	besuch**te**	ging	bekam
wir	mach**ten**	besuch**ten**	ging**en**	bekam**en**
ihr	mach**tet**	besuch**tet**	ging**t**	bekam**t**
Sie/sie	mach**ten**	besuch**ten**	ging**en**	bekam**en**

You can find a list of commonly used irregular verbs at the end of this book.

There are, however, still a couple of points to note.

▶ For regular verbs, when the stem of an infinitive ends in a **-d**, **-t** or **-gn**, an extra **-e-** is needed before the endings are added.

anwor**t**en → Ich antwor**tete**.

re**d**en (*to talk*) → Ich re**dete**.

bege**gn**en (*to meet*) → Ich bege**gnete**.

▶ For irregular verbs, an extra **-e** is needed to 'oil the works' in the **du** and **ihr** forms when the **ich** form ends in a **-t** or a **-d**:

raten (*to advise*) → ich riet, du riet**e**st, ihr riet**e**t

finden → ich **fand**, du fand**e**st, ihr fand**e**t

Note that a number of verbs, so-called mixed verbs, change their vowel, but have the **-t** endings like the regular verbs (e.g. **bringen** → **brachte** which is rather like the English *bring* → *brought*).

Here is a reminder of how regular and irregular verbs form their simple past tense:

Regular verbs spielen		Irregular verbs gehen	
ich spielte	-te	ich ging	-
du spieltest	-test	du gingst	-(e)st
Sie spielten	-ten	Sie gingen	-en
er, sie, es spielte	-te	er, sie, es ging	-
wir spielten	-ten	wir gingen	-en
ihr spieltet	-tet	ihr gingt	-(e)t
Sie spielten	-ten	Sie gingen	-en
sie spielten	-ten	sie gingen	-en

Usage

The simple past tense is more often found in the written language than in the spoken language. This is because written language tends to be more formal than spoken language and the simple past tense does have a more formal flavour to it. A chatty letter to a friend, for instance, might well be written in the present perfect tense which would be better suited to the less formal language.

Generally speaking, the simple past tense is mainly used in narrative fiction and non-fiction and in newspaper reporting. You will, for instance, find that German fairy tales, such as those of the Brothers Grimm, are all in the simple past.

But bear in mind that these are general rules. You will certainly find examples that seem to contradict what we have said here. For instance, the first sentence in newspaper reports is usually in the present perfect tense, the rest is then in the simple past. Furthermore, it is sometimes claimed that the simple past tense is used in the ordinary spoken language more frequently in Northern Germany than it is in the south.

For regular verbs it is fairly easy to predict the forms. The best way to learn the irregular verb forms is probably to work with verb lists which you can find in any good dictionary and at the end of this book.

Note that many irregular and mixed verbs follow certain patterns when changing their stems in the simple past and the present perfect tense. Here are some examples:

Infinitive		Simple Past	Perfect	
ei –ie · ie	bleiben	blieb	geblieben	to *stay*
	schreiben	schrieb	geschrieben	to *write*
e – a · o	sprechen	sprach	gesprochen	to *speak*
	sterben	starb	gestorben	to *die*
i – a · u	singen	sang	gesungen	to *sing*
	trinken	trank	getrunken	to *drink*
ie – o · o	fliegen	flog	geflogen	to *fly*
	verlieren	verlor	verloren	to *lose*

2 SAYING *THE YEARS* IN GERMAN

Here are a few examples of how you say *the years* in German:

1820	achtzehnhundertzwanzig
1976	neunzehnhundertsechsundsiebzig
2011	zweitausend(und)elf

Note that Germans usually don't use the preposition **in** when referring to years:

Peter ist 1989 geboren.

You could say **im Jahre** but this is normally only used in a formal context:

Im Jahre 1786 ist Goethe nach Italien gereist.

Practice

1 22.04 **Wie spricht man diese Jahreszahlen aus? Überprüfen Sie Ihre Antworten dann auf der Audioaufnahme.**

    a 1842   **b** 1978   **c** 2004   **d** 2012

2 22.05 **Claudia Schulte, von Beruf Journalistin, erzählt über ihr Leben. Hören Sie zu und versuchen Sie die Fragen zu beantworten:**

    a In welchem Jahr ist sie geboren? _____

    b Was machte sie nach der Schule? _____

    c Wann machte sie ihr Praktikum? _____

    d Wo studierte sie? _____

    e Wie lange arbeitete sie bei der *Tageszeitung*? _____

    f Seit wann arbeitet sie beim *Spiegel*? _____

 3 **Lesen Sie jetzt den Lebenslauf von Claudia Schulte. Then help her complete a description of her job history.**

<u>LEBENSLAUF</u>

Name:	Claudia Schulte
geboren:	1.6.1983 in Bremen
Nationalität:	deutsch
Familienstand:	ledig
Wohnort:	Hamburg

<u>Werdegang</u>

1989–1993	Grundschule in Bremen
1993–2002	Heinrich-Heine-Gymnasium in Bremen
	Abschluss: Abitur
2002–2003	Reisen durch Asien
2003–2004	Praktikum bei der Hamburger Zeitung
2004–2009	Studium der Journalistik an der Universität Hamburg
	Abschluss: M.A. phil.
2009–2012	Journalistin bei der Tageszeitung in Berlin
seit 2012	Journalistin bei Der Spiegel in Hamburg

<u>Besondere Kenntnisse</u>
Englisch, Spanisch und Französisch fließend

4 Helfen Sie ihr. Setzen Sie die fehlenden Wörter ein.

arbeitete	ging	machte	studierte	wechselte
reiste	machte	zog	machte	

Ich bin am 1. Juni 1983 in Bremen geboren. Von 1989 bis 1993 _____ ich in die Grundschule in Bremen. Danach _____ ich auf das Heinrich-Heine-Gymnasium. 2002 _____ ich mein Abitur. Nach der Schule _____ ich durch Asien.

Von 2003 bis 2004 _____ ich ein Praktikum bei der *Hamburger Zeitung*.

Anschließend _____ ich Journalistik an der Universität Hamburg und 2009 _____ ich meinen Abschluss.

Nach dem Studium _____ ich von 2009 bis 2012 bei der *Tageszeitung* in Berlin.

2012 _____ ich wieder nach Hamburg und ich arbeite seitdem beim Nachrichtenmagazin *Der Spiegel*.

Writing

Schreiben Sie einen tabellarischen Lebenslauf wie Herr Frankenthal oder Frau Schulte. Benutzen Sie die folgenden Rubriken: Name, geboren, Nationalität, Familienstand, Wohnort, Werdegang, Besondere Kenntnisse.

Then write a description of your education and job history. Use Claudia Schulte's or Peter Frankenthal's texts as a model. Write in the simple past tense.

Go further

 22.06 Numbers can be difficult to understand and produce, particularly when they are said quickly. Here is a reminder of a few points about German numbers.

▶ The numbers 21–99 are 'back-to-front' compared with English numbers.

21 einundzwanzig   37 siebenunddreißig   98 achtundneunzig

▶ The numbers 101–120 tend not to have 'and' to link them together.

101 hunderteins   111 hundertelf   120 hundertzwanzig

▶ All numbers up to one million are written all as one word.

2 843 zweitausendachthundertdreiundvierzig

10 962 zehntausendneunhundertzweiundsechzig

▶ Numbers after a million are written as follows:

4 800 543 vier Millionen achthunderttausendfünfhundert dreiundvierzig

Note that a comma can be used in German where a decimal point would be used in English:

81,5 Millionen. Say: **einundachtzig Komma fünf Millionen**

1 Wie heißen die Zahlen? Schreiben Sie die Zahlen.

a 47 = *siebenundvierzig*

b 123 = _____

c 3796 = _____

d 10 659 = _____

e 57 388 = _____

f 200 541 = _____

g 2 612 470 = _____

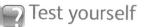

1 Here is an adapted extract from the fairy tale **Schneewittchen** (Snow White). Complete the story using the appropriate verbs from the box.

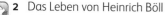

ging	trank	war	dachte	schlief	sah	blieb
standen	gab	war	aß	legte	stand	

Da **a** _____ das Mädchen ein kleines Häuschen und
b _____ hinein. In dem Haus **c** _____ alles klein: da
d _____ ein Tisch mit sieben kleinen Tellern (plates). Außerdem
e _____ es sieben Messer (knives) und Gabeln (forks) und
sieben Becher. An der Wand **f** _____ sieben Betten.
Schneewittchen **g** _____ von jedem Teller ein wenig Gemüse
und Brot und **h** _____ aus jedem Becher einen Tropfen Wein.
Dann **i** _____ es sich in ein Bett. Es **j** _____ im Bett liegen,
k _____ an den lieben Gott und **l** _____ ein.

2 Das Leben von Heinrich Böll
Schreiben Sie einen Lebenslauf des Schriftstellers Heinrich Böll. Look back at Unit 14, Writing and Reading and use the information to write a report about the popular German author in the past simple. For some irregular verbs you might need to look up the correct forms in the list at the end of the book. Note that you need to make no changes to the first sentence:
a 1917 ist Heinrich Böll am 21. Dezember in Köln geboren.
b Von 1924 bis 1928 besuchte er die Volksschule Köln-Raderthal.

SELF CHECK

	I CAN. . .
○	. . . read and understand job adverts.
○	. . . write a basic CV in German in tabular format.
○	. . . write a description of my education and job history.
○	. . . form the simple past tense with regular and irregular verbs.

23 Geschichte und Allgemeinwissen

History and general knowledge

In this unit you will learn how to:

▶ *talk about German-speaking countries.*
▶ *talk about historical events.*
▶ *use subordinate clauses (with dass, weil, obwohl).*
▶ *use the passive form.*

CEF: *Can scan quickly through long and complex texts, locating relevant details (B2); Can depart from a prepared text (B2); Can pass on detailed information reliably (B2); Can write an essay or report (B2); Can understand extended speech (B2)*

German history after 1945

In 1945, after the end of World War II, Germany and Berlin were divided into four **Besatzungszonen** (*occupation zones*). In 1949 the western zones were merged to form the **Bundesrepublik Deutschland** (*Federal Republic of Germany*) while the Soviet Zone became the **Deutsche Demokratische Republik** (*German Democratic Republic*). They were informally known as **Westdeutschland** (*West Germany*) and **Ostdeutschland** (*East Germany*).

In 1961, alarmed at the number of **Facharbeiter** (*skilled workers*) leaving East Germany, the **Regierung** (*government*) gave the order to build the **Berliner Mauer** (*Berlin Wall*) and seal off all **Grenzen** (*borders*) between both countries.

Following the **Mauerfall** (*fall of the Wall*) in 1989 and the subsequent collapse of the East German regime, Germany was finally **wiedervereinigt** (*reunited*) on 3 October 1990.

What are the German words for *government, economy, skilled workers* and *borders*? And what happened in 1961, 1989 and 3 October 1990?

Vocabulary builder

EXPRESSING OPINIONS

 23.01 Read the expressions for making opinions. Listen and match the English translations to the German words.

a   meinen _____   1   *to have no idea*

b   glauben _____   2   *to believe*

c   denken _____   3   *to mean*

d   keine Ahnung haben _____   4   *to think*

Interview

Ein Reporter fragt Leute über Deutschland, Österreich und die Schweiz. Lesen Sie die Interviews. Note that **dass** means *that*.

NEW EXPRESSIONS

Look at the expressions that are used in the next readings. Note their meanings.

Reading 1

die Muttersprache (-n)	*mother tongue*
die Grenze (-n)	*border*
das Fürstentum (¨er)	*principality*
die Minderheit (-en)	*minority*
insgesamt	*in total*
umfassen	*to comprise*
die Fläche (-n)	*area*
km² = der Quadratkilometer (-)	*square metre*
bekannt	*famous, well known*
das Arzneimittel (-)	*drugs*
die Sehenswürdigkeit (-en)	*sight*
beliebt	*popular*
die Wiedervereinigung	*reunification*
ehemalig	*former*
die Gesellschaft (-en)	*society*
der Ausländer (-)	*foreigner*
der Asylant (-en)	*asylum seeker*

Reading 2

der Weltkrieg (-e)	*World War*
teilen	*to divide*
die Gründung (-en)	*founding, foundation*
gründen	*to establish, to found*
die Berliner Mauer	*Berlin Wall*
bauen	*to build*
die innerdeutsche Grenze	*the border between the two Germanies*
wiedervereinigt	*reunited*
wählen	*to elect, to choose*
Bundeskanzler(-)/-in (-nen)	*Federal Chancellor*

Readings

1 23.02 **Lesen Sie den Text und beantworten Sie die Frage. Then listen and read to check your pronunciation.**

  a What is the main purpose of the text?

   1 to give general information about German, Austria and Switzerland
   2 to show which is the best place to live
   3 to talk about the languages spoken in each country

Deutschland, Österreich und die Schweiz

Deutschland, Österreich und die Schweiz – das sind die drei Länder, wo man Deutsch als Muttersprache spricht. Aber es gibt auch noch einige andere Regionen, wo die Leute Deutsch sprechen, zum Beispiel in Belgien an der Grenze mit Deutschland, in Luxemburg, im Fürstentum Liechtenstein und in Südtirol, Italien. Deutschsprachige Minderheiten findet man auch in Kanada, den USA, Rumänien, und sogar in Namibia! Insgesamt sprechen etwa 110 Millionen Deutsch als Muttersprache.

Von den drei Ländern ist die Schweiz das kleinste. Sie umfasst 41 293 km² und hat 7,5 Millionen Einwohner. Die Hauptstadt ist Bern, nicht Zürich, aber Zürich ist die größte Stadt mit 367 000 Einwohnern. Interessant ist, dass man in der Schweiz vier Sprachen spricht: Deutsch, Französisch, Italienisch und Rätoromanisch. Bekannt ist die Schweiz für ihre Uhren, Arzneimittel und für die Berge – ideal für einen Wanderurlaub im Sommer und einen Skiurlaub im Winter.

Österreich ist etwa doppelt so groß wie die Schweiz. Österreich hat 8,3 Millionen Einwohner und eine Fläche von 83 853 km². Die Hauptstadt ist Wien, mit 2,1 Millionen Einwohnern. Bekannte Sehenswürdigkeiten sind das Schloss Schönbrunn, die Hofburg oder das Sigmund-Freud-Haus. Andere Städte in Österreich sind Linz, Graz, Innsbruck und Salzburg. Salzburg ist die Geburtsstadt von Wolfgang Amadeus Mozart und viele Leute besuchen die Stadt im Sommer. Sehr beliebt sind die Mozartkugeln, eine Süßigkeit aus Marzipan.

Seit der Wiedervereinigung am 3. Oktober 1990 umfasst die Bundesrepublik Deutschland insgesamt 356 974 km² und hat 82,4 Millionen Einwohner. Seit 1990 ist auch Berlin wieder Hauptstadt. Davor war es Bonn für die Bundesrepublik und Ost-Berlin für die ehemalige DDR (Deutsche Demokratische Republik).

Berlin ist auch die größte Stadt in Deutschland, jetzt mit 3,6 Millionen Einwohnern.

Nach Berlin ist Hamburg die zweitgrößte Stadt mit 1,75 Millionen Einwohnern vor München mit 1,33 Millionen. München ist aber von allen Städten am beliebtesten. Die meisten Deutschen wollen hier leben, denn das Wetter ist meistens schön im Sommer und im Winter sind die Alpen nicht weit. Vielleicht gehen aber auch viele Leute gern in die Biergärten oder aufs Oktoberfest.

Deutschland ist aber auch schon längst eine multikulturelle Gesellschaft: hier leben insgesamt 7,28 Millionen Ausländer, die meisten aus der Türkei (rund 2 Millionen), aber auch Menschen aus dem früheren Jugoslawien, Griechenland, Spanien, Italien, Irland und aus der ehemaligen Sowjetunion. Unter den Ausländern gibt es auch Asylanten aus Ländern wie Afghanistan, Sri Lanka, dem Irak, dem Iran usw. Prozentual hat Frankfurt am Main mit 27 Prozent die meisten Ausländer und ist am multikulturellsten.

2 Beantworten Sie die Fragen.

  a Welches Land ist größer: Österreich oder die Schweiz? _____

  b Wie heißt die Hauptstadt der Schweiz? _____

  c Wie viele offizielle Sprachen gibt es in der Schweiz? _____

  d Wie viele Städte kennen Sie in Österreich? _____

  e Wo ist das Schloss Schönbrunn? _____

  f Wie viele Einwohner hat die Bundesrepublik Deutschland? _____

  g Wie heißt die Hauptstadt von Deutschland? _____

  h Welche Stadt ist größer: Hamburg oder München? _____

  i In welcher Stadt findet das Oktoberfest statt? _____

  j Welche Stadt in Deutschland ist am multikulturellsten? _____

3 Ordnen Sie zu! Put the following features into the correct column.

Wiedervereinigung	Sigmund-Freud-Haus
Mozart-Kugeln	Biergärten
Uhren	Arzneimittel
82,4 Millionen Einwohner	Schloss Schönbrunn
Oktoberfest	viele Leute aus der Türkei
vier Sprachen	8,3 Millionen Einwohner
neue Hauptstadt	multikulturelle Gesellschaft
7,28 Millionen Einwohner	etwa doppelt so groß wie die Schweiz

Schweiz	Österreich	Deutschland
Uhren	Sigmund-Freud-Haus	Wiedervereinigung
_____	_____	_____
_____	_____	_____
_____	_____	_____
_____	_____	_____
		_____

4 Finden Sie die Zahlen.

a Fläche der Bundesrepublik Deutschland: *__356 974 km²__*

b Fläche von Österreich: ____

c Fläche der Schweiz: ____

d Einwohnerzahl von Deutschland: ____

e Einwohnerzahl von Österreich: ____

f Einwohnerzahl der Schweiz: ____

g Deutsche Wiedervereinigung: ____

h Seit wann Berlin Hauptstadt ist: ____

i Ausländeranteil in Frankfurt: ____%

5 **23.03** Read the history of Germany after 1945 and answer the question. Then listen and check your pronunciation.

   a What kind of history does the list focus upon?

     1 natural history   **2** political history   **3** cultural history

---

Die Geschichte Deutschlands nach 1945

1945	Das Ende des 2. Weltkrieges. Deutschland wird in vier Zonen geteilt.
1949	Die Gründung der Bundesrepublik Deutschland in den drei Westzonen. In der Ostzone wird die Deutsche Demokratische Republik gegründet.
1961	Der Bau der Berliner Mauer.
1989	Die Öffnung der Berliner Mauer und der innerdeutschen Grenze.
1990	Am 3. Oktober wird Deutschland offiziell wiedervereinigt. Berlin wird als neue Hauptstadt gewählt.
2005	Angela Merkel wird als erste Frau zur Bundeskanzlerin gewählt.

---

6 **Welche Wörter fehlen? Ergänzen Sie.**

   a 1945 teilen die Alliierten Deutschland in _____ _____ .

   b Ab 1949 gibt es zwei deutsche Staaten: die _____ _____ und die Deutsche Demokratische Republik.

   c 1989 fällt die Berliner _____ .

   d Angela Merkel wird 2005 zur _____ gewählt.

It is quite common in German to use genitive constructions when referring to historical events:

die Gründung der Bundesrepublik	*the founding of the Federal Republic*
der Bau der Mauer	*the building of the Wall*

In this context, it is also common to use passive constructions, often in the present tense: *is divided* → **wird geteilt**, *is founded* → **wird gegründet**.

Language discovery

1 **Look at these sentences from the interview section. Can you figure out where the verbs are placed in clauses introduced by dass (that)?**
   a Ich meine, <u>dass</u> Deutschland ungefähr 82 Millionen Einwohner hat.
   b Ich glaube, <u>dass</u> er aus Österreich kommt.
   c Ich denke, <u>dass</u> St. Moritz in der Schweiz liegt.

2 **Read the text about the history of Germany after 1945 again and identify the missing words. Can you translate the sentences into English?**
   a Deutschland wird in vier Zonen _____ .
   b In der Ostzone wird die Deutsche Demokratische Republik _____ .
   c Am 3. Oktober 1990 wird Deutschland offiziell _____ .
   d Berlin wird als neue Hauptstadt _____ .

Learn more

1 USING DASS (THAT)

The word **dass** can be useful when you want to express an opinion in German. It is very similar to *that* in English, except that **dass** sends the main verb to the end of the sentence or clause.

   Ich denke, **dass** St. Moritz in der Schweiz **liegt**.*

When you use **dass** with the perfect tense, **haben** or **sein** go right at the end:

   Ich glaube, **dass** Frau Schulte in Hamburg **studiert hat**.*

*Note that the **dass** part of the sentence starts with a comma.

You can leave out the word **dass** if you want to. The verb then comes earlier in the sentence:

   Ich denke, St. Moritz **liegt** in der Schweiz.
   Ich glaube, Frau Schulte **hat** in Hamburg **studiert**.
   Ich glaube, Frau Schulte **ist** nach dem Abitur durch Asien **gereist**.

Dass can also be used to report what someone has said:

Er hat gesagt, dass Schwarzenegger aus Österreich kommt.	*He said, that Schwarzenegger comes from Austria.*

Dass can also be used to give an indirect command:

Bitte sag ihm, dass er mich anrufen soll.   *Please tell him to phone me (lit. that he should phone me).*

2 CONJUNCTIONS (THAT, WHEN, BECAUSE, ALTHOUGH)

Words like *that*, *when*, *because*, *although* which join two sentences or clauses together are known as conjunctions:

I am learning German. I often go to Germany. →
I am learning German **because** I often go to Germany.

In German **dass** and **wenn** are examples of conjunctions that change the word order (i.e. the verb is sent to the end of the sentence). Other examples are **weil** (*because*) and **obwohl** (*although*):

Ich lerne Deutsch, **weil** ich oft nach Deutschland **fahre**.
Ich fahre oft nach Italien, **obwohl** ich kein Wort Italienisch **spreche**.

3 THE PASSIVE VOICE

There are usually two ways of looking at an action. The sentence *The cat ate the mouse* is said to be in the *active voice*, whereas *The mouse was eaten by the cat* is in the *passive voice*. The passive is frequently used in the past, for instance to talk about historical events and inventions.

Alexander Fleming entdeckte 1928 das Penizillin.
Das Penizillin wurde 1928 von Alexander Fleming entdeckt.

Both sentences have more or less the same meaning, but it is possible in most passive sentences to omit the agent, the initiator of the action:

Das Penizillin wurde 1928 entdeckt.

This structure therefore lends itself particularly well to:

a scientific and technical processes:

Die Lösung wird in einem Reagenzglas geheizt.   *The solution is heated in a test tube.*
Die Bremsen werden in der Werkstatt geprüft.   *The brakes are tested in the workshop.*

b historical events:

Die Bundesrepublik Deutschland wurde 1949 gegründet.

Here is an overview of how you form the passive in the present tense, the simple past tense and the present perfect tense:

▶ For the present tense, use **werden** (present tense) + past participle of main verb:

Der Text **wird** in unserem Büro **übersetzt.**

*The text is being translated **in our office.***

In der Schweiz **werden** vier Sprachen **gesprochen.**

In Switzerland four languages are spoken.

In German the passive is constructed by using the verb **werden** together with the past participle of the main verb. As a reference here are all *present tense* forms of **werden**:

ich werde	wir werden
du wirst	ihr werdet
Sie werden	Sie werden
er/sie/es wird	sie werden

▶ For the simple past tense, use **wurden** (simple past) + past participle of main verb.

Die Berliner Mauer **wurde** 1961 **gebaut.**

*The Berlin Wall **was built** in 1961.*

Wann **wurden** diese Bücher geschrieben?

*When **were** these books **written**?*

As a reference, here are all *simple past* forms of **werden**:

ich wurde	wir wurden
du wurdest	ihr wurdet
Sie wurden	Sie wurden
er/sie/es wurde	sie wurden

▶ For the present perfect tense, use **worden** + past participle.

Der Euro **ist** 2002 **eingeführt worden.**

*The Euro **was introduced** in 2002.*

Nach der Wiedervereinigung sind viele Häuser restauriert worden.

*After reunification many houses **were restored**.*

Note that when **werden** is not used in a passive structure it can mean *to become*.

Er möchte Rennfahrer **werden.**

*He wants **to become** a racing driver.*

Practice

1 Was denken Sie? Beantworten Sie die Fragen mit Ja, ... oder Nein, ... und benutzen Sie *dass*.

Beispiel: Denken Sie, dass die Schweiz ein teures Land ist?

Ja, ich denke, dass die Schweiz ein teures Land ist. /

Nein, ich denke nicht, dass die Schweiz ein teures Land ist.

a   Glauben Sie, dass die Schweizer langweilig sind? _____

b   Denken Sie, dass die Deutschen viel Bier trinken? _____

c   Glauben Sie, dass man in Berlin gut ausgehen kann ? _____

d   Denken Sie, dass man in Österreich gut Urlaub machen kann?

_____

e   Glauben Sie, dass die Österreicher in bisschen konservativ sind?

_____

2 *Weil* oder *obwohl*? Was passt besser?

a   Herr Groß fährt oft nach Wien, _____ er geschäftlich dort zu tun hat.

b   Claudia gefällt ihr Beruf, _____ sie oft unter Termindruck arbeitet.

c   Sie arbeitet gern im Team, _____ alle Kollegen freundlich sind.

d   Er möchte eine andere Stellung finden, _____ die Bezahlung schlecht ist.

e   Sie lernt Chinesisch, _____ die Sprache sehr schwer ist.

3 Was passierte außerdem in der Welt? Benutzen Sie das Passiv und schreiben Sie die Sätze a-f um.

Beispiele   1949 Mehrere westliche Staaten gründeten die NATO.

1949 wurde die NATO von mehreren westlichen Staaten gegründet.

1963 ermordete man John F. Kennedy.

1963 wurde John F. Kennedy ermordet.

a 1969 betrat zum ersten Mal ein Mensch den Mond.

b 1981 ermordete man John Lennon.

c 1990 entließ man Nelson Mandela nach 27 Jahren aus der Haft.

d 2002 führte man in Europa den Euro als neue Währung ein.

e 2009 wählte man Barack Obama zum Präsidenten der USA.

f 2012 feierte man in London das 60. Thronjubiläum von Queen Elizabeth.

 NEW WORDS

ermorden	*to murder, to assassinate*
betreten	*here: to walk on*
der Mond	*the moon*
entlassen	*to release*
die Haft	*detention, custody*
einlführen	*to introduce*
die Währung (-en)	*currency*

 # Pronunciation

23.04 At the end of a word or syllable the letter **d** in German is pronounced more like an English **t**:

Abend, Freund, Geld, Fahrrad, Land
abendlich, Freundschaft, Geldschein, Radfahrer, Landschaft

When the d is no longer at the end of the word or syllable it is pronounced as an English **d**:

Abende, Freunde, Gelder, Fahrräder, Länder

How would you pronounce these words?
Lied, Lieder, Bad, Bäder, Hund, Hunde.

Listening

 23.05 Hören Sie das folgende Radioprogramm über Johann Wolfgang von Goethe und beantworten Sie die Fragen.

1 **Richtig oder falsch? Korrigieren Sie die falschen Aussagen.**

   a Goethe wurde 1747 in Weimar geboren. _____

   b Er studierte in Leipzig und Straßburg. _____

   c Mit seiner Novelle ‚Die Leiden des jungen Werther' wurde er in Europa bekannt. _____

   d 1780 ging er nach Weimar. _____

   e 1786 reiste er für zwei Jahre nach Italien und Griechenland. _____

   f ‚Faust' ist eines seiner wichtigsten Werke. _____

   g Das Goethe-Institut wurde nach seinem Sohn benannt. _____

2 **Hören Sie die Audioaufnahme noch einmal an und ergänzen Sie dann die Sätze.**

   a Johann Wolfgang von Goethe wurde_____.

   b Er studierte _____.

   c In ganz Europa berühmt wurde er durch _____.

   d 1775 ging er _____.

   e 1786 reiste Goethe _____.

   f 1808 erschien _____.

   g Ein Philosoph verkauft seine Seele _____.

   h 1832 starb er _____.

   i Seine Werke wurden _____.

   j Das Goethe-Institut wurde _____.

NEW WORDS

berühmt	*famous*
übersetzen	*to translate*
die Leiden	*sorrows*
benennen	*to name*
veröffentlichen	*to publish*
die Seele (-n)	*soul*
der Teufel (-)	*devil*

 Speaking

**23.06 Now you can show off your knowledge in this TV quiz show!
Schreiben Sie zuerst Ihre Antworten auf und beantworten Sie dann
die Fragen auf der Audioaufnahme.**

Frage	Wissen Sie denn, wie viele offizielle Sprachen in der Schweiz gesprochen werden?
Sie	*Say yes ... and say how many languages are spoken in Switzerland.*
Frage	Wann wurde die Bundesrepublik Deutschland gegründet?
Sie	*Say the Federal Republic of Germany was founded in ... .*
Frage	Und in welchem Jahr wurde die Berliner Mauer gebaut?
Sie	*Say the Berlin Wall was built ... .*
Frage	Ausgezeichnet. Aber an welchem Tag wurde Deutschland offiziell wiedervereinigt?
Sie	*Say when Germany was reunited.*
Frage	Aber wissen Sie auch, von wem ‚Faust' geschrieben wurde?
Sie	*Say who 'Faust' was written by.*
Frage	Phänomenal! Aber Sie wissen bestimmt nicht, in welchem Jahr es veröffentlicht wurde.
Sie	*Say, of course, and say when it was published.*
Frage	Unglaublich! Aber wissen Sie auch, welche Institution nach Goethe benannt wurde?
Sie	*Say, of course. The Goethe-Institut was named after him.*

 Writing

**Was können Sie über Ihr Land sagen? Schreiben Sie, wie groß Ihr
Land ist, wie viele Einwohner es hat, wie die Hauptstadt heißt, was
für Sehenswürdigkeiten es gibt, welche Sprache(n) es gibt etc.**

> Ich komme aus Großbritannien. Großbritannien
> besteht aus England, Schottland und Wales und hat
> etwa 60 Millionen Einwohner. Die Hauptstadt ist
> London. London ist auch die größte Stadt und …

Go further

Wissen Sie die Antworten? Create appropriate sentences from these components and put your general knowledge to the test.

Beispiel Guernica' wurde von Pablo Picasso gemalt.

a	Die neunte Symphonie		Tim Berners-Lee	geschrieben.
b	Die Fußballweltmeisterschaft 2010		Alexander Fleming	gesungen.
c	Das World Wide Web		Ludwig van Beethoven	gemalt .
d	‚Hamlet'	wurde	Spanien	komponiert.
e	‚Guernica'	von	Helen Mirren	erfunden.
f	Das Penizillin		Pablo Picasso	gespielt.
g	‚Set fire to the rain'		William Shakespeare	gewonnen.
h	Die Queen		Adele	entdeckt.

NEW WORDS

malen	*to paint*
entdecken	*to discover*
erfinden	*to invent*

 Test yourself

1 **Sagen Sie es anders und benutzen Sie *dass*.**
   Beispiel: Ich denke, viele Touristen fahren nach Heidelberg. →
   Ich denke, dass viele Touristen nach Heidelberg fahren.
   a Ich meine, Frankfurt ist das Finanzzentrum von Deutschland.
   b Ich glaube, es gibt in Wien viele alte Kaffeehäuser.
   c Ich denke, München ist eine sehr schöne Stadt.
   d Ich glaube, die Schweizer haben viel Humor.
   e Ich denke, die Deutschen trinken viel Bier.
   f Ich meine, Österreich hat viele schöne Bergregionen.

2 **Warum lernen die Leute Deutsch? Benutzen Sie *weil*. Nicht vergessen – das Verb geht ans Ende.**
   Beispiel Sharon – ihr Partner **kommt aus Zürich.**
   Sharon lernt Deutsch, weil ihr Partner aus Zürich kommt.
   a Paul – er fährt oft geschäftlich nach Frankfurt. → Paul lernt Deutsch, weil er _____ .
   b Susanna – sie liebt die Musik von Mozart und Brahms → Susanna lernt Deutsch, weil _____ .
   c Richard – er lernt gern Sprachen. → Richard lernt Deutsch, weil _____ .

d Carlo – es ist gut für seine berufliche Karriere. →

_____ .

e Myriam – sie findet die deutsche Sprache schön. →

_____ .

f Deborah – sie viele Freunde in Berlin → hat

_____ .

Und Sie? Warum lernen Sie Deutsch? Schreiben Sie.

3 **Deutschland, Österreich und die Schweiz. Ergänzen Sie den Text.**

Bekannt	Hauptstadt	Regionen	Städte	~~Muttersprache~~
Arzneimittel	Gesellschaft	Einwohner	Wiedervereinigung	
Sehenswürdigkeiten	Ausländer	Ländern		

In Deutschland, Österreich und der deutschsprachigen Schweiz
spricht man Deutsch als **a** _Muttersprache_. Man spricht Deutsch
aber auch in anderen **b** _____ , zum Beispiel in Südtirol, Italien.
Von den drei **c** _____ ist die Schweiz am kleinsten. Die **d** _____
ist Bern. **e** _____ ist die Schweiz für ihre Berge, Uhren und
f _____ .
Österreich hat 8,3 Millionen **g** _____ . Die Hauptstadt ist
Wien. Dort gibt es viele **h** _____ , wie zum Beispiel das Schloss
Schönbrunn oder die Hofburg.
Seit der **i** _____ 1990 ist Berlin die Hauptstadt von Deutschland.
Bekannte **j** _____ in Deutschland sind auch Hamburg, München
und Frankfurt.
In Deutschland leben sehr viele **k** _____ . Deutschland ist schon
lange eine multikulturelle **l** _____ .

SELF CHECK

I CAN. . .
○ . . . talk about German-speaking countries and cities.
○ . . . say something about my own country.
○ . . . use **dass, weil** and **obwohl** to express an opinion.
○ . . . use conjunctions to join sentences.
○ . . . express events in both the active and the passive voices.

Listening comprehension transcripts

Polizist	Wie heißen Sie, bitte?
Frau Gruber	Ich heiße Gertrud Gruber.
Polizist	Gruber, Gertrud ... Und Sie? Wie ist Ihr Name?
Herr Braun	Mein Name ist Braun, Martin Braun.
Polizist	Braun, Martin ... Und Sie? Wie heißen Sie?
Herr Schwarz	Ich heiße Boris Schwarz.
Polizist	Schwarz, Boris ...

UNIT 1: INTRODUCTION

69

Wie heißen Sie?

Woher kommen Sie?

Und wo wohnen Sie jetzt?

UNIT 1: LISTENING AND WRITING

1

- Guten Abend, verehrte Zuschauer ...
- Radio Bayern. Guten Morgen, liebe Zuhörer ...
- Hallo, schön' guten Morgen ...
- Gute Nacht, liebe Zuhörer ...
- Guten Tag. Hier ist die Tagesschau ...
- Unser Programm geht jetzt zu Ende. Wir wünschen Ihnen eine gute Nacht.

UNIT 2: LISTENING

Frau Bachmann	Guten Tag, Frau Huber!
Frau Huber	Tag, Frau Bachmann! Und wie geht's Ihnen?
Frau Bachmann	Na ja ... Mir geht es heute nicht so gut.
Frau Huber	Das tut mir aber leid.
Frau Bachmann	Und Ihnen? Wie geht's Ihnen denn?
Frau Huber	Mir geht's wirklich sehr gut ... Oh, da kommt Herr Dietz!
Bachmann u. Huber	Tag, Herr Dietz!
Herr Dietz	Tag, Frau Huber! Tag, Frau Bachmann!
Frau Huber	Und wie geht's heute?
Herr Dietz	Ach, es geht.

UNIT 3: VOCABULARY BUILDER

3

Die weiteren Ergebnisse vom 33. Spieltag:

Hamburg–Dortmund: 2 zu 1

Bochum–Hannover: 6 zu 0

Duisburg–Mönchengladbach: 4 zu 2

Bielefeld–Wolfsburg: 1 zu 3

Schalke–Freiburg: 0 zu 2

Nürnberg–Hertha Berlin: 3 zu 0

Bremen–Frankfurt: 1 zu 0

UNIT 3: THE ALPHABET

2

– Guten Tag! Wie heißen Sie, bitte?

– Baumgart, Waltraud.

– Wie schreibt man das?

– B-A-U-M-G-A-R-T.

– Ja, gut. Sie stehen auf der Liste.

– Guten Tag! Mein Name ist Schanze, Martin Schanze.

– Und wie buchstabiert man Schanze?

– S-C-H-A-N-Z-E.

– Ja, Sie sind auch auf der Liste.

– Hallo! Mein Name ist Hesse, H-E-S-S-E.

- Danke. Ja, hier ist Ihr Name.
- Und ich heiße Schidelowskaja S-C-H-I-D-E ...
- Ist schon gut! Sie sind auch dabei, Frau Schidelowskaja!

UNIT 3: SPEAKING

2

Welche Telefonnummer haben Sie?

Wie ist Ihre Handynummer?

Wie ist Ihre Faxnummer?

Wie ist Ihre E-Mail-Adresse?

Here is how Jochen replies:

Jochen	Meine Telefonnummer ist null – sieben – elf – dreiundzwanzig – achtunddreißig – einundvierzig. Meine Handynummer ist 01734 06 02 94. Meine Faxnummer ist null – sieben – elf – vierundzwanzig – neunundachtzig – null – zwo. Meine E-Mail-Adresse ist jkrause@yahoo.at

UNIT 3: LISTENING

1

Und nun der Bericht von der Börse aus Frankfurt. Ein guter Tag für die AEG, plus 9 Punkte. Von der Autoindustrie ist Positives zu vermelden: BMW legte um 3 Prozent zu und auch VW meldet ein leichtes Plus. Dagegen ein schlechter Tag für die Banken: Deutsche Bank minus 5 Prozent und die DZ Bank minus 7. Nichts Neues von der Bahn: die DB meldete plus minus 0.

UNIT 3: LISTENING

2

Kunde	Guten Tag. Ich hätte gern die Telefonnummer von Berta Schulz in Hamburg.
Frauenstimme	Schulz? Wie schreibt man das, bitte?
Kunde	S-C-H-U-L-Z.
Frauenstimme	Vorname Berta?
Kunde	Ja, richtig.
Computerstimme	Die Nummer ist 040-30 07 51.
Kunde	Hallo. Ich brauche die Nummer von Günter Marhenke hier in Hamburg.

Frauenstimme	Marhenke? Wie buchstabiert man das?
Kunde	M-A-R-H-E-N-K-E.
Frauenstimme	Können Sie das wiederholen?
Kunde	Ja, kein Problem: M-A-R-H-E-N-K-E.
Computerstimme	Die Nummer ist 040-73 45 92.

UNIT 3: GO FURTHER

38 Die Lottozahlen

Die Lottozahlen: 6 8 14 23 26 46, und die Zusatzzahl: 22.

UNIT 4: SPEAKING

1

Interviewer	Wie heißen Sie?
Jürgen	Ich heiße Jürgen Krause.
Interviewer	Sind Sie Deutscher?
Jürgen	Nein, ich bin Österreicher.
Interviewer	Woher kommen Sie?
Jürgen	Ich komme aus Wien.
Interviewer	Und wo wohnen Sie jetzt?
Jürgen	Ich wohne jetzt in Salzburg.
Interviewer	Was sprechen Sie?
Jürgen	Ich spreche Deutsch und Englisch.
Interviewer	Sind Sie verheiratet?
Jürgen	Nein, ich bin seit drei Jahren verwitwet.
Interviewer	Arbeiten Sie?
Jürgen	Ja, ich arbeite in Salzburg.

UNIT 4: SPEAKING

2

Wie ist Ihr Name?

Woher kommen Sie?

Wo wohnen Sie jetzt?

Sind Sie Amerikaner oder Amerikanerin?

Ist Ihre Muttersprache Englisch?

Verstehen Sie ein bisschen Deutsch?

Sind Sie verheiratet?

Studieren Sie?

Dialog 1

| Gür | Hallo! Mein Name ist Gür Yalezan. Ich bin Türke und komme aus Berlin. Ich wohne jetzt in der Nähe von Leipzig, in Taucha. Ich spreche Türkisch, Deutsch und ziemlich gut Englisch. Ich bin ledig und studiere in Leipzig. |

Dialog 2

| Susi | Ich heiße Susi Merkl – das buchstabiert man S-U-S-I und M-E-R-K-L – und bin Österreicherin. Ich komme aus Innsbruck, wohne aber jetzt in Rötha, hier in der Nähe von Leipzig. Ich spreche Deutsch und Englisch und ich verstehe ein bisschen Spanisch. Ich bin seit vier Jahren verheiratet und arbeite zurzeit hier in Leipzig. |

UNIT 6: SPEAKING

Interviewer	Sind Sie Deutsche?
Gudrun	Ja, ich bin Deutsche.
Interviewer	Ist Ihr Mann auch Deutscher?
Gudrun	Nein, er ist Ire.
Interviewer	Und wo wohnen Sie?
Gudrun	Ich wohne seit 17 Jahren in Münster.
Interviewer	Sind Sie berufstätig?
Gudrun	Ja, ich bin Sekretärin bei Mannesmann.
Interviewer	Und was ist Ihr Mann von Beruf?
Gudrun	Er ist Taxifahrer.

UNIT 6: LISTENING

Jochen	Willkommen in Dresden! Mein Name ist Jochen Krenzler. Können Sie vielleicht Deutsch?
Rainer	Guten Tag! Ja, ich spreche Deutsch. Ich heiße Rainer Tietmeyer.
Jochen	Das ist ja großartig! Sind Sie denn Deutscher?

Rainer	Ja, aber meine Frau ist Engländerin und ich wohne seit 24 Jahren in England.
Jochen	Ach so. Und was sind Sie von Beruf?
Rainer	Ich bin Tischler.

UNIT 6: GO FURTHER

4

Heike	Hallo! Ich heiße Heike und das ist Martina. Wie heißt ihr?
Paul	Hallo! Ich heiße Paul und komme aus Bremen.
Daniel	Grüß euch! Ich bin der Daniel und komme aus Hamburg. Und woher kommt ihr?

Heike	Ich komme aus Düsseldorf und Martina kommt aus Köln. Seid ihr Studenten?
Paul	Ja, wir studieren in Bremen. Ich studiere Germanistik.
Daniel	Und ich Anglistik. Ihr seid wohl auch Studenten?
Heike	Ja, in Aachen. Ich studiere Informatik und Martina studiert Mathematik.

UNIT 8: GO FURTHER

– Was kostet eine Flasche Wein?
– 4 Euro 90.

Und jetzt Sie!
– Was kostet ein Roggenbrot?
– 1 Euro 10.
– Und wie teuer ist eine Flasche Olivenöl?
– 5 Euro 40.
– Was kostet eine Dose Tomaten?
– 89 Cent.
– Und eine Packung Müsli?
– 1 Euro 65.

- Und was kosten die Äpfel?
- 1 Kilo 2 Euro 5.
- Und wie teuer ist der Emmentaler Käse?
- 1 Kilo 12 Euro 25.
- Und was kostet ein Blumenkohl?
- 1 Euro 95.

UNIT 9: LISTENING

6 Was ist ihr Hobby?

Interview 1

| Reporter | Guten Tag. Wir sind vom Radio und machen eine Umfrage. Was ist Ihr Hobby, bitte? |
| Touristin | Mein Hobby? Also, mein Hobby ist mein Garten. Und ich wandere gern. |

Interview 2

Reporter	Entschuldigen Sie, bitte. Haben Sie ein Hobby?
Tourist	Ein Hobby? Ja, ich schwimme gern, ich gehe gern ins Kino und ich lese gern.
Reporter	Lesen Sie gern Krimis?
Tourist	Nein, ich lese nicht gern Krimis. Ich lese gern Romane und Biographien.

UNIT 10: DIE 12-STUNDEN-UHR

3 & 4

Dialog 1

Female voice	Mmh. Das riecht ja lecker. Ist das Essen fertig?
Male voice	Es dauert noch einen kleinen Moment, Schatz. Wie spät ist es denn?
Female voice	Genau 6 Uhr 28.

Dialog 2

Female voice	Richard, aufstehen! Es ist schon zehn vor neun!
Male voice	Was? Zehn vor neun? Nein, das glaube ich nicht.
Female voice	Doch. Doch. Aufstehen.

Dialog 3

Female voice	Anke, weißt du wie spät es ist?
Female voice	Ja, es ist halb fünf.

Dialog 4

Male voice 1	Entschuldigung, wie viel Uhr ist es, bitte?
Male voice 2	Äh, Viertel vor neun.
Male voice 1	Vielen Dank.
Male voice 2	Gern geschehen.

UNIT 10: MORGENS ODER ABENDS?

2 Sagen Sie die Uhrzeit.

Es ist ein Uhr mittags. / Es ist vier Uhr nachmittags. / Es ist acht Uhr abends. / Es ist elf Uhr abends. / Es ist neun Uhr morgens. / Es ist sechs Uhr morgens.

UNIT 10:

3

Es ist dreizehn Uhr. / Es ist fünfzehn Uhr zwanzig. / Es ist sieben Uhr fünfundvierzig. / Es ist achtzehn Uhr zwölf. / Es ist dreiundzwanzig Uhr fünfunddreißig. / Es ist vier Uhr siebzehn.

UNIT 10: PRACTICE

Renate	Herr Fabione, Sie arbeiten als Automechaniker in einer Autowerkstatt. Wie sieht denn ein typischer Tag bei Ihnen aus?
Harr Fabione	Nun, normalerweise stehe ich früh auf, so gegen halb sieben Uhr. Oft kaufe ich morgens frische Brötchen und frühstücke mit meiner Frau und den Kindern.
Renate	Wann fängt denn Ihre Arbeit an?
Herr Fabione	Um acht Uhr.
Renate	Wie lange arbeiten Sie denn?
Herr Fabione	Bis 16 Uhr.
Renate	Und haben Sie eine Pause?
Herr Fabione	Nun, Mittagspause machen wir um 12 Uhr.
Renate	So, Feierabend ist so gegen vier. Was machen Sie denn dann?

Herr Fabione	Tja, ich fahre nach Hause und spiele oft mit den Kindern. Manchmal gehen wir in den Park oder spielen Fußball.
Renate	Und wann essen Sie zu Abend?
Herr Fabione	Meistens um halb sieben. Danach bringen wir dann die Kinder ins Bett.
Renate	Bleiben Sie zu Hause oder gehen Sie oft aus?
Herr Fabione	Oft bleiben wir zu Hause. Wir sehen nicht viel fern, wir lesen viel und meine Frau und ich lernen im Moment auch zusammen Spanisch. Manchmal kommt meine Schwiegermutter als Babysitterin und passt auf die Kinder auf. Dann gehen meine Frau und ich aus, ins Kino oder ins Restaurant oder wir besuchen Freunde.
Renate	Und wann gehen Sie normalerweise ins Bett?
Herr Fabione	Meistens um halb 12, manchmal erst später.

UNIT 13: LISTENING

1 and 2

Angela	Hallo, Ulrike. Na, wie geht's?
Ulrike	Ganz gut, ich bin noch ein bisschen müde.
Angela	Oh, habe ich dich geweckt?
Ulrike	Nein, nein, ich habe gerade gefrühstückt.
Angela	Gerade gefrühstückt? Was hast du denn gestern gemacht?
Ulrike	Am Morgen war ich in der Stadt und habe eingekauft. Am Nachmittag habe ich Britta und Georg besucht. Am Abend waren wir dann zusammen in der neuen ‚Mondschein-Bar' und haben bis drei Uhr getanzt. Wir haben viel Spaß gehabt. Und du?
Angela	Ich habe gestern Morgen einen neuen Computer gekauft und, na ja, dann den ganzen Tag mit dem Computer gespielt.
Ulrike	Hast du auch im Internet gesurft?
Angela	Genau, das war schon interessant.
Ulrike	Und wie viel hast du für den Computer bezahlt?
Angela	€900. Er hat €100 weniger gekostet.
Ulrike	Und was habt ihr am Abend gemacht?
Angela	Bernd und ich haben gekocht und dann noch ein bisschen klassische Musik gehört. Ganz romantisch; wie früher, weißt du. Was machst du denn heute, Ulrike?
Ulrike	Tja, ich weiß noch nicht so genau. Vielleicht können wir ja …

UNIT 14: LISTENING

15 Mehr über Peter Wichtig

Moderator	Herr Wichtig, vielen Dank, dass Sie heute zu uns ins Studio kommen konnten. Ich weiß, Sie sind sehr busy im Moment.
Peter Wichtig	Ja, das stimmt. Wir bereiten eine neue Tournee vor und wir haben gerade eine neue CD auf dem Markt.
Moderator	Ja, bevor wir Ihren neuen Song spielen, Herr Wichtig, ein paar Fragen zu Ihrer Person. Wie lange machen Sie denn schon Musik?
Peter Wichtig	Seit 10 Jahren genau. Auch meinen ersten Hit habe ich genau vor 10 Jahren geschrieben: ‚Um acht Uhr aus dem Bett, das finde ich nicht nett.' Wir haben 400.000 CDs verkauft.
Moderator	Und wie viele CDs haben Sie insgesamt gemacht?
Peter Wichtig	Insgesamt 10. Jedes Jahr eine, das ist nicht schlecht, oder?
Moderator	Schreiben Sie alle Lieder selber?
Peter Wichtig	Ja, ich komponiere die Musik und schreibe auch die Texte, klar.
Moderator	Sie sind ein Allround-Mensch, Herr Wichtig, schreiben und komponieren, geben viele Interviews, gehen zweimal im Jahr auf Tournee, haben Sie denn überhaupt Freizeit?
Peter Wichtig	Wenig, wenig.
Moderator	Und wenn, was machen Sie dann?
Peter Wichtig	Im Winter fahre ich gern Ski. Und im Sommer, nun ich surfe, spiele Tennis – ich bin ein guter Freund von Boris. Und dann die vielen Partys, New York, Berlin, Nairobi, Los Angeles, Monte Carlo... Und die vielen Freunde, die ich sehen muss: Robert de Niro, Michelle Pfeiffer, meinen Kollegen Mick Jagger, Claudia Schiffer, Franz Beckenbauer...
Moderator	Äh, Herr Wichtig, ich muss Sie leider unterbrechen, aber wir müssen im Programm weitermachen. Hier ist also die neueste Single von Peter Wichtig: ‚Dich kann man vergessen' – aah, pardon: ‚Ich kann dich nicht vergessen'. Puh.

UNIT 14: GO FURTHER

Bernd	Hallo, Dieter, na, 25 Jahre ist das her. Kaum zu glauben.
Dieter	Tja, 25 Jahre, und du hast immer noch so lange Haare wie früher, Bernd. Fantastisch. Ich dagegen, na, kein Haar mehr, schon seit fünf Jahren und dabei hatte ich früher auch so schöne, lange Haare.

Bernd	Na komm, Dieter, charmant wie Yul Brynner. Sag mal, trinkst du denn immer noch so gern Rum und Cola wie früher?
Dieter	Cola und Rum, oh, das ist lange her. Nein, ich trinke jetzt sehr gern Wein, französischen Wein. Aber sag mal Bernd, du trinkst Mineralwasser? Früher hast du doch immer Viel Kognak getrunken, das war doch dein Lieblingsgetränk.
Bernd	Ja, das stimmt. Aber, na ja, mein Arzt hat gesagt, ich soll mit dem Alkohol aufhören. Und jetzt trinke ich eben mehr Wasser, Tee, Orangensaft, weißt du. Hörst du eigentlich immer noch so gern Blues-Musik, du hast doch damals alle Platten von Eric Clapton gehabt, oder?
Dieter	Ja, das ist lange her. Am meisten höre ich jetzt klassische Musik, vor allem Beethoven. Und du, immer noch der Elvis-Fan?
Bernd	Elvis forever, haha. Nein, Rock'n Roll höre ich nicht mehr. Ich höre viel Jazz-Musik.
Dieter	Und machst du noch selber Musik? Du hast doch früher in einer Band gespielt?
Bernd	Nein, das ist lange vorbei. Wenn ich Zeit habe, reise ich. Letzten Monat war ich erst für eine Woche in Moskau. Du warst doch früher ein guter Fußballspieler?
Dieter	Tja, das stimmt, aber im Moment spiele ich nur noch Tennis, ich bereite mich auf Wimbledon vor, haha. Guck mal, da drüben ist Gerd.
Bernd	Hallo, Gerd, na, wie geht es ...

UNIT 15: SPEAKING

1

Moderator	Wohnen Sie in einem Haus oder in einer Wohnung?
Frau Martini	Wir wohnen in einer Wohnung.
Moderator	Wie viele Zimmer hat die Wohnung?
Frau Martini	Die Wohnung hat vier Zimmer, plus Küche und Bad.
Moderator	Wie sind die Zimmer?
Frau Martini	Die Zimmer sind groß und hell.
Moderator	Haben Sie einen Garten?
Frau Martini	Nein, wir haben leider keinen Garten.
Moderator	Ist die Miete oder die Hypothek teuer?
Frau Martini	Die Miete ist nicht so teuer, 465 Euro, plus Nebenkosten.

Moderator	Wie ist die Umgebung?
Frau Martini	Die Umgebung ist ruhig und sehr grün.
Moderator	Haben Sie gute Verkehrsverbindungen?
Frau Martini	Ja, die Verkehrsverbindungen sind sehr gut.
Moderator	Wie lange fahren Sie zur Arbeit?
Frau Martini	Ich fahre nur 10 Minuten zur Arbeit.
Moderator	Fahren Sie mit dem Auto, mit dem Bus oder mit der U-Bahn?
Frau Martini	Ich fahre mit der U-Bahn. Im Sommer kann ich mit dem Fahrrad fahren.

UNIT 17: LISTENING

Interviewer	... Und Sie Frau Martens. Sind Sie berufstätig?
Frau Martens	Ja, ich bin Verkäuferin in der Kaufhalle hier in Hanau. Ich arbeite seit sieben Jahren dort und finde meinen Beruf eigentlich ganz interessant.
Interviewer	Interessant, aber sicher auch anstrengend?
Frau Martens	Ich arbeite nur halbtags, von acht Uhr bis um 12.30 Uhr. Meine Arbeit ist also nicht besonders anstrengend. Doch wenn meine Kinder um eins nach Hause kommen – dann wird's anstrengend! Und wenn mein Sohn im Fernsehen ein neues Computerspiel sieht – dann muss er das unbedingt haben! Die eine Tochter möchte neue Schuhe von Bruno Magli, die andere eine neue Jeans-Jacke von Calvin Klein.
Interviewer	Und für Sie? Ist Mode auch für Sie wichtig?
Frau Martens	Ich persönlich finde Mode uninteressant. Ich ziehe nur an, was ich mag.
Interviewer	Und wie sind im Allgemeinen die Kunden?
Frau Martens	Wir haben meistens ganz nette Kunden. Nur selten sind sie unfreundlich. Also, ich versuche dann immer, besonders freundlich zu sein.

2

Dialog 1

Richard	Was tragen Sie denn normalerweise für Kleidung bei der Arbeit?
Mareike	Ich arbeite in einem Büro und die Atmosphäre ist sehr relaxed. Normalerweise trage ich eine bequeme Hose, meistens mit einer Bluse, wenn es kälter ist, mit einem Pulli.
Richard	Und zu Hause?
Mareike	Eigentlich dasselbe. Eine Hose, oft auch eine Jeans – bei der Arbeit trage ich kaum Jeans – T-Shirt, Pullover. Ich mag bequeme Sachen. Eigentlich trage ich alles, was bequem ist. Was ich aber nicht mag sind Röcke. Röcke ziehe ich fast überhaupt nicht an.

Dialog 2

Richard	Herr Scholz, was tragen Sie denn normalerweise bei der Arbeit?
Günther	Bei der Arbeit trage ich immer einen Anzug, meistens einen dunkelblauen. Dazu ein weißes Hemd und eine Krawatte.
Richard	Und zu Hause?
Günther	Zu Hause, nun, etwas Bequemeres, ein sportliches Hemd oder ein Poloshirt.
Richard	Gibt es etwas, was Sie nicht gerne anziehen?
Günther	Nun, wie gesagt, ich trage sehr gern sportliche Kleidung in meiner Freizeit, ich spiele auch Golf und Tennis. Ich mag elegante Kleidung, was ich nicht mag ist bunte Kleidung. rote Hemden, Hawaii-Hemden, bunte Hosen und solche Sachen.

UNIT 18: LISTENING

Was bringen wir der Familie mit?

Saskia	Was für ein Stress, jetzt müssen wir auch noch nach den Geschenken suchen. Wir haben mal wieder bis zum letzten Tag gewartet.
Sys	Na ja, das ist ja nichts Neues. Aber was kaufen wir bloß?
Saskia	Wie wär's mit einer kleinen Freiheitsstatue für Mutti? Sie mag solche Sachen.

	Und Vati? Was bringen wir ihm mit? Das ist doch schwierig, oder?
Sys	Vati sieht gern Baseball-Spiele im Fernsehen. Kaufen wir ihm doch einfach eine Baseball-Mütze von den New York Yankees.
Saskia	Toll! Vati mit einer Baseball-Mütze – das möchte ich sehen!
Sys	Und Oma hat gesagt, sie möchte einen neuen Bademantel.
Saskia	Gut, dann schenken wir ihr einen Bademantel. Hoffentlich ist er aber nicht zu teuer.
Sys	Oh, Tante Heidi müssen wir Turnschuhe von Nike kaufen. Nike-Turnschuhe sind in Amerika viel billiger als in Europa.
Saskia	Und Onkel Georg sammelt U-Bahn-Pläne. Ihm können wir einen U-Bahn-Plan von New York mitbringen.
Sys	Das wär's also. Gehen wir schnell einkaufen. Und vergiss nicht, deine Kreditkarte mitzunehmen!

UNIT 20: WEATHER

3

Bärbel Specht	Wir waren diesen Frühling auf Kreta. Das war fantastisch. Ich war einmal im Sommer dort, oh, das war nicht auszuhalten: über 40 Grad. Aber diesmal: meistens so um 28 Grad. Ideal. Und auch kein Regen. Jeden Tag Sonne und ein leichter Wind. Zum Windsurfen war das wirklich toll. Das kann ich nur jedem empfehlen. Kreta im Frühling: Das ist ein Erlebnis.
Jutta Weiß	Mein Traum war es immer, einmal nach Australien zu fahren und eine alte Schulfreundin von mir dort zu besuchen. Und letzten Dezember hat es endlich geklappt, da hatte ich Zeit und auch genug Geld. In Deutschland war Winter, minus 12 Grad, alle haben hier gefroren, und als ich in Sydney ankam, da war dort Sommer: über 35 Grad. Und Weihnachten haben wir im T-Shirt gefeiert, die machen dort Straßenpartys, unglaublich. Drei Wochen nur Sonne, nur manchmal hat es ein Gewitter gegeben. Aber – ganz ehrlich – mir war das manchmal einfach zu heiß.

UNIT 20: LISTENING

Nun die Wettervorhersage für Sonntag, den 25. Mai. Nachts kühlt es bis auf 6 Grad ab. Tagsüber im Südosten 23, in den übrigen Gebieten 13 bis 20 Grad Celsius. Die weiteren Aussichten: Montag im Norden und Osten Wolken und Regen. Dienstag in ganz Deutschland Schauer. Am Mittwoch ab und zu sonnige Abschnitte, und nur noch im Osten Schauer.

Dialog 1

Receptionist	Berchtesmeier und Company. Guten Tag. Was kann ich für Sie tun?
Herr Giesecke	Guten Tag. Giesecke von der Firma Krönke, Maschinenbau. Könnte ich bitte mit Frau Dr. Martens sprechen?
Receptionist	Einen Moment bitte, ich verbinde ... (Pause) Herr Giescke, es tut mir leid, aber Frau Dr. Martens telefoniert gerade. Die Leitung ist besetzt. Wollen Sie warten?
Herr Giesecke	Äh, Giesecke, mit e, nicht Giescke.
Receptionist	Oh. Entschuldigung, Herr Giesecke.
Herr Giesecke	Wie lange kann es denn dauern?
Receptionist	Ja, das ist schwer zu sagen. Soll ich Frau Dr. Martens vielleicht etwas ausrichten? Oder soll sie Sie zurückrufen?
Herr Giesecke	Nein, nein, nein. Das ist nicht nötig. Ich rufe später noch mal an. Auf Wiederhören.
Receptionist	Auf Wiederhören, Herr Giescke ... äh (Pause). Puh.

Dialog 2

Nadine möchte ihre Freundin, Sandy, sprechen. Hören Sie zu.

Nadine	Hallo, Frau Stoll, hier ist Nadine. Ist die Sandy da?
Frau Stoll	Hallo, Nadine. Na, wie geht's dir?
Nadine	Ganz gut, danke.
Frau Stoll	Das ist ja schön, Nadine. Aber leider ist die Sandy im Augenblick nicht da.
Nadine	Oh, das ist schade. Wo ist sie denn?
Frau Stoll	Sie ist gerade beim Zahnarzt.
Nadine	Oh, nein. Wann kommt sie denn wieder?
Frau Stoll	Ich denke, so in einer Stunde. Soll sie dich dann zurückrufen?
Nadine	Ja, das wäre toll. Ich bin zu Hause.
Frau Stoll	Gut, ich sage es ihr. Und grüß deine Familie.
Nadine	Klar, das mache ich.
Frau Stoll	Tschüss, Nadine.
Nadine	Tschüss, Frau Stoll.

Dialog 3

Corinna	Hallo Peterle, bist du's?
Herr Schulz	Äh, meinen Sie Herrn Fink? Der ist im Moment nicht da, der ist auf Geschäftsreise.
Corinna	Oh, äh, das wusste ich gar nicht.
Herr Schulz	Ja, er musste für drei Tage nach Wien.
Corinna	Wann kommt er denn wieder?
Herr Schulz	Wahrscheinlich morgen. Wollen Sie vielleicht eine Nachricht hinterlassen?
Corinna	Wenn das geht, ja, gerne.
Herr Schulz	Natürlich. Kein Problem.
Corinna	Können Sie ihm sagen, Corinna hat angerufen und er soll mich morgen zurückrufen. Ich habe ein fantastisches Geschenk für ihn.
Herr Schulz	Gut. Das sage ich ihm.
Corinna	Vielen Dank. Auf Wiederhören.
Herr Schulz	Auf Wiederhören.

UNIT 22: PRACTICE

2

Frau Schulte Mein Name ist Claudia Schulte und im Moment lebe und arbeite ich in Hamburg. Geboren bin ich aber 1983 in Bremen, wo ich dann auch zur Schule gegangen bin und zwar zunächst von 1989 bis 1993 auf die Grundschule und danach aufs Heinrich-Heine-Gymnasium. Nach dem Abitur 2002 war ich dann nicht so sicher, was ich eigentlich machen sollte und habe dann ein bisschen gejobbt, um genug Geld zu haben und bin dann für ein Jahr durch Asien gereist. Das war eine wichtige Erfahrung für mich.

Als ich dann nach Deutschland zurückgekommen bin, habe ich mit etwas Glück eine Praktikumsstelle bei der *Hamburger Zeitung* gefunden und dort für zwei Jahre, von 2003 bis 2004 als Praktikantin gearbeitet.

Nach den zwei Jahren Praxis habe ich dann ein Studium an der Universität Hamburg angefangen und von 2004 bis 2009 studiert, nebenbei natürlich für verschiedene Zeitungen geschrieben.

Nach dem Studium habe ich gleich eine Stelle bei der *Tageszeitung* in Berlin gefunden und dort drei Jahre – von 2009 bis 2012 – gearbeitet.

Seit 2012 arbeite ich beim *Spiegel*, wieder in Hamburg – das ist natürlich ein Traum für jeden Journalisten.

UNIT 23: LISTENING

Johann Wolfgang von Goethe gilt heute über 175 Jahre nach seinem Tod als einer der universalen Repräsentanten europäischer Kultur. Geboren am 28.8.1749 in Frankfurt am Main, erhielt er als Kind Privatunterricht und ging dann auf die Universitäten von Leipzig und Straßburg, wo er Jura studierte. Beeinflusst wurde er durch einen anderen bekannten Schriftsteller, Johann Gottfried Herder, der ihn dazu bewegte, zu schreiben.

Berühmt wurde Goethe 1774 durch seine Novelle ‚Die Leiden des jungen Werther', die ihn über Nacht in ganz Europa bekannt machte.

1775 ging Goethe an den Hof von Weimar, wo er in den Staatsdienst eintrat und auch politisch tätig wurde. Weiterhin schrieb er Theaterstücke und andere Werke.

1786 reiste er für zwei Jahre nach Italien und wurde stark vom Klassizismus beeinflusst. Zurück in Weimar begann er eine sehr produktive Zeit: Er veröffentlichte Bücher über naturwissenschaftliche Themen und schrieb einige seiner bekanntesten Werke. 1808 erschien dann sein wohl bekanntestes Theaterstück ‚Faust', in dem ein Wissenschaftler und Philosoph seine Seele an den Teufel verkauft. Bis zu seinem Tod 1832 in Weimar blieb Goethe ein äußerst produktiver Schriftsteller, dessen Werke in fast alle Sprachen übersetzt wurden. Das Goethe-Institut, das Kulturinstitut Deutschlands, ist nach ihm benannt.

ANSWER KEY

Unit 1

Discovery questions: Mr is Herr; Mrs is Frau; You say Grüß Gott in Austria, southern Germany, Servus in Austria and Grüezi in Switzerland.
Vocabulary builder 2: Good evening. My name is … **3 Sample answer: a** Hallo. Mein Name ist Ruth Laufer. **b.** Hallo. Ich heiße Ruth Laufer. 4 **a** 3; **b** 1; **c** 4; **d** 2.

5

	Guten Morgen	Guten Tag	Guten Abend	Gute Nacht
14:00		✔		
8:00	✔			
23.00				✔
11.00		✔		
18.00			✔	

Introductions 1 a Wie heißen Sie? **b** Wie ist Ihr Name? **2** name; you
3 a Gertrud Gruber; **b** Martin Braun; **c** Boris Schwarz **4 a** True; **b** False;
c True; **d** True. **5** I; from **Interviews 1 a** Where do you come from?
b Where do you live? **2**

Name	Geburtsort	Wohnort
Ich heiße ...	Ich komme aus ...	Ich wohne jetzt in ...
Jochen Kern	Aachen	Bonn
Dana Frye	Stuttgart	Hannover

Language discovery 1: Sie means you; Ich means I **2** The –en endings
goes with Sie and the –e ending with ich: **a** kommen; **b** komme; **c** wohnen;
d wohne. **Practice: 1** en; en; en **2** e; e; e **Listening and writing 6:** Six
greetings. Guten Abend; Guten Morgen (x2); Gute Nacht (x2); Guten Tag.
Test yourself 1: a 2; **b** 1; **c** 2 **2 a** Wie; **b** Wo; **c** Woher; **d** Wie **3 a** -e, -en;
b –e, -en; **c** –e, -en **4** Sie; Ich; Sie; Ich

Unit 2

Discovery questions: Deutschland means Germany, München Munich,
Österreich Austria, Wien Vienna and die Schweiz Switzerland. The word for
German is Deutsch. **Vocabulary builder: Saying how you are 2 a**3; **b**5;
c6; **d**2; **e**4; **f**8; **g**7; **h**1 **Conversations 1** Conversation 3 **2**

	ausgezeichnet	sehr gut	gut	es geht	nicht so gut	schlecht
Frau Renger			✔			
Frau Müller		✔				
Herr Schulz					✔	
Frau Koch				✔		
Herr Krämer	✔					
Herr Akdag				✔		

3 a Rainer Görner comes from Berlin (in Germany). **b** Martina Schümer comes from Basle (in Switzerland). **c** Susanne Vermeulen comes from Brussels (in Belgium). **d** Michael Naumann comes from Leipzig (in Germany). **4 a** richtig **b** falsch; Zürich liegt nicht in Österreich, sondern in der Schweiz. **c** richtig **d** falsch; Susanne Vermeulen kommt nicht aus Delft in den Niederlanden, sondern aus Brüssel in Belgien. **e** richtig **f** falsch; Michael Naumann kommt nicht aus Dresden, sondern aus Leipzig. Er wohnt jetzt nicht in Linz, sondern in Salzburg, Österreich. **Language discovery 1** Er means he, sie means she and es means it. **2** Er, sie and es all have a –t ending: **a** kommt; **b** wohnt; **c** kommt; **d** liegt. **Practice 1 a** Danke, mir geht's sehr gut. **b** Mir geht's heute schlecht./Mir geht's heute nicht so gut. **c** Ach, es geht. **d** Mir geht's heute nicht so gut./Mir geht's heute schlecht. **2 a** -t; **b** -t; **c** -t; **d** -et **3 b** Nein, Wien liegt nicht in Deutschland. **c** Nein, sie heißt nicht Claudia. **d** Nein, Frankfurt liegt nicht in Österreich. **e** Nein, ich komme nicht aus Berlin. **f** Nein, sie arbeitet nicht im Hotel Lindenhof. **4** ein, mein, in, sie, geht, es, prima, aus, ausgezeichnet, ich, wirklich, wir, noch, heute, er, nicht, danke, sehr, gut. **Did you find any others? Let us know if you did! Listening** e, c, b. **Go further 1** BELgien; DÄNemark; DEUTSCHland; GroßbriTANNien; IRland; ITALien; SPANien; die TürkEI. The first syllable is most often stressed. GroßbriTANNien, ITALien and die TürkEI do not fit into this category. **2 a** richtig; **b** falsch; Heidelberg liegt nicht in Österreich, sondern in Deutschland. **c** falsch; Köln liegt nicht in den Niederlanden, sondern in Deutschland. **d** richtig; **e** falsch; Amsterdam liegt nicht in Belgien, sondern in den Niederlanden. **Writing**

a Naomi Campbell kommt aus Großbritannien. Sie wohnt jetzt in den USA. **b** Johnny Depp kommt aus den USA. Er wohnt jetzt in Frankreich. **c** Karl Lagerfeld kommt aus Deutschland, aber wohnt jetzt in Frankreich. **d** Michael Schuhmacher kommt aus Deutschland. Er wohnt jetzt in Österreich. **e** Arnold Schwarzenegger kommt aus Österreich. Er wohnt jetzt in den USA. **f** Heidi Klum kommt aus Deutschland, aber wohnt jetzt in den USA. **Speaking:** Sheena: Guten Tag! Ich heiße Sheena McDonald. / Ich komme aus Edinburg in Schottland. Und Sie? Wo wohnen Sie? / München ist schön. **Test yourself 1 a 1** aus; **2** aber; **3** jetzt; **b 1** aus; **2** Belgien; **3** aber; **4** arbeitet. **2 a** Wie heißen Sie? **b** Woher kommen Sie? **c** Wo wohnen Sie jetzt? **d** Wie geht es Ihnen heute? **3 a** -t, -t; **b** -et, -e; **c** -t; **d** -e, -t.

Unit 3

Discovery questions: They are: ä,ö,ü,ß. **Vocabulary builder**: Numbers 1–10 **2**. 9, 3, 8, 4, 6, 2 **3** Hamburg–Dortmund: 2 zu 1; Bochum– Hannover: 6 zu 0;

Duisburg–Mönchengladbach: 4 zu 2; Bielefeld–Wolfsburg: 1 zu 3; Schalke–Freiburg: 0 zu 2; Nürnberg–Hertha Berlin: 3 zu 0; Bremen–Frankfurt: 1 zu 0. **The Alphabet 2** Baumgart, Waltraud √ 1; Henning, Sebastian; Hesse, Patrick .√ 3; Hoffmann, Silke; Ludwig, Paul; Schanze, Martin .√2; Schidelowskaja, Tanja .√4; Schulte, Christel. **Conversation 1 a** Jena and Stuttgart. **b** No. One couple speaks a little. **2 a** richtig; **b** falsch; Sie sprechen kein Französisch. **c** falsch; Marga und Peter sind aus Jena. **d** richtig; **e** falsch; Sie sprechen ziemlich gut Englisch. **f** Sie arbeiten bei Carl Zeiss. **Language discovery 1** Wir and sie both have the ending –en: **1** heißen; **2** kommen; **3** arbeiten; **4** sprechen; **5** kommen; **6** sprechen; **7** Arbeiten. **Practice 1 a** Wohnen Tim und Julia wirklich in München? **b** Arbeiten Tim und Julia wirklich im Apple Store? **c** Kommt Julia wirklich aus Italien? **d** Spricht Tim wirklich ein bisschen Spanisch? **2 a** Sie means she; **b** Sie means you (formal); **c** sie means they. **3** –en; -en; -en; -en; -en. **Speaking** Telefon 0711-23 38 41; Handy 01734 06 02 94; Fax 07 11 24 89 02; E-Mail jkrause@yahoo.at **Listening 1** AEG, BMW, DB, DZ Bank, VW **2 a** Schulz 040 - 30 07 51; **b** Marhenke 040 - 73 45 92. **Go further** 2 99 neunundneunzig; 48 achtundvierzig; 87 siebenundachtzig; 26 sechsundzwanzig; 52 zweiundfünfzig 3 **Winning numbers Lotto:** 6 8 14 23 26 46, **Bonus number:** 22. 9 **Test yourself 1 a** Kommen; **b** Sprechen; **c** Heißen; **d** Arbeiten; **e** Wohnen **2 b** 23; **c** 27; **d** 38; **e** 92; **f** 59; **g** 46 **3 a** –e; **b** –e; **c** –en; **d** –t; **e** –t; **f** -en; **g** –en 4 **Visitenkarte A** Ich heiße Matthias Peters. Ich wohne in Hamburg. Meine Telefonnummer ist 040-300526. Meine Faxnummer ist 040-376284. Meine E-Mail-Adresse ist m.peters@delta.com **Visitenkarte B** Ich heiße Dorothea Johannsen. Ich wohne in Münster. Meine Telefonnummer ist 0251 - 514386. Meine E-Mail-Adresse ist johannsen@artdeco.de

Unit 4

Discovery questions: One of your parents: du; a group of people at a meeting: Sie; a person you don't know: Sie; two of your good friends: ihr **Vocabulary builder Nationalities and languages 2 a** *–er, -e*; **b** *-in*; **c** *–isch* **Conversation 1 a 2 1** H; **2** N; **3** N; **4** N; **5** H; **6** N. **Language discovery 1 a** –st; **b** –t **Practice 1 b** Engländerin; **c** Japanerin; **d** Schotte; **e** Amerikanerin; **f** Österreicher **2 b** –t; **c** –st; **d** –st; **e** –st; **f** –st, –est; **g** deine; **h** deine **3 a** Ihnen; **b** geht es dir? or wie geht's dir? **c** geht es euch or wie geht's euch?; **d** geht es Ihnen? **Speaking** Jürgen Krause: Ich heiße Jürgen Krause./ Nein, ich bin Österreicher. /Ich komme aus Wien. /Ich wohne jetzt in Salzburg. /Ich spreche Deutsch und Englisch. /Nein, ich bin seit drei Jahren verwitwet. /Ja, ich arbeite in Salzburg.

Listening

Name	Gür Yalezan	Susi Merkl
Nationalität	Türke	Österreicherin
Geburtsort	Berlin	Innsbruck
Wohnort	Taucha	Rötha
Sprachen	Türkisch, Deutsch, Englisch	Deutsch, Englisch, Spanisch
Familienstand	ledig	verheiratet
Arbeit? Studium?	studiert in Leipzig	arbeitet in Leipzig

Reading and writing 1 Michael speaks German, English and French. He understands a bit of Spanish and is learning Japanese **2. a** Nein, er ist Österreicher. **b** Nein, er ist Student. / Nein, er studiert. **c** Nein, er studiert in Wien. **d** Ja, er spricht Deutsch. / Ja, Deutsch ist seine Muttersprache. **e** Nein, er spricht Englisch und Französisch. **f** Ja, er versteht ein wenig Spanisch. **g** Nein, er lernt im Moment Japanisch. **Go further 1 Markus:** Hallo! Ich heiße Markus. Und wie heißt du? **Christian:** Ich bin Christian. Woher kommst du? **Markus:** Aus München. Kommst du auch aus München? **Christian:** Nein, aus Nürnberg. Sprichst du Englisch? **Markus:** Ja, ziemlich gut. Und du? **Christian:** Na ja, es geht. **2 Klaus:** Guten Tag! Ich heiße Klaus Thomas. Wie heißen Sie? **Gerhard:** Ich bin Gerhard Braun. Woher kommen Sie? **Klaus:** Aus München. Kommen Sie auch aus München? **Gerhard:** Nein, aus Nürnberg. Sprechen Sie Englisch? **Klaus:** Ja, ziemlich gut. Und Sie? **Gerhard:** Na ja, es geht. **Test yourself 1 a** 3; **b** 5; **c** 1; **d** 2; **e** 6; **f** 4. **2 a** Wie heißt du? **b** Woher kommst du? **c** Und wo wohnst du jetzt? **d** Wie geht's dir heute? **e** Sprichst du Englisch? **f** Bist du aus Hamburg? **g** Wie ist deine Handynummer? **3 a** Wie heißt ihr? **b** Woher kommt ihr? **c** Und wo wohnt ihr jetzt? **d** Wie geht's euch heute? **e** Sprecht ihr Englisch? **f** Seid ihr aus Hamburg? **g** Wie ist eure Handynummer?

Unit 5

Discovery questions: Kirchen mean churches, Gebäude buildings, Garten means garden, Altstadt old town and Essen food. **Vocabulary builder 1 a** Das ist ein Hotel. Das Hotel Schmidt in Celle **b** Das ist ein Bahnhof. Das ist der Bahnhof in Hannover. **c** Das ist eine Bäckerei. Die Stadtbäckerei. **d** Das ist ein Flohmarkt. Der Flohmarkt in Hannover. **e** Das ist ein Kino. Das Abaton-Kino. **f** Das ist eine Kneipe. Die Kneipe heißt ‚Das Weinloch'. **2 a** = ein, eine; the = der, die, das **3 a**2, **b**5, **c**6, **d**3, **e**1, **f**4 **Reading 1** Sie ist in München. **2 a** Die Stadt ist sehr schön. **b** Das Stadtzentrum und

der ‚Englische Garten' sind besonders schön. **c** Die Sprachschule heißt
‚Superlang'. **d** Nein, sie spricht ziemlich viel Deutsch. **e** Das Bier ist auch
sehr gut in München. **Language discovery** das Stadtzentrum, der
Englische Garten, die Sprachschule, das Bier **Practice 1**

ᵃB	Ä	C	K	E	R	E	I
ᵇB	A	H	N	H	O	F	
ᶜH	O	T	E	L			
			ᵈK	I	R	C	H	E
			P				
	ᵉB	I	E	R			

die Bäckerei; der Bahnhof; das Hotel; die Kirche; das Bier; die Kneipe

2 a ein Kino; **b** Das Hotel; **c** eine Bäckerei; **d** Ihr Name; **e** das
Bahnhofshotel; **f** ein Café; **g** deine Telefonnummer; **h** Die Kneipe **Speaking**
1 Eins ist eine Kneipe. Die Kneipe heißt *Bierstübl*. **2** Zwei ist ein Biergarten.
Der Biergarten heisst *Mönchbräu*. **3** Drei ist eine Kirche. Die Kirche heißt
Jakobskirche. **4** Vier ist ein Hotel. Das Hotel heißt *Bahnhofshotel*. **5** Fünf
ist ein Café. Das Café heißt *Café Krause*. **6** Sechs ist ein Markt. Der Markt
heisst *Buttermarkt*. **Go further 3 1** b; **2** c; **3** a; **4** c; **5** b; **6** a.

Writing

Heidelberg	143 000	(ein)hundertdreiundvierzigtausend
Dresden	502 000	fünfhundertzweitausend
Frankfurt am Main	660 000	sechshundertsechzigtausend
München	1 326 000	eine Million dreihundert-sechsundzwanzigtausend
Hamburg	1 750 000	eine Million siebenhundert-fünfzigtausend
Berlin	3 402 000	drei Millionen vierhundert(und)-zweitausend

Test yourself 1 a Ihr, Mein; **b** Ihre, Meine; **c** Ihre, Meine; **d** Ihre, Meine;
e Ihr, Mein; **f** Ihre, Meine. **2** geht's; fantastisch; eine; Die; schön; das; der;
eine; Die; heißt; spreche; bald.

Unit 6

Discovery questions Jura means law, Universitäten universities, Maschinenbau mechanical engineering and Informatik computer science. The Ruprecht-Karls-Universität in Heidelberg is the oldest. **Vocabulary builder Occupations 1 a** Taxifahrer; **b** Automechanikerin; **c** Musikerin; **d** Tischler; **e** Kellner; **f** Ärztin; **2 a** Das ist Peter Meier. Er ist Taxifahrer. **b** Das ist Helga Neumann. Sie ist Automechanikerin. **c** Das ist Heike Müller. Sie ist Musikerin. **d** Das ist Manfred Lustig. Er ist Tischler. **e** Das ist Kurt Leutner. Er ist Kellner. **f** Das ist Ulrike Wagner. Sie ist Ärztin. **More professions a** Lehrerin; **b** Maurer; **c** Journalist; **d** Sekretärin; **e** Koch **Conversation 1 a** She is German. **b** She's lived in England for 18 years. **2 a** They both work. **b** Ingrid's husband. **3 a** falsch; Ingrid ist Deutsche. **b** richtig; **c** richtig **d** falsch; Jutta ist Krankenschwester. **e** falsch; Herr Sammer ist Mechaniker bei Opel. **f** richtig **Language discovery**

singular	plural
ich *bin*	wir *sind*
du bist	ihr *seid*
Sie *sind*	Sie sind
er/sie/es *ist*	sie sind

Practice 1 b –n; **c** –n; **d** –n; **e** –nen; **f** –nen; **g** -e; **h** –e **2** ist; bin; bin; ist; sind; ist; ist **Speaking** Mrs Murphy-Heinrichs' responses: Ja, ich bin Deutsche. Nein, er ist Ire. Ich wohne seit 17 Jahren in Münster. Ja, ich bin Sekretärin bei Mannesmann. Er ist Taxifahrer. **Listening a** Deutscher; **b** Engländerin; **c** 24 Jahren; **d** Tischler von Beruf. **Go further 2** Karin and Anke. **3 a** falsch; Sie kommen aus Gießen. **b** richtig **c** falsch; Er studiert Romanistik. **d** richtig **e** richtig **f** falsch; Sie finden es ein bisschen langweilig.

Name	Paul	Daniel	Heike	Martina
Geburtsort	Bremen	Hamburg	Düsseldorf	Köln
Studienort	Bremen	Bremen	Aachen	Aachen
Studienfach	Germanistik	Anglistik	Informatik	Mathematik

Test yourself 1 e 2 b 3 c 4 f 5 a 6 d 7 g or **1 e 2 b 3 a 4 d 5 g 6 c 7 f 2 a** Engländer; **b** Ire; **c** Schottin; **d** Studenten; **e** Studentin; **f** Journalist; **g** Sekretärinnen; **h** Verkäuferin; **i** Kellnerin. **3 a** bin; **b** Sind; **c** ist, ist; **d** bin; **e** ist; **f** Bist; **g** Seid **4 a** von Beruf? **b** wo arbeiten; **c** wann; **d** sind ... verheiratet? **e** was; **f** studiert

340

Discovery questions Kuchen means cake, Getränke drinks, Brötchen roll and Apfelstrudel apple strudel. a cup= eine Tasse; a bottle = eine Flasche, a glass = ein Glas. **Vocabulary builder** Menu items and prices

1

MENU			
Hot drinks	€	Ice-cream specialities	€
Cup of coffee	2,50	Assorted ices	3,00, 4,00, 5,00
Cappuccino	2,75		
Hot chocolate	2,80	Peach Melba	4,50
Black tea	2,50	Ice cream cone	4,75
CAKES		NON-ALCOHOLIC DRINKS	
Butter cake	2,25	Coca Cola	2,50
Black Forest gateau	3,50	Lemonade	2,50
Various fruit flans	3,00	Orange juice	2,50
Portion of cream	0,90	Mineral water	2,80
BEERS			
König Pils (0,33l)	2,75		
Wheat beer (0,5l)	3,25		

2 a–3; **b**-4; **c**-2; **d**-5; **e**-6; **f**-1 **3 a** Butterkuchen: 2 Euro 25; Schwarzwälder Kirschtorte 3 Euro 50; Diverse Obstkuchen: 3 Euro. **4 a** 2 Euro 50; **b** 2 Euro 75; **c** 3 Euro 50; **d** 4 Euro 75; **e** 4 Euro 50; **f** 3 Euro 25. **Conversation 1 a** At a Café or restaurant **2 a** richtig; **b** falsch; Er möchte ein Bier. **c** richtig. **d** falsch; Sie bestellt ein Mineralwasser und einen Kaffee. **e** falsch; Er bekommt einen Orangensaft. **f** richtig. **3 a** No. The waitress gives the foods to the wrong people, the beer is too warm and the coffee is too cold. **4 a** falsch; **b** richtig; **c** richtig; **d** falsch. **Language discovery 1 a** einen; **b** eine; **c** ein; **d** ein, einen. **2 a** den; **b** die; **c** das. There are three words and *den* goes with masculine nouns. **Practice 1 b** eine; **c** einen; **d** einen, ein; **e** einen, einen; **f** ein **2 b** –en; **c** –ie; **d** –as; **e** –as; **f** –en

3 a (N); **b** (A); **c** (A); **d** (N); **e** (A); **f** (N) **4 a** m; **c** nt; **d** nt; **e** m; **g** m **Go further 1 b** trinken, trinke; **c** bekommen, bekomme; **d** nehmen, nehme **Containers and their contents 2 a**-4; **b**-5; **c**-3; **d**-1; **e**-2 **Speaking a** Ich möchte einen Kaffee, bitte. **b** Ich möchte ein Mineralwasser und einen Orangensaft. **c** Ich nehme eine Tasse Tee, bitte. **d** Ich nehme eine Cola und ein Glas Bier. **Test Yourself 1 a** (m); **b** (nt); **c** (m); **d** (m); **e** (f) **2 a** -en; **b** -; **c** -en, -e; **d** den, den; **e** der; **f** der; **g** das, den **3 a** Becher; **b** Dosen; **c** Flaschen; **d** Tassen **4 a**-6; **b**-4; **c**-5; **d**-2; **e**-1; **f**-3

Unit 8

Discovery questions Brot means bread, Obst and Gemüse fruit and vegetables. Vegetarier = vegetarians. **Vocabulary builder**

2 Here are some items you might have listed. We have also included the appropriate plural forms and some words that might be new for you; can you guess what they mean?

Lebensmittel	Obst	Gemüse	Getränke
das Brot, Brote (pl)	der Apfel,	der Blumenkohl,	das Bier, Biere (pl)
das Brötchen,	Äpfel (pl)	zwei Köpfe	die Cola, Colas (pl)
Brötchen (pl)	die Banane,	Blumenkohl (pl)	der Kaffee, Kaffees (pl)
das Ei, Eier (pl)	Bananen pl)	die Karotte,	die Limonade, Limonaden (pl)
das Fleisch	die Orange,	Karotten (pl)	die Milch
das Müsli, Müslis (pl)	Orangen (pl)	die Kartoffel,	das Mineralwasser
das Öl, Öle		Kartoffeln (pl)	der Orangensaft,
der Reis		der Salat, Salate	Orangensäfte (pl)
das Salz		(pl)	der Schnaps, Schnäpse (pl)
das Würstchen,		der Brokkoli,	der Sekt
Würstchen (pl)		Brokkoli (pl)	der Tee, Tees (pl)
der Zucker			der Wein, Weine (pl)

3 These are just some of the possibilities: a Gemüse und Käse; **b** Fleisch und Würstchen; **c** Bier, Wein und Orangensaft; **d** Tee, Kaffee und Zucker. **More Containers and quantities 1 a**-2; **b**-5; **c**-3; **d**-1; **e**-4 **2 a** Tomaten; **b** Wein; **c** Cornflakes; **d** Bonbons; **e** Salami **Conversations 1** Brötchen, Tomaten **2 a** Sie kauft zehn Brötchen. **b** Ein Kilo kostet €1,80. **c** Sie kauft den Riesling. **d** Alles zusammen kostet €12,35. **3** Seven **4 a** richtig; **b** falsch; **c** falsch; **d** falsch; **e** falsch. **Language discovery 1 a** Tomaten; **b** Flaschen; **c** Brötchen **2 b** Ich (S) nehme (V) ein Perrier. **c** Ich (S) möchte (V) aber keine Pommes frites. **d** Als Vorspeise nehme (V) ich (S) eine Gemüsesuppe. **e** Als Hauptgericht nehme (V) ich (S) das Pfeffersteak mit Grilltomaten. **f** Als Nachtisch bekomme (V) ich (S) einen gemischten Eisbecher. **Practice 1 a**-3; **b**-1; **c**-6; **d**-2; **e**-4; **f**-5 **2 b** Dosen; **c** Tüten; **d** Packung; **e** Gläser; **f** Becher; **g** Kännchen **3 a** Ich möchte bestellen. **b** Ich nehme Spaghetti mit Tomatensoße. **c** Zum Trinken nehme ich ein Glas Rotwein. **d** Als Vorspeise bekomme ich die Gemüsesuppe. **e** Als Nachtisch esse ich einen Apfelstrudel mit Sahne. **f** Wir möchten bezahlen. **Reading 2** Ich möchte bitte bestellen./Als Vorspeise möchte ich eine französische Zwiebelsuppe./Als Hauptgericht nehme ich das Schnitzel mit Pommes frites. Und ich möchte auch einen gemischten Salat./Ich möchte ein Glas Weißwein. Und als Nachtisch (als Dessert) nehme ich den Apfelstrudel./Mit Sahne. Und nachher möchte ich einen Kaffee. **Writing**

ᵃK ⁱ	Ä	S	E				
ᵇS	A	L	A	T			
	ᶜB	R	O	T			
		ᵈO	B	S	T		
			ᵉT	E	E		
	ᶠT	O	M	A	T	E	N
			ᵍE	I	E	R	
	ʰK	U	C	H	E	N	

Test yourself 1 b-5; **e**-2; **c**-1; **f**-6; **a**-4; **d**-3 **2 a** die Apfelsäfte **b** die Salate **c** die Tomaten **d** die Flaschen **e** die Tassen **f** die Kartoffel **g** die Brötchen **h** die Gläser **i** der Vater **j** die Restaurants **k** die Partys **3 a** Als Vorspeise möchte ich eine Gemüsesuppe. **b** Als Hauptgericht nehme ich das Schnitzel. **c** Zum Trinken möchten wir eine Flasche Mineralwasser bestellen. **d** Als Dessert bekommen wir den Obstsalat mit Sahne. **e** Nachher trinken wir eine Tasse Kaffee und eine Tasse Tee. **f** Jetzt möchten wir bitte bezahlen.

Discovery questions Freizeit means free time, fernsehen watching TV, Radfahren is cycling and Wandern is hiking. A Gesangsverein is a singing club and a Sportverein is a sports club. **Vocabulary builder**

1 a-4; **b**-7; **c**-1; **d**-6; **e**-8; **f**-2;**g**-3; **h**-5 **2 a** fahren / fliegen; **b** schwimmen; **c** spielen; **d** spielen; **e** hören (or: spielen); **f** kochen / essen. **Conversation 1** Sandro **2 a** richtig; **b** richtig; **c** falsch; (Sie liest gern Romane). **d** richtig. **e** richtig **Reading 1** Leisure activities **2 a** Er geht viermal pro Woche ins Fitnesscenter. **b** Er geht lieber ins Restaurant. **c** Er bleibt zu Hause und sieht fern. **d** Sie geht normalerweise zweimal im Monat ins Museum. **e** Mit ihren Kindern (und mit ihrem Mann) geht sie oft ins Kindertheater. **f** Sie geht meistens zweimal die Woche in die Disco. Ins Museum geht sie sehr selten. **g** Sie findet Brad Pitt sehr attraktiv. **Language discovery 1 a** lese; **b** liest; **c** esse; **d** isst. Lesen und essen have different vowels when used with du and er/sie/es. **2** After the verb. **3 a** ins; **b** in den; **c** in die; **d** ins; **e** in die. Masculine: in den; feminine: in die; neuter: ins. **Practice 1 a** spricht; **b** Sprichst; **c** fahre; **d** fährt; **e** nimmst; **f** nehme; **g** liest; **h** lesen; **i** isst; **j** essen **2 a** Ich gehe gern ins Theater. **b** Er trinkt gern französischen Rotwein. **c** Wir essen sehr gern Baguette mit Käse. **d** Angela geht nicht gern in die Oper. **e** Ich koche nicht gern. **f** Thomas und Uta gehen nicht gern ins Fitnesscenter. **3 a** Magst; **b** mag; **c** Mögen; **d** mag; **e** Mögt; **f** mögen **4 a** Nein, sie gehen nicht ins Kino, sie gehen ins Restaurant. **b** Nein, sie geht nicht ins Café, sie geht ins Konzert/in die Oper. **c** Nein, sie geht nicht in die Oper, sie geht ins Café. **d** Nein, er geht nicht ins Restaurant, er geht ins Fußballstadion. **e** Nein, er geht nicht ins Museum, er geht in die Kneipe. **f** Nein, er geht nicht ins Fitnesscenter, er geht ins Kino. There may be other possibilities.

Listening

Lesen	☑	Golf	☐	Fitness	☑
Reisen	☐	Surfen	☐	Fotografieren	☐
Fußball	☐	Schwimmen	☑	Popmusik	☐
Facebook	☐	Kino	☑	Garten	☑
Klassische Musik	☐	Tennis	☐	Segeln	☐
Twittern	☐	Wandern	☑	Joggen	☐

Writing Possible answers: 1 Ja, ich lese gern Zeitung. / Nein, ich lese nicht gern Zeitung. **2** Ja, ich höre gern Elvis Presley. / Nein ich höre nicht gern Elvis Presley. / Ja, Elvis Presley höre ich gern. / Nein, Elvis Presley höre ich nicht gern. **3** Ja, ich esse gern Pizza. / Nein, ich esse nicht gern Pizza. / Ja, Pizza esse ich gern. / Nein, Pizza esse ich nicht gern. **4** Ja, ich reise gern. / Nein, ich reise nicht gern. **5** Ja, ich arbeite gern im Garten. / Nein, ich arbeite nicht gern im Garten. / Ja, im Garten arbeite ich gern. / Nein, im Garten arbeite ich nicht gern. **6** Ja, ich trinke gern Bier. / Nein, ich trinke nicht gern Bier. / Ja, Bier trinke ich gern. / Nein, Bier trinke ich nicht gern. **7** Ja, ich twittere gern. / Nein, ich twittere nicht gern. **8** Ja, ich koche gern. / Nein, ich koche nicht gern. **Go further Sample answers:** Ich schwimme selten. / Ich höre oft Musik. / Ich spiele selten Fußball. / Ich lese immer morgens Zeitung. / Ich mache manchmal ein Picknick. / Ich spiele nie Schach. **Test yourself 1 a** Isst; **b** fährt; **c** Sprichst; **d** spielt; **e** Sprecht; **f** fotografiere; **g** liest; **h** sind. **2 a** Ich trinke gern Rotwein. **b** Ich esse gern Pommes frites. **c** Wir hören gern klassische Musik. **d** Wir spielen gern Schach. **e** Ich lese gern die Süddeutsche Zeitung. **f** Trinkst du gern Kaffee? **3 a** Schwimmen; **b** Musik; **c** Wandern; **d** Kochen; **e** Tauchen; **f** Fußball; **g** Twittern; **h** Lesen **4 a** in die; **b** in den; **c** ins; **d** ins; **e** in die; **f** ins

Unit 10

Discovery questions Arbeitstag means working day, Mittagspause lunch break and Stunden hours. At 8 o'clock is um 8.00 Uhr and at 12 noon is um 12 Uhr mittags. **Vocabulary builder 2 b.** o'clock; **c** please; **d.** It's **Die 12-Stunden-Uhr 2 a**-4; **b**-3; **c**-1; **d**-5; **e**-2 **3 a** 4.30–3; **b** 8.50–2; **c** 8.45–4; **d** 6.28–1 **4 b** Es ist zehn vor neun. **c** Es ist halb fünf. **d** Es ist Viertel vor neun. **Morgens oder abends? 1 a**-2; **b**-3; **c**-6; **d**-1; **e**-5 **2** Es ist ein Uhr mittags; Es ist vier Uhr nachmittags; Es ist acht Uhr abends; Es ist elf Uhr abends; Es ist neun Uhr morgens; Es ist sechs Uhr morgens; Es ist dreizehn Uhr; Es ist fünfzehn Uhr zwanzig; Es ist sieben Uhr fünfundvierzig; Es ist achtzehn Uhr zwölf; Es ist dreiundzwanzig Uhr fünfunddreißig; Es ist vier Uhr siebzehn. **Reading 1 a** About 16 hours. **2 a**-3; **b**-5; **c**-4; **d**-2; **e**-1; **f**-7; **g**-6 **Language discovery 1 a** steht auf; **b** fängt ... an; **c** ruft ... an; **d** kauft ein; **e** holt ... ab; **f** sieht ... fern. **2 b** Frau Haase (S) arbeitet (V) in einer Bank. **c** Danach schreibt (V) sie (S) E-Mails. **d** Um sechs Uhr ist (V) sie (S) wieder zu Hause. **e** Normalerweise isst (V) sie (S) ein Brötchen und sie (S) trinkt (V) zwei Tassen Kaffee. **f** Anschließend gehen (V) sie (S) zusammen ins Kino und dann gehen (V) sie (S) in die Kneipe. After und the verb is normally in 2nd position and can be preceded by a subject or a word such as *dann*. **Practice 1 a** steht … auf. **b** sieht fern. **c** fängt … an. **d** kauft … ein. **2 a** falsch; **b** richtig; **c** falsch; **d** richtig **3 a** Er steht gegen halb sieben auf. **b** Feierabend ist gegen vier. **c** Nein, er sieht nicht viel fern. **d** Meistens um halb 12. **4 a** Zum Frühstück esse ich Müsli und ich trinke grünen Tee. **b** Ich checke meine E-Mails und dann gehe ich aus dem Haus. **c** Ich bin in zwanzig Minuten an der Universität und meine Seminare fangen um zehn Uhr an. **d** Um ein Uhr habe ich Mittagspause und meistens esse ich Sushi. **e** Normalerweise bin ich um 18.00 Uhr wieder zu Hause, aber manchmal muss ich länger studieren. **Listening a** 20.00 **b** 14.30 **c** 13.00 **d** 7.57 **e** 15.44 **f** 17.03. **Test yourself 1 a** an; **b** fern; **c** auf; **d** ab; **e** ein; **f** an; **g** an; **h** ab. **2** Um halb sieben steht er auf. Um sieben Uhr fährt er zur Arbeit. Um neun Uhr ruft er eine Kundin an. Um halb eins geht er zur Bank. Um fünf Uhr kauft er ein. Um sieben Uhr geht er mit Helga in die Kneipe. Um zehn Uhr sieht er fern. **3 a** Ich komme aus Deutschland, aber mein Mann ist aus Schottland. **b** Ich dusche und danach frühstücke ich. **c** Ich bin pensioniert und ich kann morgens lange schlafen. **d** Ich gehe gern ins Theater, aber ich gehe gern nicht in die Oper. **e** Mein Mann und ich reisen viel und wir fahren oft nach Großbritannien. **f** Wir sind oft in London und dann gehen wir in die Tate Gallery oder ins Britische Museum.

Unit 11

Discovery questions Theaterstücke mean plays, Ausstellungen exhibitions and Konzerte concerts. Touristeninformation is tourist information. **Vocabulary builder 1 3** Mittwoch; **5** Freitag; **6** Samstag / Sonnabend; **1** Montag; **4** Donnerstag; **2** Dienstag; **7** Sonntag **2 1** Montag; **2** Dienstag; **3** Mittwoch; **4** Donnerstag; **5** Freitag; **6** Samstag / Sonnabend; **7** Sonntag **Reading 1 a** lecture. **2 a** richtig; **b** falsch; **c** falsch; **d** richtig. **3 a** Man kann ein Theaterstück für Kinder und Erwachsene (Die Abenteuer von Aladdin) sehen. **b** Man kann anschließend spielen, Eis und Bratwurst essen. **c** Um halb neun kann man Oldies und Goldies hören. **d** Sie können ‚Mission Possible' sehen. **Conversation 1 a** To the cinema. **2 a** falsch; Sie möchte einen Film mit Cate Blanchett sehen. **b** richtig; **c** falsch; Am Mittwochabend muss Petra ihre Schwester abholen. **d** richtig; **e** richtig; **f** falsch; Sie treffen sich um acht. **Language discovery 1 a** muss; **b** muss; **c** muss; **d** muss **2 a** = movement; **b** = location **Practice 1 a**-6; **b**-5; **c**-8; **d**-1; **e**-7; **f**-4; **g**-3; **h**-2 **2 a** Am Montag muss er um 20.00 Uhr Dr. Schmidt treffen. **b** Am Dienstag muss er abends zum Geburtstag von Bernd gehen. **c** Am Mittwoch muss er bis 22 Uhr arbeiten. **d** Am Donnerstag muss er mit den Kollegen essen gehen. **e** Am Freitag muss er mit Tante Gisela in die Oper gehen. **f** Am Wochenende muss er nach München fahren.

3 b 1 (position), **b 2** (movement); **c 1** (position), **c 2** (movement); **d 1** (movement), **d 2** (position); **e 1** (position), **2** (movement). **4 a** ins Kino **b** Im Café; **c** ins Café; **d** im Restaurant; **e** in die Sprachschule; **f** ins Restaurant; **g** Im Kino; **h** In der Sprachschule. **Speaking** There may be other possibilities: Hallo, Jutta. Mir geht's gut. Und dir? /Ja, das ist eine gute Idee. Wann denn? / Tut mir leid. Dienstagabend kann ich nicht. Da muss ich arbeiten. / Tut mir leid. Am Freitag muss ich nach Köln fahren. Geht es Samstagabend? / Wann treffen wir uns? / Acht Uhr ist gut. Wir können uns im Restaurant treffen. / Tschüss, bis Samstagabend. **Go further 2 Sample answers: a** Ja, ich komme gern mit. / Tut mir leid, aber ich habe leider keine Zeit. **b** Ja, das ist eine tolle Idee. / Da muss ich arbeiten. **c** Ja, gern. / Ich möchte mitkommen, aber ich muss lernen. **d** Ja, ich komme gern mit. / Ich möchte mitkommen, aber ich habe leider keine Zeit.**Test yourself 1 a** Im Theater kann man ein Stück von Shakespeare sehen. **b** Er möchte heute Abend in die Kneipe gehen. **c** Er kann sehr gut Tango tanzen. **d** Was kann man in London machen? **e** Ich möchte am Dienstag essen gehen. **f** Frau Johnson kann sehr gut Deutsch sprechen. **2** Am Dienstag möchte sie Klaus treffen, aber sie muss das Mathe-Examen machen. Am Mittwoch möchte sie lange schlafen, aber sie muss morgens um 7.30 Uhr ins Fitnesscenter. Am Donnerstag möchte sie in die Kneipe gehen, aber sie muss für Hannelore Babysitting machen.

Unit 12

Discovery questions Sparpreise means economy prices, eine Fahrt means journey, Ermäßigung means discount and Fahrkarte ticket. With a Länder-Ticket you can travel cheaper within a German state and a Schönes-Wochenende-Ticket offers special travel at weekends.
Vocabulary builder

1 a-3; **b**-7; **c**-1; **d**-2; **e**-4; **f**-6;**g**-5 **Conversation 1 a** A return ticket **2 a** Sie fährt nach Berlin. **b** Sie kostet €53. **c** Nein, der Zug ist direkt. **d** Er fährt in 10 Minuten. **e** Er fährt von Gleis 14. **Language discovery 1 a** dem; **b** dem; **c** der; **d** der; **e** dem; **f** dem. **Der** changes to **dem** (masculine nouns), **die** to **der** (feminine nouns), and **das** to **dem** (neuter nouns). **Practice**

1 a dem; **b** der; **c** der; **d** dem; **e** dem. **2 a** zum; **b** zur; **c** vom, zum; **d** zum.
3 a-3; **b**-2; **c**-2; **d**-1. **Speaking** Was kostet eine Fahrkarte nach Frankfurt?/
Einfach./Ja, gut./Wann fährt der nächste Zug nach Frankfurt?/Und von
welchem Gleis fährt er?/Muss ich umsteigen?/Vielen Dank. **Reading**
Donnerstag um 9.30 Uhr – **1** Der nächste Zug fährt um 9.50 Uhr. **2** Ja,
Sie müssen in Frankfurt und Mannheim umsteigen. **3** Ja, es gibt einen
Speisewagen. **4** Er kommt um 13.05 Uhr in Heidelberg an. Sonntag um
06.30 Uhr – **1** Der nächste Zug fährt um 7.24 Uhr. **2** Ja, Sie müssen in
Frankfurt umsteigen. **3** Ja, es gibt einen Speisewagen. **4** Er kommt um
10.43 Uhr in Heidelberg an. **Go further**

1

Person	Wie fahren sie?	Wie lange brauchen sie?
Person 1	mit dem Fahrrad	20 Minuten
Person 2	mit dem Bus und der U-Bahn	50 Minuten
Person 3	mit dem Auto	eine Stunde
Person 4	geht zu Fuß	10 Minuten

2 b Sie braucht ungefähr 20 Minuten. **c** Er fährt meistens mit dem Bus
zum Bahnhof. **d** In der U-Bahn liest er. / Er liest in der U-Bahn. **e** Sie ist
nicht gut. / Die Verbindung mit Bus und Bahn ist nicht gut. **f** Er fährt eine
Stunde. **g** Er geht meistens zu Fuß. **Test yourself 1 a** m; **b** f; **c** nt; **d** nt;
e f **2** Wie komme ich zum Flughafen, zur Gedächtniskirche, zum Hotel
Ramada, zum Bahnhof, zur Universität, zum Café Extrablatt? **3. a** dem,
zur; **b** der, zur; **c** dem, zum; **d** dem; **e** der **4 c**-5; **e**-2; **d**-6; **b**-1; **f**-3; **a**-4

Unit 13

Discovery questions Kneipen means pubs, Umfrage survey and bekannt
well-known. Glücklich und zufrieden mean happy and content. **Vocabulary
builder 1** 1-e; **2**-b; **3**-d; **4**-a; **5**-f; **6**-c **Listening 1 a** Saturday's **2 a** U **b** A **c** U **d**
A **e** A **f** U **g** A **h** U **i** A **Reading 1 a** Visitors to the flea market **2 a** Sie haben
eine alte Platte von den Rolling Stones gekauft. **b** Er fährt diesen Sommer
nach Mexiko. Er reist gern. **c** Sie hat ein neues Hemd gekauft. Sie hat €7,50
bezahlt. **d** Er kann morgens schlecht aufstehen. **Language Discovery**

1a Was <u>hast</u> du denn gestern <u>gemacht</u>? **b** Wir <u>haben</u> viel Spaß <u>gehabt</u>.
c Ich <u>habe</u> gestern Morgen einen neuen Computer <u>gekauft</u>. **d** Ich <u>habe</u>
gerade <u>gefrühstückt</u>. **e** Bernd und ich <u>haben gekocht</u>. Haben is the 2nd
'idea' or gramatical element; the past participle is in last position.
2 a fantastische; **b** interessantes; **c** tolle; **d** alten, mechanischen.

Practice 1 b getanzt; **c** gemacht; **d** gefrühstückt; **e** gekostet; **f** gekocht;
g telefoniert; **h** bezahlt; **i** besucht; **j** eingekauft. **2 b** getanzt; **c** besucht;

d eingekauft; **e** bezahlt; **f** gekocht; **g** telefoniert. **3 a** –en; **b** –es; **c** –e; **d** –en; **e** –es; **f** –e **4 b** groß; **c** teuer; **d** langweilig; **e** neu; **f** arm; **g** schwer; **h** altmodisch. **Writing One possible version:** Am Samstagmorgen war Bettina in der Stadt und hat eingekauft. Danach hat sie ein Paket abgeholt. Am Nachmittag hat sie dann ihren Freund Georg im Krankenhaus besucht. Am Abend hat sie mit Pia Schach gespielt. Sie hat Nudeln mit Pesto gekocht. Am Sonntagmorgen hat Bettina einen Ausflug gemacht. Danach hat sie um halb vier im Garten gearbeitet. Am Abend hat sie mit Christina telefoniert und für das Deutsch-Examen gelernt. **Go further a** richtig; **b** falsch; **c** falsch; **d** richtig **Test yourself 1 Possible answers:** Um 10 Uhr hat sie mit Frau Martini telefoniert. Danach hat sie die Firma Schmidt + Consultants besucht. Um 12.45 Uhr hat sie Mittagspause gemacht. Am Nachmittag hat sie Texte diktiert und Tickets für die Reise nach Rom gebucht. Um 17 Uhr hat sie einen schönen Mantel gekauft. Um 18.30 Uhr hat sie mit Michael Badminton gespielt. **2 a** war; **b** warst; **c** Waren; **d** war; **e** Wart; **f** waren. **2 d** -es; **e** -e; **f** -es; **g** -e; **h** -en; **i** -e; **j** -es; **k** -es.

Unit 14

Discovery questions Ausflug means day trip, Nachbarn neighbours and durstig and hungrig mean thirsty and hungry. Wanderwege are hiking paths and a Wanderurlaub is a hiking holiday. **Vocabulary builder 1 1**-h; **2**-g; **3**-e; **4**-c; **5**-b; **6**-a; **7**-d; **8**-f **Reading 1 a** visited New York; **2** visited Florida; **3**. sang on MTV; **4**. went to Salzburg; **5**. went to the casino; **6**. saw a clip of his new video **2 a** Er ist nach New York geflogen. **b** Auf einer Party hat er Kaviar gegessen und Champagner getrunken. **c** Er hat Robert de Niro getroffen. **d** In Florida ist er im Meer geschwommen. **e** Er hat neue italienische Anzüge gekauft. **f** Am Freitag ist er ins Kasino gegangen. **g** Am Wochenende ist er Ski gelaufen. **h** Das neue Lied heißt: Ich kann dich nicht vergessen. **Language discovery**

1

sein	haben
sein - gewesen	bekommen – bekommen
fliegen – geflogen	treffen – getroffen
bleiben – geblieben	sprechen – gesprochen
schwimmen – geschwommen	fragen – gefragt
zurückkommen – zurückgekommen	essen – gegessen
fahren – gefahren	trinken – getrunken
gehen – gegangen	geben – gegeben
laufen - gelaufen	kaufen – gekauft
	singen – gesungen
	sehen - gesehen

2 b treffen; **c** gegessen; **d** gesprochen; **e** gegangen; **f** gefahren; **g** fliegen; **h** bleiben **Practice 1 b** gegeben; **c** getrunken; **d** gesungen; **e** getroffen; **f** genommen; **g** gekommen; **h** gegangen; **i** gefahren; **j** aufgestanden **2 b** hat; **c** Haben; **d** ist; **e** Bist; **f** hat; **g** habe; **h** habe **3 a** bin ... aufgestanden; **b** habe ... gegessen; **c** bin ... gegangen; **d** bin ... gefahren; **e** habe ... getroffen; **f** haben ... gesehen, habe ... verstanden; **g** habe ... gekannt. **Listening 1 a** Seit 10 Jahren genau. **b** Um acht Uhr aus dem Bett, das finde ich nicht nett. **c** Insgesamt 10. **d** Er komponiert die Musik selber und schreibt auch die Texte. **e** Im Winter fährt er gern Ski. Im Sommer surft er oder spielt Tennis. Er geht auch auf viele Partys und sieht viele Freunde. **2 Reading and writing 1 a** Von 1928 bis 1937 hat er das Kaiser-Wilhelm-Gymnasium in Köln besucht. **b** 1937 hat er das Abitur gemacht. **c** 1937 hat er auch in Bonn eine Buchhandlungslehre begonnen. **d** 1939 hat er an der Universität Köln Germanistik studiert. **e** Von 1939 bis 1945 ist er Soldat im Zweiten Weltkrieg gewesen. **f** 1942 hat er Annemarie Zech geheiratet. **g** Von 1946–1949 hat er Kurzgeschichten in Zeitschriften geschrieben. **h** 1949 ist sein erstes Buch (Der Zug war pünktlich) erschienen. **i** Von 1949 bis 1985 hat er viele literarische Werke geschrieben. **j** 1972 hat er den Nobelpreis für Literatur bekommen. **k** 1985 ist er am 16. Juni in Hürtgenwald/Eifel gestorben. **Go further 2 a** falsch; **b** richtig; **c** falsch; **d** richtig; **e** falsch; **f** falsch; **g** richtig.

3

Früher	Haare	Trinken	Musik	Freizeit
Bernd	hat lange Haare gehabt	hat viel Kognak getrunken	hat Elvis Presley gehört	hat in einer Band gespielt
Dieter	hat lange Haare gehabt	hat Rum und Cola getrunken	hat viel Eric Clapton gehört	hat viel Fußball gespielt

Heute	Haare	Trinken	Musik	Freizeit
Bernd	hat immer noch lange Haare	trinkt Wasser, Tee, Orangensaft	hört viel Jazz-musik	reist viel
Dieter	hat keine Haare mehr	trinkt gern französischen Wein	hört klassische Musik	spielt Tennis

Test yourself 1 a geflogen; **b** besucht; **c** abgeholt; **d** gegangen; **e** gesehen; **f** geschlafen. **2 a** sind; **b** haben; **c** haben; **d** haben; **e** sind; **f** haben **3 b** verstanden; **c** vergessen; **d** besucht; **e** empfohlen; **f** erhalten.

Discovery questions Mieten means rents, Wohnungen apartments and Häuser houses. Unmöbliert means unfurnished. **Vocabulary builder**
1 1-e; **2**-a; **3**-c; **4**-d; **5**-b **2 a**-6; **b**-8; **c**-5; **d**-2; **e**-3; **f**-4; **g**-7; **h**-1 **At home**
2 b das Schlafzimmer; **b** das Kinderzimmer; **c** die Küche; **d** das Badezimmer; **e** das Wohnzimmer; **f** der Balkon; **g** das Arbeitszimmer.
3 The conventional answers are as follows. Perhaps you have other ideas! **3** Der Schrank kommt ins Wohnzimmer. **4** Das Bett kommt ins Schlafzimmer. **5** Der DVD-Player kommt ins Wohnzimmer. **6** Der Küchentisch kommt in die Küche. **7** Die Pflanze kommt ins Wohnzimmer. **8** Die Waschmaschine kommt in den Keller. **9** Der Kühlschrank kommt in die Küche. **10** Das Sofa kommt ins Wohnzimmer. **11** Der Sessel kommt ins Wohnzimmer. **12** Der Fernseher kommt ins Wohnzimmer. **13** Das Bild kommt auch ins Wohnzimmer. **14** Die Magazine kommen auch ins Wohnzimmer. **15** Das Regal kommt ins Arbeitszimmer. **16** Die Bücher kommen auch ins Arbeitszimmer. **17** Der Topf kommt in die Küche. **18** Die Gummiente kommt ins Badezimmer. **19** Die Teller kommen in die Küche.

[interview]

1 Wer?	Wo wohnen sie?	Wie ist es?
Person 1	in einem Hochhaus	nicht zu teuer
Person 2	in einem Einfamilienhaus	grün und ruhig
Person 3	in einer Wohngemeinschaft	nett und interessant
Person 4	in einer Altbauwohnung	hell und ruhig

2 a falsch. Er zahlt €375 Miete und er ist ganz zufrieden. **b** richtig; **c** richtig; **d** falsch. Sie wohnt seit 50 Jahren in einer Altbauwohnung. **e** richtig. **Reading 1** c **2** b interessanter, bunter; **c** stressiger; **d** besser, freundlicher; **e** länger; **f** entspannter. **Language discovery 1** The ending is –er **2 a** meiner, einem; **b** einer; **c** meiner; **d** meinem. They are all in the dative case. **Practice 1 a** So ein Quatsch! Der Eiffelturm ist jünger als die Akropolis. **b** So ein Quatsch! In Deutschland ist es kälter als in Südafrika. **c** So ein Quatsch! Das Essen im ‚Gourmet-Restaurant' ist besser als in der Mensa. **d** So ein Quatsch! Der Toyota Prius ist billiger als der Porsche. **e** So ein Quatsch! Tokio ist größer als Paris. **f** So ein Quatsch! Berlin ist interessanter als Stuttgart. **2 a** Ihr; **b** ihr; **c** seine; **d** ihre; **e** meine; **f** unsere; **g** ihren **3 a** -em; **b** -er; **c** -em; **d** -em; **e** -er; **f** -em; **g** -en -n. **Reading 2 a** Fast sechs Monate; **b** Vier Zimmer, plus Küche und Bad; **c** €465, + Nebenkosten; **d** Relativ zentral, in der Nähe vom Stadtpark; **e** Sie sind sehr gut.

3

Vorteile (+)	Nachteile (−)
Sie haben jetzt mehr Platz. Es ist eine sehr große Wohnung. Die Wohnung liegt relativ zentral, in der Nähe vom Stadtpark. Die Umgebung ist ruhig und sehr grün. Die Zimmer sind groß und hell. Die Miete ist nicht so teuer, €465. Die Verkehrsverbindungen sind sehr gut.	Bis zum nächsten Supermarkt ist es ein bisschen weit. Das Arbeitszimmer ist sehr klein. Leider hat die Wohnung keinen Garten.

Speaking 1 a Wir wohnen in einer Wohnung. **b** Die Wohnung hat vier Zimmer, plus Küche und Bad. **c** Die Zimmer sind groß und hell. **d** Nein, wir haben leider keinen Garten. **e** Die Miete ist nicht so teuer, €465, plus Nebenkosten. **f** Die Umgebung ist ruhig und sehr grün. **g** Die Verkehrsverbindungen sind sehr gut. **h** Ich fahre nur 10 Minuten zur Arbeit. **i** Ich fahre mit der U-Bahn. Im Sommer kann ich mit dem Fahrrad fahren. **Writing** One possible answer: Liebe Frau Löschmann, ich danke Ihnen für Ihren Brief vom 13. Mai. Ich bin gerne bereit, Ihre Fragen zu beantworten. Die Wohnung liegt sehr zentral – nur zwei Minuten bis zur Hauptstraße, aber sie liegt auch sehr ruhig, in der Nähe vom Stadtpark. Die Verkehrsverbindungen sind sehr gut – nur fünfzehn Minuten bis zum Hauptbahnhof und fünf Minuten bis zur Bushaltestelle. Die Wohnung hat drei Schlafzimmer und zwei Badezimmer. Die Küche ist sehr groß, da kann man auch essen. Wir haben zwei Fernseher und einen DVD-Player. Man kann Satellitenprogramme, also auch deutsche Programme bekommen. Wir haben einen großen, schönen Garten. Dort kann man im Sommer auch essen. Mit freundlichen Grüßen Ihr Peter Smith **Go further 2 a** außerhalb; **b** klein; **c** dunkel; **d** interessant; **e** teuer; **f** neu; **g** antik; **h** laut. **Test yourself 1 b** größer; **c** älter; **d** lauter; **e** besser; **f** teurer; **g** höher; **h** billiger; **i** interessanter; **j** stressiger **2 a** sein; **b** ihr; **c** meine; **d** unsere; **e** mein; **f** ihre **3 a** –er; **b** –em, -en; **c** –em; **d** –em; **e** –em; **f** -em; **g** -em;

Unit 16

Discovery questions Pensionen means B & Bs, Jugendherbergen youth hostels and Ferienwohnungen means holiday flats. Hotelketten are hotel chains, Preisklassens mean price ranges and Sehenswürdigkeiten sites. **Vocabulary builder 1 a**-3; **b**-4; **c**-3; **d**-1; **e**-2 **2 a**-8: **b**-6; **c**-3; **d**-9; **e**-7; **f**-5; **g**-2; **h**-4; **i**-1 **Conversations 1** Monday **2 a** falsch; Er nimmt ein

Doppelzimmer. **b** richtig; **c** falsch; Er möchte mit seiner Frau auf eine Antiquitätenmesse gehen. **d** falsch; Er nimmt ein Zimmer mit Bad. **e** falsch; Das Zimmer kostet €77,50. **f** richtig. **3** A hotel room for two nights.

4

Hotels/ Pension	Zimmer	Preis für Einzelzimmer	Entfernung	Pluspunkte
Offenbach	80	€90	5 Minuten vom Zentrum	sehr zentral, gute Bar
Atlanta	120	€130	30 Minuten (eine halbe Stunde) vom Zentrum	Swimming- Pool und Park
Schneider	28	€67,50	20 Minuten vom Zentrum	nette Atmosphäre, ruhig

Language discovery a zentralsten; **b** zentralsten; **c** billigsten; **d** billigsten; **e** am; **f** weitesten; **g** am komfortabelsten; **h** komfortabelsten **Practice 1 a**-3; **b**-4; **c**-5; **d**-6; **e**-7; **f**-2; **g**-1 **2 a** am größten; **b** am billigsten; **c** am zentralsten; **d** am ruhigsten **3 b** neben; **c** gegenüber; **d** zwischen; **e** hinter; **f** neben **4 a**-7; **b**-3; **c**-6 ; **d**-5 or 1; **e**-5 or 1; **f**-4; **g**-2 **Speaking 1 a** Guten Tag. Haben Sie ein Zimmer frei? **b** Ein Einzelzimmer, bitte. **c** Für drei Nächte. **d** Mit Dusche, bitte. **e** Um wie viel Uhr gibt es Frühstück? **2** Gehen Sie geradeaus. Die Bibliothek ist auf der rechten Seite, neben dem Museum. / Ja, natürlich. Gehen Sie geradeaus und nehmen Sie die erste Straße links. Die Post liegt hinter dem Brunnen. / Ja, natürlich. Gehen Sie links, dann rechts. Die Apotheke liegt neben dem Imbiss und dem Hotel Hotel da Vinci. / Gehen Sie geradeaus. Der Supermarkt ist gegenüber dem Museum. / Natürlich. Gehen Sie links, dann wieder links. Da finden Sie eine Kneipe auf der linken Seite neben der Bäckerei. Die Kneipe ist sehr gut. **Test yourself 1 c** Die Waschmaschine steht jetzt im Keller. **d** Das Foto von Oma Lisbeth hängt jetzt im Esszimmer. **e** Die CDs stehen jetzt im Regal. **f** Die Pflanze steht jetzt auf dem Balkon. **g** Das Poster von Lionel Messi hängt jetzt im Kinderzimmer. **h** Das Sofa steht jetzt zwischen dem Regal und dem Tisch. **2 a** warm, am wärmsten; **b** kälter; **c** interessanter, am interessantesten; **d** billiger, am billigsten; **e** höher, am höchsten; **f** teurer, am teuersten; **g** gern, am liebsten; **h** besser, am besten **3 a** Der Nil ist länger als der Rhein, aber der Amazonas ist am längsten. **b** Kanada ist größer als Deutschland, aber Russland ist am größten. **c** Der Tower of London ist älter als das Empire State Building, aber das Colosseum ist am ältesten. **d** Gold ist härter als Silber, aber Granit ist am härtesten. **e** Der BMW M6 ist teurer als der VW Passat, aber der Ferrari F430 ist am teuersten.

Unit 17

Discovery questions Kleidung means clothes and Kaufhaus is department store. Modeindustrie means fashion industry, Modegeschäft fashion shop and Modemarken fashion labels. **Vocabulary builder a**-7; **b**-4; **c**-6; **d**-1; **e**-8; **f**-3; **g**-10; **h**-2; **i**-9; **j**-5 Clothing **2 a** falsch; Der Mann trägt einen blauen Anzug und eine rote Krawatte. **b** richtig; **c** richtig; **d** falsch; Außerdem trägt sie einen braunen Rcck, eine gelbe Strumpfhose und braune Schuhe. **e** richtig. **f** falsch; Der Junge trägt eine schwarze Jeans, ein grünes T-Shirt, eine gelbe Baseball-Mütze und gelbe Turnschuhe.
3 a Anzug; **b** Mantel; **c** Hemd; **d** Sachen; **e** Rock **Interview 1 Ist Mode wichtig oder unwichtig?**

Bettina Haferkamp	☐	☑
Johann Kurz	☑	☐
Boris Brecht	☐	☑
Ulrike Maziere	☑	☐

2 b Sie zeigt, was Leute denken und fühlen. **c** Die Leute sollen immer etwas Neues kaufen. **d** Schwarze Sachen finde ich am besten. **e** Ich ziehe nur an, was ich mag. **f** Mode ist ein wichtiger Ausdruck unserer Zeit./ Mode bedeutet viel für mich.

3

pro (+)	contra (−)
Mode ist ein wichtiger Ausdruck unserer Zeit. Sie zeigt, was Leute denken und fühlen. Mode bedeutet viel für mich. Eine modische Frisur, ein modernes Outfit – das ist sehr wichtig für mich.	Die Leute sollen immer etwas neues kaufen. Modetrends finde ich langweilig.

Reading 1 a It's their birthdays. **2 a** falsch, Jutta und Christian machen jedes Jahr eine Party. **b** richtig; **c** richtig; **d** falsch, Die Person, die am schlechtesten, am hässlichsten aussieht, bekommt einen Preis. **e** falsch; Die Gäste bringen etwas zum Trinken mit. **Language discovery 1** It means something new. **2 a** –er; **b** –er; **c** –er; **d** -e; **e** –es. Masculine: -er; feminine: -e; neuter: -es **Practice 1 a**-4; **b**-5; **c**-1; **d**-2; **e**-3 **2 b** Das war ein langweiliger Film. **b** Das ist ein starker Kaffee. **c** Das ist ein interessantes Buch. **d** Das ist ein schwieriges Problem. **e** Das ist ein neuer Computer. **f** Das sind unfreundliche Leute. **g** Das ist ein billiges Hotel. **h** Das ist eine komplizierte Frage. **3 a** -en, -em, -en. **b** -en, -en. **c** -em, -en, -er, -en, -en, -en. **d** -em, -en, -er, -en, -en, -en. **e** -er, -en. **f** -em, -en, -en, -en. **Speaking** Guten Tag. Ich suche eine neue Jacke. / Eine graue Jacke, für eine Party.

/Ich suche etwas Modisches. /Ja, gut, aber italienische Jacken sind sehr teuer. /Ja, das stimmt und das ist auch eine sehr modische Party in New York **Listening 1 a** Sie sagt, Verkäuferin ist ein interessanter Beruf. **b** Die Arbeit im Haushalt ist anstrengend. **c** Ihr Sohn findet Computerspiele interessant. **d** Sie findet, sie ist kein modischer Typ. **e** Die Töchter von Frau Martens finden Mode wichtig. **f** Kunden sind manchmal unfreundlich **Writing Sample answers: a** Bei der Arbeit trage ich meistens eine weiße Bluse und einen blauen Rock. / An der Universität trage ich meistens eine Jeans und ein T-Shirt. **b** Zu Hause trage ich am liebsten bequeme Kleidung. **c** Ich trage gern modische und bunte Sachen. Ich trage nicht so gern dunkle Kleidung. **d** Meine Lieblingsfarbe ist blau. **e** Ja, Mode ist ziemlich wichtig für mich. **f** Zu einer Bad-Taste-Party ziehe ich eine gelbe Bluse mit einer grünen Hose und einer roten Jacke an. **Go further**

2

	bei der Arbeit	zu Hause	was sie gern tragen	was sie nicht gern tragen
Mareike Brauer	eine bequeme Hose, eine Bluse, einen Pulli	eine Hose, oft eine Jeans, T-Shirt, Pullover	bequeme Sachen; alles, was bequem ist	Röcke
Günther Scholz	einen Anzug, ein weißes Hemd, eine Krawatte	ein sportliches Hemd oder ein Poloshirt	sportliche Kleidung, elegante Kleidung	bunte Kleidung, rote Hemden, Hawaii-Hemden, bunte Hosen usw.

Test yourself 1 a Neues; **b** Modisches; **c** Billiges; **d** Elegantes; **e** Sportliches; **f** Dummes; **g** Wichtiges **2 a** m; **b** f; **c** f; **d** m; **e** nt **3 a** Verkäuferin Ich arbeite in einem großen Kaufhaus in München. Bei der Arbeit trage ich einen schwarzen Rock und eine weiße Bluse. Im Winter trage ich zu meinem schwarzen Rock auch eine schwarze Jacke. **b** Student Im Moment arbeite ich bei Burger King und muss eine hässliche Uniform tragen. An der Uni trage ich aber immer eine blaue Levi-Jeans mit einem modischen T-Shirt. Mir gefallen am besten amerikanische oder britische T-Shirts. Alte Sachen vom Flohmarkt gefallen mir manchmal auch.

Unit 18

Discovery questions Geburtstage means birthdays, Hochzeiten weddings, Weihnachten Christmas. Silvester is the German word for New Year's Eve, Neujahr means New Year's Day and Kater means hangover. Germans exchange presents on Christmas Eve (Heiligabend). **Vocabulary builder 1 a** Geburtstagsparty; **b** Hochzeit; **c** Grillparty; **d** Hauseinweihungsfeier **2 a**-5; **b**-6; **c**-1; **d**-3; **e**-2; **f**-4 **3 a** falsch; Susanne und Michael heiraten am 8. Mai in Marburg. **b** richtig; **c** falsch; Uschi und Matthias haben ihr ‚Schloss' gefunden. **d** falsch; Mareike und Jörg wollen in ihrem Haus eine Grillparty machen. **e** falsch; Sie haben auch Essen für Vegetarier. **Reading 1** CDs **2 a** falsch; Er hat Geburtstag, aber er ist Frankreich-Fan. **b** richtig; **c** richtig; **d** falsch; Sie machen eine Hauseinweihungsfeier. **Conversation 1** A gift for his wife. **2 a** Er möchte seiner Frau etwas schenken. / Seiner Frau möchte er etwas schenken. **b** Beide kosten €49,99. **c** Seine Frau hat schon eine. **d** Er sieht altmodisch aus. **e** Er nimmt den blauen Schal. **Language discovery 1** a –e; **b** –e; **c** –e; **d** –e; **e** -e. Yes, masculine and neuter forms differ. In the nominative case after ein, masculine forms take –er and neuter forms –es: ein schöner Tag, ein gutes Buch. **2 a** ihm; **b** ihr; **c** ihm; **d** ihnen. him = ihm, her = ihr and them = ihnen. The dative case is used. **Practice 1 a** –e; **b** –e; **c** -e; **d** –e; **e** –e; **f** –en **2 a** Sie kauft den Kindern *(DI)* ein Eis *(IO)*. **b** Magda bringt ihrer Mutter *(IO)* Blumen *(DI)* mit. **c** Hast du dem Verkäufer *(IO)* schon das Geld *(DI)* gegeben? **d** Kannst du mir *(IO)* bitte eine Flasche Wasser *(DI)* mitbringen? **e** Sie haben ihrem Sohn *(IO)* ein Auto *(DI)* gekauft. **f** Petra hat den Leuten *(IO)* ihre neue Wohnung *(DI)* gezeigt. **3 a** ihr; **b** ihm; **c** ihnen; **d** ihr; **e** ihnen; **f** ihm **Speaking 1** Guten Tag. Können Sie mir helfen?/Ich suche ein Buch über New York. Können Sie mir etwas empfehlen?/Nein. Er gefällt mir nicht. /Das gefällt mir. Wie viel kostet es?/Das Buch nehme ich. Haben Sie das neue Buch von Dan Brown?/Danke schön, und wo ist die Kasse, bitte?

Listening

Wem?	Was bringen sie mit?	Warum?
Vater	Sie bringen ihm eine Baseballmütze von den New York Yankees mit.	Er sieht gern Baseballspiele im Fernsehen.
Oma	Sie bringen ihr einen neuen Bademantel mit.	Sie hat gesagt, sie möchte einen neuen Bademantel.
Tante Heidi	Sie bringen ihr Turnschuhe von Nike mit.	Nike-Turnschuhe sind in Amerika viel billiger als in Europa.
Onkel Georg	Sie bringen ihm einen U-Bahn-Plan von New York mit.	Er sammelt U-Bahn-Pläne.

Go further 2 a-4; **b**-1; **c**-8; **d**-6; **e**-7; **f**-5; **g**-2; **h**-3 **Test yourself 1 a** -en; **b** -e; **c** -e; **d** -en; **e** -e; **f** -en **g** –en **2 1 a** Man kann ihm eine CD von Maria Callas schenken. **b** Man kann ihr ein Buch über Indien schenken. **c** Man kann ihm Turnschuhe schenken. **d** Man kann ihnen eine Flasche Wein schenken. **e** Man kann ihr ein Buch über Blumen und Pflanzen schenken. **f** Man kann ihm ein Computerspiel schenken.

Unit 19

Discovery questions Allgemeinarzt is the word for GP, Facharzt means specialist, eine Apotheke pharmacy and ein Apotheker is a pharmacist. Eine Notfallbehandlung is emergency treatment. **Vocabulary builder Here are the singular and plural forms: 1** das Gesicht (-er); der Kopf (ë); das Auge (-n) ; die Nase (-n) ; der Zahn (ë); der Mund (ër); die Brust (ë); der Arm (-e); der Bauch (ë); der Finger (-); die Hand (ë); der Fuß (ë); das Haar (-e); das Ohr (-en); die Lippe (-n); die Zunge (-n); der Hals (ë); der Busen (-); der Rücken (-); das Bein (-e); das Knie (-); die Zehe (-n); die Ferse (-n) **Was tut hier weh? 1** a-6; **b**-7; **c**-5; **d**-2; **e**-1; **f**-4; **g**-3. **2 1**-d; **2**-c; **3**-b; **4**-g; **5**-e; **6**-h; **7**-f; **8**-a **Reading 1** Michael Warnke **2 a** Wer joggt abends? MW; **b** Wer möchte mehr relaxen? ES-T; **c** Wer hat früher Volleyball gespielt? MF; **d** Wer lebt sehr gesund? GT; **e** Wer treibt viel Sport? GT; **f** Wer darf nicht mehr Ski fahren? MF

3

	Was tun sie im Moment?	Was dürfen sie nicht tun?	Was sollen sie tun?	Was wollen sie tun?
Gabriela	treibt viel Sport, spielt Fußball, Handball, ein bisschen Tennis; raucht nicht, trinkt sehr wenig Alkohol; isst gesund	X	X	will vielleicht einen Fitnessurlaub machen
Michael	joggt abends	darf nicht mehr rauchen	soll weniger Fett essen; soll mehr Sport treiben	will am Wochenende mehr mit dem Rad fahren
Marianne	geht vier- bis fünfmal in der Woche schwimmen	darf nicht mehr Volleyball spielen; darf auch nicht mehr Ski fahren	soll viel schwimmen gehen	will wieder aktiver leben
Egbert	geht Windsurfen und Tauchen; geht auch Ski fahren	X	soll nicht mehr so viel Sport machen	will mehr relaxen

Conversation 1 She has backache. **2 a** richtig; **b** falsch; Die Schmerzen hat sie seit fast vier Wochen. **c** richtig; **d** richtig; **e** falsch; Sie darf nicht Volleyball spielen. Sie soll lieber zum Schwimmen gehen. **f** falsch; Sie sagt, es ist nichts Schlimmes. **Language discovery 1 a** will; **b** darf, soll; **c** soll;

d darf; **e** will. Dürfen and wollen have a vowel change. **2** They go to the end. **Practice 1 a** soll; **b** will; **c** soll; **d** darf; **e** dürfen; **f** soll; **g** will

2

gesund	ungesund
• Salat essen	• fernsehen und Kartoffelchips essen
• zweimal in der Woche schwimmen gehen	• jeden Tag vier Flaschen Bier trinken
• ein Glas Rotwein pro Tag trinken	• fünf Stunden ohne Pause vor dem Computer sitzen
• Fahrrad fahren	
• lange spazieren gehen	

Possible answers: Es ist gesund, wenn man Salat isst. / Ich finde es ungesund, wenn man fernsieht und Kartoffelchips isst. / Es ist gesund, wenn man zweimal in der Woche schwimmen geht. /Ich finde es ungesund, wenn man jeden Tag vier Flaschen Bier trinkt. / Ich finde es aber gesund, wenn man ein Glas Rotwein pro Tag trinkt. / Es ist ungesund, wenn man fünf Stunden ohne Pause vor dem Computer sitzt. / Es ist gesund, wenn man Rad fährt und auch wenn man lange spazieren geht. **Speaking** Ich habe ziemlich starke Halsschmerzen. / Etwa drei Tage und es wird immer schlimmer./Ich bin Lehrer(in)./Ja, aber was soll ich tun? /Ja, nächste Woche fliege ich nach Florida. / Gut und vielen Dank. **Writing 3 Possible answers a** Ja, es ist gut, wenn man manchmal (aber nicht zu oft!) einen Schnaps trinkt. **b** Ja, es ist schlecht, wenn man zu viel Fernsehen sieht. **c** Ja, man ist eigentlich ein bisschen altmodisch, wenn man keine Jeans trägt. **d** Nein, es ist nicht ungesund, wenn man jeden Tag fünf Tassen Kaffee trinkt. (Aber es ist auch nicht besonders gesund!). **e** Ja, es ist gesund, wenn man viermal pro Woche ins Fitnesscenter geht. **Go further a** Ich habe Kopfschmerzen; **b** Ich habe seit einer Woche Rückenschmerzen; **c** Ich habe seit zwei Tagen Magenschmerzen; **d** Wie oft muss ich die Tabletten nehmen? **e** Muss ich zu Hause bleiben? **f** Was soll ich essen? **Test yourself 1 a** soll; **b** soll; **c** will; **d** wollen; **e** Darfst; **f** darf; **g** dürfen **2 a** Wenn du Englisch lernen möchtest, musst du in eine Sprachschule gehen. **b** Wenn Bodo ein altes Buch über Deutschland finden möchte, musser bei Amazon suchen. **c** Wenn ihr nächste Woche nach New York fliegen wollt, müsst ihr bald eure Tickets buchen. **d** Wenn Sie Rückenschmerzen haben, müssen Sie zum Arzt gehen. **e** Wenn Marcus ein Jahr in Madrid leben möchte, muss er vorher Spanisch lernen. **f** Wenn du Hunger hast, musst du etwas essen.

Unit 20

Discovery questions Urlaub means holiday and Feiertage public holiday, Die Ostseeküste means Baltic Sea coast, der Schwarzwald is Black Forest and die Bayerischen Alpen are the Bavarian Alps. **Vocabulary builder 1 a** der Frühling; **b** der Sommer; **c** der Herbst; **d** der Winter **2 a**-6; **b**-1; **c**-3; **d**-4; **e**-2; **f**-5

3

	wo sie waren	Jahreszeit	Temperaturen	Wetter
Bärbel Specht	auf Kreta	Frühling	um 28 Grad	Ideal. Kein Regen. Jeden Tag Sonne und ein leichter Wind.
Jutta Weiß	Australien	Dezember (Sommer in Australien)	über 35 Grad	Sonne. Manchmal ein Gewitter.

Interview 1 a Er hat abends gut gegessen und ist manchmal in die Hotelbar gegangen. **b** Nein, er konnte auch richtiges deutsches Bier kaufen. **c** Sie machen jedes Jahr im Winter einen Skiurlaub. **d** Nächstes Jahr wollen sie vielleicht mal in die Schweiz fahren. **e** Das Wetter war eine Katastrophe. Sie hatten meistens Regen. Außerdem war es sehr kalt. **f** Nein, nächstes Jahr fliegen sie lieber in den Süden, nach Spanien oder Griechenland. **g** Nein, er sucht jetzt einen Job. **h** Vor zwei Jahren ist er nach Mexiko-City geflogen. **Conversation 1** She could not go skiing. **2 a** falsch; **b** richtig; **c** richtig; **d** falsch; **e** falsch; **f** richtig. **Language discovery 1** They take a –te ending. **2 a** nach; **b** nach; **c** in, in; **d** in; **e** auf; **f** an **Practice 1 b** war; **c** hatten; **d** waren; **e** hatte; **f** hatte, hatten **2 a** –e; **b** –est; **c** –en; **d** –et; **e** -en; **f** -e; **g** –e; **h** –est **3 a** nach; **b** in; **c** in; **d** aufs; **e** auf; **f** in; **g** an **Speaking** Eine einzige Katastrophe./ Die ersten drei Tage hatten wir Regen. Deshalb konnten wir nicht spazieren gehen./ Ein Freund und ich sind mit dem Wagen gegen einen Baum gefahren./ Ja, meine Beine haben mir wehgetan, aber es war nichts Schlimmes./ Nur zwei Tage, aber dann musste ich wieder nach Hause fahren./ Jetzt geht es mir wieder gut. **Listening a** 6 Grad. **b** 23 Grad. **c** Wolken und Regen. **d** Schauer. **e** besser. **Reading a** richtig **b** falsch; 22 Millionen Deutsche finden kurze Urlaube besser. **c** richtig **d** richtig **e** falsch; Es fahren mehr Leute nach London als nach Amsterdam. **Writing** Letztes Jahr war ich in Heidelberg im Urlaub. Dort habe ich in einer Jugendherberge gewohnt. Abends bin ich in eine Karaoke-Kneipe gegangen. In der Kneipe habe ich ein Lied von Elvis Presley gesungen. Dort hat mich ein Produzent gehört. Ihm hat meine Stimme sehr gut gefallen. Am nächsten Tag bin ich mit ihm nach Berlin geflogen. In einem Studio habe ich eine neue CD gemacht. In Berlin bin ich 10 Tage geblieben. Dann habe ich im Fernsehen und im Radio gesungen. Nächstes Jahr will ich in Las Vegas singen. **Go further 2 a** In München ist es wärmer. **b** 20 Grad Celsius. **c** Ja, es gibt Schauer. **d** Nein.

In Wien ist es bedeckt. **e** In Spanien gibt es Gewitter. **f** In Kairo scheint die Sonne. Die Temperatur beträgt 35 Grad. **5 a Test yourself 1 a** -; **b** –en; **c** -; **d** –t; **e** –test; **f** –te; **g** -, -te **2 a** wollte, musste; **b** konnten; **c** sollte, konnte; **d** durfte; **e** Mussten **3** Na, wie geht's? Dieses Jahr sind wir nicht nach Indien geflogen oder in die Berge gefahren. Nein, wir haben Urlaub an der Ostsee gemacht, auf der Insel Rügen. Rügen liegt im Nordosten Deutschlands. Das Wetter war gut, wir sind viel im Meer geschwommen. Außerdem haben wir einen Ausflug nach Berlin gemacht. Dort war es natürlich auch sehr interessant. So viel hat sich verändert. Wir sind ins Pergamonmuseum gegangen und waren auch im Museum für Deutsche Geschichte.

Unit 21

Discovery questions Pünktlichkeit means punctuality, Telefongespräch telephone conversation and ein Blumenstrauß is a bouquet of flowers. They say Auf Wiederhören. **Vocabulary builder 1 a**-3; **b**-2; **c**-1 **2 a**-3; **b**-1; **c**-2 **3 a**-3; **b**-4; **c**-1; **d**-2

4

informell	formell
– Hallo, Bernd, bist du es? – Ist Inga da?	– Guten Tag, Herr Preiß. Hier spricht Frau Weber. – Spreche ich mit Frau Schmidt? – Ich möchte mit Herrn Klaus sprechen. – Kann ich bitte mit Frau Groß sprechen?

5 Hier ist der telefonische Anrufbeantworter von Evelyn und Michael Schweighofer. Wir sind im Moment leider nicht da. Sie können uns aber gerne nach dem Pfeifton eine Nachricht hinterlassen. Bitte sagen Sie uns Ihren Namen und Ihre Telefonnummer und wir rufen Sie dann so schnell wie möglich zurück. **Conversations 1 b**-5; **c**-1; **d**-2; **e**-3; **f**-4 **2 b** Nein, links vorne war das Büro der Sekretärin, Frau Schüller. **c** richtig. **d** Nein, auf der rechten Seite in der Mitte war das Zimmer der Texter, Michaela und Günther; **e** Und ganz hinten rechts war der Raum der Chefin, Frau Conrad. **f** Ganz hinten links war dann das Zimmer des Managers, Guido Kafka. **3 a 2** He's on a business trip. **4 a** richtig; **b** falsch; Herr Schneider hat am Ende der Woche einen Termin mit ihr; **c** falsch; Er fährt auf Geschäftsreise in die USA; **d** richtig; **e** falsch; Sie machen einen Termin für Donnerstag um 14.00 Uhr. **Language discovery 1 a** des; **b** des; **c** der; **d** der; **e** der. Masculine nouns = des, feminine nouns = der, plural nouns = der. An s is added to masculine nouns in these examples. **Practice 1 b** Ich habe den

Namen der Designerin vergessen. **c** Die Telefonnummer der Kundin ist 45 76 98. **d** Die Rechnung des Hotels war astronomisch. **e** Die Reparatur des Computers hat drei Wochen gedauert. **f** Mir gefällt die Farbe des neuen Firmenautos nicht. **g** Die Anzahl der Leute ohne Arbeit beträgt etwa drei Millionen. **2 a**-2; **b**-6; **c**-1; **d**-5; **e**-3; **f**-4; **g**-

1. APPARAT
ANR
2. ZURÜCKRUFEN
3. PFEIFTON
4. VERBINDE
5. BESETZT
6. HINTERLASSEN
7. ANSCHLUSS
8. LEITUNG
W
O
9. NACHRICHT
T
10. NAMEN
11. AUSRICHTEN

Speaking Guten Tag, ich möchte gern mit Frau Conrad sprechen. / Vielen Dank. / Hier spricht ... . Ich habe einen Termin für Anfang der Woche. / Es tut mir sehr leid, aber ich muss den Termin absagen. / Ja. Passt es Ihnen am Ende der Woche? / Ich habe keine Termine für Freitagmorgen. Das passt mir gut. Auf Wiederhören.

Listening 1

Sie ist beim Zahnarzt.	☐	☒	☐
Die Leitung ist besetzt.	☒	☐	☐
Er ist auf Geschäftsreise.	☐	☐	☒

Soll sie zurückrufen?	☐	☒	☐
Wollen Sie warten?	☒	☐	☐
Wollen Sie eine Nachricht hinterlassen?	☐	☐	☒
Er möchte mich morgen zurückrufen.	☐	☐	☒
Ich bin zu Hause.	☐	☒	☐
Ich rufe später noch mal an.	☒	☐	☐

2 a Sie telefoniert. **b** Sie ist beim Zahnarzt und kommt in einer Stunde wieder nach Hause. **c** Er ist auf Geschäftsreise (in Wien) und ist wahrscheinlich morgen wieder im Büro. **d** Sie möchte ihm ein (fantastisches) Geschenk geben.**Test yourself 1 a** 3; **b** 1; **c** 5; **d** 6; **e** 2; **f** 4. **2 a** 1; **b** 6; **c** 2; **d** 3; **e** 8; **f** 5; **g** 7; **h** 4 **3 a** Das Auto meines Bruders fährt sehr schnell. **b** Der Computer meiner Kollegin ist fantastisch. **c** Die Firma meines alten Schulfreundes war letztes Jahr sehr erfolgreich. **d** Die Kollegen meines Mannes sind alle schrecklich langweilig. **e** Die Managerin der exquisiten Boutique ‚La dame' kommt aus Paris. **f** Das Büro unseres neuen Designers ist sehr schick. **g** Der Laptop meines Sohnes hat €500 gekostet. **h** Das Geschenk meiner Kollegen hat mir gut gefallen.

Unit 22

Discovery questions Schule means school, Grundschule primary school, Abschlüsse qualifications and Lebenslauf CV. The Abitur is comparable to A-Levels in the UK or the High School Diploma in the US. **Vocabulary builder 1 a**-4; **b**-6; **c**-1; **d**-5; **e**-3; **f**-2 **Readings 1a** office job; **b** nanny; **c** magazine editor; **d** cook; **f** night porter **2 a**-4; **b**-5; **c**-3; **d**-2; **e**-4; **f**-3; **g**-1 **3 a**-5; **b**-1; **c**-3; **d**-4; **e**-2 **1 a** 2 – banking **2 a** falsch; Herr Frankenthal ist verheiratet. **b** richtig; **c** falsch; Er hat in Offenbach seinen Realschulabschluss gemacht. **d** richtig; **5 e** falsch; Seinen ersten Job hatte er bei der Dresdner Bank. **f** richtig; **g** richtig **4 a** Grundschule; **b** Realschulabschluss; **c** Banklehre; **d** Filialleiter **Language discovery a** ging; **b** wechselte; **c** machte; **d** bekam; **e** arbeitete; **f** besuchte **Practice 1 a** achtzehnhundertzweiundvierzig; **b** neunzehnhundertachtundsiebzig; **c** zweitausendvier; **d** zweitausendzwölf **2 a** 1983. **b** Sie ist durch Asien gereist. **c** 2003–2004. **d** An der Universität Hamburg. **e** Drei Jahre. **f** Seit 2012. **4** Ich bin am 1. Juni 1983 in Bremen geboren. Von 1989 bis 1993 ging ich in die Grundschule in Bremen. Danach wechselte ich auf das Heinrich-Heine-Gymnasium. 2002 machte ich mein Abitur. Nach der Schule reiste ich durch Asien. Von 2003 bis 2004 machte ich ein Praktikum bei der Hamburger Zeitung. Anschließend studierte ich Journalistik an der Universität Hamburg und 2009 machte ich meinen Abschluss. Nach dem Studium arbeitete ich von 2009 bis 2012 bei der Tageszeitung in Berlin. 2012 zog ich wieder nach Hamburg und ich arbeite seitdem beim Nachrichtenmagazin *Der Spiegel*. **Go further 1 b** (ein) hundertdreiundzwanzig; **c** dreitausendsiebenhundertsechsundneunzig; **d** zehntausendsechshundertneunundfünfzig; **e** siebenundfünfzigtausenddrei-hundertachtundachtzig; **f** zweihunderttausendfünfhunderteinundvierzig; **g** zwei Millionen sechshundertzwölftausendvierhundertsiebzig **Test yourself 1 a** sah; **b** ging; **c** war; **d** stand; **e** gab; **f** standen; **g** aß; **h** trank; **i** legte; **j** blieb; **k** dachte; **l** schlief. **2** Das Leben von Heinrich Böll. **c** Von 1928 bis 1937 besuchte er das Kaiser-Wilhelm-Gymnasium in Köln. **d** 1937 machte er das Abitur. **e** 1937 begann er in Bonn eine Buchhandelslehre. **f** 1939 studierte er an der Universität Köln Germanistik. **g** Von 1939 bis 1945 war er Soldat im Zweiten Weltkrieg. **h** 1942 heiratete er Annemarie Zech. **i** Von 1946 bis 1949 schrieb er Kurzgeschichten in Zeitschriften. **j** 1949 erschien sein erstes Buch *Der Zug war pünktlich*. **k** Von 1949 bis 1985 schrieb er viele literarische Werke. **l** 1972 bekam er den Nobelpreis für Literatur. **m** 1985 starb er am 16. Juni in Hürtgenwald / Eifel.

Unit 23

Discovery questions Regierung means government, Wirtschaft economy, Fachkräfte skilled workers and Grenzen borders. In 1961 the Berlin Wall was built and all borders between West and East Germany were sealed off. In 1989 the Wall came down and on 3rd October 1990 Germany was officially reunited. **Vocabulary builder a**-3; **b**-2; **c**-4; **d**-1 **Reading 1 a** 1 to give general information about Germany, Austria and Switzerland **2 a** Österreich ist größer als die Schweiz. **b** Die Hauptstadt der Schweiz heißt Bern **c** Es gibt vier offizielle Sprachen in der Schweiz: Deutsch, Französisch, Italienisch und Rätoromanisch. **d** In Wien. **e** Wolfgang Amadeus Mozart ist in Salzburg geboren. **f** Die Bundesrepublik Deutschland hat 82,4 Millionen Einwohner. **g** Die Hauptstadt der Bundesrepublik Deutschland ist Berlin. **h** Hamburg ist größer als München. **i** Das Oktoberfest findet in München statt. **j** Frankfurt ist am multikulturellsten.

3 Schweiz	Österreich	Deutschland
Arzneimittel	Mozart-Kugeln	82,4 Millionen Einwohner
vier Sprachen	Schloss Schönbrunn	Biergärten

7,5 Millionen	etwa doppelt so groß	Oktoberfest
Einwohner	wie die Schweiz	viele Leute aus der Türkei
	Einwohner	neue Hauptstadt
	8,3 Millionen	multikulturelle Gesellschaft

4 b 83 853 km²; **c** 41 293 km²; **d** 82,4 Millionen; **e** 8,3 Millionen; **f** 7,5 Millionen Einwohner; **g** am 3. Oktober 1990; **h** 3.10.1990; **i** 29,1%
5 a b – political history **6 a** vier Zonen; **b** Bundesrepublik Deutschland; **c** Mauer; **d** Bundeskanzlerin **Language discovery 1 a** Ich meine, dass Deutschland ungefähr 82 Millionen Einwohner hat. **b** Ich glaube, dass er aus Österreich kommt. **c** Ich denke, dass St. Moritz in der Schweiz liegt. The verb goes into last position. **2 a** geteilt; **b** gegründet; **c** wiedervereinigt; **d** gewählt. Translation: **a** Germany is divided into four zones. **b** In the eastern zone the German Democratic Republic is founded. **c** On 3rd October Germany is officially reunited. **d** Berlin is chosen as the new capital. **Practice 1 Sample answers: a** Nein, ich glaube nicht, dass die Schweizer langweilig sind. **b** Ja, ich denke, dass die Deutschen viel Bier trinken. **c** Ja, ich glaube, dass man in Berlin gut ausgehen kann. **d** Ja, ich denke, dass man in Österreich gut Urlaub machen kann. **e** Nein, ich glaube nicht, dass die Österreicher ein bisschen konservativ sind. / Ja, ich glaube, dass die Österreicher ein bisschen konservativ sind. **2 a** weil; **b** obwohl; **c** weil; **d** weil; **e** obwohl **3 a** 1969 wurde der Mond zum ersten Mal von einem Menschen betreten. **b** 1981 wurde John Lennon ermordet. **c** 1990 wurde Nelson Mandela nach 27 Jahren aus der Haft entlassen. **d** 2002 wurde in Europa der Euro als neue Währung eingeführt. **e** 2009 wurde Barack Obama zum Präsidenten der USA gewählt. **f** 2012 wurde in London das 60. Thronjubiläum von Queen Elizabeth gefeiert. **Listening 1 a** falsch; **b** richtig; **c** richtig; **d** falsch; **e** falsch; **f** richtig; **g** falsch. **2 a** (am 28. August) 1749 in Frankfurt am Main geboren. **b** Jura. **c** Seine Novelle ‚Die Leiden des jungen Werther'. **d** an den Hof von Weimar. **e** nach Italien. **f** ‚Faust'. **g** an den Teufel. **h** in Weimar. **i** in fast alle Sprachen übersetzt. **j** nach ihm benannt. **Speaking** Ja, in der Schweiz werden vier Sprachen gesprochen. / Die Bundesrepublik Deutschland wurde 1949 gegründet. / Die Berliner Mauer wurde 1961 gebaut./ Deutschland wurde am 3. Oktober 1990 wiedervereinigt. / ‚Faust' wurde von Johann Wolfgang von Goethe geschrieben. / Natürlich. Es wurde 1808 veröffentlicht./ Natürlich. Das Goethe-Institut wurde nach ihm benannt. **Go further a** Die neunte Symphonie wurde von Ludwig van Beethoven komponiert. **b** Die Fußballweltmeisterschaft 2012 wurde von Spanien gewonnen. **c** Die World Wide Web wurde von Tim Berners-Lee erfunden. **d** ‚Hamlet' wurde

von William Shakespeare geschrieben. **e** ‚Guernica' wurde von Pablo Picasso gemalt. **f** Das Penizillin wurde von Alexander Fleming entdeckt. **g** ‚Set fire to the rain' wurde von Adele gesungen. **h** Die Queen wurde von Helen Mirren gespielt. **Test yourself 1 a** Ich meine, dass Frankfurt das Finanzzentrum von Deutschland ist. **b** Ich glaube, dass es in Wien viele alte Kaffeehäuser gibt. **c** Ich denke, dass München eine sehr schöne Stadt ist. **d** Ich glaube, dass die Schweizer viel Humor haben. **e** Ich denke, dass die Deutschen viel Bier trinken. **f** Ich meine, dass Österreich viele schöne Bergregionen hat. **2 a** ..., weil er oft geschäftlich nach Frankfurt fährt. **b** ..., weil sie die Musik von Mozart und Brahms liebt. **c** ..., weil er gern Sprachen lernt. **d** ..., weil es gut für seine berufliche Karriere ist. **e** ..., weil sie die deutsche Sprache schön findet. **f** ... weil sie viele Freunde in Berlin hat. **3 a** Muttersprache; **b** Regionen; **c** Ländern; **d** Hauptstadt; **e** Bekannt; **f** Arzneimittel; **g** Einwohner; **h** Sehenswürdigkeiten; **i** Wiedervereinigung; **j** Städte; **k** Ausländer; **l** Gesellschaft.

Glossary of grammatical terms

The glossary covers the most important grammar terminology used in this book. qv (quod vide) means 'which see', i.e. please see the entry for this word.

Adjectives Adjectives are used to provide more information about nouns. In English they remain unchanged whether they stand on their own after a verb, such as *to be* or *to seem* (The car is *new*.) or whether they appear in front of a noun (The *new* car wasn't cheap.). In German the adjective does not change after a verb, such as **sein** or **scheinen** (**Das Auto ist neu**.), but endings *are* needed on adjectives that come in front of a noun (**Das *neue* Auto war nicht billig**.).

Adverbs Just as adjectives provide more information about nouns, so adverbs tend to provide more information about verbs: Wayne ran *quickly* down the stairs. But adverbs can also provide more information about adjectives: I was *completely* exhausted. In English adverbs often (but not always) end in *-ly*. In German adverbs often have the same form as adjectives: **Deine Arbeit ist gut**. Your work is *good*. **Du hast das sehr *gut* gemacht**. You did that very *well*.

Articles There are two main types of articles: *definite* and *indefinite*. In English the definite article is *the*. In German there are three definite articles: **der**, **die** and **das**, referring to the three different genders in German. The term indefinite article is given to the words *a* and *an*. In German the indefinite articles are **ein**, **eine**, etc. (See also **Gender**.)

Auxiliary verbs Auxiliary verbs are used as a support to the main verb, e.g. I *am* working; he *has* gone. The most important auxiliary verbs in German are **haben**, **sein** and **werden**. These are used in the formation of the present perfect tense (qv) and of the passive (qv): **Ich *habe* gerade einen sehr guten Film gesehen**. I *have* just seen a very good film. **Die neue Schule *wurde* 1998 gebaut**. The new school *was* built in 1998. (See also **Modal verbs**.)

Cases There are four cases in German: the *nominative*, the *accusative*, the *genitive* and the *dative*. Cases are used in German to express relationships between the various parts of the sentence. Here is a short summary:

Nominative: this is the term used for the case that indicates the **subject** (qv) of the sentence:

Der Mann kauft einen Computer. *The man* buys a computer.

Accusative: this is the term used for the case that indicates the direct object (**object qv**) of the sentence:

Der Mann kauft *einen Computer*. The man buys *a computer*.

Dative: this is the term used for the case that indicates the indirect object (**object qv**) of the sentence:

Wir haben den Computer meinem Bruder gegeben.	We gave the computer ***to my brother***.

Genitive: this is the term used for the case that indicates possession:

Das ist der Computer *meines Bruders*.	That's ***my brother's*** computer.

Note that **prepositions** (qv) in German are followed by the accusative, dative or genitive case.

Comparative When we make comparisons, we need the comparative form of the **adjective** (qv). In English this usually means adding **-er** to the adjective or putting **more** in front of it:

*This shirt is **cheap*er** than that one. This blouse is **more** expensive than that one.*

Making comparisons in German follows the first example and adds **-er** to the adjective:

Dieses Hemd ist *billiger* als das da. Diese Bluse ist *teurer* als die da. (See also **Superlative**.)

Conjunctions Conjunctions are words such as ***and***, ***but***, ***when***, ***if***, ***unless***, ***while*** and ***although***. They link words, clauses or sentences together: Bread ***and*** butter. **Brot *und* Butter**. He comes from Berlin ***but*** now lives in London. **Er kommt aus Berlin, *aber* lebt jetzt in London**. In German a distinction is made between ***co-ordinating conjunctions*** and ***subordinating conjunctions***. Co-ordinating conjunctions such as **und *and***, **aber *but*** and **oder *or*** simply join two main clauses together and do not affect the word order: **Anna kommt aus München *und* ist 21 Jahre alt**. Anna comes from Munich *and* is 21 years old.

Subordinating conjunctions include such words as **wenn *when*, *if*, weil *because*, obwohl *although*** and **seitdem *since*** and send the verb to the end of the clause: **Er kann nicht kommen, *weil* er krank ist**. He can't come, ***because*** he is ill.

Demonstratives Words such as ***this***, ***that***, ***these***, ***those*** are called demonstratives or ***demonstrative adjectives:*** *This* book is interesting. ***Dieses* Buch ist interessant**. *These* exercises are very difficult. ***Diese* Übungen sind sehr schwer**.

In German **dieser** (masculine), **diese** (feminine & plural), **dieses** (neuter) are the most commonly used demonstratives.

Gender In English gender is usually linked to male and female persons or animals, so for example we refer to a man as ***he*** and to a woman as ***she***. Objects and beings of an indeterminate or no sex are referred to as having neuter gender. For instance, we refer to a table as ***it***.

In German nouns have a gender irrespective of sex. For instance, the gender of the word for ***girl*** (**das Mädchen**) is neuter. In German there are three genders, ***masculine***, ***feminine*** and ***neuter***: **der Tisch *the table*, die Lampe *the lamp*, das Haus *the house***.

Imperative The imperative is the form of the verb used to give orders or commands: ***Help me***, please.

In German there are three main forms of the imperative because of the various forms of address. ***Helfen* Sie mir, bitte!** (**Sie** form); ***Hilf* mir, bitte!** (**du** form); ***Helft* mir, bitte!** (**ihr** form).

Infinitive The infinitive is the basic form of the verb. This is the form that you will find entered in the dictionary. In English the infinitive is usually accompanied by the word *to*, e.g. *to go*, *to play*. In German the dictionary entry for the infinitive usually ends in **-en**: **gehen *to go*, spielen *to play*, machen *to do*,** etc.

Irregular verbs **see** Verbs

Modal verbs Verbs which express concepts such as permission, obligation, possibility, etc. (***can***, ***must***, ***may***) are referred to as modal verbs. Verbs in this category cannot in general stand on their own and therefore also fall under the general heading of *auxiliary verbs* (qv). Modal verbs in German include **wollen *to want to*, können *to be able to*, dürfen *to be allowed to***.

Nouns Nouns are words like ***house* Haus**, ***bread* Brot** and ***beauty* Schönheit**. They are often called 'naming words'. A useful test of a noun is whether you can put ***the*** in front of it: e.g. ***the house*, *the bread***. Nouns in German have one of three ***genders*** (qv) and take a capital letter.

Object The term object expresses the 'receiving end' relationship between a noun and a verb. Look at the following sentence: The dog bit the postman. **Der Hund biss den Postboten**. The postman is said to be the object of the sentence as he is at the receiving end of the action. (See also **Subject**.)

Sentences such as: 'My mother gave my wife an expensive ring' have both a **direct object** (an expensive ring) and an **indirect object** (my wife). In German the direct object requires the **accusative case** and the indirect object the **dative case**: **Meine Mutter gab *meiner Frau*** (dative) ***einen teuren Ring*** (accusative).

Passive voice Most actions can be viewed in two different ways: 1 The dog bit the postman. **active voice**

2 The postman was bitten by the dog. **passive voice**

In German you will also find both the active and passive voice. The passive is normally formed with the verb **werden** rather than with the verb **sein**:

1 Der Hund biss den Postboten.

2 Der Postbote *wurde* vom Hund gebissen.

Personal pronouns Personal pronouns refer to persons. In German they are: **ich** *I*; **du** *you* (informal singular); **Sie** *you* (formal singular); **er**, **sie**, **es** *he*, *she*, *it*; **wir** *we*; **ihr** *you* (informal plural); **Sie** *you* (formal plural); **sie** *they*. (See also **Pronouns**.)

Plural see Singular

Possessives Words such as **mein** *my*, **Ihr** *your* (formal), **dein** *your* (informal), **ihr** *her*, **sein** *his* are given the term possessives or **possessive adjectives** because they indicate who something belongs to.

Prepositions Words like **in** *in*, **auf** *on*, **zwischen** *between*, **für** *for* are called prepositions. Prepositions often tell us about the position of something. They are normally followed by a noun or a pronoun: **a** This present is *for* you. **b** *Despite* the weather I'm going to walk. **c** Your book is *on* the table.

In German prepositions require the use of a **case** (qv), such as the accusative, genitive or dative: **a Dieses Geschenk ist *für* dich.** (accusative) **b *Trotz des* Wetters gehe ich zu Fuß.** (genitive neuter) **c Dein Buch liegt *auf dem* Tisch.** (dative masculine)

Pronouns Pronouns fulfil a similar function to nouns and often stand in the place of nouns mentioned earlier. The *lamp* (noun) is modern.

It (pronoun) is ugly. **Die *Lampe* ist modern. *Sie* ist hässlich.** Note that in German the pronoun has to be the same gender as the noun which it stands for (***die Lampe → sie***).

Singular and plural The terms singular and plural are used to make the contrast between 'one' and 'more than one': **Hund/Hunde** *dog/dogs*; **Buch/Bücher** *book/books*, **Hut/Hüte** *hat/hats*.

Most plural forms in English are formed by adding an -s, but not all: *child/children, woman/women, mouse/mice*. There are many different plural forms in German. Here are just three: **Kind/Kind*er*, Frau/Frau*en*, Maus/Mäuse.**

Some nouns do not normally have plurals and are said to be *uncountable*: **das Obst** *fruit*.

Subject The term subject expresses a relationship between a noun and a verb. Look at the sentence 'The dog bit the postman'. Here the dog is said to be the subject of the verb ***to bite***, because it is the dog that is doing the biting.

In German the subject of the sentence needs to be in the ***nominative case***: ***Der Hund* biss den Postboten.**

Superlative The superlative is used for the most extreme version of a comparison: **a** This shirt is the ***cheapest***. **b** This blouse is the ***most*** expensive of all.

The superlative in German follows a similar pattern:

a Dieses Hemd ist *am billigsten*. b Diese Bluse ist die *teuerste* von allen.

(See also **Comparative**.)

Tense Most languages use changes in the verb form to indicate an aspect of time. These changes in the verb are traditionally referred to as tenses, and the tenses may be ***present***, ***past*** or ***future***. Tenses are often reinforced with expressions of time:

Present: ***Today*** I am staying at home. **Heute bleibe ich zu Hause.**

Past: ***Yesterday*** I went to London. **Gestern bin ich nach London gefahren. / Gestern fuhr ich nach London.**

Future: ***Tomorrow*** I'll be flying to Berlin. **Morgen werde ich nach Berlin fliegen.**

The German tenses dealt with in this book are the present, the simple past and the present perfect tense.

Verbs Verbs often communicate actions, states and sensations. So, for instance, the verb ***to play* spielen** expresses an action, the verb *to exist* **existieren** expresses a state and the verb ***to see* sehen** expresses a sensation. A verb may also be defined by its role in the sentence or clause and usually has a **subject** (qv). It may also have an **object** (qv).

Verbs in German can be *regular* (often called *weak verbs*), or *irregular* (also often referred to as *strong verbs*). The forms of irregular verbs need to be learned. A list of the most common irregular verbs is provided on the next page.

Abbreviations

The following abbreviations are used in this book:

QV   *Quick vocab*
UE   *Useful expressions*

List of common irregular verbs

*These verbs normally form their present perfect tense with **sein**.

Infinitive	Simple past tense (er/sie/es form)	Past participle	Vowel Changes: present tense er/sie/es form
anlfangen *to start, begin*	fing an	angefangen	fängt an
anlrufen *to call up*	rief an	angerufen	
auflstehen *to get up*	stand auf	aufgestanden*	
beginnen *to begin*	begann	begonnen	
bleiben *to stay*	blieb	geblieben*	
bringen *to bring*	brachte	gebracht	
denken *to think*	dachte	gedacht	
einlladen *to invite*	lud ein	eingeladen	lädt ein
empfehlen *to recommend*	empfahl	empfohlen	empfiehlt
essen *to eat*	aß	gegessen	isst
fahren *to go (by vehicle)*	fuhr	gefahren*	fährt
finden *to find*	fand	gefunden	
fliegen *to fly*	flog	geflogen*	
geben *to give*	gab	gegeben	gibt
gefallen *to be pleasing*	gefiel	gefallen	gefällt
haben *to have*	hatte	gehabt	
halten *to hold; to stop*	hielt	gehalten	hält
heißen *to be called*	hieß	geheißen	
helfen *to help*	half	geholfen	hilft
kennen *to know, be acquainted with*	kannte	gekannt	
laufen *to run*	lief	gelaufen*	läuft
lesen *to read*	las	gelesen	liest
nehmen *to take*	nahm	genommen	nimmt
raten *to advise; to guess*	riet	geraten	rät
schlafen *to sleep*	schlief	geschlafen	schläft
schreiben *to write*	schrieb	geschrieben	
schwimmen *to swim*	schwamm	geschwommen*	
sehen *to see*	sah	gesehen	sieht
sein *to be*	war	gewesen*	ist
singen *to sing*	sang	gesungen	

sitzen *to sit*	saß	gesessen	
sprechen *to speak*	sprach	gesprochen	spricht
tragen *to carry; to wear*	trug	getragen	trägt
treffen *to meet*	traf	getroffen	trifft
trinken *to drink*	trank	getrunken	
tun *to do*	tat	getan	
um|steigen *to change (transport)*	stieg um	umgestiegen*	
verbinden *to connect, put through*	verband	verbunden	
vergessen *to forget*	vergaß	vergessen	vergisst
verlassen *to leave*	verließ	verlassen	verlässt
verlieren *to lose*	verlor	verloren	
verstehen *to understand*	verstand	verstanden	
waschen *to wash*	wusch	gewaschen	wäscht
werden *to become*	wurde	geworden*	wird
wissen *to know (a fact)*	wusste	gewusst	weiß
ziehen *to go, move; to pull, draw*	zog	gezogen*	

English-German vocabulary

This reference vocabulary is intended to help you recall and use some of the most important words that you have met during the course. It is not intended to be comprehensive.

* indicates this verb or its root form is in the verb list preceding the German–English vocabulary, and is irregular.

| indicates that a verb is separable (e.g. an|rufen).

about **ungefähr**

actually **eigentlich**

address **die Adresse (-n)**

adventure **das Abenteuer (-)**

to advise **raten* (+ dative)**

afternoon **der Nachmittag (e)**

afterwards **anschließend, nachher**

again **wieder**

against **gegen**

ago **vor (+ dative);** *a year ago* **vor einem Jahr**

air **die Luft (¨e)**

alarm clock **der Wecker (-)**

already **schon**

also **auch**

although **obwohl**

always **immer**

and **und**

to answer **beantworten**

answer **die Antwort (-en)**

apartment **die Wohnung (-en)**

apparatus **der Apparat (-e)**

to appear (seem) **aus|sehen***

to appear **erscheinen***

apple **der Apfel (¨)**

application **die Bewerbung (-en)**

appointment **der Termin (-e)**

apprenticeship **die Lehre (-n)**

approximately **ungefähr**

area **das Gebiet (-e)**

arm **der Arm (-e)**

armchair **der Sessel (-)**

to arrive **an|kommen***

to ask **fragen**

aunt **die Tante (-n)**

Austrian (person) **der Österreicher (-) / die -in (-nen)**

autumn **der Herbst (-e)**

awake **wach**

baby **das Baby (-s)**

back **der Rücken (-)**

bad **schlecht; schlimm**

bag **die Tüte (-n)**

bakery **die Bäckerei (-en)**

balcony **der Balkon (-s/-e)**

balloon **der Luftballon (-s)**

Baltic **die Ostsee**

bank **die Bank (-en)**

bath **das Bad (¨er)**

bathroom **das Badezimmer (-)**

to be **sein***

be able to **können**

to be called **heißen***

beach **der Strand ("e)**

beautician **der Kosmetiker (-) / die -in (-nen)**

beautiful **schön**

because **weil**

to become **werden***

bed **das Bett (-en)**

bedroom **das Schlafzimmer (-)**

beef **das Rindfleisch**

beer **das Bier (-e)**

to begin **anlfangen*; beginnen***

beginning **der Anfang ("e)**

to believe **glauben**

belly **der Bauch ("e)**

bicycle **das Fahrrad ("er); das Rad ("er)**

big **groß**

birthday **der Geburtstag (-e)**

bit: a bit (of) **bisschen: ein bisschen**

black **schwarz**

blouse **die Bluse (-n)**

blue **blau**

body **der Körper (-)**

to boil **kochen**

book **das Buch ("er)**

to book **buchen**

border **die Grenze (-n)**

boring **langweilig**

boss **der Chef (-s) / die Chefin (-nen)**

bottle **die Flasche (-n)**

boy **der Junge (-n)**

boyfriend **der Freund (-e)**

bread roll **das Brötchen (-)**

bread **das Brot (-e)**

breakfast **das Frühstück (-e)**

bricklayer **der Maurer (-) /die -in**

bridge **die Brücke (-n)**

bright **hell**

to bring **bringen***

brother **der Bruder (")**

brown **braun**

to build **bauen**

building **das Gebäude (-)**

bus stop **die Bushaltestelle (-n)**

bus **der Bus (-se)**

business **das Geschäft (-e)**

but **aber**

butter **die Butter**

to buy **kaufen**

café **das Café (-s)**

cake **der Kuchen (-)**

to call **rufen***

to call (on the phone) **anlrufen***

to call back **zurücklrufen***

can **die Dose (-n)**

cap **die Mütze (-n)**

capital city **die Hauptstadt ("e)**

car **das Auto (-s)**

carpenter **der Tischler (-) / die -in (-nen)**

to carry **tragen***

cash desk **die Kasse (-n)**

castle **das Schloss ("er)**

cauliflower **der Blumenkohl (-e)**

CD **die CD (-s)**

to celebrate **feiern**

celebration **die Feier (-n)**

cellar **der Keller (-)**

central heating **die Zentralheizung (-en)**

central(ly) **zentral**

certain(ly) **sicher**

to change **wechseln**

to change (a train, bus, etc.) **umlsteigen***

to chat **schwatzen**

cheap **billig**

cheese **der Käse**

cherry **die Kirsche (-n)**

chest **die Brust ("e)**

child **das Kind (-er)**

church **die Kirche (-n)**

cinema **das Kino (-s)**

climate **das Klima (-s)**

clock **die Uhr (-en)**

clothing **die Kleidung**

cloudy **wolkig**

coast **die Küste (-n)**

coat **der Mantel (")**

coffee **der Kaffee (-s)**

cold **kalt**
colleague **der Kollege (-n) / die Kollegin
(-nen)**
to collect **sammeln**
colour **die Farbe (-n)**
to come **kommen***
comfortable **bequem**
computer **der Computer (-)**
concert **das Konzert (-e)**
to connect **verbinden***
connection **die Verbindung (-en)**
to cook **kochen**
cool **kühl**
corner **die Ecke (-n)**
corridor **der Flur (-e)**
to cost **kosten**
country **das Land (¨er)**
course **der Kurs (-e)**
cream **die Sahne**
cup **die Tasse (-n)**
cupboard **der Schrank (¨e)**
currency **die Währung (-en)**
customer **der Kunde (-n) / die Kundin
(-nen)**
to cut **schneiden***
CV **der Lebenslauf (¨e)**
to cycle **Rad fahren***

to dance **tanzen**
dangerous **gefährlich**
dark **dunkel**
date **der Termin (-e)**
daughter **die Tochter (¨)**
day **der Tag (-e)**
dear **teuer**
delicious **lecker**
dentist **der Zahnarzt (¨e) / die
Zahnärztin (-nen)**
to depart **abIfahren***
department store **das Kaufhaus (¨er)**
desk **der Schreibtisch (-e)**
dessert **die Nachspeise (-n)**
devil **der Teufel (-)**

to die **sterben***
different **verschieden**
direction **die Richtung (-en)**
directory enquiries **die Auskunft (¨e)**
disco **die Disco / Disko (-s)**
to discover **entdecken**
to divide **teilen**
diving **das Tauchen**
divorced **geschieden**
to do **machen; tun***
doctor **der Arzt (¨e) / die Ärztin (-nen)**
dreadful **scheußlich**
dream **der Traum (¨e)**
to dress (oneself) **sich kleiden**
to drink **trinken***
drink **das Getränk (-e)**
to drive **fahren***
driving licence **der Führerschein (-e)**
drop **der Tropfen (-)**
dry cleaner's **die Reinigung (-en)**

ear **das Ohr (-en)**
early **früh**
to earn **verdienen**
Earth **die Erde**
to eat **essen***
ecology **die Ökologie**
economics **die
Wirtschaftswissenschaften (pl.)**
editor **der Redakteur (-e) / die -in (-nen)**
egg **das Ei (-er)**
end **das Ende (-n)**
engaged (phone line etc.) **besetzt**
Englishman, -woman **der Engländer (-) /
die -in (-nen)**
enough **genug**
environment **die Umwelt**
especially **besonders**
euro **der Euro (-)**
even **sogar**
evening; in the evening **der Abend (-e);
abends**
every **jeder / jede / jedes**

everything **alles**

exact(ly) **genau**

examination **die Prüfung (-en); das Examen (-)**

example **das Beispiel (-e)**

excellent **ausgezeichnet**

exciting **aufregend**

excursion **der Ausflug (¨e)**

to excuse **entschuldigen**

exercise **die Übung (-en)**

expensive **teuer**

experience **die Erfahrung (-en)**

expression **der Ausdruck (¨e)**

eye **das Auge (-n)**

face **das Gesicht (-er)**

fair (trade) **die Messe (-n)**

fairly **ziemlich**

fairy tale **das Märchen (-)**

family **die Familie (-n)**

famous **berühmt**

far **weit**

fashion **die Mode (-n)**

fashionable **modisch**

fat **das Fett; dick**

father **der Vater (¨)**

favourite colour **die Lieblingsfarbe (-n)**

to feel **fühlen**

to fetch **holen; ablholen**

figure **die Zahl (-en)**

film **der Film (-e)**

to find **finden***

finger **der Finger (-)**

to finish **beenden**

flat **die Wohnung (-en)**

flea market **der Flohmarkt (¨e)**

flight **der Flug (¨e)**

flower **die Blume (-n)**

flu **die Grippe (-n)**

fluent(ly) **fließend**

to fly **fliegen***

fog **der Nebel**

food **die Lebensmittel (pl.)**

foot **der Fuß (¨e)**

football **der Fußball (¨e)**

forbidden **verboten**

foreigner **der Ausländer (-) / die -in (-nen)**

to forget **vergessen***

former **ehemalig**

fortune **das Glück**

to found **gründen**

free **frei**

French (language) **Französisch**

French fries **die Pommes frites (pl.)**

Frenchman/ -woman **der Franzose (-n) / die Französin (-nen)**

frequently **häufig**

fresh **frisch**

friend **der Freund (-e) / die Freundin (-nen)**

fruit **das Obst**

fun **der Spaß**

furniture **das Möbel (-)**

game **das Spiel (-e)**

garden **der Garten (¨)**

garlic **der Knoblauch**

gentleman **der Herr (-en)**

German (language) **Deutsch**

German (person) **ein Deutscher / eine Deutsche**

to get up **auflstehen***

to get **bekommen***

girl **das Mädchen (-)**

girlfriend **die Freundin (-nen)**

to give **geben***

to give (as a present) **schenken**

glass **das Glas (¨er)**

to go **gehen***

to go for a walk **spazieren gehen***; einen Spaziergang machen**

good **gut**

Goodbye! **Auf Wiedersehen!; Auf Wiederhören! (on radio or phone)**

gram **das Gramm (-)**

grammar school **das Gymnasium (Gymnasien)**

grandson / -daughter **Enkelsohn (¨e) /-tochter (¨)**

grant **das Stipendium (-ien)**

graphic designer **der Grafiker (-) / die -in (-nen)**

green **grün**

grey **grau**

to grow **wachsen**

guest **der Gast (¨e)**

gym **das Fitnesscenter (-)**

hair **das Haar (-e)**

hairdresser **der Friseur (-e) / die Friseurin (-nen)**

hairstyle **die Frisur (-en)**

ham **der Schinken (-)**

hand **die Hand (¨e)**

to hang **hängen**

happiness **das Glück**

happy **glücklich**

hat **der Hut (¨e)**

to hate **hassen**

to have **haben***

to have to **müssen**

head **der Kopf (¨e)**

health **die Gesundheit**

health insurance **die Krankenversicherung (-en)**

healthy **gesund**

to hear **hören**

heart **das Herz (-en)**

hectic **hektisch**

heel **die Ferse (-n)**

to help **helfen*** **(+ dative)**

here **hier**

to hike **wandern**

history **die Geschichte (-n)**

hobby **das Hobby (-s)**

to hold **halten***

holiday **der Urlaub (-e)**

holiday (public) **der Feiertag (-e)**

holidays **die Ferien (pl.)**

to hope **hoffen**

hopefully **hoffentlich**

hospital **das Krankenhaus (¨er)**

hot **heiß**

hotel **das Hotel (-s)**

hour **die Stunde (-n)**

house **das Haus (¨-er)**

how? **wie?**

how many? **wie viele?**

how much? **wie viel?**

however **aber**

human being **der Mensch (-en)**

to hurt **wehtun**

ice cream **das Eis**

idea **die Idee (-n)**

ill, sick **krank**

important **wichtig**

information **die Auskunft (¨e)**

inhabitant **der Einwohner (-)**

interesting **interessant**

to introduce **einlführen**

invitation **die Einladung (-en)**

to invite **einlladen***

island **die Insel (-n)**

jacket **die Jacke (-n)**

job **der Job (-s)**

joke **der Witz (-e)**

journal **die Zeitschrift (-en)**

journey **die Reise (-n)**

juice **der Saft (¨e)**

key **der Schlüssel (-)**

kilo **das Kilo (-[s])**

kitchen **die Küche (-n)**

knee **das Knie (-)**

to know (a fact) **wissen***

to know (be acquainted with) **kennen***

knowledge **die Kenntnis (-se) (often pl.)**

lady **die Dame (-n)**

lamp **die Lampe (-n)**

language **die Sprache (-n)**

large **groß**

to last **dauern**

late **spät**

to lay **legen**

to learn **lernen**

least, at least **mindestens**

to leave **verlassen***

to leave (a message) **hinterlassen**

lecture **die Vorlesung (-en)**

left **links**

leg **das Bein (-e)**

lemonade **die Limonade (-n) / die Limo (-s)**

library **die Bibliothek (-en)**

to lie (in the sun, etc.) **liegen***

life **das Leben (-)**

lip **die Lippe (-n)**

to live **leben; wohnen**

living room **das Wohnzimmer (-)**

long **lang**

to look **auslsehen***

to look for **suchen**

to lose **verlieren***

loud **laut**

to love **lieben**

lunch **das Mittagessen (-)**

magazine **die Zeitschrift (-en)**

main course **das Hauptgericht (-e)**

to make **machen**

man **der Mann ("er)**

market **der Markt ("e)**

married **verheiratet**

to marry **heiraten**

to mean **bedeuten**

meat **das Fleisch**

mechanic **der Mechaniker / die -in (-nen)**

to meet **treffen***

menu **die Speisekarte (-n)**

message **die Nachricht (-en)**

message: pass on a message to someone **jemandem etwas auslrichten**

middle **die Mitte**

milk **die Milch**

mineral water **das Mineralwasser**

minority **die Minderheit (-en)**

minute **die Minute (-n)**

mixed **gemischt**

moment **der Augenblick (-e); der Moment (-e)**

money **das Geld (-er)**

month **der Monat (-e)**

morning **der Morgen (-)**

mostly **meistens**

mother **die Mutter (¨)**

mother tongue **die Muttersprache (-n)**

motor bike **das Motorrad ("er)**

mountain **der Berg (-e)**

mouth **der Mund ("er)**

much **viel**

mushroom **der Pilz (-e)**

music **die Musik**

musician **der Musiker (-) /die -in**

name **der Name (-n)**

near **die Nähe; in der Nähe von**

necessary **nötig**

neck **der Hals ("e)**

to need **brauchen**

neighbour **der Nachbar (-n)**

never **nie**

nevertheless **trotzdem**

new **neu**

newspaper **die Zeitung (-en)**

nice **nett; schön**

night **die Nacht ("e)**

nightmare **der Alptraum ("e)**

noisy **laut**

North Sea **die Nordsee**

nose **die Nase (-n)**

not **nicht**

not a **kein**

novel **der Roman (-e)**

now **nun**

now **jetzt**
number **die Nummer (-n); die Zahl (-en)**
nurse *(female)* **die Krankenschwester (-n)**
nurse *(male)* **der Krankenpfleger (-)**

occupation **der Beruf (-e)**
of course **natürlich**
office **das Büro (-s)**
often **oft**
old **alt**
old-fashioned **altmodisch**
omelette **das Omelett (-e or -s)**
once **einmal**
open **offen**
to open **öffnen**
opinion **die Meinung (-en)**
opposite **das Gegenteil (-e)**
or **oder**
orange juice **der Orangensaft (¨e)**
to order **bestellen**
otherwise **sonst**
outing **der Ausflug (¨e)**
outside **außerhalb**

packet **die Packung (-en)**
pain **der Schmerz (-en)**
to paint **malen**
parents **Eltern (pl.)**
park **der Park (-s)**
to park **parken**
party **die Party (-s)**
past **die Vergangenheit (-en)**
pasta **die Nudeln (pl.)**
to pay **bezahlen**
pedestrian **der Fußgänger (-)**
people **die Leute (pl.)**
perfume **das Parfüm (-s)**
perhaps **vielleicht**
person **der Mensch (-en); die Person (-en)**
to pick up **abholen**
picture **das Bild (-er)**
piece **das Stück (-e)**

to play **spielen**
play **das Theaterstück (-e)**
please **bitte**
police **die Polizei**
poor **arm**
popular **beliebt**
possibility **die Möglichkeit (-en)**
possible **möglich**
postcard **die Postkarte (-n)**
pot **das Kännchen (-)**
potato **die Kartoffel (-n)**
pound **das Pfund**
to prefer: I prefer drinking coffee. **Ich trinke lieber Kaffee.**
to prepare **vorlbereiten**
to prescribe **verschreiben***
present **das Geschenk (-e)**
price **der Preis (-e)**
probably **wahrscheinlich**
problem **das Problem (-e)**
producer **der Produzent (-en) / die -in (-nen)**
prospect **die Aussicht (-en)**
pub **die Kneipe (-n)**
to publish **veröffentlichen**
to pull **ziehen***
pullover **der Pullover (-), Pulli (-s)**
to put **stellen**
to put on *(clothes)* **anlziehen***

quarter **das Viertel (-)**
question **die Frage (-n)**
quiet **ruhig**

radio **das Radio (-s)**
railway **die Bahn**
railway station **der Bahnhof (¨e)**
rain **der Regen**
to rain **regnen**
to ramble **wandern**
rare(ly) **selten**
to read **lesen***
really **wirklich**

to receive **erhalten***
to recommend **empfehlen***
record **die Schallplatte (-n)**
red **rot**
refrigerator **der Kühlschrank (¨e)**
rent **die Miete (-n)**
to rent **mieten**
to reserve **reservieren**
responsibility **die Verantwortung**
responsible **verantwortlich**
to retire **in den Ruhestand treten***
retired **pensioniert**
return (ticket) **hin und zurück**
reunification **die Wiedervereinigung**
rice **der Reis**
rich **reich**
right **rechts**
room **das Zimmer (-)**
to run **laufen***

sailing **das Segeln**
salad **der Salat (-e)**
salami **die Salami (-s)**
salesperson **der Verkäufer (-) / die -in (-nen)**
same **gleich**
sausage **die Wurst (¨e); das Würstchen (-)**
to say **sagen**
school **die Schule (-n)**
to scream **schreien***
sea **das Meer (-e)**
season **die Jahreszeit (-en)**
seat **der Platz (¨e)**
secretary **der Sekretär (-e) / die -in (-nen)**
to see **sehen***
to seek **suchen**
seldom **selten**
to sell **verkaufen**
sentence **der Satz (¨e)**
to share **teilen**
shelves **das Regal (-e)**

to shine **scheinen***
shirt **das Hemd (-en)**
shoe **der Schuh (-e)**
shop assistant **der Verkäufer (-) / die -in (-nen)**
shop **das Geschäft (-e); der Laden (¨)**
to shop **einlkaufen**
short **kurz**
to shout **schreien***
to show **zeigen**
shower **die Dusche (-n)**
sight (worth seeing) **die Sehenswürdigkeit (-en)**
sign **unterschreiben*; unterzeichnen**
silk **die Seide**
simple **einfach**
to sing **singen***
singer **der Sänger (-) / die -in (-nen)**
single **ledig**
sister **die Schwester (-n)**
to sit **sitzen***
to ski **Ski laufen* / fahren***
skin **die Haut (¨e)**
skirt **der Rock (¨e)**
to sleep **schlafen***
slope **der Hang (¨e)**
small **klein**
to smoke **rauchen**
snack **der Imbiss (-e)**
snow **der Schnee**
to snow **schneien**
sock **die Socke (-n)**
sofa **das Sofa (-s)**
soldier **der Soldat (-en)**
sometimes **manchmal**
son **der Sohn (¨e)**
song **das Lied (-er)**
soon **bald**
sorry **leid**; I am sorry **Das tut mir leid**
soup **die Suppe (-n)**
space **der Raum (¨e)**
to speak **sprechen***
to spell **buchstabieren**

to spend (money) **auslgeben**
to spend (time) **verbringen**
sport **der Sport**
spring **der Frühling (-e)**
square (in a town) **der Platz (¨e)**
stadium **das Stadion (Stadien)**
to stand **stehen***
to start **anlfangen***
starter **die Vorspeise (-n)**
to stay **bleiben***
stay **der Aufenthalt (-e)**
still **noch**
stocking **der Strumpf (¨e)**
stomach **der Magen (¨)**
story **die Geschichte (-n)**
straight ahead **geradeaus**
straight away **gleich; sofort**
street **die Straße (-n)**
streetcar **die Straßenbahn (-en)**
strenuous **anstrengend**
strong **stark**
student **der Student (-en) / -in (-nen)**
study **das Studium (Studien)**
to study **studieren**
subject **das Fach (¨er)**
subway (train) **die U-Bahn (-en)**
successful **erfolgreich**
sugar **der Zucker**
suit **der Anzug (¨e)**
summer **der Sommer (-)**
sun **die Sonne (-n)**
sunglasses **die Sonnenbrille (-n)**
sunny **sonnig**
supermarket **der Supermarkt (¨e)**
sure **sicher**
surfing **das Surfen**
survey **die Umfrage (-n)**
sweet **der Bonbon (-s); süß**
sweetcorn **der Mais**
to swim **schwimmen***

table **der Tisch (-e)**
tablet **die Tablette (-n)**

to take **nehmen***
to talk **reden**
to taste **schmecken**
taste **der Geschmack (¨er)**
taxi **das Taxi (-s)**
tea **der Tee (-s)**
teacher **der Lehrer (-) / die -in (-nen)**
telephone **das Telefon (-e)**
to telephone **telefonieren; anlrufen***
to tell **erzählen**
temperature **die Temperatur (-en)**
tennis **das Tennis**
terraced house **das Reihenhaus (¨er)**
terrible **schrecklich**
thank you; thank you very much **danke; danke schön**
theatre **das Theater (-)**
then **damals; dann**
there **dort; da**
therefore **deshalb**
thing **die Sache (-n)**
to think **denken***
thirsty **durstig**
throat **der Hals (¨e)**
thunderstorm **das Gewitter (-)**
ticket **die Fahrkarte (-n)**
tie **die Krawatte (-n)**
tights **die Strumpfhose (-n)**
time **die Zeit (-en)**
timetable **der Fahrplan (¨e)**
tired **müde**
tiring **anstrengend**
today **heute**
toe **die Zehe (-n)**
together **zusammen**
tomato **die Tomate (-n)**
tomorrow **morgen**
tongue **die Zunge (-n)**
tooth **der Zahn (¨e)**
topic **das Thema (Themen)**
tour **die Tournee (-n)**
tower block **das Hochhaus (¨er)**

town **die Stadt ("e)**
town/city hall **das Rathaus ("er)**
track **das Gleis (-e)**
traffic **der Verkehr**
train **der Zug ("e)**
trainer **der Turnschuh (-e)**
tram **die Straßenbahn (-en)**
to translate **übersetzen**
to travel **reisen**
treaty **der Vertrag ("e)**
tree **der Baum ("e)**
trip **die Reise (-n)**
trousers (a pair of) **die Hose (-n)**
true **wahr**
to try **versuchen**
to try out **auslprobieren**
tube (train) **die U-Bahn (-en)**
Turk **der Türke (-n) / die Türkin (-nen)**
TV set **der Fernseher (-)**
type **der Typ (-en)**
typical **typisch**

ugly **hässlich**
umbrella **der Regenschirm (-e)**
uncle **der Onkel (-s)**
understand **verstehen***
unemployed **arbeitslos**
university **die Universität (-en)**
until **bis**
useful **nützlich**

vacation **der Urlaub (-e)**
various **verschieden**
vegetable(s) **das Gemüse**
verb **das Verb (-en)**
very **sehr**
vest **das Unterhemd (-en)**
village **das Dorf ("er)**
to visit **besuchen**
voice **die Stimme (-n)**

to wait **warten**
waiter/waitress **der Kellner (-) / die -in (-nen)**

walk **der Spaziergang ("e)**
to walk **(spazieren) gehen**
wall **die Mauer (-n)**
warm **warm**
to wash **waschen***
to watch TV **fernlsehen***
water **das Wasser**
to wear **tragen***
weather **das Wetter**
weather forecast **die Wettervorhersage (-n)**
weather report **der Wetterbericht (-e)**
wedding **die Hochzeit (-en)**
week **die Woche (-n)**
weekend **das Wochenende (-n)**
weight **das Gewicht (-e)**
well-known **bekannt**
what? **was?**
wheel **das Rad ("er)**
when? **wann?**
whenever **wenn**
where ... from? **woher?**
where? **wo?**
white **weiß**
why? **warum?**
widowed **verwitwet**
to win **gewinnen***
wind **der Wind (-e)**
windy **windig**
wine **der Wein (-e)**
winter **der Winter (-)**
woman **die Frau (-en)**
work **die Arbeit (-en)**
to work **arbeiten**
world **die Welt (-en)**
World War **der Weltkrieg (-e)**
to write **schreiben***

year **das Jahr (-e)**
yellow **gelb**
yoghurt **der / das Joghurt (-s)**
young **jung**
youth hostel **die Jugendherberge (-n)**

Taking it further

If you have enjoyed working your way through *Complete German* and want to take your German further, why not try *Perfect your German?* You should find it ideal for building on your existing knowledge and improving your listening, reading and writing skills.

Here are just three examples of websites that you might find helpful:

http://www.goethe.de The *Goethe Institut* is represented in most countries and staff may be able to inform you about German language courses in your area. They will also have information on short intensive courses based in Germany.

http://www.austria.org for information about Austrian life and culture.

http://www.swissinfo.org for information about Swiss life and culture.

TRY SOME REAL GERMAN!

Have a go at listening to German-speaking radio and TV stations and reading German newspapers and magazines.

Whatever you try, it's best to concentrate on small extracts at first – either a video or audio clip or a short article. See how much you can work out, going over the material several times. Then look up any key words that you have not understood, and go on till you are satisfied that you have grasped the main ideas. If you do this on a regular basis, you'll find that your command of German increases steadily.

Sources of real German

▶ Newspapers, magazines (e.g. *Bild-Zeitung*, *Stern*, *Focus*).
▶ Satellite and cable TV channels (e.g. ARD, RTL, SAT1, ZDF).
▶ Radio stations via satellite and, within Europe, on Medium Wave after dark.
▶ Internet – most German newspapers have websites where you can browse for short articles that interest you. TV and radio stations, too, have websites where you can often find audio and video clips of the latest newscasts. In some cases you will also find transcripts of the newscasts to help you if you run into difficulties with the spoken language.

- You can use our homepage or a German-language search engine or portal such as http://www.google.de or http://de.yahoo.com to find any of the above and lots more besides.
- Last but not least, we would highly recommend that you try speaking German with native-speakers, whether in your home country or in a German-speaking country. Explore Berlin, Vienna or Zürich (or any other German-speaking city) and make contact with the locals!

Viel Spaß beim Weiterlernen!

Index to grammar

The numbers after each entry refer to the units. For a summary of grammatical terminology used in this book, see the Glossary of grammatical terms.

Photo credits